THE OFFICIAL

LIVERPOOL FC

ILLUSTRATED HISTORY
SECOND EDITION

This edition published in 2004
First published in Great Britain in 2002 by
Carlton Books an imprint of Carlton Publishing Group
20 Mortimer Street
London W1T 3JW

10 9 8 7 6 5 4 3 2

ISBN 1 84442 855 9

Project editors: Nicky Paris and Chris Hawkes
Managing art director: Jeremy Southgate
Design: David Hicks
Picture research: Debora Fioravanti
Production: Alastair Gourlay

Printed in Italy

CONTRIBUTORS

Broadcaster, author and journalist JOHN KEITH has featured in several television programmes including Granada's hit series *Reds in Europe*. He presents BBC Radio Merseyside's *Saturday Football Phone-In*, reports for Ireland's national radio service RTE and is an after-dinner speaker. He joined the *Daily Express* sports staff just before the 1966 World Cup and spent more than 30 years on the paper. His many books include *The Essential Shankly*, *Bob Paisley – Manager of the Millennium*, *The Ian Callaghan Story* and *A–Z of Mersey Soccer*.

RIC GEORGE has been covering Liverpool FC since breaking into journalism with Mercury Press Agency in 1984. He began a 15-year career at the *Liverpool Echo* two years later and became their Liverpool FC correspondent in 1992. Merseyside-born, he graduated from Liverpool University before pursuing his studies in France. A fluent French speaker, Ric has been the English correspondent for *France Football* for over ten years. He often appears as a match analyst for Radio Merseyside, and on national radio in France. Since leaving newspapers, he has worked for Internet companies Sportprofile International and Icons Worldwide. Ric also contributes to the Liverpool FC website, official magazine and programme. He has written two books.

THE OFFICIAL

LIVERPOOL FC

ILLUSTRATED HISTORY
SECOND EDITION

JEFF ANDERSON
WITH STEPHEN DONE

CARLTON
BOOKS

Contents

1972

1981

1989

The Coca-Cola Cup Winners 1994/5 The

1995

2001

FEW FOOTBALL CLUBS generate as much passion and loyalty as Liverpool FC; the fervour of its supporters is unmatched anywhere in England and the humour of those fans is recognised throughout the world.

The story of how Liverpool Football Club came to occupy such an important place in people's hearts is an enthralling one, with each episode of the club's history captured here in impressive detail.

As a lifelong fan of the Club I have always been fascinated by the story of its birth, its turbulent first years and its early success.

This book takes us through the life of Liverpool FC with entertaining descriptions of the legendary managers, players and matches through the years, together with some of the more unusual episodes in Liverpool's history.

Through the pioneering tours of Europe during the depression years, the games played at Anfield in the shadow of a world war, we follow the Reds' story and watch the Club's development chapter by chapter.

For me, perhaps the most compelling theme in the book is the relationship between the club and its supporters. Liverpool FC has an extraordinary bond with its fans stretching back to the dawn of the twentieth century when thousands began to gather on the newly-built terrace known as the Spion Kop.

In spite of the appalling economic circumstances of the 1930s, when many supporters struggled to scratch a living – let alone attend a football match – and throughout the dark days of the 1950s when the team languished in the old second division of the football league, the fans stood firm.

The 1950s, of course, ended with the arrival of Bill Shankly and the birth of a sporting phenomenon both on the pitch and on the terraces. Shankly's inspired leadership set Liverpool on a course that would bring every domestic honour allowing his successors to conquer Europe repeatedly.

The huge highs and terrible lows that have followed since then are richly documented in these pages. The accounts of players and managers – along with some arresting photographs – help us to recall those events in the most vivid way.

My own involvement in the Liverpool story began in 1998. Since then, we hope we have been able to contribute one or two more episodes to add to this rich historic tale. The players have played an enormous role in the success of the club as have the supporters in their own way. That is why this book belongs to them as it is as much of a celebration of the fans as of the club itself.

Gérard Houllier

JOHN HOULDING IS THE MAN TO THANK. IF IT WASN'T FOR HIM, WE MIGHT ALL BE EVERTONIANS.

It's not as far-fetched as you may think. Until the late nineteenth century there was only one professional club in Liverpool. The team was Everton and their ground was Anfield. Then came a blazing row that tore the club in two and led to the team decamping to a new home at Goodison Park. Houlding was left behind with an empty ground and no one to play on it. He could have walked away and concentrated on his other business interests. Instead, he stayed ... and gave birth to the most successful club in the history of English football.

Houlding was a tycoon who made his money the hard way. He was born in 1833 in Tenterden Street, just off Scotland Road, where his father was a cow-keeper. It was a successful business, but any wealth the family had built up was destroyed when their stock of animals fell victim to a "cattle plague". All had to be destroyed and replaced.

The young John was a brilliant maths pupil but – at the age of just 11 – he left school to help bring some much-needed cash into the household. He became an office boy, then a door-to-door milk salesman, and spent much of his teens working as a porter at the city's Cotton Exchange. But by the mid-nineteenth century, work was much harder to come by. Liverpool's population was exploding due to mass immigration from Ireland, and in one six-month period alone some 300,000 people arrived to escape the famine across the sea. As the city's workforce trebled, competition for jobs was intense, and for a while

JOHN HOULDING
Brewer, former Lord Mayor, and founder of Liverpool Football Club.

Houlding returned home to work in the family business.

In 1854 he began earning an independent income again. He was taken on by a local brewery where his head for figures led to a rapid rise from drayman to book-keeper. He worked hard, saved hard, and was eventually made manager. By the end of his twenties he had bought two pubs and a brewery of his own, and by his mid-thirties he was a rich man. In later life he built up a formidable business empire. He also became influential in local politics and ended up as the city's Lord Mayor.

Houlding had a lifelong interest in sport, and was a keen swimmer and cricketer. He also loved football, spending weekend afternoons watching amateur matches from his elevated rear terrace overlooking Stanley Park. The players came from all over the city – church clubs, factory teams, makeshift sides put together by local community leaders – all eager to escape the slums and the smog; all keen to develop their skills in the quiet, clean, rural backwater that was nineteenth-century Anfield.

It was the team known as Everton that captured Houlding's attention. It may have been the all-dark strip that earned them the nickname "the Black Watch", but more likely it was the sizeable following they attracted – and the fact that they usually won their matches. Enthusiasm led to involvement. In 1883, when the club was forced to move from Stanley Park, he persuaded a cattle-dealer named James Cruitt to rent out a field on nearby Priory Road for home games. A year later, when Cruitt grew tired of the "vociferous" fans who spoiled his peace and quiet at weekends, Houlding looked for a solution closer to home.

Standing virtually opposite his grand red-bricked house on Anfield Road was a patch of land owned by fellow brewers John and James Orrell. Houlding approached the brothers and asked if they would be willing to grant a lease to the club, with him acting as its "representative tenant". The brothers were happy to do a deal. They asked for £100 annual rent, and Houlding's signature on this agreement:

"That we, the Everton Football Club, keep the existing walls in good repair, pay the taxes, do not cause ourselves to be a nuisance to other tenants adjoining, and pay a donation each year to the Stanley Hospital in the name of Mr Orrell."

Houlding put pen to paper, and Everton moved to Anfield. The ground was enclosed and, on 27 September 1884, it staged its first-ever football match – with the home side beating Earlestown by five goals to nil.

Providing Everton with vision, energy and money, he rose to the position of president. There were other prominent local clubs in the 1880s – notably Bootle, Liverpool Caledonian and Liverpool Ramblers – but it was Everton, under Houlding's leadership, who occupied the premier position on Merseyside. In fact, in organizational terms, they were one of the best in the country. They were the first to publish a match programme listing home and visiting players. They also pioneered the use of goal nets – a welcome development for referees, who often found themselves in the middle of violent disputes over whether a ball had crossed the line.

When professionalism was introduced in 1885, Everton's players immediately went full time, and new signings were recruited from as far away as Scotland and Ireland. Three years later the club joined with eleven others from the North-west and Midlands to found the English Football League. One of those was Accrington – whom Everton faced in the inaugural League match at Anfield, on 8 September 1888.

Despite soccer's growing popularity in the late nineteenth century, Liverpool was still primarily a rugby union city. But in 1890 the city's dockers won the right to a five-and-a-half-day week, and suddenly thousands of them were looking for a way to spend their Saturday afternoons. Interest in football soared, just as it had done in East Lancashire a decade earlier, when the mills and textile factories adopted the same working week. Attendances showed a rapid rise too, with Everton suddenly attracting up to 15,000 fans to home games. An early club document shows gate receipts in 1890 topping £5,000 – alongside an annual wage bill of just over £2,000. With a salary of £10 a month,

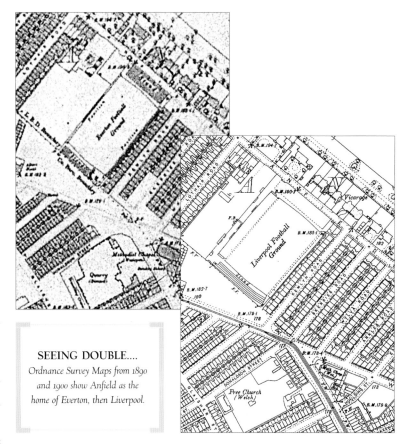

SEEING DOUBLE....
Ordnance Survey Maps from 1890 and 1900 show Anfield as the home of Everton, then Liverpool.

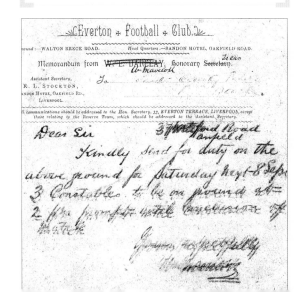

Anfield's first League game was between Everton and Accrington on 8th September 1888. This letter to the police requests "three constables to be on ground at 2pm prompt until conclusion of match."

Nick Ross was the best-paid player, but, in an early indication of wage inflation, the club was also attempting to lure the Glasgow Celtic star Dan Doyle to Anfield – offering him £5 a week and the tenancy of a local pub.

If costs were rising, Houlding did not mind. His association with a successful football club was good for his other interests. Christened by the press as "King John of Everton", he gained powerful positions in both the Freemasons and the Orange Order. He led the local carters' union, was active in the Conservative Working Men's Association, and got elected as a Tory city councillor. His business boomed, too. The brewery he had built in Tynemouth Street was working to full capacity, churning out the bottles of 'Houlding's Everton Beacon Ale' that had helped to make his fortune. And he had expanded further into the licensed trade, buying up more pubs in the surrounding districts, as well as the city centre.

But it was this involvement in the drinks trade that first brought him into conflict with some of his football colleagues. Everton, which had started life as the St Domingo Football Club, still had a number of strict Methodists among its members. And in Victorian Liverpool, where drunkenness and destitution were rife, they formed part of an active Temperance Movement which blamed alcohol for all the city's social problems.

The militant tee-totallers had a particular dislike for Houlding. No matter that he was a philanthropist, a Guardian of the Poor and a prominent fund-raiser for local hospitals. To them, he was chairman of the all-powerful Liverpool Brewers' Association; the man who had vigorously opposed a local by-law making it illegal for pubs to serve alcohol to children under 13; and the man who had led a successful campaign to allow pubs to keep their back doors open throughout the day. This

THE BEER THAT MADE HOULDING'S FORTUNE...
Houlding's Amber and Beacon Ales.

despite objections from magistrates who claimed that it encouraged drinking by women, who would have been 'too ashamed' to enter through the front.

Some of the Everton members also accused him of using the football club to promote his own drinks business. From the earliest days he had ignored suggestions to build proper administrative offices at Anfield, preferring to run affairs from the Sandon Hotel – the pub he owned on Walton Breck Road, and which doubled as the players' changing room. While this undoubtedly boosted the pub's popularity with thirsty football fans, it did little for Everton's professional image.

One letter in the *Liverpool Echo* claimed that Houlding did not want the players to move out while his business continued to benefit. And it concluded: "It's a disgrace that at a big club such as Everton, players have to walk through hordes of people on match days."

In 1891 Everton landed their first League championship – with those same "hordes" carrying the triumphant players back to the Sandon on their shoulders, following the final home game. In the same year Houlding, acting in an individual capacity, paid the Orrell brothers £5,845 to buy Anfield outright. As the newly installed landlord, he began drawing up some fresh rules. The first involved drink: his beer would be the only alcoholic refreshment on sale at the ground. The second involved the club's annual rent: it would go up from £100 to £250.

When the inevitable objections came, Houlding asked Everton's members to consider a way forward: they should transform the club into a limited company and buy Anfield from him. He would have made a handsome profit on the deal but, in Houlding's defence, he had been bankrolling Everton for years. He had paid their rent, built grandstands, even dug into his own pocket to help meet the cost of travel to away games. According to his own figures he had pumped in £6,045 – a figure more like £370,000 in 2002 terms. It had been a huge personal outlay. And now the team was becoming successful, he saw nothing wrong in reaping the benefit of his investment.

But the response could not have been more hostile. The members, led by the St Domingo church organist George Mahon, refused to buy, and, in a clear challenge to their new landlord's authority, they offered him a reduced rent of £180 to stay at Anfield for the coming year. "I cannot understand why a gentleman that has done so much for the club and its members should be given such treatment," wrote an offended Houlding.

The relationship between him and his fellow members worsened, and on 12 March 1892 Mahon and his followers called Houlding to a crisis summit. But there was to be no meeting of minds. As the *Liverpool Review* magazine reported: "There were mumblings and grumblings and, finally, the storm burst. 'King Houlding' insisted he was in the right; the great majority of members insisted he was in the wrong. The 'King' began to assert his power; his subjects broke out in open rebellion. Very soon it became a war to the knife.

"On the one side was the 'King', the sinews of war and a small and chosen band; on the other side were a big army of malcontents. Finally, the 'King' has been 'kicked', and the victorious have elected to migrate to fresh fields and pastures new."

Mahon left the meeting bound for Goodison Park, along with the vast majority of Everton's 279 members, and all but three of the first-team squad. Houlding was left behind with a handful of loyalists, and little idea of what to do next.

The uncertainty, however, did not last for long. Just three days after the split, he called a few of his supporters

DOWN WENT "KING JOHN."

MORAL.—A "King" may be knocked down in various ways. · If we were a "King" we would prefer that the blow came from another than a football quarter.

ABOVE: *Liverpool Review cartoon 1892.*
BELOW: *Stanley House, Houlding's home at 73 Anfield Road where LFC was formed.*

to his home at 73 Anfield Road, and asked for their backing to form an entirely new club. The Football League had already rejected his plan to call the club "Everton", ruling that the name should stay with the existing team and the majority of its members. So finding a replacement title was the next item on Houlding's agenda.

It was his friend William E. Barclay who came up with the best, and simplest, idea. He argued that if the new club was to attract support away from Goodison Park it needed a name that would inspire loyalty and affection across the entire city. Everyone agreed to his suggestion; and so, on 15 March 1892, Liverpool Football Club was born.

1878 ST DOMINGO FC FORMED

1879 NAME CHANGED TO EVERTON

1884 EVERTON MOVE TO ANFIELD

1888 FORMATION OF FOOTBALL LEAGUE

1892 BIRTH OF LIVERPOOL FC

CHAPTER ONE
1892–1902

The Old Masters

1893 LIVERPOOL JOIN FOOTBALL LEAGUE

1894 PROMOTION TO DIVISION ONE

1895 RELEGATION TO DIVISION TWO

1896 WIN DIVISION TWO TITLE

TOM WATSON APPOINTED MANAGER

1899 CHANGE SHIRT COLOURS TO RED

1900 BATTLE OF SPION KOP

1901 DIVISION ONE CHAMPIONS

DEATH OF QUEEN VICTORIA

PLAYERS' MAXIMUM WAGE INTRODUCED

1902 DEATH OF JOHN HOULDING

"HE IS A MAN OF ENERGY, DETERMINATION, AND HONESTY OF PURPOSE, AND UNDER HIS PRESIDENCY THE LIVERPOOL CLUB IS SURE TO PROSPER, THE SAME WAY THE EVERTON CLUB DID."

PROGRAMME TRIBUTE TO JOHN HOULDING

One of the earliest known photographs of Liverpool FC – taken at the Sandon Hotel bowling green in 1892.

IT WAS ANOTHER THREE MONTHS BEFORE THE CLUB RECEIVED ITS OFFICIAL "BIRTH CERTIFICATE" – THE NOTE FROM THE BOARD OF TRADE RECOGNIZING THE NAME CHANGE FROM EVERTON TO LIVERPOOL. THERE WAS A SLIGHT HOLD-UP WHEN THE CITY'S MAIN RUGBY UNION OUTFIT – ALSO CALLED LIVERPOOL FC – COMPLAINED ABOUT POTENTIAL CONFUSION, BUT WHEN HOULDING AGREED TO ADD THE WORD "ASSOCIATION" TO HIS NEW CLUB'S TITLE, THEY WITHDREW THEIR OBJECTION.

Bureaucracy aside, there was real work to be done. Houlding gave the new club a £500 loan, then began hiring a small group of men who would build it from scratch. His most important lieutenants were William Barclay and John McKenna (see page 21), who were both given the title "director". In reality, they were Liverpool's first joint managers, with Barclay looking after the administration and McKenna handling team affairs.

Although three of the Everton team – Andrew Hannah, Pat Gordon and Duncan McLean – had decided to throw in their lot with the new Anfield side, McKenna desperately needed to recruit new players. His search took him to Scotland, a country where football remained strictly amateur, and where the best players still spent the bulk of the week labouring down the mines, at the steelworks or in the shipyards. Not surprisingly, many of them were keen to move to England, where they could earn much better money for playing a game they loved. The Scottish press may have described them as mercenaries and traitors, but that was not enough to put them off. By the time McKenna finished his tour, he had persuaded ten of them to sign.

Back on Merseyside, Barclay was having less success. The Football League had rejected Liverpool's application for membership, so the club would miss out on glamour games against the Prestons and Aston Villas. Instead they would be playing in the Lancashire League, facing unfashionable rivals like West Manchester, South Shore and Fairfield.

Their first game at Anfield was to be a friendly against Midland League side Rotherham Town. The kick-off was scheduled for Thursday, 1 September at 5.30 pm – the same time that Everton would face Bolton in their opening game at Goodison Park. As the local papers speculated on who would be the biggest draw, Liverpool's directors tried some early-season hype, predicting that "no better game will be witnessed on any of the plots in the neighbourhood". But the spin failed.

A crowd of around 10,000 flocked to Goodison, while Anfield was almost deserted.

The one-penny match programme consisted of two sheets of foolscap, with most of the space taken up with advertisements and a lengthy explanation of the offside rule. There was also a glowing portrait of Houlding:

"To know him is to like him, though there are some who are hostile to him, because they never tried to know him. He is a man of energy, determination, and honesty of purpose, and under his presidency the Liverpool Club is sure to prosper, the same way the Everton Club did."

It certainly prospered in that

first Anfield game, as Liverpool hammered Rotherham 7–1. The team turned out – as they would for the next six years – in blue-and-white-quartered shirts. Admission to the ground cost threepence, and the line-up for that historic fixture was: Ross, Hannah, McLean, Kelso, McQue, McBride, Wyllie, Smith, Miller, McVean and Kelvin.

The following Saturday the same team was in action for Liverpool's opening Lancashire League fixture against Higher Walton. It was another meagre Anfield crowd, but at least the 200 who bothered to turn up got value for money: the home side won 8–0. It was the shape of things to come in that first season. Liverpool dominated the League from the outset, and ended it on top, having won 17 of their 22 games. Still, the players were not immune from public criticism – even from their own directors. The programme notes for the home game against Cliftonville in April 1893 were typical:

"A word to one or two of our players: why will McLean persist in marring his really brilliant and effective play by getting too far away from his own goal? By all means back up the halves, but a full-back has no business whatever amongst the forwards, except on the defensive. If Mac will only get rid of this one fault he will be as good a back as there is in England today.

"Then let Smith not dally so long with the ball; let him either pass or shoot. He is playing a good game at present, but for a little dilatoriness.

"And finally, just a little more dash in front of goal amongst the forwards. Their passing is fine, but they may well take a lesson from another quarter and not overdo it."

Even the hard-to-please directors should have been satisfied with the outcome of the following week's game – the victory over Everton in the Liverpool Senior Cup final (see page 17). But we can imagine their feelings just a few weeks later when both the Cup and the Lancashire League trophy were stolen while sitting on display in a shop window. Liverpool were ordered to replace both – at a cost of £127.

MALCOLM McVEAN
Scored Liverpool's first League goal.

Up Among the Big Boys

In the summer of 1893 the Football League's AGM agreed to extend the First Division to 16 clubs, which meant they needed more teams to make up the numbers in Division Two. McKenna – allegedly without the knowledge of his fellow directors – immediately drafted Liverpool's fresh application.

At least half a dozen longer-established clubs were in competition for the initial two places, but McKenna put up a strong Liverpool case: the club had a successful squad of players, a sound financial footing, excellent rail links for visiting teams, and huge potential for growth. The League's Management Committee were obviously impressed by his argument. Together with Woolwich Arsenal – the first-ever London side to be granted Football League status – Liverpool were duly elected.

They could not have hoped for more in that first year. From the opening game at Middlesbrough Ironopolis (a 2–0 win, with Malcolm McVean scoring Liverpool's first-ever League goal) they were irresistible, scoring 77 goals and conceding only 18. By the end of the season, they had won 22 of their 28 matches, drawing six and losing none. Promotion, though, depended on a "test match" – an early play-off system, with the teams at the top of the Second Division facing the clubs at the bottom of the First. Newton Heath were the opponents. And Liverpool's 2–0 victory must have been as sweet as any over the club that would soon rename itself Manchester United.

We can only guess at the level of excitement on Merseyside as the next season got under way, with two local teams both playing in the top flight. It was a time when thousands of children went barefoot, when the workhouse provided the only form of social security, and when an estimated 40 per cent of the city's men earned just £1 a week or less. Yet, amid all the desperation and poverty, Liverpool's football fans were prepared to pay to watch their teams in record numbers.

Everton's attendances had been growing steadily since the split, and in season 1892–93 the club had an average home gate of 16,500. But the Anfield fan base was also widening rapidly. Chiefly, this was the result of Liverpool's early success, but it was also partly due to another Merseyside team's demise. Bootle FC's fans had lived through an intense rivalry with Everton for more than a decade. At the beginning of the 1893–94 season, when their cash-strapped club was forced to resign from the Football League, those who wanted to watch professional action needed to find a new team to follow. Few could stomach the idea of cheering on their former enemies – so Liverpool became the club to benefit.

The fervour surrounding the city's two teams reached its height in October 1894 when they came face to face in the first-ever League derby. An unprecedented Football League crowd of 44,000 crammed into Goodison Park, generating receipts of more than £1,000, mostly handed over in sixpences. Hundreds of others climbed on to nearby rooftops to get a glimpse of the action for free. Thousands more were locked out.

The historic kick-off was scheduled for 2.15 pm, so the game could be completed before the fading of the autumn afternoon light. Liverpool, who had spent the week in training at Hightown, started as rank outsiders, after failing to win any of their previous seven games. Everton, who had started the season with six straight wins, prepared for the game as if it were any other.

True to that season's form Liverpool won the toss, but little else. The players put up a spirited fight but were overwhelmed by their more experienced rivals: Everton ran out 3–0 winners. A month later came the return at Anfield. This time another bumper crowd of 30,000 saw the two teams play out a 2–2 draw. While it was generally agreed that Liverpool were the better side, they very nearly lost again. Only a last-minute penalty from captain Jimmy Ross stopped Everton claiming all four points from the two games.

Ross – "fast, brilliant and a deadly shot," according to one report – ended the season with 23 goals from 25 League matches. But his heroics were not enough to save Liverpool from a miserable campaign. They ended up with just seven wins from 30 games, finished second from bottom, then lost a test match against Bury. Just a year after arriving in Division One, they were on their way back down again.

Sam Raybould

TOP 10
GOALSCORERS 1892–1902

1.	GEORGE ALLAN	50
2.	HARRY BRADSHAW	45
3.	SAM RAYBOULD	39
4.	FRANCIS BECTON	37
5.	JIMMY ROSS	37
6.	MALCOLM McVEAN	33
7.	JACK COX	24
8.	TOMMY ROBERTSON	19
9.	JOHN WALKER	18
10.	MATT McQUEEN	16

ALL COMPETITIONS

REBUILDING

If Liverpool had received a bloody nose in their first season in Division One, McKenna was at least determined to learn the lessons. He toured Britain looking for the sort of high-calibre players who would propel the club back to the top flight – and be strong enough to keep them there. In came the likes of Leith's George Allan – soon to become Liverpool's first Scottish international – and Archie Goldie from Clyde. Striker Francis Becton – already an England international – followed Ross by making the journey from Preston North End to Anfield.

The tactics paid off. Liverpool's new-look team laid waste to their opponents throughout the 1895–96 season, finishing top of the division with 106 goals – a club record that stands to this day. Along the way they notched up three 6–1 home victories, a 7–0 away win against Crewe, and the record 10–1 home rout of Rotherham Town.

As they prepared for their return to Division One, McKenna put in place the second part of his strategy: the recruiting of an expert coach who knew exactly what it would take to win the championship. For him,

MATCH THE FIRST **MERSEYSIDE DERBY**

Most football historians point to October 1894 as the starting point for this fixture, but in fact the first meeting between Liverpool and Everton came 18 months earlier. The date was Saturday, 22 April 1893. The venue was Bootle Football Club. And the occasion: the final of the Liverpool Senior Cup.

With the wounds of the split still fresh, the tension surrounding the game was intense. The Liverpool Football Association were worried about the potential for trouble, and had done their best to keep the two teams apart in the qualifying rounds. But, as both sides advanced, the chances of a meeting grew stronger. And, on 15 April, when Liverpool beat Bootle in the semi-final at Anfield, the clash became inevitable.

As the city's Football League club, Everton were the undoubted favourites. But they were also nervous of losing. Just a few days before the final, their directors arranged a meaningless friendly against Scottish club Renton – and scheduled it to take place on the same Saturday. It gave them an excuse to field a weakened side for the final – but led to accusations that they were running away from the fight.

If anything, the controversy added more spice to the game. On the day itself, 10,000 spectators packed into the Wadham Road ground as the teams took to the pitch. Liverpool fielded 11 senior players; Everton a mixture of first-team regulars and reserves. Match reports refer to a hard, physical contest played out in sunshine and intense heat. Liverpool's Joe McQue played like a man possessed, lunging into tackles, and getting a lecture from the referee about his conduct.

After half an hour Liverpool went ahead, thanks to a low shot from Wyllie. From then on Everton threw men forward in search of an equalizer, putting pressure on the Liverpool defence but leaving themselves exposed at the back. In a frantic last 30 minutes, Liverpool had a second goal disallowed, Everton saw a shot cleared off the line, and McQue had to be separated from the Everton

Joe McQue (second from right)

"Match reports refer to a hard, physical contest played out in sunshine and intense heat. Liverpool's Joe McQue played like a man possessed, lunging into tackles, and getting a lecture from the referee about his conduct."

wing-half, Murray. In the final minute Everton's players claimed a Liverpool defender had handled in the box, and demanded the referee award them a penalty, but, after consulting a linesman, he waved their protests aside, and blew for time just 30 seconds later.

Everton's fans and players reacted with such fury that the Liverpool FA officials did not dare to present the Cup. The Everton directors then handed them a written protest about the result, along with a letter complaining about the "general incompetence" of referee Herbie Arthur. Two days later the officials met at the city's

Neptune Hotel and rejected the complaints outright. They also issued a stern statement criticizing Everton's conduct and poor sportsmanship in the face of defeat.

The Liverpool players were finally presented with their gold medals – sponsored by Bovril – after a home friendly against Preston the next day. Houlding received the trophy in front of the fans, just as he had done in previous seasons when president of Everton. Placing the Cup in the Anfield boardroom, he said he was proud to "welcome the piece of plate back as an old friend".

LFC V. SHEFF. UTD 1899
The team's colours have changed to red.

Sunderland's Tom Watson was the ideal candidate (see page 30). And when Watson agreed to Liverpool's offer, McKenna was happy to stand aside from both team selection and recruitment.

In the new boss's first season, Liverpool finished fifth. In the FA Cup they went further than ever, thanks to victories over Burton Swifts, West Bromwich Albion and Nottingham Forest. Cup fever was a fresh experience for Liverpool supporters, and the semi-final at Bramall Lane brought the first reports of those fans travelling in significant numbers. Sadly, their vocal backing was not enough to see the team through to the final: Liverpool lost 3–0 to Aston Villa.

But at least they were on the road to fulfilling their potential. Playing in their new red and white colours, and led by their brilliant new Scottish captain Alex Raisbeck (see page 19), Liverpool finished runners-up in the 1898–99 championship race. And by the time the old century drew to an end they were closing in on their first-ever League title.

CHAMPIONS!

The 1900–01 season started well for Liverpool, with the team winning five of their first seven matches. A series of indifferent results followed which saw them slip from the top of the table by Christmas. It was not until February, with the country still in mourning over Queen Victoria's

death, that the team got back into their stride. Then they hit blistering form, winning nine of their last 12 games, and collecting just enough points to pip Watson's old club Sunderland to the title.

The trophy itself was secured on Monday, 29 April thanks to a 1–0 win at bottom-of-the-table West Brom. There was no civic reception, but when the team train pulled into Central Station at 11.30 pm the players were mobbed. A drum and fife band greeted them on the platform, directors and officials were held aloft, and thousands of well-wishers lined Bold Street and Church Street as their horse-drawn carriages headed back to Anfield in the early hours. It was time for the team and their fans to bask in the glory. Less than a decade after coming into existence, Liverpool FC had reached the summit of English football.

FAREWELL TO "THE KING"

Sadly, the man to whom they owed that existence said his final farewell just a few months later. John Houlding had been gradually reducing his involvement in the club, concentrating more and more on politics. The city's tee-totallers had continued to hound him – calling for a ban on Town Hall meetings when he was elected first citizen in 1897. But the so-called "Brewster Mayor" continued to face them down, attracting such a high

TOP 10 HAT-TRICKS 1892–1902	
1. GEORGE ALLAN	5
2. SAM RAYBOULD	3
3. FRANCIS BECTON	2
4. MALCOLM McVEAN	2
5. JIMMY ROSS	2
6. DAVY HANNAH	1
7. "SAILOR" HUNTER	1
8. ANDY McGUIGAN	1
9. TOMMY ROBERTSON	1
10. JAMES STOTT	1

A mix of strength, speed and skill made Alex Raisbeck Liverpool's first superstar. A combination of Hollywood looks and a boxer's physique turned him into football's original pin-up boy.

As a teenager, Raisbeck quickly made a name for himself as a centre-half with Larkhall Thistle, then Hibernian. In 1898, he moved to Stoke, but was so unhappy with life in the Potteries that he headed back to his native Stirlingshire after just two months. When Liverpool's Tom Watson heard the news he followed him over the border and persuaded him to move to Anfield. The fee: the paltry sum of £350.

For the next decade he was the commanding presence at the heart of the Liverpool defence, becoming renowned for his phenomenal tackling and stamina. He was the first Liverpool skipper to lift the League title, and later went on to win another championship medal and eight Scotland caps. He also appeared three times for the Scottish League.

Standing at 5ft 9³/4in, and weighing just under 13 stone, he was an arresting sight. One contemporary sports journalist noted: "A man of Raisbeck's proportions, style and carriage would rivet attention anywhere. He is a fine and beautifully balanced figure." He was also fast, superb at heading and a brilliant distributor of the ball. Other football journals routinely referred to him as the best defender in Britain, and at least one authoritative book on Scottish internationals still rates him as probably the finest centre-back the country has ever produced

In 1901, when the maximum wage rule prevented clubs from paying players more than £4 a week, it became difficult for Liverpool to hold on to stars like Raisbeck.

However, his additional job as so-called "bill inspector" meant he continued to top up his earnings.

Although from Scotland, Raisbeck became an adopted scouser, fiercely committed to the team, and particularly relishing the derby clashes with Everton. He appeared in 24 of them, scoring on two occasions, including a victorious FA Cup first round replay in 1902.

By 1909 he had made 340 first-team appearances and was probably past his peak. But at the age of 32 he was still good enough for Liverpool to realize a profit in the transfer market, with Partick Thistle paying £500 to take him back to Scotland.

He subsequently finished his playing days with Hamilton Academicals before going into management. He was boss of Bristol City for eight years, before spells at Halifax Town and Chester. In 1938 he finally returned to Anfield as a talent scout.

The entrance to the Kop in the early 1900s.

HOULDING HAD FOUNDED A FOOTBALL EMPIRE. AND ONE DAY IT WOULD BECOME THE WORLD'S MOST POWERFUL.

level of support in his Everton ward that the Tories asked him to stand in one of their safest Parliamentary seats.

He rejected the offer on health grounds. He was already suffering recurring bouts of illness and baulked at the additional stresses of an MP's life. In the spring of 1902 he followed his doctor's advice and took a holiday in the south of France to convalesce, but on 17 March, while staying at a hotel in Nice, he died.

Back on Merseyside there was an outpouring of grief and sentiment. Public functions were cancelled, and – throughout Anfield, Everton and Kirkdale – many people drew their curtains and blinds as a mark of respect. On the day of his funeral, silent mourners lined the streets as

the coffin was taken to Everton Cemetery. Liverpool players acted as pallbearers, and – with the bitterness of the split long forgotten – officials from Everton FC also turned up to pay their respects.

Houlding's life was an extraordinarily successful one. The man who started with nothing left £45,000 in his will – equivalent to almost £3m in 2002 terms. He had, as one Everton historian noted, "risen from the humblest beginnings to the most prominent position in the place of his birth – at the time when it was the second city in the largest Empire the world had ever known."

Houlding had also founded a football empire. And one day it would become the world's most powerful.

TOP 10
LEAGUE APP'S 1892–1902

1.	BILLY DUNLOP	173
2.	JOHN McCARTNEY	141
3.	ARCHIE GOLDIE	125
4.	WILLIAM GOLDIE	124
5.	JOE McQUE	121
6.	ALEX RAISBECK	121
7.	WILLIAM WALKER	118
8.	HARRY BRADSHAW	118
9.	JACK COX	117
10.	MALCOLM McVEAN	110

MANAGER JOHN McKENNA

John McKenna was an Irishman from County Monaghan. He arrived in Liverpool as a 19-year-old, working first as a grocer's boy, then as a vaccinations officer. He was active in the Church and joined the West Derby Union, helping to administer the many workhouses that housed the city's poor and destitute.

His charity work – and involvement with the Orange Order – brought him into contact with John Houlding. As their friendship developed, McKenna received an invitation to watch Everton play at Anfield. Soon he was a regular spectator, with football replacing his earlier sporting passions – rifle shooting and rugby union.

When the split came, Houlding appointed his friend as a director of the new Liverpool club. Working full time, McKenna quickly became its driving force, securing Liverpool's acceptance into the Football League, and bringing together the so-called "Team of the Macs" – the players he signed during two whirlwind tours of Scotland in the 1890s. He also recruited Tom Watson – at that time the most successful coach in England.

Following that appointment, McKenna decided to take more of a back seat in team affairs, concentrating instead on administration. He remained on the Liverpool board until 1922, enjoying two spells as chairman. He also served as an FA Council member from 1905, and in 1910 was elected as president of the Football League – a position he was to hold for 26 years.

A reputation for integrity led to McKenna being known throughout the football world as "Honest John". He was said to be a kindly employer who took a great interest in players' welfare. However, with his "military bearing and staccato voice", he was not a man to trifle with. This *Liverpool Echo* report described how he handled an angry Manchester City director after one game at Anfield:

"When the director entered the Liverpool boardroom vehemently declaring that City had been robbed of the game, McKenna immediately called for quiet using his well-known phrase 'A moment, please, a moment'. He then proceeded to ask the director if he knew what the word 'robbed' meant. Did he believe the referee was a thief? He promptly proceeded to insist on the director making an apology in the presence of everyone in the room."

One aspect of McKenna's character – his high-profile Ulster Protestantism – may have led to early stories about sectarian divisions between Liverpool and Everton. But they are myths. Everton, the supposedly Catholic club, started life as a Methodist church team, and several Protestants remained as directors and shareholders after the 1892 split. There were no clergymen on the board of either club, and McKenna – despite his own beliefs – never considered religion when recruiting his players. Contrast all this with Glasgow, where Rangers only signed Protestants, and Celtic allowed priests into their ground for free.

In fact, nothing got in the way of football for John McKenna. By the time he died, aged 82, he had devoted more than half his life to the development of the sport, both locally and nationally. And today, nearly 70 years on, a marble plaque remains on display in the Anfield entrance hall, in memory of "Honest John".

"By the time he died, aged 82, John McKenna had devoted more than half his life to the development of the sport, both locally and nationally."

1904   •   RELEGATION TO DIVISION TWO

1905   •   PROMOTED TO DIVISION ONE

  •   EINSTEIN'S THEORY OF RELATIVITY PUBLISHED

1906   •   FIRST DIVISION CHAMPIONS

| CHAPTER TWO *1902–1919* | Uncle Tom Watson and All |

  •   BUILDING OF THE KOP

  •   SAN FRANCISCO EARTHQUAKE

1909   •   LOUIS BLERIOT FLIES ACROSS THE ENGLISH CHANNEL

1910   •   CORONATION OF GEORGE V

1914   •   FIRST FA CUP FINAL APPEARANCE

  •   OUTBREAK OF FIRST WORLD WAR

1915   •   MATCH-FIXING SCANDAL

  •   DEATH OF TOM WATSON

1918   •   WAR ENDS

YOU'LL NEVER WALK ALONE

LIVERPOOL FOOTBALL CLUB

EST·1892 ®

"IF THERE IS A FINER INSIDE MAN PLAYING FOOTBALL AT THE PRESENT TIME I DO NOT KNOW HIM, FOR LACEY IS RIGHT AT THE TOP OF HIS FORM, AND EVERTON MUST BE SORRY THEY PARTED WITH HIM."

DISPATCH NEWSPAPER

Liverpool fans at the 1914 FA Cup final.

LIVERPOOL WENT INTO SHARP DECLINE AFTER THEIR FIRST CHAMPIONSHIP SEASON, AS THE TEAM THAT HAD PERFORMED SO WELL BEGAN TO DISINTEGRATE. IF IT WAS FRUSTRATING FOR THE FANS, IT MUST HAVE BEEN AGONY FOR WATSON. FOR THE PROBLEM WAS NOT OF HIS MAKING.

Just a few weeks before they had clinched the title, Liverpool received news from the Football League: from now on, all professional players in England would have their earnings capped at £4 a week. The ruling followed a campaign by small clubs who resented seeing their best players poached by richer rivals. The League thought it was in every club's interests to stamp out wage discrepancies. But for Liverpool, who had been paying their players up to £10 a week, plus generous win bonuses, the ruling had dire consequences.

John McKenna fiercely opposed the new rule, arguing that it would make it almost impossible to recruit players from other parts of the country: "Why should they move away from home when they can now earn as much money playing for their local teams?" he asked. He also believed that many of the existing squad would be tempted to seek transfers back to their home-town sides once the financial incentive to stay on Merseyside was removed. He even predicted that some would quit the game completely and return to their old trades, where better money could be made.

With the League refusing to back down, McKenna had to come up with inventive ways to pay his players more than the legal maximum. Most famously, he gave

Alex Raisbeck the additional job of "bill inspector" – supposedly checking the advertising hoardings around the ground – so the captain could earn extra cash legitimately. But that sort of creative accounting could only go so far. McKenna's predictions came true, several players left – and it all began to show in the results.

In the 1901–02 campaign Liverpool finished 11th, having won only ten of their 34 games. They scored just 42 goals, with seven coming in a single home game against Stoke when the visitors were ravaged by food poisoning. Nine Stoke players started the match, but emergency trips to the Gents meant that at one stage there were only seven of them on the pitch. Liverpool's Andy McGuigan took full advantage by hitting the net a record five times in one afternoon – something Anfield would not see again for another 52 years.

The team ended the 1902–03 season in fifth place, but the following year was a disaster. Unrest over the maximum wage ruling worsened, and other clubs tried to take advantage. In May 1903 the Football League discovered that Portsmouth had made "financial inducements" to three Liverpool players to get them to sign. The south-coast club were fined £100 while the Liverpool three – Archie Goldie, Sam Raybould and John Glover – were prohibited from playing for Portsmouth for life. All

Robbie Robinson

TOP 10
LGE GOALSCORERS 1902–1919

1.	JACK PARKINSON	123
2.	ARTHUR GODDARD	73
3.	JOE HEWITT	64
4.	ROBBIE ROBINSON	64
5.	JACK COX	49
6.	SAM RAYBOULD	49
7.	TOM MILLER	37
8.	GEORGE LIVINGSTON	31
9.	FRED PAGNAM	24
10.	ARTHUR METCALFE	23

returned to Merseyside – but they were banned from playing for seven months.

Those who did turn out at Anfield in 1903–04 performed badly. Sixteen defeats sent the team tumbling towards the foot of the table. And on the last day, when they lost to fellow strugglers Blackburn, they were condemned to relegation.

When Liverpool had last gone down to Division Two, John McKenna had kept his promise to get them back up within a year. This time, Watson was determined to follow his example. He reorganized at the back, strengthening a defence that had conceded 62 goals the previous season. Then he reinforced it further, travelling back to the north-east to snap up his former 'keeper, Ned Doig, for £150. The Scot was a legendary figure in Sunderland, having helped them to three championships. He made his first appearance for Liverpool in September 1904 – and at the age of 37 years and 11 months, he remains the club's oldest debutant.

With Doig between the sticks, the Reds' defence proved to be the meanest in Division Two: the team conceded just 25 goals all season. But promotion was also achieved thanks to three prolific strikers. Liverpool scored 93 times during the campaign, with Robbie

Robinson (24 goals), Jack Parkinson (20) and Raybould (19) all at the peak of their form.

MERSEYSIDE REIGNS SUPREME

Things got even more exciting the following year. A dazzling FA Cup run brought victories over Leicester Fosse, Barnsley, Brentford and Southampton. Then came the semi-final at Villa Park – against Everton. According to that day's press reports, all trains to Birmingham were booked and all roads to the stadium jammed. By the time the gates were locked, an hour before kick-off, there were 37,000 people inside the ground, the vast majority from Merseyside.

Liverpool started as favourites, thanks to their terrific form in the League. But, despite the performance of Raisbeck ("worth any two men on the field," according to Football League founder William McGregor) they failed to live up to their promise. At the end of the afternoon, it was the Evertonians who were going home happy after seeing their side win 2–0. In fact, Everton went on to win the Cup itself three weeks later, thanks to a 1–0 victory over Newcastle at Crystal Palace. Back on Merseyside an estimated 200,000 people turned out to welcome them home. And among the first to greet

Bowden Bros.]
WOOLWICH ARSENAL v. LIVERPOOL AT PLUMSTEAD, SEPTEMBER 2, 1905.
If a forward is allowed to break through the defence the position is well nigh hopeless. Yet on this occasion Parkinson, of Liverpool, perhaps the fastest forward playing League football, fell at the critical moment as he was about to net the ball. The result was a fractured wrist, which kept the gallant fellow out of the field a number of weeks. The ball went just wide of the post, and Ashcroft is seen watching its course with some concern. Woolwich won the match by 3 goals to 1.

"The club makes nothing out of its visit to Craven Cottage today ... they go up to town for the bare railway and hotel expenses," said a newspaper report. Still, the players could look forward to at least one reward for their season's efforts. Flushed with success, the directors took them to Paris, fitting each of them with straw boaters complete with a red ribbon and Liver Bird crest.

THE BIRTH OF THE KOP

There was a reward for the fans that year, too. Success on the pitch had sent average gates up to 18,000, and – in the summer of 1906 – the board authorized an increase in Anfield's capacity. At that time the ground could hold around 20,000, with many choosing to stand on the exposed wooden terraces at the Anfield Road and Walton Breck Road ends. They could pay a little extra to sit in the Main Stand, a modest pavilion built in 1895, with its distinctive mock tudor central gable. Or they could arrive early and get one of the few vantage points in the Kemlyn Road Stand, a narrow strip of seats squeezed between the touchline and the back-to-back terraced houses that once stood on the current Centenary Stand car park.

The key to getting more fans into the ground was the construction of a huge new banking at the southern end, behind the Walton Breck Road goal. Originally it was just a vast, roofless mound of soil and cinders, with nothing more than a white picket fence to keep the crowd from spilling on to the pitch. But it offered spectacular views, and thousands began to gather there as the new season got under way.

Soon it would have a name – "Spion Kop" – derived from Spioenkop, a hill in South Africa, and the scene of one of the Boer War's bloodiest battles. In January 1900 British soldiers were attempting to break the siege of Ladysmith when they were attacked by Boer troops. At the end of the battle, 300 of them lay dead. All belonged to the Lancashire Fusiliers – a regiment which recruited locally and which included many Merseysiders in its ranks.

But, despite the local connection, Liverpool were not the first club to name a section of their ground after the battle. In fact the original "Kop" appeared in 1904 at Manor Field, the south London home of Woolwich Arsenal. By the time Liverpool adopted it – apparently at the suggestion of a local sports journalist – it was

the players at Central Station were ... the directors of Liverpool FC.

They could afford to be generous – their own players had just won the League championship. A disastrous opening sequence of three defeats had been corrected with a run of eight wins in ten games. They had vied with Preston for top spot all season, but finally moved ahead when they went to Deepdale in March and claimed a 2–1 victory. A 3–1 home win over Sheffield United on the last day of the season saw them finish as champions with four points to spare. The unique double success of the city's two teams led to widespread celebrations. And a famous *Liverpool Echo* cartoon of the two victorious captains arm-in-arm summed up everyone's feelings with a simple one-word caption: "Supremacy".

In fact, there were even more honours for Watson's team that year. With the title in the bag, his players went on to complete a modest treble by lifting the Liverpool Senior Cup and Dewar Shield. The latter was an early forerunner of the Charity Shield, and – standing at more than five feet tall – it was probably the largest trophy ever displayed in the Anfield cabinet. It was contested at the end of each season by the country's top professional and amateur clubs, with the prize presented by Sir Thomas Dewar, City of London Sheriff, and head of the famous whisky firm.

Liverpool won it after a 5–1 victory over Corinthians at Fulham, but there was no cash bonus for the team:

PLAYER EPH **LONGWORTH**

It was homesickness that brought Ephraim Longworth to Anfield. In 1910 the Bolton-born full-back had left his local Wanderers side and was playing for Southern League club Leyton. But he yearned for a move back to the North-west, and jumped on the first train to Lime Street when Liverpool expressed their interest.

After making his debut in a home defeat against Sheffield United, Longworth soon established a reputation as one of the most stylish and accomplished defenders in Britain. In 1920 he made the first of five England appearances, as his country came from 4–2 behind to beat Scotland 5–4. And, in 1921, when England played Belgium, he became the first Liverpool player to lead out the national side as captain.

Longworth formed part of a formidable back line that, at different times, included fellow England international Tom Lucas and Scotland's Don McKinley. But, even as competition for places increased, he always had the advantage of being able to play on either the left or right side. His versatility and consistency made him an automatic first-team choice in the pre-World War One years, and he was among the team who played in Liverpool's first-ever FA Cup final. When the hostilities ended he resumed his place and assumed the captaincy, leading the club to successive League championships in 1922 and 1923.

> **"Eph Longworth never once found the net for Liverpool, and to this day holds the club record for the most number of games without scoring."**

Throughout his career he was noted for a distinctive quiff – a long lock of hair swept from right to left over his forehead. He was blessed with supreme fitness and stamina, and those qualities meant he could continue playing top-class football until the age of 40. He was also an honest man – he was one of the players who refused to take part in the notorious 1915 match-fixing scandal and, according to the League's inquiry, had tried to persuade his guilty team-mates to scrap the idea.

By the time he finished playing in 1928, Longworth had made 371 senior appearances for Liverpool. He never once found the net, and to this day holds the club record for the most number of games without scoring.

Following his retirement he joined the coaching staff and held several backroom jobs with the club. He was still there when the team won the 1947 title, and lived long enough to see Liverpool finally lift the FA Cup in 1965.

already in use at several other grounds. No matter. In years to come there would only be one Kop to achieve fame around the world. And that belonged at Anfield.

But who were the original Kopites? Social historians say early-twentieth-century crowds were largely made up of skilled or semi-skilled workers – tradesmen, engineers, shipbuilders and repairers. In Liverpool, their numbers were swelled by the high number of white-collar clerks employed in the booming shipping and insurance industries. For some reason, Anfield was also popular with policemen. In 1907 you could buy a seven-shillings-and-sixpence (38 pence) season ticket, and get a single share in the club as a reward. By the time war broke out in 1914, almost a quarter of Liverpool's shareholders belonged to the local constabulary.

While English crowds were overwhelmingly male, one newspaper claimed that Liverpool, along with Everton, had the highest percentage of "Lady Supporters" among all League clubs. The Liverpool fans were also known for their sporting behaviour, with journalists noting how they applauded opposition players – particularly goalkeepers – as early as 1901.

Other reports refer to Anfield fans as "noisy", and describe how they celebrated goals by throwing their hats and caps into the air. But, according to a 1905 article in *Porcupine* magazine, they were reluctant to display their support in other ways: "We in Liverpool are either more reserved or less enthusiastic than our brethren up country. When Sheffield, Birmingham or Blackburn come to town we know it. But Liverpudlians rarely wear their colours conspicuously, even when travelling."

We know, from accounts passed down the generations, that the Kop was not a fixed vantage point throughout the game. Many home fans stood there only when Liverpool were attacking that end, switching sides when the players were kicking towards the Anfield

Road. That might explain why – when singing was first reported on the Kop in 1907 – the noise came from Blackburn Rovers supporters. Hard to imagine now, although present-day fans will easily recognize another aspect of the visitors' behaviour: "They waved their colours to a set motion, and sent forth a weird unearthly cry ... but they were silent after Liverpool had scored," reported one magazine.

AS THEY LAY ON THE BATTLEFIELD DYING...
The Battle of Spion Kop, 1900.

WILDERNESS YEARS

There was little for Liverpudlians on the Kop to sing about following the 1906 championship. The team slumped to 15th the following season, and soon afterwards some of their best players began reaching the end of their careers. A near-decade of mediocrity followed with mid-table positions, one runners-up spot – and the odd relegation scare – the main features.

There were individual matches to savour, and some have passed into legend. December 1909 brought the famous fightback against Newcastle, when the visitors led 5–2 at Anfield, only to be beaten 6–5. It also saw the Christmas Day match against Bolton, when left-half Jim Bradley had to play in goal because regular 'keeper Sam Hardy missed his train: Liverpool still won – 3–0. And in 1910 the team travelled to Manchester for the first-ever game at Old Trafford. The result: United 3, Liverpool 4.

There were some great individual players, too. Hardy – reckoned to have been one of England's finest-ever 'keepers – was replaced in 1912 by the brilliant Scottish international Kenny Campbell. Don MacKinlay, another Scot to be capped by his country, became a commanding figure at the back alongside the stylish and long-serving Eph Longworth (see page 27). And, in attack, Irish winger Bill Lacey formed a dangerous partnership with the Bootle-born centre-forward, Jack Parkinson.

Lacey, who arrived from Everton in 1912 in an exchange deal, was one of the first to cross directly from

Goodison to Anfield. His form won him 24 international caps and his wild – and distinctly modern – goal celebrations made him a crowd favourite. Half-back Tom Fairfoul told the *Liverpool Echo* how Lacey behaved during one 1914 pre-season friendly game: "The ball was only centred when Billy fired on it, and, beating all opposition, scored a glorious goal – a real old-fashioned individual effort. Billy was so pleased he performed a somersault – to the amazement and amusement of the spectators."

Despite the entertainment value, Liverpool's players were providing little real excitement for their fans. But in 1914 the one prize that had eluded them came into view.

Bill Lacey

A CUP FINAL AT LAST

Britain strengthened its armed forces, suffragettes took to the streets, dockers came out on strike, and Charlie Chaplin made his first film appearance dressed as a tramp. There was plenty to talk about that spring, but Liverpool fans were obsessed with another question: could their team actually make it to an FA Cup final?

They had seen Everton do it, and then go on to lift the trophy. They had watched their own side reach the semis on three separate occasions, only to go out after disappointing displays. But this time there was a swagger about Liverpool that made their prospects in the competition look different. The fans sensed it: the four rounds played at Anfield drew an average attendance of more than 40,000.

The high point of the run was an emphatic 5–1 victory over West Ham in a third round replay. Gates were locked and thousands turned away from the turnstiles. Inside, the supporters – once shy of wearing team colours – sported scarves and rosettes. There was even a report of a huge red flag being unfurled by a

spectator on the Kop. They witnessed a terrific all-round display by the home side, but two goals from Liverpool's ex-Goodison forward made him man of the match: "If there is a finer inside man playing football at the present time I do not know him, for Lacey is right at the top of his form, and Everton must be sorry they parted with him," said the *Dispatch* newspaper.

A fortnight later, and the fourth round tie with Queen's Park Rangers brought 43,000 to Anfield. If Liverpool's players had become used to such crowds by then, the visitors had not: the *Liverpool Echo* wondered whether the noise and atmosphere had made them "lose their heads", and added that "the best thing Rangers did was to pass prettily". That clearly was not enough: Liverpool won the game 2–1.

And so the Reds marched on to their fourth FA Cup semi-final, this time against the holders, Aston Villa. With the Midlands side also challenging strongly for the title, most newspapers thought they had it sewn up. But they were wrong. The 27,000 who watched the game at White Hart Lane saw Jimmy Nichol score a goal in each half ... and Liverpool reach the final at last (see page 32).

Sadly, that April day at Crystal Palace did not turn out as the players or the fans had hoped. But within just four months all the disappointment was forgotten. Everyone had far more important matters on their minds.

WARTIME

When Britain declared war on 4 August 1914, the Rugby Football Union scrapped its forthcoming programme. The Football League, led by John McKenna, faced immediate calls to do the same. But with the new season just four weeks away – and with confident predictions that the fighting would be over by

TOP 10 HAT-TRICKS 1902–1919		
1.	JACK PARKINSON	8
2.	SAM RAYBOULD	5
3.	CHARLIE HEWITT	2
4.	JOE HEWITT	2
5.	SAM BOWYER	1
6.	FRED PAGNAM	1
7.	WILLIAM McPHERSON	1
8.	ARTHUR METCALFE	1
9.	RONALD ORR	1
10.	JAMES STEWART	1

ALL COMPETITIONS

MANAGER TOM **WATSON**

They like their football "messiahs" in the North-east – and Tom Watson was the original Geordie miracle worker. The former school teacher and amateur player went into management early, taking the reins at Newcastle West End and making it the city's most successful club. He then repeated the trick with their main rivals East End – who would eventually evolve into Newcastle United. But it was at Sunderland that Watson really made his reputation, assembling the so-called "Team of All Talents" and leading them to three championships in the 1890s.

To this day, he ranks as the Wearsiders' most successful boss. His decision to leave must have been a terrible blow to the club and its fans. But it is a measure of John McKenna's powers of persuasion that he opted for a future on Merseyside.

His arrival brought a new professionalism to Anfield. At Sunderland he had presided over a strict diet and fitness regime, and he was quick to introduce Liverpool's players to the same discipline. While they increased their stamina and speed, Watson set about recruiting the new players who would lead the title assault. It took him the best part of five years, but in 1901 he put together a side that finally landed the championship.

After seeing them falter after that first success, Watson then faced the humiliation of dropping down a division. But his determination, tactical nous and astute movements in the transfer market soon returned Liverpool back to the top flight – and gave them a second championship trophy in 1906.

Although he brought many brilliant players to Liverpool, he had a particular knack for signing world-class goalkeepers. The first –

Sunderland veteran Ned Doig – became a crucial part of the 1905 promotion-winning side. His successor, Sam Hardy, was a £500 signing from Chesterfield who went on to become England's first-choice 'keeper for many years. Then there was Kenny Campbell, a Scotsman who was subsequently capped eight times by his country. And coming up through the ranks was a certain young Irishman named Elisha Scott.

Rules for Training.

7.30 a.m.   Rise, half-an-hour's stroll.
8.30   „   Breakfast, weak tea, chops, eggs, dry toast or stale bread.
9.45   „   Exercise, bath to follow.
1.0 p.m.   Dinner of plain roast or boiled joints of mutton or beef, with an occasional fowl, fresh vegetables, rice or tapioca puddings, stale bread, a glass of beer or claret.
3.30   „   Exercise.
5.30   „   Tea, fresh fish, light boiled eggs, or chops.
7.30   „   An hour's stroll.
9.0   „   Supper, glass of beer or claret and bread.
10.0   „   Retire to bed.

N.B.   Butter, sugar, milk, potatoes, and tobacco must be sparingly used.

When out walking the whole of the players must keep together and accompany the trainer. This rule must be observed.

The orders of the trainer must be strictly obeyed. Any player who neglects to comply with the above rules will be reported and dealt with as the Committee think fit.

By Order of the Directors.

Like many subsequent Liverpool managers, Watson lived and breathed football. He could not take his mind off the game, even when the season was over. According to a *Liverpool Echo* report he was "in the habit of taking his holidays abroad. It is not too much to say that he has had a distinct influence on popularizing the game on the Continent".

Back home, he loved to be near his workplace and made sure he lived just a few hundred yards from the ground. On match days he refused to sit in the stands, preferring to observe the game from his so-called "lair" in the dug-out. But once the action started he was prone to nerves. In a 1909 home game against Newcastle, Liverpool fell 5–2 behind. Watson – unable to bear watching any longer – left his seat and locked himself in his office.

Half an hour later he answered a knock on his door and was told that the scores were level. He ran back to watch the final few minutes – and saw his team win 6–5!

With the outbreak of war in 1914, football clubs were criticized for pressing ahead with their League programme. Players who decided against joining the Army were also frowned upon. Watson reacted angrily to the attacks, and wrote a letter to *The Times* underlining Liverpool's commitment to the war effort. *"We have 27 professionals, 13 married and 14 single. Recruiting has taken place at the ground all season, with military bands at all games. One director, one player, a great many shareholders and two sons of directors have joined the Army. The players are donating 12 1/2 per cent of their salaries to the assistance of the needy and to war funds. The donations have been:*
The club: £413 7s 6d
Ground collections: £114 3s 5d
From staff, directors and players:
£25 15s 9d. Total: £553 16s 5d
Eighteen footballs have also been sent to the front for supporters in the King's uniform. £10 10s has been sent to Princess Mary's Fund. Players are drilled twice a week by a retired Army officer. 1,000 soldiers and sailors are given free admission to each match, as are wounded men and Belgian refugees."

Just six months after writing that letter, the English game's most successful manager died at his home in Priory Road, aged 56. On the day of the funeral, several of his most famous players – including Raisbeck and Doig – carried his coffin to Anfield Cemetery.

Today, Watson should be remembered as one of Anfield's all-time greats: the original championship winner who guided the team to a second title and their first-ever Cup final appearance. Only death could prise him away from the club he loved. With 19 years' service, he remains Liverpool's longest-serving manager.

Christmas – the fixtures went ahead as planned.

If the clubs hoped football would provide a welcome distraction from the hostilities, they were wrong. Attendances plummeted. Partly, it was due to factories working compulsory overtime, but mainly it was the decision by hundreds of thousands of young men to join the British Army. There was particular enthusiasm in Liverpool, where Lord Derby led a determined campaign to get people to enlist. In one three-day period at the end of August, he personally persuaded 2,000 men to accept the King's Shilling.

As the year went on, the military chief Lord Kitchener was given space in the Liverpool match-day programme to tell spectators "Your Country Needs You". But gates had dropped by more than half, and Anfield could attract only 10,000 people to a Cup tie against Stockport.

On the pitch, the players were having a miserable time. They went out of the Cup in the second round, slumped to mid-table mediocrity in the League, and could only watch as a resurgent Everton climbed to the top. But as the fighting continued beyond Christmas, and the horrific scale of the casualties began to come through, football took on a meaningless air. As the 1914–15 season drew to a close, it became obvious that it would be the last – at least until the war was over.

It was in this climate that a group of Liverpool and Manchester United players decided to award themselves one final big pay-day. They got together in a Manchester pub several days before the two teams met in a Good Friday League fixture at Old Trafford. The reason? To agree the scoreline, organize pre-match betting, and collect the rewards.

They might have got away with it if Liverpool had not played so indescribably badly. The players had agreed to make sure United won by two goals to nil – a victory that would give them valuable points in their fight against relegation. But once that score had been reached, Liverpool showed no willingness to fight back. And even when they did manage to pump the ball upfield their forwards squandered chance after chance. The referee later described the match as the most extraordinary he had ever been involved in.

The bookies were immediately suspicious. Large sums of money had been laid on the result in betting shops all over the country. Facing heavy losses, they announced an inquiry and refused to pay out on any of the bets until it was completed. The Football League responded with its own investigation and called each of the players and officials in to give evidence.

As the truth gradually emerged, it became clear that eight players – four from each side – were involved in the betting scandal. Jackie Sheldon, Tom Miller, Tom Fairfoul and Bob Purcell were the Liverpool conspirators, while the United four included the former Anfield favourite Enoch "Knocker" West. Although all the players were suspended from playing indefinitely, seven of them had their sentences lifted after the war, probably in recognition of their service to their country. However, West – who always maintained his innocence – had to wait until the age of 62 before his suspension was finally removed.

It had been an awful year for the club, and there was even worse news to come. On the last day of the season Tom Watson complained of feeling ill while watching his team win at Oldham. He was taken home and confined to bed, but died two weeks later. In a front-page tribute, the *Daily Post* described him as "'Owd Tom' – the most popular man in football."

For the rest of the war – as Liverpool played in a makeshift, and largely meaningless, Lancashire League – the team operated without a recognized manager. The patriotic Watson, who had positively encouraged young players to enlist in the Army, would surely have been appalled by the war's progress, had he lived to see it. Three Liverpool players – Joe Dines, Wilfred Bartrop and Tom Gracie – were all killed in the fighting. Many other clubs lost star players; others were so badly wounded they never put on a pair of football boots again.

As for the city of Liverpool, an estimated 100,000 of its young men went off to join the battles on the Western Front and elsewhere. One in six of those "Scouser Tommies" never came home.

MATCH LIVERPOOL v. BURNLEY 1914 FA CUP FINAL

The entrance to Crystal Palace, FA Cup final morning, 1914.

During the early part of the 20th century, football became the most popular spectator sport in England. But as hundreds of thousands of fans flocked to the grounds, not everyone shared their enthusiasm for the game's growth. In fact, many of the country's "elite" frowned upon football, along with other early forms of mass entertainment like the music hall and the cinema. Gradually, though, it grew so big that even the wealthy middle classes began to embrace it. Then, in 1914, came the ultimate sign of football's acceptance by the Establishment – the decision by a reigning monarch to attend an FA Cup final.

Kenny Campbell

Cup Final Day.

It was a clever idea by George V's advisers, who – even then – were looking for ways to make the Royal Family appear less remote from the people. And when they discovered that the game was to be an all North-west affair, they came up with an even smarter PR stroke: the King would wear the red rose of Lancashire in his button hole.

When he took his seat in the Royal Pavilion, he was one of an official 72,778 crowd to see Liverpool take on Burnley. But, as photographers captured pictures of fans perched on telegraph poles, and clinging to nearby trees, their newspapers estimated that as many as 100,000 were watching. We will never know the true figure as no tickets were issued. The authorities at Crystal Palace reckoned the vast bowl-shaped stadium would be big enough to accommodate all supporters – no matter how many turned up.

What we do know is that packed trains began arriving in London at 11 o'clock the previous night. From then on the five lines which dealt with the rail traffic recorded the following arrivals: London & North Western, 45 trains; Great Northern, 41 trains; Great Western, 40 trains; Great Central, 25 trains; and Midland, 20 trains. The vast majority of fans arrived in the early hours of the morning – 15,000 from Burnley and at least 20,000 from Merseyside. According to press reports, Liverpool's fans plastered their carriages with rosettes, scarves, flags and team photos. Many sang during the journey – with "You Made Me Love You" one of the most popular songs on board. And, despite such an unprecedented number of people travelling, transport police made just one arrest for drunkenness.

As the supporters enjoyed their first mass excursion, the players prepared for their first FA Cup final. Earlier in the week Tom Watson had taken his squad to a hotel near Epping Forest, where he kept a strict eye on their diet and put them through a special training programme. But, despite all the careful preparations, he suffered a major blow on the morning of the game, when skipper Harry Lowe failed a fitness test. Watson drafted in Donald MacKinlay as Lowe's replacement, and handed the captaincy to Robert Ferguson.

As Liverpool's players arrived in a fleet of taxis from Chingford, the roads around Crystal Palace were clogged. Outside the stadium, both sets of fans wore their team's colours –

Burnley's Bert Freeman scores the winning goal.

The King wears the Red Rose of Lancashire.

100,000 fans watched the final.

with thousands sporting mini-replicas of the trophy on their lapels. Inside, the crowd were being entertained by a drum and fife band from Liverpool's own regiment, the 1st Kings. Five minutes before the kick-off the King himself arrived. The band struck up the national anthem, the monarch shook hands with the two captains, and the game got under way.

By all accounts, it was no classic. Typical Cup final nerves got the better of both teams in the first half, with neither willing to risk any mistakes. A hard, uneven playing surface also made control difficult, and – apart from one Burnley effort hitting the crossbar – there was little goalmouth action before the interval. The

"Liverpool's hopes of lifting the elusive trophy had come to an end. But they had played their part in a historic final – the first to be witnessed by royalty, and the last to be played at Crystal Palace."

second half provided better entertainment, but it was the sort of tight game in which a single goal was always likely to be the decider. When it came, in the 58th minute, it was Burnley's fans who had reason to celebrate: a Bert Freeman volley had given Liverpool 'keeper Kenny Campbell no chance.

It remained 1–0 until the final whistle: Liverpool's hopes of lifting the elusive trophy

had come to an end. But they had played their part in a historic final – the first to be witnessed by royalty, and the last to be played at Crystal Palace. The fans were disappointed, but grateful for the excitement the team had provided throughout their longest-ever Cup run. When the players' train arrived home, there were thousands waiting to thank them.

1919 • DAVID ASHWORTH APPOINTED MANAGER

1921 • IRISH FREE STATE FORMED

1922 • LEAGUE CHAMPIONS

1923 • ASHWORTH LEAVES

• MATT McQUEEN TAKES OVER

CHAPTER THREE
1919–1939

This Was Anfield

• LEAGUE CHAMPIONS

1926 • GENERAL STRIKE

1928 • KOP ROOF BUILT

• GEORGE PATTERSON APPOINTED MANAGER

1932 • GREAT DEPRESSION

• FIRST MERSEY TUNNEL OPENS

1933 • GORDON HODGSON SETS SCORING RECORDS

1936 • GEORGE KAY APPOINTED MANAGER

• ABDICATION CRISIS

1939 • WORLD WAR TWO BEGINS

YOU'LL NEVER WALK ALONE
LIVERPOOL FOOTBALL CLUB
EST·1892 ®

"HE DOMINATED HIS PENALTY AREA COMPLETELY.
HE HAS THE EYE OF AN EAGLE, THE SWIFT
MOVEMENT OF A PANTHER WHEN FLINGING
HIMSELF AT A SHOT, AND THE CLUTCH OF A VICE
WHEN GRIPPING THE BALL."

THE TIMES

Anfield in 1922, with the uncovered Kop to the left.

THE FIRST POST-WAR SEASON SAW AN EXPANSION OF DIVISION ONE TO 22 CLUBS. THE PLAYERS' MAXIMUM WAGE WAS RAISED TO £9 A WEEK, WHILE THE GOVERNMENT'S NEW ENTERTAINMENT TAX TOOK THE MINIMUM COST OF WATCHING A MATCH UP TO A SHILLING.

But increased prices could not dampen public enthusiasm. The fans were hungry for football, and throughout 1919–20 attendances boomed. In Liverpool the average Anfield gate approached 40,000, with 48,000 turning up for the December League derby, and 50,000 packing the ground for a third round FA Cup tie against Birmingham.

A few of the pre-war players – like Longworth, MacKinlay, Lacey and Sheldon – were still going strong, though there were also several new faces. One who would become a favourite over the next few years was a bow-legged Geordie named Harry Chambers. The man the fans called "Smiler" made his debut in 1919 and soon became a goalscoring great – finding the net, on average, once every two games.

Other new arrivals included three local boys: Widnes-born inside-forward Dick Forshaw; full-back Tom Lucas from St Helens; and Liverpool's own Tom Bromilow. As a soldier invalided out of the Army, Bromilow must have looked an unlikely prospect when he arrived at Anfield – in uniform – asking for a trial. But he made an immediate impression, breaking into the first team within weeks of the new season, and winning the first of five England caps just two years later.

That year also saw the emergence of two other men, both destined to make a massive impression on

The Liverpool and Everton squads in the 1920s – note the large number of Liverpool players from Merseyside.

Liverpool FC. The first was goalkeeper Elisha Scott (see page 37), whose brilliant form in the reserves allowed him to claim the senior-team jersey from Kenny Campbell. The second was a former referee from Watford named David Ashworth.

Before hiring Ashworth as team boss that December, Liverpool were still managerless. Since Watson's death, all recruitment and selection had been dictated by the board, with training left to a succession of ex-players. But the appointment gave the club a new focus. And from then on it was Ashworth, in consultation with chairman W.R. Williams, who would make all the key decisions.

He offered a complete contrast to the club's previous manager. Whereas Watson was large and charismatic, Ashworth was quiet, tidy and precise. He was also diminutive, with some accounts describing him as just a whisker over five feet tall. His background was different, too. Watson was a championship-winner three times over when he started work at Anfield, but Ashworth had won nothing. He had earned respect for making Oldham a First Division force. But since he'd left Boundary Park – apparently in a row over money – he had achieved little with Stockport County.

At Liverpool, Ashworth had the chance to prove himself on the big

TOP 10 LEAGUE APP'S 1919–1939		
1	ELISHA SCOTT	402
2.	GORDON HODGSON	359
3.	TOM BROMILOW	341
4.	TOM LUCAS	341
5.	JIMMY McDOUGALL	339
6.	FRED HOPKIN	335
7.	DON MACKINLAY	325
8.	ARTHUR RILEY	322
9.	HARRY CHAMBERS	310
10.	TOM BRADSHAW	27

PLAYER ELISHA **SCOTT**

The Belfast boy was just 17 when he came to Anfield. By the time he crossed back over the Irish Sea, he was nearly 40, a vastly experienced international – and the most legendary figure the club had ever produced.

It was his elder brother Billy who gave Liverpool the tip off about his extraordinary talent. Scott snr – who had himself kept goal for Everton's 1906 FA Cup-winning side – told John McKenna and Tom Watson they should see the precocious teenager in action for his hometown club, Belfast Celtic. As soon as they did, they knew he could be the latest in a long line of world-class Liverpool 'keepers.

They bought him as a long-term replacement for Scottish international Kenny Campbell, but watched as he staked a claim for the first-team jersey within a matter of months. When Campbell was injured on New Year's Day, 1913, Scott made his debut – and was so impressive that the opponents, Newcastle United, offered him £1,000 for his signature immediately after the final whistle. Facing the prospect of a lengthy spell back in the reserves, Scott was tempted to accept, but Watson persuaded him to bide his time, promising that he would be Liverpool's first-choice 'keeper within two years.

The manager kept his word. Scott was seriously challenging Campbell for a regular place towards the end of the 1914–15 season, and only the interruption of the First World War halted his progress. When the fighting ended, his supremacy was unquestioned. He was missing only three

area completely". Another said: "He has the eye of an eagle, the swift movement of a panther when flinging himself at a shot, and the clutch of a vice when gripping the ball."

He was also one of the game's great characters. He practised obsessively, training longer than anyone else, and spending hours throwing the ball against a wall to catch it on the rebound. His fitness regime would continue even when training was over. He shunned the trams, and could usually be seen walking the three miles from Anfield to the Mersey Ferry terminals, en route to his Wirral home.

On match days he would stride out in his trademark long-johns and knee pads, to be greeted by the Kop's chant of "Lisha, Lisha". Then, as soon as the action was underway he'd keep the crowd entertained with his industrial-strength language. As one newspaper politely put it: "His piping Belfast brogue could be heard issuing his defenders with instructions, and, sometimes, imprecations."

Although an automatic choice

On match days he would stride out in his trademark long-johns and knee pads, to be greeted by the Kop's chant of "Lisha, Lisha".

times during Liverpool's 1921–22 championship campaign, and was an ever-present when they retained the title the following year. Playing 81 games in those two seasons, he conceded just 61 goals.

At 5ft 9½in, Scott was no bigger than average, but his skill and agility made him an imposing figure. One contemporary newspaper said he "dominated his penalty

throughout the 1920s and early '30s, Scott gradually began to struggle for a place. A £250 bid from Everton was rejected after Liverpool fans bombarded the local newspapers with protest letters, but, when his old club Belfast Celtic offered him the player-manager's post, even his most ardent admirers could recognize the emotional pull.

His last game for the Reds came at

Chelsea in February 1934. Three months later he said goodbye to the Liverpool fans, with a tearful speech from the directors box on the final day of the season, but even though Anfield had seen the last of him he continued to play at the top level, winning his 31st international cap two years later – at the age of 42. As a manager he remained at the helm of the Belfast club until, in 1949, it folded.

TEAM OF THE TWENTIES
*The 1922 side featuring Don MacKinlay
(front centre) and Fred Hopkin (front right)*

TOP 10
LGE GOALSCORERS 1919–1939

1.	GORDON HODGSON	135
2.	DICK FORSHAW	117
3.	BERRY NIEUWENHUYS	69
4.	ADOLF ("ALF") HANSON	50
5.	DICK EDMED	44
6.	JIMMY SMITH	38
7.	FRED HOWE	36
8.	DICK JOHNSON	36
9.	JACKIE BALMER	34
10.	VIC WRIGHT	33

season, however. Boasting a team containing the best 'keeper in the land, a defence with four internationals, plus two free-scoring strikers, Liverpool lost just one of their opening 15 matches. A series of five straight wins in January and February made them title favourites. Then they made up for a late loss of form with home wins over Cardiff and Burnley, plus a 4–1 victory at West Brom on the last day of the season. Spurs, who had been heading the chasing pack, could not make up the lost ground – and the championship trophy headed back to Anfield for the first time in 16 years.

For a city suffering from the post-war economic downturn it was a massive morale boost, and MPs, councillors and civic dignitaries rushed to offer their congratulations. They were all there six weeks later when the club laid on a lavish reception for the team at the Adelphi Hotel. The entire squad were pictured outside in their smart lounge suits before being wined, dined, entertained and, finally, presented with gold watches as a mark of thanks for all their efforts. Even the old 1906 championship-winning team were invited, and the evening ended with a toast in their honour.

GROWING STRONGER

Ashworth's team reached the height of its powers during the following season. Once again the defence was the envy of the League, but this time the forward line also showed others the way. At home, the early form was awesome: six wins, no defeats, 26 goals scored, seven conceded. "Smiler" Chambers did most of the damage, finding the net 22 times during the campaign. He was at his most lethal in the 5–1 derby rout – scoring a hat-trick in front of a then-record 54,368 house at Anfield.

It was a season when Forshaw weighed in with another 19 goals and Johnson, 14. Even Fred Hopkin, the shot-shy winger, managed to score in one of his 42 appearances, but his goal – in a home victory over Bolton – was so rare that it set off riotous, and dangerous, celebrations. Lifelong Reds' fan Billy O'Donnell remembered it well:

stage. He made a solid, if unspectacular, start, guiding the team to fourth place at the end of his first season. Highlights included 15 goals from Chambers, a 3–1 home victory over Everton, and a game at Manchester City's Hyde Road ground in front of the King. Unfortunately, the monarch was proving to be something of an unlucky charm for Liverpool by then. As in the 1914 Cup final, they ended up being beaten.

They finished fourth again the following year, although this time they scored more goals and conceded fewer. Scott had consolidated his position as first-choice 'keeper, while up front Chambers, Forshaw and Dick Johnson shared 44 goals. In one memorable week in October 1920, Liverpool did the double over Everton in front of a combined attendance of 105,000. When Forshaw grabbed the winner at Anfield, reporters claimed the Kop "rocked with the convulsion of a volcano".

They had much more to celebrate in the 1921–22

The 1922 title was won with a team that cost virtually nothing. Immediately after the First World War, Liverpool's policy was to recruit locally and to promote from the reserves. At the club's annual meeting, chairman W.R. Williams mocked those who went in for big money transfers: "We believe that it is in blending, not in paying, that a club succeeds."

It was difficult to argue with this approach. Liverpool had won the League with six points to spare, losing just seven of their 42 games, and conceding only 36 goals. With Elisha Scott between the posts, Eph Longworth marshalling the defence, and Harry Chambers getting the goals, they were destined for more honours the following year.

This photograph was taken before the team's lavish commemoration dinner at Liverpool's Adelphi Hotel, where they were treated to comedy, music, French cuisine, in addition to gold watches presented by a grateful Board. It brings together the club's best-known faces of the 1920s, along with all its directors and officials, and – on the left of the front row – three former managers.

Back Row (L to R): H. Beadles, F. Wood, J Lillie, G. Owen, J. Kane.

Third Row: H. Riley (Groundsman), R. Forshaw, H. Chambers, D. Shone, T. Lucas, W. Lacey, F. Checkland, H. Wadsworth, R. Johnson, H. Lewis, F. Mitchell, F. Hopkin.

Second Row: G. Gillespy, E. Parry, J. Bamber, P. McKinney, W. Cunningham, E. Scott, T. Bromilow, C. Harrington, J. McNabb, W. Matthews, W. Wadsworth, W. Constantin (Asst. Groundsman), C. Wilson (Players' Coach), W. Connell (Trainer).

Front Row: G. Patterson (Secretary), D. Ashworth (Manager), M. McQueen (Director), J. Hill (Director) R. Martindale (Director), W.R. Williams (Chairman), J. Asbury (Vice Chairman) E. Bainbridge (Director), T. Compton (Director), W. cartwright (Director), W. Webb (Director).

Foreground: E. Longworth, D. MacKinlay.

A quarter of an hour before the end of the game they opened the main gate, and hundreds of fellows, like myself, used to get in for nothing. You'd see a good quarter of an hour's football, and when I got in it always seemed that there was a corner.

Hopkin was the outside-left for Liverpool. He scored one goal and the Anfield Road Stand went on fire. A furore went up: 'Fire' ... all we could see was smoke.

It was all anyone else could see, too. With the pitch and players hardly visible, the referee seriously considered abandoning the game. Only after the police evacuated the stand, and the Westminster Road Fire Brigade contained the flames, did he allow play to restart. Liverpool went on to win 3–0.

It was just one episode in an eventful season. The team rounded off 1922 with five straight wins throughout December, and when they racked up another three victories in January they began to look unassailable. Everything was on course for a second successive title, but then came a decision that put all those plans in jeopardy.

ASHWORTH QUITS

On 23 January 1923 David Ashworth walked out of Anfield – becoming the first Liverpool manager ever to resign. The reasons were shrouded in secrecy, and his decision to rejoin struggling Oldham Athletic baffled football fans everywhere. Some newspapers speculated that he had had a row with the Anfield board; others thought he retained a strong emotional attachment to a club he had brought into the Football League back in 1905. Ashworth himself remained silent on the issue, and his departure has continued to puzzle club historians for 80 years.

The truth, however, is simple: he left for cash. At the end of 1922, Oldham were rooted to the bottom of Division One and looking certainties for relegation. On Christmas Day Liverpool went to Boundary Park and

ARSENAL V. LIVERPOOL, 1923
The Reds won this FA Cup replay.

put another nail in their coffin, with a 2–0 victory. Afterwards, the directors invited Ashworth to the boardroom and tried to persuade him to come back and save his former club from the drop. They succeeded. As reported in the Lancashire club's own official history: "It seemed a strange decision for him to return because Liverpool were top. But, as with his leaving in 1914, money seemed to be the all-important motivation in Ashworth's decision. The Oldham Athletic directors are believed to have offered him a lucrative deal to entice him away."

Ashworth may have looked forward to a healthy payday, but his decision proved to be a personal disaster. Oldham's performances failed to improve and they were duly relegated. As their gates dwindled he was left with virtually no money to strengthen the squad, and he chose to leave after little more than a year. Short and unhappy spells followed at Manchester City, Stockport and Walsall. Finally, he dropped out of management altogether and ended up as a talent scout for Blackpool.

His departure from Anfield, though, had given Liverpool their own headaches. With 17 games left the board had no time to look for an outside replacement. Instead, they reshuffled the backroom staff and put fellow director Matt McQueen in charge of team affairs. As one of the original Team of the Macs in the 1890s, McQueen had played in every position, including goalkeeper. Now the man who had proved so versatile on the pitch was being asked to take on another role – and it would be his most demanding yet.

He succeeded, but it was tighter than Liverpool would have hoped. As the season drew to a close, the team's form dipped and they took just seven points from their final seven games. Luckily, their earlier performances had given them a substantial points cushion, and when they beat Stoke 1–0 at Anfield in the final match of the season, the trophy had already been secured for the second year running.

BEHIND THE TIMES

McQueen had earned his place in history, but he never tasted success again. His next five years as manager were undistinguished, with the team finishing no higher than fourth in the table. But while he failed to land any more silverware, he deserves credit for bringing some exceptionally gifted players to Anfield.

One of his most notable – if unusual – signings was the Aberdeen full-back "Parson" Jimmy Jackson, who combined playing football with religious studies. As a devout Presbyterian, Jackson was vigorously opposed to smoking, drinking and gambling. His dislike of strong language also led to regular on-the-field rows with Elisha Scott. As late Reds fan Joe Anderson recalled:

"Scott used to swear like a trooper. If the other team had a corner, and you were standing behind the goal, you could hear him cursing, effing and blinding at his defenders. When the ball had been cleared the Parson used to have a real go at him, wagging his finger, and tut-tutting. He'd walk away shaking his head – then Scott would give him a mouthful, too."

Jackson went on to make 224 appearances, many as captain. He played in every outfield position and won the distinction of being selected for both the Football League and a Scottish League XI. But his personal goals lay elsewhere. He used his football career to finance courses at university, where he read philosophy and Greek. On retirement he went to Cambridge to finish his religious education, and eventually achieved a lifetime's ambition by being ordained as a Presbyterian minister.

Jackson may have been a crowd favourite, but the real hero of the

M. McQUEEN, Esq.
Manager

MATT McQUEEN
*Played in every position for Liverpool,
and became manager in 1923.*

time was the South African-born striker Gordon Hodgson. As one of the Springbok team who toured Britain in 1925, the free-scoring Hodgson made a huge impression. McQueen persuaded him to remain in England, where he could combine top-flight professional football with his other great passion, cricket. He stayed for 11 years – turning out as centre-forward for Liverpool, and as a fast bowler for Lancashire.

From the outset, Hodgson was a goalscoring sensation; a genuine answer to Everton's legendary Dixie Dean. He found the net 232 times in 359 appearances – and was leading marksman in seven of his nine seasons with Liverpool. Although his tally of goals was eventually eclipsed by Roger Hunt and Ian Rush, his total of 17 hat-tricks remains a club record. At 32 he left for Aston Villa, then went on to rewrite the record books at Leeds, scoring 67 goals in 120 appearances – and hitting the target five times in one match.

But while McQueen was recruiting talented individuals, his competitors were building complete playing units. As the decade progressed, the Huddersfield manager Herbert Chapman emerged as the king of tactical football, putting strong emphasis on teamwork and ball skills. He also became the first manager to wrest complete control of team selection from the directors – a position that would not be copied at Anfield until the late 1950s. Chapman's success put rival clubs in the shade. Under his leadership, Huddersfield emulated Liverpool by winning two successive League titles. By the time he left, they were on their way to a third.

A ROOF OVER OUR HEADS

When the Yorkshire club's grip finally

TOP 10	
HAT-TRICKS 1919–1939	
1. GORDON HODGSON	17
2. DICK FORSHAW	6
3. HARRY CHAMBERS	5
4. FRED HOWE	3
5. DICK JOHNSON	2
6. WILLIAM DEVLIN	2
7. HAROLD BARTON	2
8. HENRY RACE	1
9. JIMMY WALSH	1
10. DANNY SHONE	1
REID & WRIGHT ON 1 EACH	

ALL COMPETITIONS

loosened, it was Everton, Sheffield Wednesday, then Chapman's new team, Arsenal, who dominated Division One. Liverpool, meanwhile, struggled to find consistency and were never more than also-rans. In 1928 Matt McQueen retired as manager after a horrific car crash in which he lost a leg. He was replaced by club secretary George Patterson, an ex-Marine FC amateur player who had worked as Tom Watson's assistant before the war.

His arrival coincided with another major development at Anfield, one that would cement its reputation as the noisiest, and most atmospheric, ground in the country. The landmark was the rebuilding of the Kop, extended to 425 feet x 131 feet, designed to house nearly 30,000 standing spectators – and finished with a vast iron cantilever roof that amplified their roars to deafening levels.

On match days the dark, imposing new enclosure

"OH, I AM A LIVERPUDLIAN..."
A rare picture of the Kop before it was covered, and when only a wooden fence kept the fans from the pitch.

would begin to fill up well ahead of kick-off. Queues often started forming as early as 11.30 am. And, for the 1928 derby, there were 45,000 in the ground two hours before play started. The normal pre-match entertainment would include a schoolboy game and a set routine from the Edge Hill Silver Prize Band. Interviewed for Liverpool's Radio City in 1993, these elderly fans recalled some more sights and sounds:

Syd Rogers: "In the old days the Spion Kop was just a mound of ashes and rubble, and it wasn't very comfortable to stand on because it was a steep slope and it wasn't terraced. In fact it wasn't terraced until after the last war."

Billy O'Donnell: "They had the boys walking round with the chewing gum and chocolates on a tray, and the crowd would throw money down. They were quite good at throwing the packets. If anyone else caught it, they'd hand it over: 'Here y'are.'"

Alf Smithies: "The Kop used to have quite a sense of humour. You'd get a fellow shout out something, perhaps he wasn't in favour of the game, and if he was wrong, he'd get an offering from round about. Perhaps he'd get a custard on the back of his head. It was all good tempered, as a general rule."

Jack Payne: "To add a little bit of sport, especially with the opposing spectators (no segregation in them days), the thing was, 'Lads, what about a shilling in the hat?' Consequently, the ten forwards were put in the hat. Someone would tear the edge off the morning paper. The names were all screwed up and put in a cap. You shook them all up. A shilling each was taken up by one fellow. The one with the first forward to score got ten bob [50 pence] ... which wasn't bad, them days.'

Harold Atkinson: "When [opposing] fans met one another they were quite cordial. In fact they used to laugh and joke, and a few friendships were set up. Sometimes they'd arrange to go to their ground for the return game, and some stayed the weekend. This was the way it was."

Going to the match had become a way of life for many on Merseyside. But as the Great Depression of the 1930s began to bite, fewer of them could find the money to attend. In the 1932–33 season – with local unemployment at around 30 per cent – the combined average League gate at Anfield and Goodison fell below 50,000. Still, the fanaticism remained. A 1938 study by the Pilgrim Trust charity reported how jobless fans still used to turn up at

Anfield on match days – simply to watch their fellow supporters going through the turnstiles.

THE TWO GEORGES

The trophy cabinet remained bare during Patterson's eight-year reign. Liverpool finished no higher than fifth in the table, and never progressed beyond the sixth round of the FA Cup. Lack of goals was often the major problem, and their record would have been worse still without Hodgson's formidable firepower.

But Patterson – like McQueen before him – proved to be a shrewd operator in the transfer market. He recruited a mixture of unknowns – like Liverpool-born striker Jack Balmer, and future manager Phil Taylor – plus established internationals, such as the 6ft 3in centre-back Tom "Tiny" Bradshaw, signed from Bury in 1930 for a then-record club fee of £8,000.

He was also keen on South Africans, and employed talent scouts in that country to keep him informed of any up-and-coming teenagers who fancied a football career in England. During the early 1930s, seven Springboks made the long journey north, among them Berry Nieuwenhuys, a winger who would become an Anfield favourite for the next 15 years. The tall, slim "Nivvy" terrorized opposing defences with his strong running, tricky dribbling and cannonball shot. By the time he left in 1947 he had made 250 appearances, scored 79 goals and won a championship winner's medal.

Patterson's other notable signings included Glasgow Rangers striker Sam English, who arrived in 1933 after breaking the Scottish scoring record with 44 goals in a season. English scored in eight of his first 11 games, and was on the mark twice when Liverpool beat Tranmere in a 1934 FA Cup tie, before a staggering 61,036 Anfield crowd. The same year saw the arrival of Sheffield Wednesday's international defender Ernie Blenkinsop, along with his England colleague Tom Cooper, from Derby.

In the summer of 1935, Patterson took his team off on a pre-season tour of the Canary Islands. International travel was still considered wildly exotic then, and as their cruise liner docked in Las Palmas, the Depression gloom of Merseyside must have seemed a world away. Touring the beaches, town squares and street cafés, the players found themselves treated as celebrities by the

JOURNEY TO THE SUN
The 1935 tour of the Canaries, where the players soaked up the sun – and met Miss Spain.

MANAGER GEORGE **KAY**

Who knows what George Kay would have achieved at Anfield if ill-health – and Hitler – had not intervened. Liverpool looked certainties for relegation when he took charge in 1936, but within three years he had put them in shape to challenge for the title once again.

In later years Bob Paisley would list Kay as one of the great managers. And Sir Matt Busby would describe him as a model of dedication and determination: "I grew to admire George Kay for the resolute way he set about transforming Liverpool. But for the war, I feel the club would have been among the major honours in the 1940s."

Kay was a gifted centre-back whose playing days were disrupted by World War One. He fought in the trenches on the Western Front before resuming his career with Belfast Celtic, and became the first Englishman to skipper the Irish League club. In 1923 he captained West Ham in the famous "White Horse" Cup final, when more than 200,000 people attended the Wembley clash with one of his old clubs, Bolton.

He came to Merseyside after a five-year managerial spell with Southampton. Two of his earliest signings – Paisley and Billy Liddell – would prove to be among the most important in the club's history. But when World War Two broke out, his promising new squad were scattered around the globe. And, for the next seven years, he had to cobble together makeshift teams for the chaotic wartime Regional League programme.

When hostilities ended, Kay got back to the job in hand. Along with chairman Bill McConnell, he masterminded Liverpool's 1946 pre-season tour of America – giving players time to get reacquainted, and the chance to build up their physiques on unrationed steaks. His team came back confident and fighting fit. Nine months later they lifted the championship trophy.

Kay was a Mancunian, burly and blunt. He never wore a tracksuit, preferring instead his trademark three-piece suit. On team photos he usually looked like he had come straight

from the set of a gangster movie, but despite the tough appearance, he was a deep and subtle thinker. He believed in careful planning, packing the entire squad off to Southport for two nights before every home game, so he could monitor their diet and exercise regime. He also made sure that everyone got plenty of sleep – and no sex.

Among the players his word was law. When an American journalist asked if they were looking forward to nights on the town during the New York trip, he replied: "The boys are professionals. If they are

intemperate in anything they do they won't keep their jobs. They know that. So far no one has lost his job."

A naturally shy man, Kay found it difficult to communicate – even with his favourite stars. Bill Shankly, who guested in one of Anfield's wartime teams, once recalled his style of team selection: "All the players were in the passageway including Billy Liddell and myself. But George Kay didn't speak. He just went round touching people on the shoulder. If he touched you then you were playing."

But in later years Liddell did develop a close friendship with Kay. He became concerned as his manager chain smoked, lost weight and grew visibly stressed by the demands of the job. In the run-up to the 1950 FA Cup final, Kay collapsed and needed medical attention. He recovered in time to see his team walk out at Wembley, but suffered a relapse shortly afterwards. In January 1951 he was forced to quit his job on doctors' orders, and, in 1954 – after a long spell in hospital – he died.

"He was the Shankly of his day. He ate, slept and lived for one thing only – football." CYRIL DONE

Liddell was convinced that overwork had contributed to Kay's illness. And, in his autobiography, described his friend's obsessive dedication: "He had no other thought but for the good of Liverpool during his waking hours, and also during many of his nights. He told me often of the times he had lain in bed, unable to sleep, pondering over the manifold problems that beset every manager, but which can be a curse to the oversensitive or excessively conscientious ones ... If ever a man gave his life for a club, George Kay did so for Liverpool."

curious islanders. Even Miss Spain turned up at one match to see how the pasty-faced boys from England coped with the heat.

But a few weeks later they were back at home ... and down to earth with a bump. Their form veered wildly throughout the campaign, and every time they appeared to get a run going, their performances dipped again. The most extreme example of inconsistency came in a four-day period when they hammered Everton 6–0 at home – then went to Maine Road and got thrashed by the same margin.

No wonder Patterson began to fall ill. In 1936, the Liverpool boss also decided to make way for another man. He stayed on as club secretary, but from that moment on it was new manager George Kay who had the job of keeping the team up (see page 44).

His appointment coincided with the £8,000 capture of Matt Busby, from Manchester City. Years later the man who conquered Europe as a manager recalled the scene that greeted him at Anfield: "Liverpool were really struggling then and in danger of being relegated to the Second Division. It was a time when men who had been great players were coming towards the close of illustrious careers ... George Kay worked like a Trojan to put things right."

With Kay installed as manager, and Busby as half-back, Liverpool managed to avoid the drop, finishing 19th at the close of the 1935–36 season. They ended the following year just one place higher, and suffered humiliation in the FA Cup, losing 3–0 to Division Two strugglers Norwich in the third round.

But Kay started to rebuild. In defence he brought in reserve full-back Jim

MATT BUSBY
Signed for Liverpool from Manchester City in 1936.

Harley, a former Scottish sprint champion. Up front he introduced Willie Fagan, a 20-year-old recruit from Preston, where he had played alongside both Jimmy Milne – father of Gordon – and Bill Shankly. Results started to improve, and within a year Liverpool had jumped to 11th in the table. However, the time for playing football was fast running out.

WAR APPROACHES

On 30 September 1938 Britain agreed to Germany's demand to be allowed to take over part of Czechoslovakia – in return for Hitler's promise to expand no further. Prime Minister Neville Chamberlain arrived home clutching a piece of paper promising "peace in our time". And just 24 hours later 60,000 Merseyside football fans marked his return from Munich by singing the National Anthem before the League derby at Goodison.

But relief from the threat of war was only temporary, as football continued to be played against the backdrop of much more significant events. On 15 March 1939, as Liverpool were drawing away at Huddersfield, German tanks were rolling into Prague. Two weeks later, as the Reds beat Brentford at Anfield, the Nazis issued threats against Poland.

The season ended with Liverpool in 11th place once again, and with Everton as champions, but any hopes of capturing the trophy from their great rivals were short lived. The new campaign had only just got under way when, on 3 September 1939, Britain declared war on Germany. Liverpool had played three games when soccer was suspended. It would be another seven years before their next League match.

RED AND BLUE IN WHITES:
A Liverpool and Everton cricket team, starring Gordon Hodgson (front row, left) next to fellow scoring legend Dixie Dean

1940 • "BLITZ" BOMBING OF LIVERPOOL

• BILLY LIDDELL'S WARTIME DEBUT

1945 • WORLD WAR TWO ENDS

1946 • PRE-SEASON TOUR OF AMERICA

1947 • FIRST DIVISION CHAMPIONS

CHAPTER FOUR
1939–1959

War and Peace

1950 • FA CUP RUNNERS-UP

1951 • DON WELSH APPOINTED MANAGER

1952 • RECORD ANFIELD ATTENDANCE

• QUEEN ELIZABETH II CROWNED

1954 • RELEGATION TO DIVISION TWO

1956 • PHIL TAYLOR BECOMES MANAGER

1957 • FLOODLIGHTS INSTALLED AT ANFIELD

1959 • FA CUP DEFEAT BY WORCESTER CITY

• ROGER HUNT'S DEBUT

• BILL SHANKLY APPOINTED MANAGER

YOU'LL NEVER WALK ALONE
LIVERPOOL
FOOTBALL CLUB
EST·1892 ®

"I WOULD NOT LIKE TO PLAY AGAINST PAISLEY. HE HAS LITTLE HEIGHT, TWO STOUT LIMBS, A HEART OF GOLD AND A TACKLE THAT IS RIOTOUS. HE HAS TENACITY WRITTEN ALL OVER HIS FACE."

THE SPORTS SPECTATOR, 1947

Ready for action ... Liverpool players in uniform, 1939.

ALTHOUGH THE LEAGUE PROGRAMME WAS SUSPENDED IN 1939 THE GOVERNMENT WANTED FOOTBALL TO CONTINUE, AS A WAY OF MAINTAINING MORALE THROUGHOUT THE COUNTRY. WITHIN WEEKS, THE GAME'S AUTHORITIES HAD SET UP A NEW REGIONAL COMPETITION THAT WOULD SURVIVE FOR ALMOST THE ENTIRE WAR PERIOD.

The organizational problems were huge. Crowds were initially limited to 8,000 maximum, entry had to be all-ticket, and teams were forbidden from travelling more than 50 miles to a match. Players often cancelled appearances at the last minute because they had been called up. Sometimes they were replaced with volunteers from the crowd, and hopeful spectators even started taking their boots along in case they were called upon to play. As the war went on, kits became scarce

as clothing coupons ran out. The matches themselves were sometimes abandoned because of air raid warnings.

As in 1914, Liverpool FC displayed great support for the war effort. In July 1939, the Anfield players were the first to respond to the FA's appeal for professionals to join the Territorial Army. Everyone who was old enough put their names forward: Matt Busby and Phil Taylor were among volunteers for the 9th King's Liverpool Battalion; Jim Harley signed up for the Royal Navy; Berry Niewenhuys elected to join the RAF. Bob Paisley – who had only joined the club in May that year – became a gunner in the Royal Artillery. He was destined to become one of Britain's wartime heroes, helping the Desert Rats sweep to victory at El Alamein, and driving a tank during the battle to liberate Rome in 1944.

With so many professionals away on active service, the Football League introduced a "guest" system whereby players could turn out for any club. Usually they played for the team that was nearest to their barracks, so they often found themselves appearing at the most unlikely venues. It also meant that clubs like Blackpool and Aldershot – with huge military bases nearby – suddenly had the cream of English football available on their doorsteps.

But Liverpool's talent shortage was not too severe, and throughout the war a succession of top-class internationals turned out for the team. They included Charlton 'keeper Sam Bartram, Arsenal's Welsh

Bootle-born centre-forward Cyril Done (right of picture) made his debut in the last game before World War Two. His second league apperance came seven years later.

international Horace Cumner, Stan Cullis of Wolves and Cliff Britton from Everton. Charlton's Don Welsh – later to be Liverpool manager – was another temporary wartime recruit. In one amazing 12–1 win against Southport he was on the scoresheet six times.

Some guests, however, were even more distinguished. In February 1942 the great Irish midfielder Peter Doherty turned up to watch Liverpool take on Blackpool at Bloomfield Road – and was quickly persuaded by George Kay to pull on a red shirt. And in May that year, when Liverpool beat Everton 4–1 at Anfield, Preston's Bill Shankly was wearing the number four jersey.

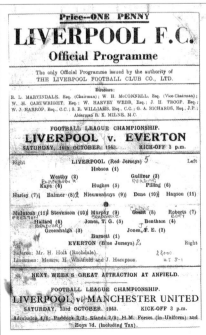

One player who took full advantage of his colleagues' absence was Billy Liddell (see page 51), who was still too young for active service when hostilities started. The 17-year-old winger made his wartime debut on New Year's Day 1940, scoring once in Liverpool's 7–1 victory over Crewe at Anfield. A week later he went to Maine Road and grabbed a hat-trick in a 7–1 win against Manchester City. As he left the field, City 'keeper Frank Swift gave the teenager a pat on the back, and a word of advice: "Well done, sonny boy – just don't do that sort of thing too often." But Swift, who would later lose his life in the Munich air disaster, knew he had just witnessed the emergence of a phenomenal talent. Within 18 months his teenage opponent was appearing for a Football League representative side against a British XI. He was also selected for Scotland, but had to withdraw because of injury.

For Liverpudlians, football was a welcome diversion from the battering the city had suffered at the hands of Hitler's Blitzkrieg bombers. As Cyril Done later recalled: "We were in the entertainment business and obviously people in Britain wanted entertaining as much as possible. The spirit in Britain I don't think has ever been better, of friendship, companionship, of helping one another. I think the powers-that-be thought it was good for the people of Merseyside that we should keep playing our game, the same as entertainers should carry on with their business."

The results were usually academic, but there were still celebrations when Liverpool were crowned champions of the Northern Region in 1943. That same year brought an incredible Anfield derby, with Liverpool scoring five times in the last eight minutes to overwhelm Everton 5–2. More than 13,000 turned up to watch – raising £946 for the Lord Mayor of Liverpool's War Fund. In 1944 the team beat Bolton to lift the Lancashire Cup after a two-legged final. And, with the Government's crowd limit lifted, Merseyside's highest wartime attendance – 44,820 – saw Liverpool beat their neighbours 3–2 at Goodison Park.

As the war came to an end the League rules were revised, the number of games increased, and the FA Cup reinstated. Liverpool went out in the fourth round, and finished 11th in the 1945–46 Northern League table. At the same time, the war heroes began to return. One of the first to be demobbed was Matt Busby,

TOM COOPER
Former Liverpool captain who lost his life during World War Two.

his playing days by then behind him. Liverpool wanted to make him part of their coaching staff, but his outstanding leadership potential had already been noted elsewhere. Reading approached him about an assistant manager's job, and Ayr United tried to tempt him back to Scotland, but the offer he could not refuse came in October 1945 – when Manchester United asked him to fill the boss's chair at Old Trafford.

Of the other players, Liddell – who had eventually qualified as an RAF navigator – came home safe following service in Europe and Canada, as did full-back Eddie Spicer, wounded and decorated for bravery; Jim Harley, mentioned in despatches; defender Bill Jones, awarded the Military Medal for helping rescue wounded comrades while under fire; Jack Balmer, who had been present at Dunkirk; and Bob Paisley, shot at and almost blinded in the North African desert.

Sadly, club captain Tom Cooper was one of the 75 professional footballers who did not make it. He had been among the first to volunteer for the 9th Kings, serving as a sergeant in the Infantry Unit, and later joining the Military Police. In April 1940 the Stoke-born full-back turned out for Liverpool against his home-town club at Anfield. Just two months later he was killed in a motorcycle accident while on despatch duty.

THE AMERICAN WAY

It would be almost a year between the end of the war and the resumption of the normal League programme, but Liverpool's chairman, William McConnell, made good use of the time.

"Billy Mac" was a caterer whose company had helped keep Merseyside's dockers fed during the darkest days of the Blitz. As well as running a successful business he had a keen interest in nutrition, and acted as an adviser to the Government on catering matters throughout the war years. As a result

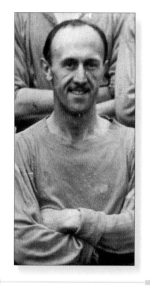

JACKIE BALMER
First Reds striker to score three consecutive hat-tricks.

Comparing players from different eras is fraught with problems, but if anyone is qualified to make an attempt it is Ian Callaghan. The man who holds Liverpool's all-time appearance record once worshipped Billy Liddell from the terraces. He has seen hundreds of players come and go since then, but has always reserved pride of place for his boyhood idol: "In my opinion, Liddell, Keegan and Dalglish were the club's best players ever, but I would put Billy ahead of the other two as being the greatest."

Many of Cally's generation would not argue. By their accounts, Liddell combined the best of everything: the strength of Tommy Smith, the pace and power of Emile Heskey, the dribbling ability of Peter Thompson, the thunderous shot of Jimmy Case. Even in an age when British wingers were the best in the world, Liddell was an awesome talent. When the selectors chose their Great Britain representative sides in 1947 and 1955 he was one of only two men to be included in both. The other? Sir Stanley Matthews.

It was Liverpool's Matt Busby who first heard rumours of a supremely gifted 16-year-old playing for the Scottish side Lochgelly Violet back in 1938. On his recommendation, Anfield boss George Kay went to watch – and within days had persuaded the teenager's parents to let him move south. At 17, he signed a £3-a-week professional contract and was on the point of forcing his way into the senior team – only for the war to prevent him taking his place in the First Division.

Liddell played in most of the club's Regional League matches during the early 1940s, making the left-wing position his own, and winning the first of his 28 Scotland caps. He later joined the RAF, serving in Europe and Canada, and turning out for its wartime team, Bomber Command. He was demobbed just a few weeks into the 1946–47 season, then made 35 League appearances for a Liverpool team that went on to lift the championship. He supplied the crosses for Albert Stubbins and Jack Balmer to convert. He cut inside to score with shots of fierce accuracy. And he terrorized First Division defences with the marauding runs for which he would become famous: "Billy was so strong he was

unbelievable," said Bob Paisley. "He would always battle, challenge and show tenacity."

The post-war side went into swift decline in the 1950s, and even the Flying Scot's best efforts were not enough to stop the slide. He had many opportunities to move – including a lucrative offer from the Colombian team Bogota shortly after the 1950 FA Cup final. But, in a show of loyalty that is hard to imagine today, he decided to stay with Liverpool even when they were relegated.

It was largely because of him that Anfield gates remained relatively high throughout the Division Two years. The Kop loved his mix of brute force and skill, happily paying to watch him run defenders ragged, and christening the team "Liddellpool" in his honour. He

switched positions with ease, moving from wing to wing, leading the line as a free-scoring centre-forward, even shoring up the defence during one stint as a full-back.

In the world of professional footballers, Liddell was a man apart. Throughout his time at Anfield he continued to hold down a nine-to-five job as an accountant – a career his parents insisted he followed when they agreed to him moving to Merseyside. He was a non-smoker, tee-totaller, and Methodist lay-preacher. He also supported many charities, gave his time freely to work as a DJ on hospital radio, and served as a magistrate.

The honesty and integrity he displayed in private life also spread to the soccer pitch. His reputation for fairness often led to ovations by opposing sets of supporters. And, in November 1957, when he made his record-breaking 430th League appearance, the entire Notts County team lined up in the centre circle to shake his hand.

He had his last League outing for the club in August 1960 – just four months short of his 40th birthday. Shortly afterwards a crowd of 39,000 – nearly 10,000 more than that season's home average – turned up for his testimonial match against an International XI at Anfield. In all, Liddell made 537 appearances for the Reds, scoring 229 goals. When he bowed out the fans were certain they would never see another player with such ability. And Liverpool FC knew they would never find a better servant.

Billy Liddell died in 2001 after a long illness. He remained a regular spectator at Anfield until the final few months of his life, and will always be remembered as one of the finest players ever to grace its turf.

PHIL TAYLOR Right Half   J. BEDFORD Toronto   HARRY EASTHAM Inside

TOP: *The Mayor of Toronto kicks off the 1946 North American tour.*
CENTRE & BOTTOM: *How the US newspapers reported it.*

DETROIT BASEBALL STAR HANK
GREENBERG HAD A CONTRACT
WORTH $60,000 A YEAR. YET HERE
WAS THE "WORLD-FAMOUS
LIVERPOOL SOCCER TEAM", EACH
EARNING JUST £10 A WEEK.

of his knowledge, he became concerned about the effects of post-war rationing on the club's players. In 1946, high-protein foods like meat, cheese and eggs were still strictly limited. Home-grown vegetables were a rarity in winter, and imported fruit such as oranges and bananas were an almost unheard-of luxury all year round.

McConnell's solution was bold and brilliant. Following discussions with Kay he organized a mammoth pre-season tour of America: six weeks aboard the Queen Mary, plus matches in ten major cities from the southern states of the USA to Canada. While away from home, the players would have time to bond as a team – and, equally important, build up their strength on an unlimited diet of T-bone, fillet and rib-eye steaks.

The trip was a massive success, with the first game against the New York All Stars attracting 20,000 fans to the city's Triboro Stadium. The following matches in Baltimore, Philadelphia and St Louis brought record soccer crowds to all three cities, and had the American press referring to the team as "England's Star Booters". Sports journalists followed them wherever they went, anxious to hear about their war records and curious about conditions back home in England. When they heard how much the players earned, the newspapers were incredulous. This was a country where Detroit baseball star Hank Greenberg had just signed a contract worth $60,000 a year. Yet here was the "world-famous Liverpool soccer team", able to attract home crowds of more than 50,000, but each earning just £10 a week during the season, and £7.50 in summer. When a reporter asked Kay where the rest of the gate money went, he was stumped for an answer, but he did explain that the best players could make a bit of extra cash thanks to win bonuses: "It can all add up to about 15 quid a week – which is still a lot better than working down the mines."

"ENGLAND'S STAR BOOTERS"
*The Reds drew record American crowds for their
match against the New York All-Stars.*

By the time the team crossed the Niagara Falls they had played before 150,000 spectators. Then, up in Toronto, they took on the city's star team, Ulster United, in front of another 14,000 – Canada's biggest-ever soccer attendance. Describing Liverpool's 11–1 victory, the *Toronto Globe & Mail* reported that "Perhaps the finer art of soccer was never better displayed in this country than was the case last night at Maple Leaf Stadium". But, aside from the performance, the players had another reason to remember their Canadian visit. Hearing that nylon was in short supply back in Britain, a local company presented them with dozens of pairs of stockings to take home to their wives.

OFFICIAL **10c.** PROGRAM

LIVERPOOL FOOTBALL CLUB OF ENGLAND
vs.
PHILADELPHIA SELECT OF AMERICAN LEAGUE

LIVERPOOL'S REGULAR LEAGUE LINE-UP

Yellow Jacket Stadium, Phila., Pa.   Sunday, May 26, 1946
PRELIMINARY GAME AT 1:30 P. M.
PHILADELPHIA AMERICAN RESERVES
vs. LIBERTY BELL POST S. C.
Music by Washington Memorial Bagpipe Band

1946 TOUR PROGRAMME
*George Kay's side played in six cities
throughout the USA and Canada.*

Following another victory back in New York, they all boarded ship bound for Southampton. They had played ten, won ten, conceded ten – and scored 70. They had won many friends, and forged links that would lead to future tours in 1948 and 1953. Most crucially, they had achieved what McConnell had planned all along. According to a *New York Times* report:

"Liverpool came to the States for a crack at our teams and our vitamins. It was a clean sweep. The Britons swept all ten of their matches and, like Jack Spratt and his wife, they also swept the platter clean. Away from

AND STUBBINS HEADS THE BALL!
Another trademark Stubbins' diving header, this time against Wolves, 1st May 1948.

the British austerity program, they plunged zestfully into our steaks, eggs, milk and other vittles. Not only was there a perceptible gain in strength on the playing field, but the squad averaged a gain in weight of seven pounds a man."

ALBERT AND THE CRAZY GANG

Kay's new muscle-bound team made a reasonable start to the new season: two wins, one defeat. But after a 5–0 hiding at Old Trafford, he made an instant decision to strengthen the squad. Rumours had been sweeping the football world that Newcastle's prolific centre-forward Albert Stubbins was looking for a move. And as soon as Kay heard that Everton were on their way to sign him, he and McConnell jumped in a car and drove to the North-east.

That same night Stubbins was in a Newcastle cinema, completely unaware that the two Merseyside clubs were in a race for his signature. In an interview for the 1993 book *Three Sides of the Mersey*, he explained what happened next:

"... a notice came up on the screen: 'Would Albert Stubbins please

NICE TO MEET YOU...
Stubbins steps out for his Liverpool debut.

[THE MOST **THRILLING** TITLE RACE IN **YEARS** WAS ABOUT TO END.
AND, FOR THE **FIRST** TIME IN ALMOST A **QUARTER**
OF A **CENTURY**, LIVERPOOL WOULD FINISH **FIRST**.]

THAT SAME OLD FEELING AGAIN...

Anfield, 4th December, 1948, and Strong, the Burnley 'keeper, dives acrobatically to turn the ball round the post, just as he did in the FA Cup semi-final in 1947.

report to St James' Park.' This was about six o'clock, and I went up there, and Mr Kay, representing Liverpool, and Theo Kelly, representing Everton, were there. Stan Seymour, the Newcastle director, said, 'Which representative would you like to see first?' I said, 'Well, flip a coin. Heads Liverpool. Tails Everton.' And it came down heads – Liverpool. Bill McConnell, the Liverpool chairman, and George Kay and myself discussed matters and I was impressed with them both, and with the possibilities of Liverpool, so I said I would go to Liverpool. I met Mr Kelly, who was very gracious about it. I told him I'd decided on Liverpool, and he wished me all the best, which I thought was very sporting."

The £12,500 signing was an inspired one. Stubbins played 36 League games that season and, with Billy Liddell supplying the crosses, scored 24 goals. It was also a vintage campaign for fellow striker Jack Balmer. He ended up with the same League tally, and – hitting a total of ten against Portsmouth, Derby and Arsenal – became the first Liverpool player to score three consecutive hat-tricks.

But it was still a rollercoaster of a season. Superb wins were followed by ridiculous losses; 6–1 victories cancelled out by 5–1 defeats. Only after a disastrous January, when they lost all their League games, did the team start winning

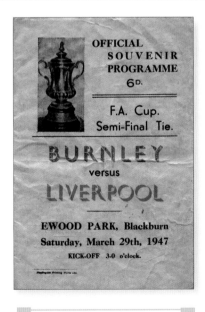

OFFICIAL
SOUVENIR
PROGRAMME
6D.

F.A. Cup.
Semi-Final Tie.

BURNLEY
versus
LIVERPOOL

EWOOD PARK, Blackburn
Saturday, March 29th, 1947
KICK-OFF 3-0 o'clock.

MATCH PROGRAMME

Liverpool's defeat in the replay cost them a shot at the Double.

consistently. They notched up five straight victories and – by the end of March – were closing in on Wolves at the top of the Division One table.

They were also making great progress in the Cup, despatching Walsall, Grimsby and Derby, before facing Birmingham in the quarter-finals at Anfield. The 4–1 win – played on ice during one of Britain's worst-ever winters – is still fondly remembered by Liverpudlians of a certain age. The reason? An incredible header from Stubbins that seemed to all to defy gravity. According to Liverpool's *Daily Post*, it was the "best goal ever seen at Anfield".

"Liddell operated with a free-kick from about 18 yards. The ball is lashed by intense driving force across the goal area. Two players trying to contact it find it too fast. The crowd are yelling their 'Ohs', feeling the ball will pass out of play, when Stubbins, out of position, flinging his body forward, connects with the rocket ball, and, at a distance of no more than a foot or two from the ground, the ball is positively rammed into the net."

Hopes of a Cup final appearance disappeared a month later, when Burnley beat them in the semis following a replay. But by then the League title had become a real possibility. The championship had

MATCH 1947 CHAMPIONSHIP PARADE

"It was the middle of summer. We'd had a bad winter and a lot of matches off. There were 50,000 there and men with handkerchiefs tied round their heads, and they were carrying some of the girls out of the terraces because it was too hot. When I took my sweater off after the game, you'd have thought I'd taken my undershirt out of the bath."

CYRIL SIDLOW, GOALKEEPER

1947 title winners.

Victory over Chelsea.

The homecoming.

When the Liverpool team went to Molineux for their final League game of the 1946–47 season, it seemed like half the city had gone with them. Thousands of fans travelled to the Midlands for a match they had to win to lift the first post-war championship trophy.

Wolves were the First Division's top scorers, with 97 goals, and lying just a point away from the title. Liverpool boasted Liddell, Fagan and the deadly striking duo of Balmer and Stubbins. But on an afternoon when temperatures hit 91 degrees in the shade, the Reds' real hero stood between the sticks: "It was ironic that the man who did most to keep Wolves from the draw which would, as things turned out, have given them the championship, was their former goalkeeper Sidlow," wrote Liddell. "Cyril made save after save when it seemed certain that he must be beaten."

Wolves did manage to put one past him, but by then Liverpool were 2–0 up. Balmer's opener followed a six-man move, and was, according to the *Liverpool Echo* report, "a picture goal that should be drawn and framed and hung in the dressing room." The second, from Stubbins, came after "he covered the half-field in record time with the ball at his toe".

Among those lying in his wake was Wolves' legendary skipper Stan Cullis, making his final appearance as a player. "At the end of the match, Stan and I shook hands," said Stubbins. "I think there was a tear or two in his eyes because he had lost his last chance of winning a League title medal. Then, of course, it was great for Liverpool. We sang all the way home on the bus."

But despite their famous victory, Liverpool still didn't know whether they were champions. Stoke were just two points behind, with a superior goal average and a game still to play. That match took place at Sheffield United on 14 June – at the same time the Reds faced Everton in the Liverpool Senior Cup final.

Anfield was packed for the tie. Balmer put Liverpool ahead, Everton equalized, then Bill Watkinson restored the home side's

Title celebrations in Lime Street.

advantage after the restart. Liverpool were heading for victory, but did anyone really care? As recounted in that night's *Football Echo*: "All interest in this match went west five minutes before the finish when Mr George Richards, the Liverpool director, announced over the loud-speaker system that Sheffield United had beaten Stoke, and that Liverpool were therefore League champions after an interval of 24 years.

"The roar which greeted this announcement made the Hampden Park one sound almost like a childish whisper. The crowd threw their arms in the air, many lost their hats and did not bother to look for them after they had tossed them high up in a burst of joyful celebration."

When the referee blew for time, fans swarmed onto the pitch from the Kop and Kemlyn Road, carrying the players shoulder high in jubilation. A day later, countless thousands lined the streets as captain Willie Fagan showed off the trophy from an open-topped bus. A campaign that had begun in America ended in triumph in Liverpool. The so-called Crazy Gang were home. They were champions.

developed into a four-cornered fight. And on the last day of their season, with United and Wolves on 56 points, and Liverpool and Stoke on 55, the Reds travelled to Molineux (see page 56). The most thrilling title race in years was about to end. And, for the first time in almost a quarter of a century, Liverpool would finish first.

THE ANFIELD FAMILY

But the team never recaptured that season's form, or entertainment value, under Kay's leadership. For the next three years they had to settle for mid-table positions as United overtook them, Arsenal reasserted themselves, and Portsmouth powered their way to two successive League titles.

There were a few changes on the field. "Nivvy" bowed out at the end of the 1946–47 season, and Harley went a year later. Up front, Done and Balmer began to struggle for their places, while Kevin Barron graduated from the reserves. And, as South African winger Bob Priday faded from view, local boy Jimmy Payne put on a series of dazzling displays that had newspapers comparing him to Tom Finney and Stanley Matthews. But the post-war line-up stayed largely intact throughout the late 1940s: Cyril Sidlow remained in goal, with Ray Lambert and Eddie Spicer as full-backs. Paisley, Phil Taylor and Bill Jones kept their places in midfield, while Liddell, Stubbins and Fagan were usually to be found in attack.

Throughout this period, football was more popular than it had ever been. Starved of first-class entertainment during the war, the fans were flocking to the grounds in unprecedented numbers. In 1947–48, a record 41 million people paid to watch English League games. On Merseyside, both the big clubs were enjoying the boom. Home gates usually hovered around the 50,000 mark during Liverpool's championship run, enabling the club to make a profit of £17,208. The

TOP 10	
LEAGUE APP'S 1939–1959*	
1. BILLY LIDDELL	476
2. RAY LAMBERT	308
3. LAURIE HUGHES	303
4. WILLIAM ("BILL") JONES	257
5. BOB PAISLEY	252
6. JIMMY PAYNE	224
7. PHIL TAYLOR	223
8. ALAN A'COURT	215
9. RONNIE MORAN	192
10. JACKIE BALMER	167

NOT COUNTED FROM 1939/40 - 1945/46 AS LEAGUE SYSTEM WAS CANCELLED

BOB PAISLEY
A fierce tackler who lost out on a place in the 1950 FA Cup final line-up.

DOWN WEMBLEY WAY...
Fans at the 1950 final against Arsenal.

following season, more than 74,000 saw them take on Manchester United in an FA Cup tie played at Goodison Park. And a year later a record 78,299 fans crammed into the same ground for the Everton-Liverpool League derby.

But, although money was pouring into the game, the players' lifestyles were modest. Eight of the Liverpool team lived in the same street in Bowring Park, renting their houses from the club for 25 shillings (£1.25) a week. New young recruits stayed in digs, sometimes owned by widows of former players. Even when the Football League raised the maximum wage to £12 a week – in response to a threatened footballers' strike – the average player earned little more than a white-collar professional. Years later, Albert Stubbins recalled how no one in the Liverpool side could afford to run a car, and how they all used to arrive at Anfield for weekday training – by bus.

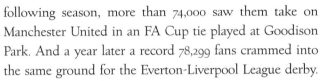

WEMBLEY AGAIN

Liverpool made the record books in the 1949–50 season, remaining unbeaten for longer than any other club in First Division history. They won ten of their opening 18 matches, drawing the rest, and looked likely candidates for the championship once again. But after they lost away to Huddersfield their form dipped and their title challenge gradually faded. By spring it was clear that the best chance of success lay with the FA Cup.

They had made impressive progress, knocking out Blackburn, Exeter and Stockport in the early rounds, before beating Blackpool 2–1 in front of 54,000 at Anfield. With Everton also doing well, there were hopes of an all-Merseyside final, but when the draw was made, the two teams found they would be facing each other in the semis. The Maine Road tie was scheduled for 25 March, Grand National Day. As thousands of punters headed towards Liverpool on the morning of the big race, the East Lancs Road was jammed in the opposite direction – with Liverpudlians and Evertonians decamping en masse to Manchester.

In the end it turned out to be Liverpool's day. The Blues had the best of the early play but failed to turn their dominance into goals. Midway through the first period Paisley picked up a clearance on the edge of the box, then saw his hopeful lob cross the line. In the second half, Liverpool soaked up more Everton pressure before Liddell pounced on a poor back pass to fire in the second. When the final whistle blew, the Reds' supporters among the 72,000 fans were ecstatic, with hundreds invading the pitch to congratulate the team and – in particular – the scorers. For Paisley, it was one of his finest moments as a player.

Sadly, he was also in for one of the biggest disappointments of his life. In the run-up to the Wembley clash with Arsenal, Kay and his fellow

1950 FA CUP FINAL
Captains Taylor and Mercer.

[LIVERPOOL HAD BEATEN ARSENAL TWICE IN THE LEAGUE THAT SEASON AND WERE RANKED AS FAVOURITES TO BRING HOME THE CUP FOR THE FIRST TIME IN THEIR 58-YEAR HISTORY.]

1950 FA CUP FINAL
A hard and physical game.

directors faced a major selection dilemma. Laurie Hughes, their first-choice centre-back, was fit again after a long lay-off through injury. That meant Bill Jones, who had deputized brilliantly, was again available to play in midfield alongside captain Phil Taylor. Kay – who was then in the early stages of a serious illness – wanted to keep Paisley, but was outvoted by the board. The Geordie half-back was, in his own words, "shattered" by the decision. And, for days afterwards, he "couldn't even bear to look at" his manager.

Back on Merseyside the excitement and sense of expectation were huge. Liverpool had beaten Arsenal twice in the League that season and were ranked as favourites to bring home the Cup for the first time in their 58-year history. The ticket allocation was snapped up within a day, and thousands who could not make it besieged the few city electrical shops that had a TV. The Islington branch of Rushworth and Dreaper charged customers a shilling to watch the match "live" on one of their sets, and hundreds began queuing outside from the early hours.

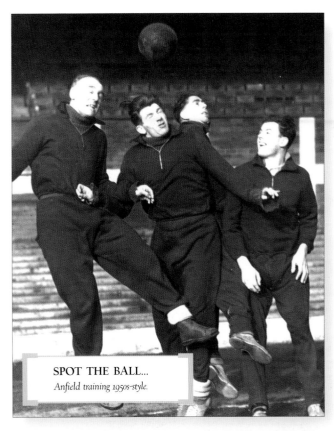

SPOT THE BALL...
Anfield training 1950s-style.

TOGA PARTY...
but the boss wisely keeps his clothes on.

But the old joke about the Liverpudlian saving up for the day his team won the Cup (and dying a millionaire) stayed intact. Arsenal dominated the game from the start and were 1–0 up after just 17 minutes. In midfield, Liverpool missed Paisley's bite; up front, Liddell was subjected to a barrage of bone-crunching tackles from the Arsenal half-back Alec Forbes. They did put the Gunners under some pressure after the interval, with Stubbins hitting the side-netting and Jones heading against the crossbar, but when Reg Lewis grabbed his second goal after 62 minutes, the contest was over: Arsenal's Footballer of the Year Joe Mercer lifted the trophy, and Liverpool returned empty handed from Wembley once more.

Not that you would have thought so when the team's train pulled into Lime Street on the Monday night. Tens of thousands of fans had turned out to welcome them home, choking the city-centre streets and lining the roads to the Town Hall. After addressing the crowds from the balcony, the team were then driven to Anfield, where thousands more had gathered for a youth match. The players were given an ecstatic reception as they walked around the touchline, and many had tears in their eyes. Afterwards, Liddell said he had almost been overcome with emotion.

DON WELSH
The first Liverpool manager to be sacked.

"That was a night I shall never forget. What sort of a reception some future Liverpool team will get when the Anfielders win the FA Cup for the first time I just cannot imagine. All I hope is that I shall be there to witness it."

Billy got his wish. But it would take another 15 years.

DECADE OF DECLINE

The next season was five months old when an increasingly frail George Kay retired on medical advice. The boss's mantle passed to Don Welsh, a colourful Mancunian who had been an outstanding player with Charlton. Unfortunately, he was one of the many footballers who are unable to make a successful leap into management. In Welsh's defence, he did inherit an ageing squad, many of whom had been around since

THERE WAS NO **DISGUISING** THE TRUTH THAT **LIVERPOOL** WERE NOW JUST A **MEDIOCRE** SECOND DIVISION SIDE, SIMPLY **NOT GOOD ENOUGH** TO **COMPETE** WITH THE **BEST** IN THE **LAND.**

MANAGER PHIL TAYLOR

As a Liverpool player, Phil Taylor had an illustrious Liverpool career, but it is his managerial record that's more likely to crop up in football quiz books. He was the last boss before Shankly, and the only Anfield manager never to have a team in the top division.

Phil Taylor(left), Bob Paisley and Eddie Spicer

Still, he was a superb club servant. He arrived as a teenager from his local team Bristol Rovers, after skippering England Schoolboys. He was a cultured, intelligent inside-right who quickly established himself among 1930s stars like Matt Busby, Tom Cooper and Berry Nieuwenhuys. But for World War Two, he would have added to his three senior England caps – and made many more than the 345 appearances for his club.

Taylor was one of the first to volunteer for action when hostilities began in 1939. He joined the 9th Kings Regiment and guarded the viaducts on the Liverpool to London railway line. But it was football that provided him with his only injury. Playing in a wartime Merseyside derby, he went for a ball with Everton's Billy Cook, got laid out flat, and

spent a week in hospital.

When the war ended, Taylor converted to a midfielder, took his place in the famous 1947 title-winning side, and later became a natural candidate for the captaincy. "Phil was the perfect Englishman," recalled team-mate Albert Stubbins. "He was a very smooth man, and totally unflappable." But by the time he'd finished playing at 35, the championship days were a distant memory and Liverpool had dropped into Division two. He took up a job on the coaching staff and was appointed manager when Don Welsh left in 1956.

During his time at the helm Liverpool constantly challenged for a promotion place. He signed the Scottish international 'keeper Tommy Younger, made an audacious and successful bid for Everton's Dave Hickson,

and gave Roger Hunt his debut. However, his teams were never quite good enough to escape, and, after more than three years of frustration, it was a stressed and exhausted Taylor who explained his decision to step down: "No matter how great has been the disappointment of the directors at our failure to win our way back to the First Division, it has not been greater than mine. I made it my goal. I set my heart on it and strove for it with all the energy I could muster. Such striving has not been enough, and now the time has come to hand over to someone else to see if they can do better.

"I shall have no official connection with the club in future, but I would like to feel that I can look in on their matches and still be welcome." He could be sure of that.

> AS THE LIKES OF **FAGAN** AND **PAISLEY** BEGAN TO FADE, **WELSH** FAILED TO BRING IN **ADEQUATE** REPLACEMENTS, RELYING ALL TOO OFTEN ON **LIDDELL** TO **CARRY** THE TEAM.

before the war. But, as the likes of Fagan and Paisley began to fade, he failed to bring in adequate replacements, relying all too often on Liddell to carry the team.

Welsh was wildly enthusiastic, if a little unpredictable: when the team won, he would celebrate by doing cartwheels in the dressing room. And former full-back Ray Lambert recalled how he once caused disbelief among the guests in a Leeds hotel.

"We've come in for our midday lunch, before the match starts, and there are people sitting in the hotel and he comes running in and he stands on his hands, legs up in the air, all his money over the floor. He starts walking on his hands. You've never seen anything like it. That was Don."

The fanatically fit ex-Army PT instructor introduced rigorous new training methods at Anfield, placing strong emphasis on stamina. But, according to Stubbins, he caused a minor dressing-room revolt by insisting on a man-to-man marking system: "Don had this defensive theory. I remember a tactical talk he gave us. He said: 'Now, in football, if the others don't score, you can't lose' ... In other words, we had to play a negative game." And it didn't work. Following four straight defeats – and a players' protest – Welsh abandoned the system.

At least he got his tactics right in one historic home

DAVE HICKSON
The former Everton striker marked his debut with two goals

ALAN A'COURT
A popular figure in Liverpool's 1950s team.

JIMMY MELIA
*1950s marksman – and the pride of
Scotland Road.*

RONNIE MORAN
*One of the few players to be kept on after
Shankly's arrival.*

match. On 2 February 1952 Liverpool faced Wolves in the FA Cup fourth round. As the teams lined up for the game Liddell was at outside-left and Cyril Done at centre-forward. But, just seconds before kick-off, the two players switched positions, with Done moving to the wing. Wolves, who had worked out a careful plan to stop Liddell, were thrown into confusion, and by the time they reorganized their defence Liverpool had already scored twice. The Reds finished as 2–1 winners, in front of 61,905 fans – the biggest-ever attendance at Anfield.

But, that victory aside, the early 1950s are usually remembered for a series of humiliating defeats. In 1951 Liverpool lost a Cup tie to Third Division Norwich; a year later they went out at the hands of Gateshead. Then, the following season, they were beaten 5–1 at Old Trafford and Portsmouth; 6–0 at Charlton and 5–2 at Chelsea. In April 1954 the team travelled to London and lost 3–0 to Arsenal. It may not have been the heaviest defeat of the campaign, but it was the one that sent them down.

SECOND DIVISION DAYS

That year must rank as one of the worst ever for Liverpudlians. They watched their team being relegated while Everton celebrated promotion. Their hopes of an immediate return to Division One vanished as the side won just one of their first seven games. And on 11 December they faced the awful prospect of a second successive drop as Liverpool were thrashed 9–1 at Birmingham.

Their worst fears faded thanks to a flurry of victories in the New Year, which helped the team to finish in 11th place. But there was no disguising the truth that Liverpool were now just a mediocre Second Division side, simply not good enough to compete with the best in the land.

Welsh lasted for almost two more seasons. During his time with the club he had spent more than

DIVISION TWO DAYS...
*Phil Taylor's team was unable
to win promotion.*

£50,000, buying the likes of ex-Wolves striker Sammy Smyth, the Charlton inside-forward John Evans and Carlisle's centre-half Geoff Twentyman. He had also given many local boys their chance: Ronnie Moran, a future captain and coach, Alan A'Court, who went on to play for England, and the teenage Jimmy Melia, who won schoolboy, youth and full international caps. But however many new players, formations and tactics Welsh tried, his team could never manage promotion. And as Liverpool headed for third place at the end of the 1955–56 season, the board decided he had had enough chances.

TOP 10
LEAGUE GOALS 1939–1959*

1. BILLY LIDDELL	211
2. ALBERT STUBBINS	82
3. JACKIE BALMER	64
4. JOHN EVANS	49
5. LOUIS BIMPSON	39
6. JIMMY MELIA	38
7. ANTONIO ROWLEY	38
8. JIMMY PAYNE	37
9. ALAN A'COURT	36
10. ALAN ARNELL	33

*NOT COUNTED FROM 1939–46
AS LEAGUE SYSTEM WAS CANCELLED

The man they turned to was former captain Phil Taylor (see page 63), who had recently followed Paisley on to the coaching staff. He was a popular choice among the players and – for a short period in his first year – he looked like the one to take the club back up. But, like Welsh, his best was never quite sufficient. In his first full season in charge Liverpool again finished third; for the next two years they were fourth.

By 1959 the average Anfield attendance had dwindled to around 30,000, and the fans were restless. They bombarded the newspapers with protest letters when Liddell lost his regular place; subjected the players to a slow handclap after a home draw with Portsmouth; and watched in disbelief as their once-mighty team crashed out of the FA Cup at non-League Worcester City.

One bright spot was the emergence of 21-year-old striker Roger Hunt (see page 79), who scored on his debut against Scunthorpe. Another came in November when Everton's Dave Hickson crossed Stanley Park for £12,000, and grabbed two goals in his first game. But in the next match Liverpool were beaten 4–2 at Lincoln, and promotion looked as far away as ever. Just two days later Taylor resigned, worn down by the strain of trying to restore his club to Division One status.

For the next fortnight the team were rudderless as the directors sought a

ROGER HUNT
Top scorer in his debut season.

replacement. Then, at the beginning of December, chairman Tom Williams announced that all applications for the post had been considered: "Of the small number who came up to the requirements, the board decided to ascertain the position of Mr W. Shankly, now with Huddersfield Town, and eventually offered the management to him. He put the position before his board and, after expressing their regret at the prospect of losing his services, they have agreed that Mr Shankly shall join Liverpool FC."

The new manager put pen to paper the following day. Life at Anfield was about to change for ever.

Mr. Shankly Arrives At Anfield

Mr. Bill Shankly, the new manager of Liverpool F.C., took over officially at Anfield today, although he was at the ground on Saturday to watch the reserves play. Left to right in the round table conference this afternoon are: Bob Paisley, first team trainer, Mr. Shankly, Mr. T. V. Williams, chairman, and Reuben Bennett, the chief coach.

1961   YEATS AND ST JOHN SIGNED

LIDDELL RETIRES

PLAYERS' MAXIMUM WAGE ABOLISHED

1962   PROMOTION TO DIVISION ONE

HUNT SETS SEASON'S GOALS RECORD

CHAPTER FIVE *1960–1966*	Building the Bastion

THE BEATLES RELEASE "LOVE ME DO"

1963   PROFUMO SCANDAL

"YOU'LL NEVER WALK ALONE" AT NUMBER ONE

SINGING ON THE KOP

1964   LEAGUE CHAMPIONS

THE BEATLES CONQUER AMERICA

1965   FIRST FA CUP WIN

1966   LEAGUE CHAMPIONS

CUP WINNERS' CUP FINALISTS

ENGLAND WIN WORLD CUP

"MY IDEA WAS TO BUILD LIVERPOOL INTO A BASTION OF INVINCIBILITY ... TO BUILD LIVERPOOL UP AND UP AND UP, UNTIL EVENTUALLY EVERYONE WOULD HAVE TO SUBMIT."

BILL SHANKLY

*Worth the wait ... the
1965 FA Cup homecoming.*

"QUITE A CHARACTER, THIS NEW LIVERPOOL MANAGER," SAID THE *DAILY POST* ON THE DAY OF SHANKLY'S ARRIVAL. THE 46-YEAR-OLD SCOT HAD JUST GIVEN HIS FIRST INTERVIEW AS ANFIELD BOSS, AND HAD STRUCK EVERYONE WITH HIS FIERCE DRIVE AND PASSION.

"I am very pleased and proud to have been chosen as manager of Liverpool FC, a club of such great potential," he said. "It is my opinion that Liverpool have a crowd of followers which rank with the greatest in the game. They deserve success and I hope in my small way to be able to do something towards helping them to achieve it.

"I make no promises, except that from the moment I take over I shall put everything I have into the job. I am not a lazy man. I like to get down to it and set the example which I will want following from the top of the club to the bottom."

Behind the scenes, he had already insisted on one cardinal rule: that he – not the board – would pick the team. The directors had agreed, although the side that lined up for his first match was chosen by the traditional selection committee.

Liverpool lost that home game 4–0 to Cardiff. Afterwards, Shankly picked up a ball and headed back to Huddersfield to take part in a pre-arranged kickabout with some of the locals. A Cardiff director who had offered commiserations was told bluntly: "Save your sympathy. I can look after myself and I can look after my team."

But he knew that team needed changing. With more than half the season gone they were lying tenth in the table, and promotion was a pipe dream. The shrinking band of fans knew it, too. For one of Shankly's first games, at home to Derby County, just 19,411 turned up. And as Manchester United powered their way to a 3–1 FA Cup victory at Anfield, even the Kop was reported to have "given up on their team" long before the final whistle.

IAN ST JOHN
An inspired record signing from Motherwell.

Results improved, but Liverpool could only finish third – a full eight points off the promotion pace. Almost immediately, the new manager showed his steel, cutting the squad of 38 by more than a quarter. Within two years, he would show 24 of those players the door.

But Shankly displayed superb judgement in deciding which players to keep. Among them was Gerry Byrne, a locally born full-back who had made only a handful of senior appearances under Phil Taylor, and who was on the transfer list when his successor arrived. Under the new boss, Byrne soon established himself as an indispensable first-teamer – and years later Shankly would describe him as his "favourite Merseyside player". Another who caught the manager's eye early on was a baby-faced Ian Callaghan. The 17-year-old winger made his League debut against Bristol Rovers in April 1960 – and would go on to make more appearances for the club than anyone else in its history.

Shankly kept faith with the backroom staff, too, retaining both Paisley and the fearsome Scottish trainer Reuben Bennett. He also held on to Joe Fagan, who – as a player – Shankly had tried to sign while manager of Grimsby. Together, these four men would become the original "Boot Room Boys" – the legendary committee who would dissect each player's performance in previous games, and then plan tactics for the next.

In the transfer market, Shankly's early performance was mixed. In fact his first signing – Motherwell winger Sammy Reid – never managed to break out of the reserve side. But in Gordon Milne, a £16,000 capture

from Preston, he discovered a midfield gem. And in Kevin Lewis, bought from Sheffield United for £13,000, he found an effective goalscorer to play alongside Hickson and Hunt.

In the 1960–61 season those strikers shared 50 of Liverpool's 87 goals. But that still was not enough to clinch promotion as the team, yet again, finished third. Dissatisfaction grew, average Anfield gates fell to 29,000, and the manager became increasingly frustrated at the lack of money to spend. He made inquiries about Denis Law, the scoring sensation he had discovered and nurtured at Huddersfield, but could come nowhere near the £50,000 asking price He then tried to sign Leeds' centre-back Jack Charlton, but was prevented from raising his offer above the initial £18,000.

For Shankly, the turning point came with the appointment to the board of Eric Sawyer, a director of the Littlewoods company, who shared his ambitions and vision. It was Sawyer who persuaded his fellow directors to start renovations on a dilapidated Anfield (famously described by Shankly as "the biggest toilet in Liverpool"). More importantly, he got them to authorize the transfer of Ian St John from Motherwell. At £37,000, St John was easily the most expensive Liverpool player ever. But, within days of his arrival in May 1961, he proved his worth by scoring a hat-trick against Everton in the Liverpool Senior Cup final.

Encouraged by this success, the board backed Shankly's move for another Scot – Dundee United's Ron Yeats. The giant centre-half had found himself placed on the transfer list for asking for a £2 a week wage increase. When he met his potential new boss at an Edinburgh hotel he had just one simple question: where's Liverpool?

"It was the worst thing I could have asked Shanks – it was like a red rag to a bull," said Yeats. "He came right up to me and said: 'What do you mean, where's Liverpool? We're in the First Division in England.'

RON YEATS
*"I've bought a Colossus,"
said Shankly.*

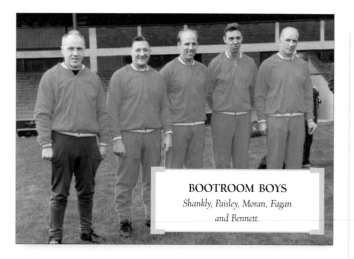

BOOTROOM BOYS
*Shankly, Paisley, Moran, Fagan
and Bennett.*

"I said: 'I thought you were in the Second Division,' and he goes: 'We are at the moment. But when we sign you we'll be in the First Division next year.' Well, how can you refuse to sign for someone who shows that sort of faith in you?"

In Shankly's view, Yeats and St John were his most crucial signings: they were, he said, "the start of it all." Throughout the 1961–62 campaign they played in almost every League game, helping push the side towards the top of the division and adding 10,000 to the average home gate. St John grabbed 18 goals that season, while Jimmy Melia weighed in with another 12. But Liverpool's most lethal striker was Roger Hunt. His incredible tally of 41 in as many League games made him the highest scorer in the country. It also brought England recognition and broke a club record of 36, set by Gordon Hodgson three decades earlier.

By the spring Liverpool were well out in front, needing just one more win to clinch their place back in the top flight. The crucial game was against Southampton at Anfield, one which St John was forced to miss because of suspension. In his place came Kevin Lewis, a player whose pre-match nerves often caused him to be violently sick. But the stand-in striker need not have worried before this game. Spurred on by an increasingly hysterical crowd, he hit both goals in Liverpool's 2–0 victory. When the final whistle blew, thousands invaded the pitch waving rattles, scarves and banners in triumph.

The match was played on 21 April 1962 – a day so overcast that floodlights had hardly made an impression. But as the victorious team emerged from the tunnel for a second lap of honour, the sun finally broke through. And an eight-year gloom was lifted from Anfield.

COMPLETING THE JIGSAW

There are several reasons to remember the first season back in Division One: the League derby when 72,488 saw Roger Hunt grab a last-minute goal in a thrilling 2–2 draw at Goodison; a 5–2 Anfield victory over Double winners Spurs (offset by a 7–2 drubbing at White Hart Lane three days later); a winter run of nine straight League victories; then defeat in an FA Cup semi-final against an ultra-defensive Leicester. It was a year when Liverpool marked their return by finishing eighth. And it was the time when Shankly showed just how ruthless he could be in pursuit of major honours.

The manager may have had a soft spot for the team that had clinched promotion with such a swagger. But from day one, when they lost 2–1 at home to Blackpool, he knew they were not strong enough to mount a title challenge. And by November – with just ten points from 16 games – critics thought they were heading straight back down.

The time for sentiment had passed. Shankly went out and signed the Glasgow Rangers half-back Willie Stevenson, dropping Tommy Leishman, who had made 41 appearances the previous season. Jim Furnell, the 'keeper who had edged out Bert Slater during the promotion push, was himself now ordered to make way. In his place came Tommy Lawrence, a long-time reserve who would make the number one jersey his own for eight years. Although the changes had an immediate effect on form, the early points dropped meant they were always at a disadvantage from winter onwards. And, when the winning sequence ended, they could not make

DIVISION TWO CHAMPIONS
*Plymouth players form a tunnel of
honour for Yeats and co.*

up ground on eventual champions Everton.

But a team that could put up a serious future challenge was starting to take shape. Lawrence, Yeats and St John had given Shankly a firm "spine" to build around. Byrne, Milne, Stevenson, Callaghan and Hunt had all become established regulars, about to enter their peak years. Preston's exciting winger Peter Thompson had agreed to switch to Anfield for a record £40,000, bringing width and speed down the left. And, in the reserves, home-gown youngsters like Chris Lawler and Tommy Smith were making strong claims for first-team places. Almost four years after arriving, Shankly had the players he wanted. The time had come for trophies.

TRAINING TO WIN

The manager planned his championship assault at the training ground. Since his arrival, he had supervised constant improvements to Melwood, making sure it was one of the best-equipped and most modern facilities in the country. He based his coaching methods on those at Preston, where "you were trained to be footballers – not marathon runners or circus artists". Sessions lasted 90 minutes, and would include sprints, stretching and turning exercises. But the main feature was fast and furious five-a-side games, played on pitches 45 yards long and 25 yards wide. "We played them all the time," said Tommy Smith. "We never practised corners, penalties, no set-pieces, nothing. It was just five-a-side, five-a-side, get fit, and five-a-side."

Usually it would be first-teamers facing reserve players, or the infamous "staff side", comprising Paisley, Fagan, Bennett and Shankly himself. The staff remained unbeaten for more than a decade, mainly because they all had whistles. But, aside from blatant cheating, they used the

PETER THOMPSON
The winger added the final flourish to Shankly's team.

games to check out who was the sharpest, strongest and fastest.

Then there was the "Sweat Box", a Shankly invention based on a training technique used by his playing hero, Tom Finney. "I'll describe it for those sadistic readers who enjoy reading about other people's torture," wrote Roger Hunt. "He sets up four numbered boards to form a hollow square. The boards are the walls and are roughly 20 yards apart. Now this operation calls for two players. One fires the ball at the board of his choice, it comes off at an angle, the other anticipates the angle, cracks the ball back at the target, and off it comes again for the first player.

"It sounds great fun but try it under Bill Shankly's eye and at his pace and you will realize it is no picnic. Some of the boards are marked off into six squares and we have to bang the ball at the square he orders, so you can see that we build up accuracy and anticipation this way. Training at Liverpool is the hardest job in soccer – and don't let anyone tell you otherwise."

The Sweat Box brought new signings to their knees. Even Hunt himself was near to collapse after trying it

TRAINING DAY
Shankly puts Gordon Milne through his paces at Melwood.

THE **SWEAT BOX** BROUGHT NEW SIGNINGS TO THEIR **KNEES**. EVEN **HUNT** HIMSELF WAS NEAR TO **COLLAPSE**. BUT **SHANKLY** WAS CONVINCED HIS **METHODS** WERE BREEDING THE **FITTEST PLAYERS** IN BRITAIN.

out for the first time. But Shankly was convinced his methods were breeding the fittest players in Britain. To make sure his work was not undone, he insisted they behave like athletes. "How my players train is vital," he said. "But equally important, perhaps more so, is how they rest and how they live. I try to control this as much as possible, short of ordering curfews. It's a full-time job of vigilance."

In the 1963–64 season all his efforts were to pay off. Liverpool's main rivals that season were Manchester United, a team rebuilt following the 1958 Munich air disaster, and now containing Bobby Charlton, Denis Law and a teenage George Best. For four months the two North-west giants slugged it out at the top. But, in March, when United lost 3–0 at Anfield, the title looked bound for Merseyside. On 18 April, with four games remaining, Liverpool needed just two more points to clinch the championship. Their visitors that day were Arsenal.

CAMERAS ON THE KOP

"The 28,000 people on the Kop begin singing together – they seem to know intuitively when to start. Their rhythmic swaying is an elaborate and organized ritual.

"Throughout the match they invent new words, usually within the framework of old Liverpool songs ... but even when they begin singing these new words, they do so with one immediate huge voice. They seem instinctively to be in touch with one another."

So said a plummy-voiced presenter from the BBC's current affairs series *Panorama*, sent to Merseyside to report on the "extraordinary cultural phenomenon" of communal singing at Anfield. It was the end of a season in which the Kopites had found their voice, graduating from simple chants to cover-versions of hits by the Beatles, Gerry Marsden and Cilla Black. After adopting songs, they adapted them: first it was the saints – then the Reds – who went marching in; the traditional "Farmer's in His Den" turned into "Ee-Ay-Adio"; and The Routers' early-

1960s single "Let's Go" was transformed into a thumping tribute to their idol: "One-two, one-two-three, one-two-three-four, St John!"

For a TV crew wanting to capture the new Anfield atmosphere, the clash with Arsenal could not have been better: glorious sunshine, 51,000 inside the ground, the Kop a heaving, steaming mass of unbridled passion. As they recorded a deafening rendition of "She Loves You", the players could feel the vibrations down in the dressing rooms. When the teams took to the field an hour later they could barely hear themselves speak. Future Liverpool star Geoff Strong, who was among the Arsenal line-up, later revealed how the crowd had punctured the Gunners' morale: "I've never heard a noise like the Kop made that afternoon in my life. It made you want to stop and listen to them calling for their team to win."

As the opposition took fright, the Liverpool players ran riot. St John's early opener was followed by a second from Alf Arrowsmith – a reserve striker who had forced his way into the first team that year, hitting 15 League goals in just 20 games. Thompson found the net with two thumping strikes after the interval. Minutes later he again tore through the Arsenal defence to set up a fifth goal for Hunt.

As Shankly took his bows before an ecstatic Kop, a TV audience of millions met the charismatic Anfield miracle-worker. In less than five years he had assembled the best players in Britain. And with his focus on discipline and hard work, he had built a team ready to take on the cream of Europe.

"We were on top of the world as we did a lap of honour at the end. I was so full of joy that I could have played another 90 minutes," wrote Hunt. "The boss and his assistants really made us sweat in training, but the effort was all worthwhile. Bill Shankly always claims that Liverpool are the fittest team in the country and he's right. In game after game we took control because, even if our opponents could match us for skill, they could not match us at producing it right to the end."

EURO-ADVENTURES
While Merseyside's footballers were conquering England, its musicians were conquering the world. In 1964 a record US television audience – an estimated 74 million – saw the Beatles play live on *The Ed Sullivan*

THE '64 TITLE CLINCHER...
Fan Adrian Killen captures the moments the League was won at Anfield.

SIXTIES PRIDE

Shankly's boys show off the championship trophy ... and their new all-red strip.

Show. The Americans were crazy about Liverpool. And, just weeks later, they tuned in to the same programme for an appearance by the men from Anfield.

Shankly had taken his team across the Atlantic as a reward for their championship success, but also in preparation for the rigours of international travel. With the title under their belt they had qualified for the European Cup, and could soon expect tours all over the Continent.

American soccer fans were already familiar with Liverpool because of their pioneering tours of the 1940s and '50s. Bob Paisley, a veteran of all those trips, was delighted to be back. But, as he later recalled, his manager found it hard to settle: "He didn't really like the States when we were on tour, even though he had this big thing about fighters like Jack Dempsey, and the gangsters of the prohibition days. When we met him in the lounge of our hotel in New York I asked him if he wanted to visit Dempsey's bar. He looked at his watch and said it was too late. I said it was only half past six. But he hadn't altered his watch and said that, as far as he was concerned, it was half past eleven and no Yanks were going to tell him what time it was."

Shankly's dislike of anything foreign would be a recurring feature of Liverpool's trips to Europe, too. Throughout their campaigns he would maintain that the locals were out to sabotage his plans. According to him, the team was deliberately put up in

COUPE D'EUROPE
EUROPESE BEKER
16-12-64

R.S.C. ANDERLECHT
LIVERPOOL F.C.

programme 10f. programma

substandard hotels; workmen would begin drilling in the early hours to disrupt their sleep; opposing players cheated and feigned injury; and foreign referees were subject to bribery.

At least he had no complaints about Liverpool's inaugural European draw – a two-legged game with Icelandic part-timers Reykjavik in August 1964. Liverpool won the away tie 5–0 with two goals each from Roger Hunt and Gordon Wallace, and a fifth from Phil Chisnall. The return at Anfield was a mere formality, although 32,500 still turned up to watch their team hit another six. But the Kop's biggest cheer of the night was reserved for the Reykjavik forward Felixson who – against all the odds – managed to grab a goal in front of them. The Icelanders left the field to warm applause – both from the crowd and the home players. Liverpool had scored an 11–1 aggregate win and could not have hoped for an easier introduction to European competition.

But the opposition was about to get tougher. In the next round they were paired with Anderlecht – a feared team who provided eight of the Belgian national side. Shortly before the tie, Shankly decided to unveil a secret weapon – a new strip he believed would strike fear into the opposition.

"He called me into his room after training," said Yeats. "He said I want you to put this all-red kit on. So I put it on and then I had to go down the Anfield tunnel and run on to the pitch where Shanks was standing with all the backroom boys. I ran towards him and he said: 'That's it! You look about nine feet tall in that kit. That's what we're going to wear!'"

But it would take more than a new strip to see off the Anderlecht threat, and Shankly knew it. He confided his worries to Paisley after watching the Belgians in action: "He came back to Melwood the next day and said: 'These fellas can't half play, Bob. They know what the game's all about.' But he never said that to the players; it was strictly between the two of us.

"He realized that we would have to pressurize these Belgians, to crowd them, or else they would destroy us."

The solution lay in tactics and some classic Shankly psychology. On the field, the manager introduced the 19-year-old Tommy Smith to add steel to the back line. In the dressing room he delivered one of his most memorable team talks: "Bill talked to all the lads before the game," said Paisley. "He said: 'You've read about Anderlecht having all these internationals, and how good they are. Well, forget it. They can't play. They're rubbish. I've seen them and I'm telling you. You'll murder them. So get out there and do it.'

"The boys went out there and murdered them. They won 3–0. And after the game Bill burst into the dressing room and said: 'Boys, you've just beaten the greatest team in Europe.'"

Even Liverpool's critics, who had scoffed at their European Cup chances, now had to admit that this team were worthy of their place in the competition. When they returned from Belgium having recorded another victory, some predicted they might go all the way.

DOMESTIC STRIFE

There was one serious downside to European glory: back home, their League form was exploding. Deprived of St John, suffering from appendicitis, and Arrowsmith, who had been badly injured in the 2–2 Charity Shield clash with West Ham, Liverpool had a disastrous opening, losing five games out of eight. There was a brief rally, triggered by a 5–1 win against Aston Villa, in which striker Bobby Graham hit a hat-trick on his debut. But soon they were back on a losing streak, recording three defeats and as many draws in a dismal late-autumn run.

As the New Year dawned, hope of

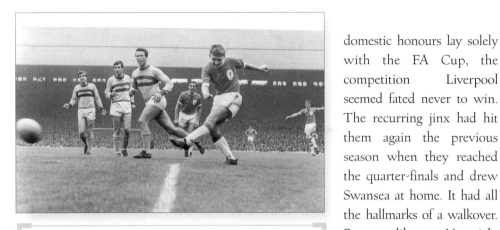

CHARITY DRAW
Liverpool and West Ham share the 1964 Charity Shield, as the game ends 2–2.

domestic honours lay solely with the FA Cup, the competition Liverpool seemed fated never to win. The recurring jinx had hit them again the previous season when they reached the quarter-finals and drew Swansea at home. It had all the hallmarks of a walkover. But, like Norwich, Gateshead and Worcester before them, the little club from south Wales had pulled off the shock of the round, humbling the Merseysiders with a 2–1 win before a stunned Anfield.

Liverpudlians had lived and died waiting for their team to lift the famous old trophy. Even while basking in their championship triumph they had to suffer the familiar Evertonian taunts of "You've never won the Cup". But Shankly never doubted that he would fill in the glaring blank on the Anfield honours board. Back in the days when he was persuading the directors to sign Yeats and St John, he had promised that those players would carry the club to Wembley glory.

THE '65 CUP RUN

The fans sensed that 1965 could be their year, and as excitement built some 5,000 of them headed for the Midlands, and a third round tie against West Bromwich Albion. But the travelling convoys caused traffic chaos on the main roads to the Hawthorns and the Liverpool team bus was caught up in the congestion. As match-time drew near, Shankly had to order his players to get changed while on board. Club chairman Sid Reakes got off the coach to seek police help, and only a motorcycle escort got them to the ground for a delayed 3.20 pm kick-off.

The game itself saw Shankly field a line-up that would become famous: Lawrence; Lawler, Byrne; Milne, Yeats, Stevenson; Callaghan, Hunt, St John,

TOP 10	
LEAGUE APP'S 1960–1966	
1. ROGER HUNT	269
2. GERRY BYRNE	233
3. GORDON MILNE	203
4. RON YEATS	192
5. IAN CALLAGHAN	188
6. IAN ST JOHN	188
7. JIMMY MELIA	165
8. TOMMY LAWRENCE	152
9. RONNIE MORAN	152
10. WILLIE STEVENSON	146

Smith and Thompson. He watched them go into a two-goal lead thanks to Hunt and St John, but had a scare when the home side pulled one back and had a penalty awarded for a Yeats handball. Luckily it went wide – and Liverpool went into round four.

The manager was so sure about winning the next tie that he decided to miss it, preferring to travel to Germany to watch the Reds' upcoming European Cup opponents, Cologne. It was easy to understand his confidence: his championship winners had been handed a home draw against Stockport County, the team lying at the bottom of Divison Four. In Football League terms, it was No. 1 versus No. 92. But this was the Cup.

A 51,000 crowd flocked to Anfield expecting to see County slaughtered. Instead, they watched in disbelief as the 5,000-1 Cup outsiders went into the lead, had a strong penalty appeal turned down, then almost added a second goal – all within the first half-hour. With acting manager Bob Paisley in shock, and the Kopites fearing another Cup humiliation, the Reds finally edged back into the game. Gordon Milne brought roars of relief after 51 minutes when he equalized with a low shot. But, despite sustained pressure throughout the rest of the match, Liverpool were unable to penetrate the defence again. After 90 minutes, County had held out for a 1–1 draw, and earned a replay back at Edgeley Park.

Shankly – who was reported to have "blown his top" when he heard the result – was back in the dug-out for that replay the following Wednesday. He named an

MAN WITH A MISSION
Roger Hunt, seen here in action against Stoke in 1967, was a goal-scoring machine.

unchanged side, but decided to dress them in the all-red strip he had used against Anderlecht. And this time his players delivered. Playing in front of a fervent capacity crowd, Liverpool dominated from the start with Hunt in his most lethal form. In a game in which County could barely get the ball out of their own half, he struck twice to give Liverpool a 2–0 victory. A potential banana skin had been avoided. But a fifth round tie at Second Division Bolton provided another.

Interest in that game was phenomenal. Liverpool had received 20,000 tickets for Burnden Park, but even after they were snapped up there was a strong demand on the black market. On the day, there were more than 57,000 in the crowd to see Ian Callaghan win the tie with a perfect header. Wanderers made frantic last-minute efforts to draw level, but it all came too late. As the referee blew for time, the huge travelling army of Kopites celebrated their passage to the quarter-finals.

Worryingly, the draw pitted them against Leicester – the "bogey" team who had beaten Liverpool in the semi-final two years earlier, and who boasted an impressive history of League wins against the Reds. On top of that, they had Gordon Banks in goal, the England 'keeper described by Tommy Smith as "the Berlin Wall – you couldn't knock him down". As expected, Banks did keep a clean sheet in that Filbert Street tie, but so did Tommy Lawrence, who had one of the games of his life in the Liverpool goal.

Four days later came the replay in front of 53,324, a

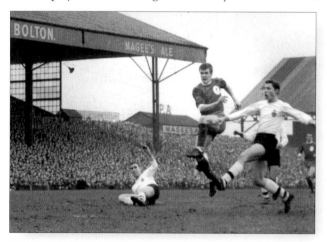

WANDERERS WILT
Alfie Arrowsmith in full flight as Liverpool win the tie at Bolton.

PLAYER ROGER **HUNT**

"Liverpool followers saw for themselves on Saturday that they have a new star in the making … it was not only Roger Hunt's goal, cracked home with the punch of a champion from over 20 yards range that created the happiest of impressions, but how he used the ball, how he fought for possession – and so often won – that stamped him as a youngster extraordinary."
Liverpool Daily Post, September 1959

Roger Hunt was 21 when he made his first Liverpool appearance. By the time he left Anfield a decade later, he had passed almost every goalscoring landmark in the book.

He reached his century in just 144 games, was leading marksman for eight successive years, and scored on his League, FA Cup, European Cup and England debuts. He found the net an amazing 41 times in the Reds' 1961–62 promotion-winning season. And his final League tally of 245 goals remains a club record.

It was former Liverpool defender Bill Jones who spotted Hunt playing for the Cheshire amateurs Stockton Heath. He recommended the Golborne teenager to his manager Phil Taylor.

He'd played only five reserve-team matches before Taylor gave him his first-team chance. But once he was in, he was impossible to dislodge. He contributed 21 goals in his first season and persuading new boss Bill Shankly to include him in his Anfield revolution.

Hunt repaid his faith. He formed an incisive partnership with new signing Ian St John, and together the young strikers pushed Liverpool to promotion. He hit 31 goals in the 1964 title-winning season, and another 30 when they lifted the championship again two years later. In between, he struck Liverpool's first-ever goal in an FA Cup final – helping the team to their historic Wembley win over Leeds.

He may have been worshipped on Merseyside, but the London-based press made him the target of constant sniping. Journalists constantly questioned his inclusion in the England squad, and were incensed as Alf Ramsey preferred his gentlemanly style to the showmanship of Jimmy Greaves. Hunt's inclusion in the 1966 World Cup final line-up was particularly badly received on Fleet

Street. And the criticism hurt.

"He had scored more goals for England than anyone in history. He was the match-winner supreme," Hunt later wrote. "Me? I had played all five matches, scored three goals, tried as hard as I could. But to the writers I was only a worker. They wanted a genius. They wanted Greaves."

But it was Hunt who appeared against the Germans at Wembley – Liverpool's sole representative on English football's greatest day. He was given a hero's welcome back at

Anfield. And as Ramsey collected his knighthood, the Kop demanded that the honours should be shared. From then on, he was always "Sir" Roger Hunt.

In all, he scored 18 times in 34 appearances for England; 286 goals in a Liverpool career spanning 492 games. He left for Bolton in 1969, still an idol for many. And his immense popularity never waned. Three years later, 56,000 fans defied the rain and wind to attend his testimonial at Anfield.

bigger crowd than Anfield had seen even in the previous championship season. It was a night of electric atmosphere – and one that belonged to Hunt. In the 72nd minute Yeats nodded down a Callaghan corner, and Liverpool's top marksman volleyed home the single goal that took them to the semi-finals. Shankly later raved about Hunt's powerful pinpoint effort, putting it down to all the hours his striker had spent in the Melwood Sweat Box. The high-pressure training was paying off again: Liverpool were just 90 minutes away from Wembley.

TOMMY LAWRENCE
Super-consistent 'keeper, nicknamed the "Flying Pig"

TAILS WE WIN

But first there was another European hurdle to clear. Exactly a week after the Leicester replay, Anfield was packed again for the visit of Cologne. Liverpool had already earned a 0–0 draw in the first leg in Germany, and went into the tie confident of getting goals. But, time and again, they were denied by the visiting goalkeeper Shumaker, whose performance was so awesome that Tommy Lawrence raced the length of the pitch to congratulate him at the final whistle. "Shumaker crammed a lifetime's glory into that game," said Shankly. "It's because of him that we have to go to a replay." That replay, seven days later, would put manager, players and fans through the ultimate emotional wringer. It would also enter soccer's history books for the most bizarre of reasons.

The match was played on neutral ground – at Rotterdam's Feyenoord Stadium. Liverpool raced into a 2–0 lead thanks to goals from St John and Hunt. But the Germans, roared on by their 20,000 travelling fans, capped a brilliant fightback by scoring twice. At full-time the scores were level; after 30 minutes of extra-time it remained at 2–2.

In the days before penalty shoot-outs and "golden goals", the referee decided that the outcome would be decided on the toss of a coin. In a scene witnessed on TV screens all over Europe, viewers watched the two captains make their way to the centre circle. After Ron Yeats chose "tails", the referee threw the coin in the air.

Then, unbelievably, the coin landed on its edge in the mud.

"I think I was trying to blow it over one way, and the Cologne skipper was trying to blow it the other," said Yeats. "But after a few seconds I said to the ref: 'I think you're going to have to do this again.' He looked at me and said: 'You're right.'"

For the Liverpool fans in the stadium – and the thousands more watching at home – the tension had become unbearable. And as the coin was flipped a second time, all they could do was watch for the reactions of Yeats and his fellow players.

What they saw was the captain, along with Tommy Smith and Roger Hunt, leaping for joy. The coin had landed tails up: Liverpool were through to the European Cup semi-finals, and a meeting with the Italian giants Inter Milan. It was a mouth-watering prospect, but no one could fail to sympathize with the Germans. Even Shankly, in the midst of wild celebrations, was scathing about the farcical rules: "Even though we came out lucky, that didn't make the procedure a good one. It was ridiculous."

RUNNING ON ADRENALINE

Liverpool officials had failed to persuade the Football Association to push back the FA Cup semi-final against Chelsea – due to take place just three days after the draining Rotterdam game. Shankly was angry at their unwillingness to help an English side who were challenging for both domestic and European honours: "We contacted the FA, but as far as I'm concerned we might as well have contacted the YMCA," he fumed.

But the players were up for the clash. The dramatic win in Holland had given them a huge psychological boost, and by the time they ran out to face Tommy Docherty's exciting youngsters their adrenaline was pumping. A massive 67,000 crowd was inside Villa Park that day, as Liverpool tore into the Londoners with confidence and passion.

With just over an hour gone the scores were still level, but then Peter Thompson went on a jinking run down the left, cut inside and hammered the ball past

Chelsea 'keeper Peter Bonetti. Fifteen minutes later, St John was brought down in the 18-yard box by Blues hard man Ron "Chopper" Harris. With regular penalty-taker Gordon Milne out injured, the spot-kick responsibility fell to Willie Stevenson. He had never taken one before, but he kept his cool and sent his shot high into the roof of the net.

The referee's whistle signalled the sort of celebrations that were now becoming commonplace for Reds fans. Hundreds invaded the pitch to congratulate the players and carry Thompson back to the tunnel on their shoulders. Chelsea trooped off disconsolately. They had gone into the game as favourites, a top-of-the-League side facing a tired team coping with a fixture pile-up. But the Cup momentum was with Liverpool, who now had a 1 May appointment with Leeds at Wembley. It was to be the greatest day in the club's 73-year history.

GOD SAVE OUR TEAM

If one thing threatened to dampen the delirious mood of Liverpool fans, it was the news that they would receive just 15,000 Wembley tickets. Although this was slightly higher than the Leeds allocation, it was 5,000 fewer than the number passed on to other Football League clubs – and less than half what county football associations were told to expect.

Faced with a barrage of begging letters, Liverpool appealed to the FA to revise their rules. City MPs backed the call, along with senior police officers, who saw the potential for a huge black market. But the Football Association refused to budge, insisting that the FA Cup final was their national showpiece event, open not just to the finalists, but to all who supported the game from the grassroots upwards.

It was an old-fashioned, idealistic view, but one which took no account of the desperate desire of supporters to see the game. This was a match that was always going to make history, as neither Liverpool nor Leeds had ever won the FA Cup. And, as the police had predicted, the huge demand led to a field-day for touts.

MANAGER BILL SHANKLY

He inherited a Division Two side, a crumbling ground and disillusioned supporters. He left a modern stadium, a world-beating team and an unbreakable bond between the club and its fans. Bill Shankly may not be the most successful manager in Liverpool's history, but he remains the most revered. He restored the pride, ignited the passion and laid the foundations for the future domination of Europe.

Shankly was tough, funny, outrageous – and dedicated to the point of obsession. He was a supreme motivator who instilled in his players a massive self-belief. And, in his adopted city, he inspired a loyalty never seen before.

His character was shaped in Glenbuck, an Ayrshire mining village now wiped off the map along with the pit that once sustained it. Determined to escape a life underground, he and his four brothers dedicated their waking hours to football. By the time they were teenagers every one of them had become a

professional.

It was Bill who showed the most talent. His career with Preston brought an FA Cup-winners' medal and 12 international caps. And his will to win impressed his legendary team-mate Tom Finney: "He honestly didn't know what the word 'defeat' meant."

Finney also noted his team-mate's ruthlessly single-minded focus on football – a a characteristic he displayed in his first managerial job, as former Reds striker Albert Stubbins recalled:

"My wife and I were on a train at Carlisle

station when there was this rap on the carriage window. It was Bill Shankly, signalling urgently that he wanted me to come out. I said 'Excuse me' to my wife and went outside. Bill never wasted any time on any preamble, not 'How's the family?' or 'How are you?' or whatever. 'Albert,' he said, 'when you move to the wing, do you like the opposing centre-half to go with you?' I said: 'Oh, yes, it can leave a gap for somebody else to go through the middle.' He said: 'Fine, that's what I wanted to hear. I've been trying for weeks to get them to play like this,

Shankly Collection ... 1966

but I'll certainly tell them next week.' He shook hands and I never saw him again for four years."

After Carlisle, came managerial stints at Grimsby, Workington and Huddersfield – then the move to Liverpool, where his huge ambitions would be realized. He clinched promotion, won the League twice and brought back the FA Cup for the first time in the club's history. He then built a second side, good enough to win more domestic honours – and a European trophy, too.

He was a wise-cracking figure, but he could be fierce in the dressing room. Tommy Smith has described how he once taunted his players by showing them pictures of old American gangsters: "You think you've got a hard time coming up this afternoon?

See about them. These lads, when they did anything wrong, they got shot."

But he also inspired deep loyalty in his players, building them up to take on the world's best – and rubbishing the opposition in the process. Kevin Keegan remembered how Shankly once watched England captain Bobby Moore get off the West Ham team coach in the Anfield car park: "He said to me 'Don't have to worry about him – he's been in the nightclubs again. He's limping, he's got bags under his eyes, and he's got dandruff."

A confident Keegan then went out and helped Liverpool to a 1–0 win. Afterwards, the boss had another word in his ear: "Aah, that Bobby Moore's some player, isn't he, son? You'll never come up against a better defender in your life!"

And as well as the affection of his players, Shankly won the adoration of the crowd. And, as Phil Thompson recalled, he gave them undying loyalty in return.

"We had just won the title and were doing a lap of honour around Anfield. Shanks came out to accept all the plaudits, and the whole place went wild – there were scarves and hats and banners being thrown on to the field. Then a policeman down by the Kop end, kicked a scarf out of the way and into the dirt. Shanks went mad. He shouted: 'Hey, someone's paid good money for that, don't be kicking it away.' He picked it up, wrapped it around his own neck and walked away. Suddenly he turned back towards the policeman. 'Don't you realize what you've just done?' he said. 'This scarf is someone's life.'"

In the weeks leading up to the game, London-based black marketeers were asking – and getting – up to 20 times the face value of a precious Wembley ticket.

No one was more sympathetic to the supporters' plight than Shankly, who promised that any spare tickets that came his way were "going to the boys on the Kop". But he had his own problems: a week before Wembley, he was battling to get three players fit.

The casualties were Milne, Callaghan and St John.

Milne had hurt his knee so badly that he had to be taken off before the game finished. Callaghan's ankle was so swollen that he travelled back from London with his foot in a bucket of ice-water – and still needed painkilling injections.

Fearing more injuries, Shankly decide fielded weakened sides in the last three League games before Wembley. Among those given the chance to impress was Geoff Strong, who had spent most of his time in the reserves since his record £40,000 capture from Arsenal. In the event, he needed the practice, as, just 48 hours before the big kick-off, Milne failed a fitness test. It was a crushing blow for a man who had played such a prominent part on the road to Wembley, but he knew he had no chance of making the line-up. He would travel with the party to London – but Strong would take his place on the pitch.

Despite the injury blow, the team set off for the capital in confident mood. Callaghan and St John had both recovered, and Shankly had supervised intensive training at Melwood for all the rest of the squad throughout the week. They spent the night before the match watching Ken Dodd on stage at the London Palladium – and were given a standing ovation when the Liverpool funnyman announced their presence to the packed theatre. The next morning they woke to hear their manager being interviewed on BBC Radio's *Desert Island Discs* – and choosing the new Kop anthem "You'll Never Walk Alone" as his favourite record.

It was just one of many songs that could be heard ringing out from Wembley that afternoon. Thousands of Liverpool fans had poured in as soon as the gates were

Top: *Shankly and Revie lead out the teams.* Middle top: *St John's winner.* Middle bottom: *The Cup is ours.* Bottom: *Yeats leads the celebration.*

opened, colonizing the north end of the stadium and producing a repertoire of chants and tunes never before heard there. At 2 pm, when Shankly walked on to the pitch and stood before them with his arms raised, they nearly took the roof off. When the national anthem was played an hour later, the millions watching at home heard the Liverpudlian version: "God Save Our Gracious Team."

The manager had told his players they should be prepared to "go out and die" for their fans. And just ten minutes into the game, full-back Gerry Byrne showed the sort of heroism that even Shankly would have found hard to match. The defender had gone in for a tackle with Leeds skipper Bobby Collins, but fell to the ground as the ex-Everton man stood on the ball and turned his shoulder towards him. When Bob Paisley ran on to the pitch he felt Byrne's collarbone and could tell immediately that it was broken. But, with no substitutes allowed, Byrne chose to carry on, playing out the rest of the game with his right arm dangling by his side – and keeping the extent of his injury a secret from his team-mates.

Apart from Byrne's bravery, there were few memorable moments. Leeds played negatively, happy to soak up long periods of Liverpool pressure and hoping to score on the counter-attack. Neither side appeared able to unlock the solid defences, and, with just a few minutes of normal time left, Shankly leaned across to Leeds boss Don Revie, remarking that it was like "watching a tight game of chess: it's stalemate".

But as the match went into extra-time – the first in a Wembley final since 1947 – the Reds' superior fitness began to tell, and, within three minutes, they were ahead. The goal came after man of the match Willie Stevenson beat two Leeds players and fed the ball to the overlapping Byrne. The courageous full-back ignored his

THE KING OF WEMBLEY

Shankly acknowledges the ecstatic cheers from the travelling fans.

pain to race to the byline and cut back a low cross. Hunt, who looked like he was going to volley, suddenly stooped to meet the ball with his head. It flew into the net, sparking wild celebrations both on the field and off.

"That's it, we've done it," screamed the scorer as his colleagues mobbed him. None of them could believe that the exhausted Leeds side could manage to claw their way back. But just eight minutes later they did – courtesy of an unstoppable Billy Bremner shot.

As the players changed ends, Shankly barked instructions, trying to gee up his men one last time: "They've shot their bolt. They've had it. Go for the kill." His own players were themselves now tiring visibly, many suffering from cramp and wearing their socks round their ankles. But then, as the rain lashed down on the Wembley turf, St John made one last supreme effort, diving to meet Callaghan's cross, and heading it past 'keeper Gary Sprake.

And that really was it. The Leeds players' heads went down, and only a couple of brilliant saves from Sprake could prevent Liverpool from pulling further ahead. With the game in its 120th minute, the Liverpool fans broke into "Ee-Ay-Addio, we've won the Cup." Seconds later, the referee's whistle went – and never has a football crowd been so euphoric.

The raucous party seemed to go on for ever. The lap of honour took an age, thousands of fans refused to leave, and those who did headed for the West End to continue their celebrations. But just a day later they were back on Merseyside, part of a half-million-strong homecoming crowd – bigger than anything Merseyside had witnessed even on VE Day. For those who were there, it was a day of unforgettable emotion: a day when players fought back tears while parading their trophy on the open-topped bus; and a day when

TOP 10	
HAT-TRICKS 1960–1966	
1. ROGER HUNT	10
2. IAN ST JOHN	2
3. JIMMY HARROWER	1
4. ALF ARROWSMITH	1
5. BOBBY GRAHAM	1
6. DAVE HICKSON	1

many elderly fans told their families: "Now I can die happy."

For the team, the season was not over. A two-legged European semi-final against Inter Milan (see page 87) would still generate the sort of drama, excitement and controversy that most other players would not experience in their entire careers. But for the supporters, the Wembley game had drawn a line under the past. And it had provided Bill Shankly with his proudest moment: "It took 73 years, and I thought it was a terrible disgrace that the Liverpool people had to suffer the taunts of others who said: 'You haven't won the Cup yet.' They were ashamed of it.

"But now we had won the Cup and it was the greatest moment of my life – because we had done it for the people of Liverpool."

1966 AND ALL THAT

Fitness was the quality that Shankly valued above all others. It had powered his team from the Second Division to the First. It had won them the championship and the FA Cup, and enabled them to live with the best in Europe. In Shankly's perfect world his men never got injured, never got tired and never needed resting. And, in the season following the Cup triumph, he almost reached his ideal – using just 14 players throughout the whole campaign.

It is a staggering statistic considering today's rotation systems, when as many players can be fielded in a single game.

And, even back in the mid-1960s, no other club could come near to matching the consistency of Liverpool's line-up. Week after week the players virtually picked themselves. Only at left-half, where Milne and Strong battled for supremacy, was the name on the team sheet ever in doubt.

Shankly's team had evolved and matured into a skilled family which functioned as a complete playing unit. Each member knew the others' characteristics off by heart. They trained as one, worked for each other and even socialized together. Fitness, ability, strength and teamwork: all were at their peak in the 1965–66 season – and no one in Britain could live with them.

The battle to reclaim the championship had begun ordinarily enough, with the first three games yielding a win, a defeat and a draw, but soon the Reds were rampant, winning 13 of their next 18 games – and hitting five past West Ham, Everton, Northampton and Blackburn. By November, they were top; by Easter, they had opened up a convincing gap. When Chelsea came to Anfield at the end of April, Liverpool needed only a draw to take the title again. Before the game, Tommy Docherty's players formed a tunnel of honour and applauded the home side on to the pitch. At the end, Ron Yeats disappeared back down the same tunnel with two points – and the championship trophy.

Liverpool had now matched Arsenal's record of seven titles, and their season's hero was – once again – Roger Hunt. He kept up his phenomenal goalscoring ratio by hitting 30 in 37 League games, the sort of form that convinced Alf Ramsey to choose him ahead of Jimmy Greaves for the 1966 World Cup campaign. But Liverpool's defence was also in inspired form all season, with Byrne, Smith and Yeats all ever-presents, and Lawler putting in 40 appearances. Together with Tommy Lawrence, who featured in every League game, the back line conceded just 34 goals.

DOUBLE SCOTCH...
Yeats and St John bring the Cup back to Merseyside.

If the greatest day was at Wembley, the greatest night belonged to Anfield. Just 72 hours after Ron Yeats lifted the FA Cup, he and his men prepared to face Inter Milan before the wildest, noisiest crowd ever gathered inside a British stadium. Gates had been locked at 5.30 pm. The 25,000 on the Kop had been singing and swaying for two hours. No one believed the atmosphere could get any more electric. Apart from Bill Shankly. Seconds after the Italians headed towards the Kop for their warm up, the Liverpool boss sent Gerry Byrne and Gordon Milne down the tunnel hoisting the one trophy Anfield had been waiting to see for 73 years. The result was a volcanic eruption on the terraces.

What followed will forever live in LFC folklore: a game in which Liverpool showed overwhelming passion, power and skill; a clash in which the Reds' home-grown stars humbled some of the world's most celebrated internationals. Nearly four decades on, it still gives former players goose-bumps. "It was the night of nights," said Ian St John. "The night when we came of age and the club came of age."

Roger Hunt set the tone after four minutes, volleying Ian Callaghan's cross into the net. Inter quickly equalized, but Liverpool then gave the Italians a footballing lesson. "We murdered them," said Tommy Smith. "We gave them a pasting," said Shankly. "We would have beaten any team in the world on that form,"

said Yeats.

Callaghan added the Reds' second – completing a dazzling free-kick routine honed at Melwood: Then, with a quarter of an hour remaining, St John followed up Hunt's shot and converted. The small number of Milan supporters who had made the journey had never seen their team so outplayed. Meanwhile the Kopites serenaded them to the tune of Santa Lucia:

> "Oh, Inter, one–two–three
> Go back to Italy!"

But if Anfield distinguished itself through humour, Milan's San Siro later proved to be

the most inhospitable arena in Europe. Facing the frenzied hatred of 90,000 people. Smoke bombs and flares rained down from the terraces; the players were spat at and pelted with coins. "It was like a war," said Shankly.

The controversy soon spread from the terraces to the pitch. After eight minutes the referee awarded Inter a free-kick on the edge of the penalty box, and appeared to signal that it should be indirect. But when Corson's curling shot hit the net, he allowed the goal to stand.

Minutes later, Tommy Lawrence, bouncing the ball in his penalty area, had it kicked from his hands by Piero, who then slotted it into the open goal. The Liverpool protests were waved away Inter were now level on aggregate.

The unfairness of the decisions, combined with the stresses of a mammoth campaign, finally began to tell on the Reds, and, when Inter added a third, and fire-crackers lit the Milan sky, they knew there was no way back.

But Shankly and Paisley learned valuable lessons about tactics, and the hostility that awaited English teams abroad. Lessons that would one day take their club to the summit of European football. But that night in Milan, the players and coaching staff were devastated. Tommy Smith later admitted to kicking the referee as they walked towards the tunnel. And, even when interviewed about the game some 15 years later, Shankly could still not forgive the referee: "Of all the people I've ever come across, he's the one man who haunts me to this day."

Despite their invincibility in the League, the team's FA Cup defence proved a huge anti-climax. A home tie with Chelsea brought 54,000 to Anfield, but the vast majority went home disappointed as the Londoners took revenge for the previous year's semi-final defeat. Hunt put Liverpool ahead after just two minutes, but that was soon cancelled out by a Peter Osgood header. Deep into the second half, another headed goal from Bobby Tambling gave Chelsea the lead and signalled the exit door for Liverpool at only the third round stage.

Although FA Cup failure would never be as hard following the 1965 win, it was still a bitter disappointment. By now Liverpool fans had grown used to the excitement of knock-out tournaments, and many feared the symptoms of adrenaline withdrawal. But they need not have worried. Another European adventure was under way.

TAKE THE HIGH ROAD

This time the Euro-highway led to Glasgow's Hampden Park, chosen as the final venue for the 1966 Cup Winners' Cup. It was a competition that lacked the glamour and prestige of the European Cup, but it still pitted Shankly's team against some of the best sides on the Continent. In the preliminary round they were drawn against Juventus – a tie that gave them a chance of quick revenge against the Italians.

The players may have been the same, but those who walked out for the first leg in Turin were a different proposition from the side who wilted in the San Siro. Liverpool were now far more organized, putting on a disciplined display that shut out the Juventus forwards. With just nine minutes left the home side did manage to score – thanks to

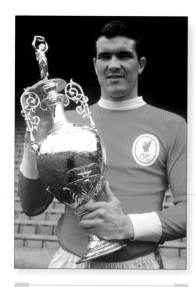

CAPTAIN FANTASTIC
Ron Yeats with the championship trophy.

TOP 10	
LEAGUE GOALS 1960–1966	
1. ROGER HUNT	186
2. IAN ST JOHN	72
3. KEVIN LEWIS	39
4. JIMMY MELIA	38
5. DAVE HICKSON	37
6. ALAN A'COURT	25
7. IAN CALLAGHAN	22
8. ALF ARROWSMITH	17
9. GORDON MILNE	16
10. PETER THOMPSON	16

a fierce long-range drive – but they now faced a trip to Merseyside with just the slenderest of leads.

While the supporters could never hope to rekindle the atmosphere of the Milan game, the 51,000 who watched the Anfield return did their best. The Kop was in full voice from the start, roaring Liverpool on against a side determined to pack all 11 players behind the ball. Hunt, St John and Thompson attacked with passion and verve, but, with almost 20 minutes gone, it was full-back Chris Lawler who prised open the defence, heading in Willie Stevenson's free-kick from close range.

Juventus came with the reputation of having the meanest defence in the meanest league. But, just five minutes after Lawler's opener, they were 2–0 down thanks to a screaming 18-yard shot from Strong. Forced to come out and attack, the Italians finally showed some of the flair for which they were renowned, but, when that failed to bring an equalizer, they unveiled a repertoire of dives and fouls that incensed the crowd and had the Liverpool bench up on their feet. The Reds hung on to their lead – but Juventus left the field to a chorus of whistles.

It was a similar story when Belgian Cup winners Standard Liège visited Anfield for the first round tie. A succession of early fouls culminated in the Liège centre-forward Claessen spitting in Ron Yeats' face – and having to limp off when the Reds' skipper repaid him with a fierce tackle. Taking a 3–1 lead to Belgium, the players faced the most partisan crowd since Milan. But despite the hostility – and yet more dirty tactics by their hosts – they came away with a famous 2–1 victory.

At the next stage Liverpool comfortably overcame the Hungarian side Honved, drawing 0–0 in Budapest and winning 2–0 at Anfield, with goals

> THE ATMOSPHERE WAS SUPERCHARGED. STEAM ROSE FROM
> THE KOP AS 25,000 FANS, DRENCHED IN A MIXTURE OF
> RAIN AND SWEAT, SWAYED IN UNISON.

from Lawler and St John. Liverpool were now just one round away from the final, but to get there they had to overcome the Scottish giants Celtic. It was a match that would be christened "the Battle of Britain".

And it lived up to its billing. Buoyed by their 1–0 win before an 80,000 home crowd, Celtic came to Anfield in confident mood. Liverpool had been poor in the first leg and, with Hunt out injured, it was always going to be a struggle to break down Jock Stein's future European Cup winners. But they piled pressure on from the beginning, forcing Celtic 'keeper Ronnie Simpson to make a series of brilliant saves. Then, with just over an hour gone, Tommy Smith finally cancelled the deficit with a rasping free-kick from 25 yards out.

The atmosphere was supercharged. Steam rose from the Kop as 25,000 fans, drenched in a mixture of rain and sweat, swayed in unison. On the Anfield Road end, the hordes of Celtic fans competed for vocal supremacy. Thousands had made the journey, so sure of victory that they had spent the afternoon celebrating in city-centre pubs. Many of them had carried on those celebrations during the match – courtesy of whisky bottles smuggled in through the turnstiles.

But they were in for a massive disappointment. Displaying courage reminiscent of Gerry Byrne in the Cup final, Geoff Strong had played through the majority of the game despite excruciating pain from a badly injured knee. With 67 minutes gone he used his one good leg as a springboard – and rose to head home an Ian Callaghan cross.

As the Kop erupted, the mood at the opposite end began to grow ugly. And when Celtic had a goal disallowed near the end, a barrage of beer and spirit bottles rained down on Tommy Lawrence's goal. As Liverpool's 'keeper ran for safety, the police went in and the referee was forced to stop play. There were a series of arrests and around 50 people at the front of the enclosure were treated for cuts caused by flying glass. But, when order was restored, the game was resumed – and Liverpool strode to a deserved victory.

So another season, another final. But sadly the glories of Wembley were not to be repeated at Hampden. In a strangely muted clash with Borussia Dortmund, the Reds could never get into gear. Torrential rain, and the counter-attraction of seeing the game on TV, had also depressed the size of the crowd: just 41,000 in a stadium designed to hold more than twice as many. The travelling Reds fans tried to generate some atmosphere, but found themselves facing a German contingent swelled by supposedly "neutral" Scots. It was a dismal spectacle, and a depressing outcome, as Borussia recorded a 2–1 win – and lifted the Cup.

But, as the spring of 1966 turned to summer, there was still plenty for Liverpudlians to savour. Their team had proved themselves the dominant force in the domestic game. The Kop's own knight, "Sir" Roger Hunt, had helped England conquer the world on another unforgettable Wembley afternoon. And Bill Shankly – the man who had indeed turned Anfield into a bastion of invincibility – pledged his future to their club by signing a new five-year contract. The cost? £4,000 per annum.

GLASGOW BELONGS TO THEM...
The 1966 European defeat at Hampden Park.

1967 ● EMLYN HUGHES SIGNS

1970 ● FA CUP DEFEAT BY WATFORD

● JOHN TOSHACK SIGNS

CHAPTER SIX
1967–1974

The Second Coming

1971 ● FA CUP RUNNERS UP

● KEVIN KEEGAN MAKES DEBUT

1972 ● ROGER HUNT TESTIMONIAL

1973 ● LEAGUE CHAMPIONS

● UEFA CUP WINNERS

● BRITAIN JOINS EEC

1974 ● FA CUP WINNERS

● BILL SHANKLY QUITS

● BOB PAISLEY APPOINTED MANAGER

YOU'LL NEVER WALK ALONE

LIVERPOOL
FOOTBALL CLUB

EST·1892 ®

"I COULD SEE THAT A FEW OF THE PLAYERS HAD STARTED TO GO A BIT. IT WAS OBVIOUS THAT, WHILE SOME STILL HAD AN APPETITE FOR SUCCESS, OTHERS HADN'T, AND MIGHT DO BETTER ELSEWHERE."

BILL SHANKLY

Ready for action at the start of the 1967/68 season

LIVERPOOL AND EVERTON RAISED THE CURTAIN TO THE 1966–67 SEASON IN A STYLE NEVER LIKELY TO BE REPEATED. FIRST, CAPTAINS RON YEATS AND BRIAN LABONE LED THEIR SIDES OUT FOR THE CHARITY SHIELD CLASH, PARADING BOTH THEIR LEAGUE CHAMPIONSHIP AND FA CUP TROPHIES. THEN ROGER HUNT AND RAY WILSON EMERGED FROM THE SAME GOODISON PARK TUNNEL – EACH WITH A HAND ON THE WORLD CUP. THREE TROPHIES, TWO CLUBS, ONE CITY: FOR MERSEYSIDE FANS, IT REALLY WAS THE DAY THAT FOOTBALL CAME HOME.

But that was as good as it got for Reds fans that year. Their team won the Charity Shield, thanks to a single Roger Hunt goal, but nothing more. And, by the end of the campaign, people were beginning to ask the unthinkable: had Shankly's great 1960s side become a busted flush? The jury was out. They had finished the season fifth in the table – nowhere near as impressive as the previous year, but high enough to re-qualify for Europe. They had also suffered a fifth round Cup exit, but a knock-out by holders Everton was certainly no disgrace.

In the European Cup, though, their performances did provide a reason to worry. Drawn against Romanian champions Petrolul Ploesti in the preliminary rounds, they struggled to find the form that had swept aside the likes of Celtic and Standard Liège the previous season. A laboured 2–0 home advantage was frittered away when they travelled behind the Iron Curtain and found themselves facing a side with no respect for reputations. In a furious, bad-tempered encounter, Willie Stevenson put through his own net before Hunt cancelled it out with an equalizer. The Romanians then struck back with two goals in six minutes – inflicting Liverpool's heaviest European defeat, and taking the tie to a replay.

EMLYN HUGHES
Anfield's "Crazy Horse" arrived from Blackpool in a £65,000 deal.

After winning that game 2–0 the Reds may have thought their Continental ride would get smoother. In fact, the wheels were about to come off. Facing Dutch champions Ajax in round two, they received a lesson in passing and finishing that made a mockery of their European ambitions. On a fog-bound night in Amsterdam, Johann Cruyff and co. put four goals past them in the first 45 minutes. By the time the final whistle blew, Liverpool were 5–1 down.

If Shankly displayed outrageous cheek in slamming the Dutch team's "defensive" tactics after the game, he also showed his incredible powers of motivation. Facing a four-goal deficit, he managed to convince his team that the cause was not hopeless. The fans were persuaded, too. Nearly 54,000 paid to watch the return leg, including a fervent Kopite named Phil Thompson: "We were hammered in Holland, but Shanks came back and had everyone believing we were going to overhaul it. Being a supporter then, if he said something, you believed it was going to happen. That was the way it was. The people thought we were going to win – and they came to Anfield in their droves."

True believers they may have been, but that night even the Kop had to admit that Shankly was fallible.

Liverpool were not outclassed like they had been in Amsterdam, but against such strong opposition they looked, at best, a mediocre side. Cruyff was their main tormentor, tearing the defence to shreds with his speed and close control, and finding the net twice. A brace from Hunt gave the home fans something to cheer, but a 2–2 draw was not nearly enough to keep them in the competition. Liverpool were out of the European Cup, and it would be another seven years before they returned.

CHANGING FACES

The Ajax defeat proved to be a mini-watershed, as Shankly began scouring the country for new talent to add to his team. One of the first to arrive was a strapping 19-year-old whom the Anfield scouts had discovered playing for Blackpool. As the manager was driving him back to Merseyside to sign for a record £65,000 fee, his car was involved in a crash with a police patrol vehicle. When the officer asked for the young passenger's name, Shankly introduced him as "Emlyn Hughes – the future captain of England".

Hughes took a little time to fulfil that international promise, but he made an immediate impression at club level. He edged out Willie Stevenson in the midfield, and by the end of the 1966–67 season had become an

H-BOMB ALERT
Striker Tony Hateley lasted little more than a season, but scored 28 goals.

established first-team regular. He had also earned the nickname of "Crazy Horse" on the Kop because of his marauding runs through the middle – and attracted a legion of female fans due to his boyish good looks.

The departure of Gordon Milne gave Shankly another excuse to reach for the Anfield chequebook. As the new season drew near he agreed to pay £96,000 for the Chelsea striker Tony Hateley, switching St John into midfield and giving Hunt a powerful new aerial partner. For a short while, the move looked inspired. The "H-Bomber" hit a hat-trick against Newcastle in Liverpool's second home game, and went on to grab a total of 16 during the season. He also got the club's European campaign off to a flyer, scoring twice in the away leg at Malmo. And, in the FA Cup, he was on target an impressive eight times in just seven appearances.

But, despite his goals, the 1967–68 season again proved to be barren. The team finished third in the League and suffered a sixth round FA Cup exit at the hands of West Brom. In the Inter City Fairs Cup (forerunner of the UEFA Cup), they followed the Malmo victory by trouncing TSV Munich 8–0 at Anfield and chalking up an aggregate 9–2 win. But in the next round they came up against the crack Hungarian side Ferencvaros, and were beaten by a single goal in both the home and away legs.

For Shankly, the experiment with the tall target man had failed. His players had found it difficult to accommodate Hateley's style, and the new season was just four games old

ALUN EVANS
The former Wolves striker was the first teenager to command a £100,000 transfer fee.

when he accepted an £80,000 bid from Coventry City. In his place came Wolves striker Alun Evans, the first teenage player in Britain to be transferred for a six-figure sum. He became an instant hit with the Kop by scoring on his debut against Leicester City in September 1968. Just a week later, he repaid more of his £100,000 fee by finding the net twice in a 6–0 win against his former club.

But Evans aside, there were few major changes. Stevenson left for Stoke, while Gerry Byrne retired to make way for a succession of replacements, including the former Wrexham full-back Peter Wall. In midfield, reserves like Ian Ross were given a few limited outings in the senior side, while in attack, the long-serving Bobby Graham finally made a serious claim for a regular starting place, scoring five times in 12 League starts.

Otherwise the core of the mid-1960s side remained intact, even as the decline became more and more evident. The team suffered early exits in both domestic cup competitions, and, although they were runners-up in the League, they finished a full six points behind the champions, Leeds. In Europe's Fairs Cup they stumbled at the first hurdle – this time falling victim to the toss of a coin following a 3–3 aggregate draw with Spain's Athletic Bilbao. As the season went on, critics noted that some of Shankly's favourites were obviously past their peak. By the time it finished, their calls for a clear-out were growing louder.

The manager resisted them until the

ROGER HUNT LEAVES
Roger Hunt leaves Anfield with the record tally of League goals intact.

next season was almost three-quarters of the way through. His team had started well, winning seven of their opening nine games and climbing to the top of the table by mid-September. That same month they opened their Fairs Cup campaign in storming fashion, running out 10–0 winners against Dundalk at Anfield and recording a 4–0 victory in the away leg in Ireland.

But it was downhill from there. In Europe, they met their match in Portugal's Vitoria Setubal, who dumped them out of the Fairs Cup thanks to the away goals rule. Back at home their early League form slumped so badly that they collected just 11 points from 13 matches. Any realistic chance of a renewed title assault came to an end in December when they were beaten 4–1 at home by Manchester United. That same week the Kop's hero Roger Hunt left for Bolton, increasingly frustrated at his inability to hold down a regular first-team place. For the fans, it was a miserable end to the 1960s. As the new decade dawned, their only hope of success lay with the FA Cup.

WATFORD WOE

For a few weeks at least, it looked as if those Wembley dreams might come true. But, following wins against Coventry, Wrexham and Leicester, the team were drawn against Second Division strugglers Watford. And, in a quarter-final that would have a huge bearing on Liverpool's future, they slumped to a disastrous 1–0 defeat at Vicarage Road.

The shock of that loss was numbing, and the fall-out immediate. Shankly decided that merely tinkering with the old side was no longer enough, and that only radical surgery would do. Even as the silent team bus headed north up the M1 he was drawing up his plans for the future: "Watford was the crucial game," he later wrote. "I could see that a few of the players had started to go a bit. It was obvious that while some still had an appetite for success, others hadn't, and might do better elsewhere."

Among the first victims of his cull

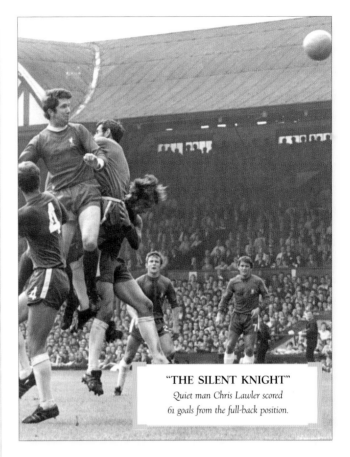

"THE SILENT KNIGHT"
*Quiet man Chris Lawler scored
61 goals from the full-back position.*

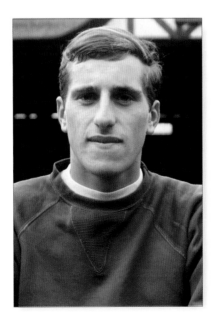

SIMPLY THE BEST
*Shankly and Paisley rated Ray Clemence as
the world's number one goalkeeper.*

were Lawrence, Yeats and St John – the three Scots who had formed the team's crucial backbone for almost a decade. Geoff Strong was sold to Coventry a few months later, and Peter Thompson found he was no longer an automatic choice. Shankly had shown the ruthlessness he had displayed ten years previously. Of the 1965–66 championship side, only the "Scouse Trio" of Smith, Lawler and Callaghan retained their regular first-team places.

Lining up alongside them for the next season were newcomers like Ray Clemence, bought as an understudy to Tommy Lawrence three years earlier, and later to be acclaimed as "the best goalkeeper in the world" by both Shankly and Bob Paisley. Classy defender Alec Lindsay arrived from Bury to fill the troublesome left-back berth. Up front, the tricky young winger Brian Hall was promoted from the reserves. And on the left flank

came fellow university graduate Steve Heighway, a former Skelmersdale United amateur whose exhilarating runs set the First Division alight.

But Shankly was also desperate for an out-and-out striker. His players had struggled to find the net the previous season, with Bobby Graham top scorer on 13, and Lawler – a full-back – next with ten. With Evans prone to injury, the team had also spent the first weeks of the 1970–71 season firing blanks. But then the manager identified a Welsh target man who he believed would transform the Reds' attack.

John Toshack was a 21-year-old who had figured in the Cardiff City first team since the age of 16. He had averaged almost a goal in every other game for his local club, and had won six international caps before switching to Liverpool for £110,000. He made his debut in a dismal 0–0 home draw against Coventry in November 1970, but just a week later he played a starring role in one of the greatest Merseyside derbies ever.

THE REVIVAL BEGINS

Everton had gone to Anfield as champions, a team that had finished 15 points ahead of their rivals the previous season, and one featuring the formidable midfield line-up of Alan Ball, Howard Kendall and Colin Harvey. True to form, they took a second-half lead when striker Alan Whittle sent a perfect lob over Clemence's head and into the Anfield Road goal. Minutes later, Joe Royle rose to convert Johnny Morrisey's cross – and it seemed the matter of Merseyside supremacy had been settled in the Blues' favour for another year.

But the game proved to be a turning point. As Liverpool conjured up a fighting spirit that had not been seen since the championship days, the Kop rediscovered the sort of voice that used to reverberate around Anfield on those memorable European nights of the mid-1960s. Spurred on by the cries of "No surrender", the Reds threw everything into attack. With 15 minutes left, Smith floated a long ball to Heighway, who skipped past his marker, ran to the byline, cut inside, and unleashed a fierce drive past 'keeper Andy Rankin.

Anfield was buzzing as the vast majority of the 54,000 crowd sensed an epic fightback. Within minutes, Heighway again collected on the wing, then left defender Tommy Wright on his backside before sending a perfectly weighted cross into the Everton box. Rising to meet it, directly in front of the Kop goal, was Toshack, whose bullet header almost burst the net.

The atmosphere became electric as Liverpool went in search of a winner, and Everton tried frantically to protect their single away point. The champions, who had once looked so assured, were run ragged by a group of unknowns with almost no derby match experience. As the game entered the dying stages, it looked like they would just hold out. But then Toshack rose to flick Lindsay's cross into Chris Lawler's path. And the quiet full-back's unstoppable shot brought the Kop's loudest roar for years.

That incredible 3–2 victory may not have set the Reds on the road to the title, but it served as a warning that they were on their way back. As the campaign progressed Shankly blooded more youngsters, such as local born striker Phil Boersma and midfielder John McLaughlin. And, with the experienced Smith as their captain, the Liverpool kids finished a respectable fifth, without losing a home League game all season.

They also went a long way to restoring the club's credibility in Europe, beating Ferencvaros, Romania's Dinamo Bucharest and the Scottish side Hibernian in the early stages of the Fairs Cup. The fifth round draw brought Bayern Munich to Anfield, complete with a glittering set of internationals led by Franz "the Kaiser" Beckenbauer. But despite the opposition's strength, the night belonged to Alun Evans, playing the game of his

THE ANFIELD IRON
"Tommy Smith was never a boy – he was born a man," said Shankly.

life and slamming a hat-trick past the West German number one, Sepp Maier.

After Liverpool had held Munich to a draw in the away leg, only Leeds stood in their way to another European final. But while Shankly's team were still in transition, Don Revie's side had reached maturity. Captain Billy Bremner's flying header provided the only goal in the Anfield leg, while his watertight defence held out for a 0–0 draw back at Elland Road. Leeds, who went on to lift the trophy that year, were fast emerging as one of the most powerful teams in the English game. That semi-final clash would become the first of many epic Merseyside-Yorkshire battles throughout the early 1970s.

DOUBLE TROUBLE

Meanwhile another English team were in the ascendant – and it was Liverpool's misfortune to come up against them at Wembley. The Reds had reached their first FA Cup final for six years thanks to wins over Aldershot, Swansea, Southampton and Tottenham. An all-Merseyside semi-final saw them come from a goal down to beat Everton 2–1 at Old Trafford – thanks to strikes from Evans and Brian Hall. The final would be against Bertie Mee's Arsenal – a team 14 points ahead of Liverpool, and sitting proudly on top of Division One.

The Gunners clinched the title on 3 May when a Ray Kennedy header gave them victory over their north London rivals Tottenham. As the champagne flowed inside White Hart Lane's visitors' dressing room, one of the jubilant team handed a ringing telephone to his manager: "Bill Shankly here," said the voice at the other end. "That was a tremendous performance, Bertie – magnificent. Your boys may even give us a game on Saturday."

Unfortunately, they did. Five days later, on an afternoon of brilliant sunshine, only a disciplined Reds defence

[AND WITH THE **EXPERIENCED SMITH** AS THEIR **CAPTAIN** THE **LIVERPOOL KIDS** FINISHED A **RESPECTABLE** FIFTH, WITHOUT **LOSING** A **HOME** LEAGUE GAME **ALL** SEASON.]

stopped Arsenal turning domination into goals. In the opening minute of extra-time, Liverpool threatened to stop their Double dream, as Heighway drew Bob Wilson from the goal-line to squeeze a shot between the 'keeper's body and the near post. But as the temperatures soared into the high 80s, Arsenal's superior

THE HEAT IS ON...
Clemence comes under pressure as the Wembley temperature rises.

experience and fitness began to tell. A goalmouth scramble ended with Eddie Kelly getting a final touch past Clemence just before the end of the first period. Then, six minutes after the interval, Charlie George hit a spectacular 20-yard drive that flew past the Liverpool 'keeper. As George lay outstretched on the Wembley turf, the travelling Merseyside fans could sense it was over. Their young team were tired and suffering from cramp. Arsenal, who had conceded just 29 League goals all year, simply were not going to allow their defence to be breached again.

The final ended with Mee's side lifting the Cup, and claiming a domestic Double. The Liverpool team, playing their 61st game of the season, looked dejected and shattered as they trooped off with their losers' medals. Equally upset was a young player who had only signed terms at Anfield earlier that week, and who had been sitting among the 100,000 crowd. "Look at him," said Shankly, pointing up at the stands. "He thinks we would have won if he'd been playing – and we probably would have done, too!" Shankly obviously had faith in the youngster, but even he could not have predicted how deep his impact would be.

SEVENTIES SUPERSTAR

The player was Kevin Keegan, who, like Clemence, had been discovered playing for lowly Scunthorpe. Shankly had monitored his progress for almost two years before agreeing to pay £33,000 to bring him to Anfield. "It's always difficult to go into the Third and Fourth Divisions and find players who can make it at the top," he later said. "But in Kevin we found a man who had the one thing we wanted. Apart from his ability he had a natural enthusiasm – and that's what made him a special player."

That enthusiasm was on display from the moment he stepped out for his debut game against Nottingham Forest at the start of the 1971–72 season. The 51,000 fans who packed into a newly renovated Anfield saw a human fireball whose speed, strength and skill tore the opposition to shreds. He scored a goal, won a penalty, then inspired the side to a 3–1 victory. No one since Billy Liddell had played with such heart. No one since Ian St John had so galvanized his team-mates. Keegan electrified grounds all over the country. He was chosen to represent England at under-23 level within six months of his debut. And, as his first season drew to an end, he looked set to win a championship medal.

It turned out to be among the closest title races in history. As it went into its last month, Liverpool were one of four clubs still in contention. As it reached its final day, they were one of three. Brian Clough's Derby County, who had completed their League programme a few days earlier, were top with 58 points. Leeds, with a game at Wolves, and Liverpool – facing a trip to Arsenal – were both on 57. For a few glorious seconds on that May afternoon, it looked like the Reds had clinched it. The game was entering its final phase when news of a Wolves goal spread among the thousands of fans who had travelled south to Highbury. Then, with just two minutes left, Toshack hammered the ball into the Arsenal net to send them into rapture. But, even as the Liverpool bench were dancing with joy, the referee Roger Kirkpatrick was consulting with his linesman and

SALE OF THE CENTURY
Kevin Keegan pledges his future to Liverpool ... for £33,000.

beginning to shake his head: according to the touchline official, the goal was offside.

The players protested vehemently, and TV evidence later appeared to support their view that Toshack was onside when he struck. But by then it didn't matter. Arsenal had held out for a draw, and the title had gone to Derby. Shankly, who had come so close to constructing a second Championship-winning side, was apoplectic: 'The referee robbed us. It's heartbreaking for my young players after their magnificent challenge for the title. The same referee disallowed a goal for us in the League game against Leeds at Anfield. Then he didn't take any notice of his linesman. Today he did.'

Neither the FA Cup nor Europe could offer any solace. Don Revie's men had ended Liverpool's Wembley hopes with a 2–0 fourth round replay victory at Elland Road. In the Cup-winners' Cup, Bayern Munich had gained revenge for the previous season

TOP 10 LEAGUE APP'S 1967-1974	
1 IAN CALLAGHAN	310
2. TOMMY SMITH	301
3. EMLYN HUGHES	294
4. CHRIS LAWLER	279
5. PETER THOMPSON	201
6. RAY CLEMENCE	180
7. RON YEATS	166
8. LARRY LLOYD	150
9. IAN ST JOHN	148
10. STEVE HEIGHWAY	145

with a 3–1 aggregate victory in round two. Alun Evans had again found the target against the Germans, but by that point his opportunities at Anfield had become limited. He left shortly afterwards with his massive potential unfulfilled, his career blighted by injuries and his confidence weakened by an appalling nightclub attack that caused severe facial injuries.

But at least those who remained had good grounds for optimism. The supporters had turned up in record numbers that season, making Anfield's home average of 47,687 the highest in the League. In April 1972 an incredible 56,000 turned out for Roger Hunt's testimonial – an emotional night when the Kop celebrated the glories of the 1960s and the promise of the new decade. On the field, Shankly's youngsters were getting stronger, and playing with an increased understanding and maturity. The close-season signing of Forest's Scottish international midfielder Peter Cormack seemed, to many observers, to be the final link.

MARATHON MEN

So it proved. In the 1972–73 season, Liverpool's line-up bore a stamp of familiarity not seen for seven years. Just 16 players were used throughout the campaign, with one of them – understudy 'keeper Frankie Lane – appearing just once. Brian Hall continued to make a claim for a regular spot, while local products like Phil Boersma in attack and Phil Thompson in defence were always ready to deputize when injuries or suspensions struck. But, for the most part, the Nos. 1–11 stayed the same: Clemence; Lawler, Lindsay; Smith, Lloyd, Hughes; Keegan, Cormack, Heighway, Toshack, Callaghan.

And they were brilliant. From the opening week, when they beat both Manchester clubs at home, Liverpool gave notice of their title ambitions. A month later they hammered Sheffield United 5–0 and went to the top, and they proved almost impossible to dislodge from then on. Arsenal – who managed a rare Anfield victory – stayed in touch for most of the season, but

TOWER OF STRENGTH
Larry Lloyd was an ever-present in the 1973 championship- and UEFA Cup-winning side.

when Liverpool beat Leeds 2–0 before a packed Anfield on a baking-hot Easter Monday, only a mathematical miracle could stop them going on to win the trophy.

Some of the performances were breathtaking, moving Shankly to declare: "The football we're playing is frightening. Frightening. Even I feel privileged to watch it." Keegan, who played in all but one League game, later explained what made that side so special:

"The secret of the Liverpool success was teamwork. Individuals were ready to sacrifice a moment's glory that accompanies flash exhibitionism for the sake of making sure that movements flowed on a conveyor belt of passes that were stunningly accurate.

"The 1970s team were one of the greatest of all passing sides. The ball would be delivered – not clobbered – from the back by players of the quality of Chris Lawler, Alec Lindsay, Tommy Smith, Larry Lloyd and the young Phil Thompson. It would then become the temporary property of accomplished midfield players like Ian Callaghan and Emlyn Hughes, with Peter Cormack and Steve Heighway always ready to fetch and carry if required.

"The final point of delivery was usually either to me or to John Toshack. Tosh and I had an almost telepathic

THE GREAT PROVIDER
Steve Heighway supplied the crosses for Toshack and Keegan. He also scored 50 goals.

BEST OF ENEMIES
The early 1970s battles with Leeds were always intense, but never dirty.

understanding and always knew where to be to get the best out of each other. During this championship season we scored 13 First Division goals each, and our little-and-large partnership proved too much of a handful for most defences.

"We always tried to be one thought and deed ahead of our opponents. We would consider how they might be planning to stop us, and then come up with a counter-plan. For instance, Tosh switching to the support striker role while I became the unlikely target man at the head of the attack. It was not always sweetness and light between the two of us, and there were times when we messed up moves and got annoyed with each other. But we were always lifted by the team spirit, and would forget our differences to produce the best efforts for the team."

The displays were all the more impressive when the sheer amount of games was taken into account. The Reds' FA Cup run lasted only until the fourth round, but both ties – against Burnley and Manchester City – went to replays. Then there was the draining saga of the League Cup. For several years Liverpool had not bothered entering the unglamorous knock-out tournament, and even when they did their performances

WELL-RED
University boys Steve Heighway and Brian Hall tackle the European press.

often seemed half-hearted. Since regular participation began in 1967 the furthest they had ever got to was the fourth round, but this time their form was so good they could hardly stop themselves progressing. By the time Christmas approached they were in the semi-final.

To get there involved playing three rounds, each with home and away legs. They beat Carlisle easily at the first stage, then scored a narrow 3–2 aggregate win over West Brom. That set up a fourth round clash with their great rivals Leeds, and two more matches played with typical intensity. They drew the Anfield leg 2–2 before losing to a single goal in a bruising encounter at Elland Road. The reward was a marathon semi-final against Tottenham – a 1–1 Anfield draw, followed by a 3–1 defeat at White Hart Lane after 30 minutes of extra-time. The result was a disappointment to Liverpool fans who had suddenly developed an interest in the much-derided competition, and quite fancied another day out at Wembley. But Shankly, who had his eyes on a bigger prize, thought it had been too much of a distraction: "I'm almost relieved we were beaten," he told reporters afterwards. "We are having to play too many games."

A EUROPEAN TROPHY AT LAST

It was the UEFA Cup that had added even more to the fixture congestion. Though not as prestigious as the European Cup, Shankly was desperate to see it in the Anfield trophy cabinet. He called for a supreme effort from his team, and convinced the fans and media that it was worth lifting: "I would say that winning this could be as difficult as winning the European Cup, because those who are in it are promising to be great teams. They are on the verge of greatness."

His players responded. Their long road to the final began back in September with a 2–0 aggregate victory over the West German side Eintracht Frankfurt. Back-to-back wins against Greece's AEK Athens followed in the second round. Then, two fine displays behind the Iron Curtain helped see off Dynamo Berlin and Dynamo Dresden.

Roger Hunt

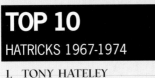

TOP 10

HATRICKS 1967-1974

1. TONY HATELEY	3
2. ROGER HUNT	1

ALL COMPETITIONS

For the April semi-final they were drawn against Tottenham Hotspur – a weird echo of the League Cup clash just four months earlier. Spurs, who had since gone on to win the Wembley final, opted for ultra-defensive tactics in the opening Anfield leg, depending on a packed defence – and the brilliance of 'keeper Pat Jennings – to prevent Liverpool from breaking through. It almost worked. Alec Lindsay's close-range shot put the Reds in front after nearly half an hour's play, but his attacking colleagues spent a frustrating night trying in vain to add to it.

A fortnight later, the north London return attracted a crowd of 47,000 – most of them expecting to see Liverpool overhauled. Former England star Martin Peters raised their hopes minutes after the interval when he beat Clemence from just a couple of yards out. But then Heighway seized on a through-pass from Keegan to level the scores on the night – and provide his team with an invaluable away goal. It proved enough in the end. Spurs threw everything at Liverpool in a frenetic last half an hour that saw Peters claim a second goal and hit the crossbar. But when the

MIGHTY MOUSE
Keegan celebrates his opening goal in the 1973 UEFA Cup final, first leg.

final whistle blew the aggregate score was 2–2 – with Heighway's crucial strike counting double.

So Liverpool prepared for another European final – the first since their ill-fated Hampden Park trip seven years earlier. This time there would be no neutral ground; instead the destination of the trophy would be settled over two games played at Anfield and at the home of their West German opponents, Borussia Moenchengladbach. In the first leg, the newly crowned English champions stepped out in torrential rain. Shankly had relegated Toshack to the bench, putting Brian Hall in his place and asking him to link up with Keegan and Heighway in attack. It was a just reward for Hall, who had played in several earlier rounds and had scored with a rare header against Dresden. He remembers how the night at Anfield promised to be one of the biggest of his life: "I thought it would be a brilliant experience to walk out in that sort of environment and pit myself against world-class players. And it really was ... for about 25 minutes."

It was at that point, midway through the first half, that the referee decided the pitch was unplayable. The rain, which had become even heavier since the kick-off, was leaving huge puddles on the pitch, holding the ball up and causing both sets of players to slip and slide. It was the ultimate anti-climax for a near-capacity crowd who had gathered for Anfield's first-ever European final. Their only consolation was a tannoy message that admission prices for the rescheduled match would be just ten pence.

Shankly, though, had more reason to be cheerful. Watching the German defence for less than half an hour had convinced him they were suspect in the air, and that a tall target man would quickly cause havoc. His observations led to a major tactical change, and a desperate disappointment for Brian Hall. When the Liverpool team took the field 24 hours later, Toshack was back in.

It worked like a dream. Just as predicted, the giant Welshman exploited the aerial weakness ruthlessly, rising above his international marker Gunter Netzer to threaten the Borussia goal from the very first attack. After 21 minutes he nodded a high cross into the path of Keegan, who scored with a diving header in front of the Kop. Just 12 minutes later Keegan collected another of Toshack's glancing headers, this time ramming home a volley from ten yards out. Liverpool dominated the

As a **WEARY** Smith **PARADED** the huge **TROPHY** around the stadium, Shankly made a **BEELINE** to the **THOUSANDS** of travelling supporters, **THRUSTING** his arms through the fencing to **SHAKE** their hands.

rest of the match, and managed to go three up when Larry Lloyd powered in another aerial effort after the break. Man of the match Keegan should have made it four, but failed to strike a penalty with sufficient power. A spot-kick at the other end gave Borussia a small glimmer of hope, but Ray Clemence's acrobatic save prevented them from claiming a precious away goal.

The final whistle was the cue for celebrations on the Kop. Liverpool had played at the top of their form, building up a commanding lead to take to Germany. And no one – least of all Shankly – thought they could lose it: "If anybody wants to know what Liverpool Football Club is about then let them study this game," he said at the after-match press conference. "Tonight we played football that was world-class against world-class opposition. The second leg will not be easy, but there's not a team on the planet that I would expect to overcome a three-goal deficit when we are playing as well as this."

Amazingly, Borussia came close. In the return match, they attacked with a ferocity that Liverpool had not experienced in any of their 65 previous games that season. The Reds were pinned back in their own half right from the kick-off, and skipper Tommy Smith found himself trying to calm frayed nerves in defence: "In that first 20 minutes we got battered," said the captain. "We were absolutely murdered."

It was Jupp Heynckes, the man who had missed from the spot at Anfield, who caused most of the trouble. His first reward came on the half-hour, when he pounced on a defensive mix-up to score from just six yards out. Nine minutes later he curled home a right-footed shot that left his rampant team trailing by just one goal – and sent the Liverpool bench into temporary panic: "After they scored the second there was a thunderstorm, and I thought we were going to get beat by about 10–0," admitted Shankly afterwards. "But then, just before half-

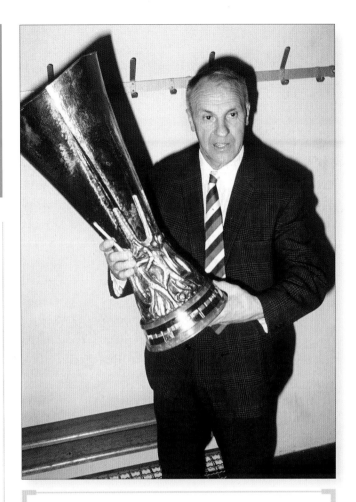

EUROPEAN GLORY
The UEFA Cup was Liverpool's first – and Shankly's only – continental triumph.

time, I could see that the steam had gone out of them. And when we were in the dressing room, I said that we may even get a draw in this match."

His prediction was over-optimistic, but his assessment correct. The Germans pressed forward again after the interval but could never match the pace they had set in the opening period. As the home side tired, Liverpool grew in confidence, tightening up at the back and even managing a few attacks themselves. At the end of 90 minutes the score remained at 2–0 with the Reds winning 3–2 on aggregate. Clemence's Anfield penalty save had proved more important than anyone had imagined.

Those close to Shankly say he reacted more joyously to that result than any other – including the 1965 FA Cup final. As a weary Smith paraded the huge trophy around the stadium with his players, the manager made a beeline to the thousands of travelling supporters, thrusting his arms through the wire-mesh fencing to

Shankly had a bond with Liverpool fans like no other.

Bill Shankly's decision to step down mystified the football world, and even now, almost three decades later, the question is still being asked: Why?

Theories have multiplied as the years have passed, including a bizarre observation from an Anfield insider that Shankly wanted his financial affairs sorted because he feared the prevailing economic climate would cause a banking collapse.

But Shankly offered the most human answers of all: "My wife Nessie and I both felt I needed a rest. She's not been well and I wanted to be fair to her. I was feeling tired and coming to my decision was like walking

Shankly inspects the silverware.

to the electric chair. But if you can't make decisions in life you're a bloody menace. I had conquered Everest so I left."

Liverpool, having seen the problems caused by Sir Matt Busby's Manchester United legacy, insisted that if Shankly was adamant about leaving it would have to be a clean break, precluding his elevation to the Board in fairness to his successor. It made life tricky at Melwood, where the former manager would continue to train, and where his old players still used to refer to him as

"boss". For Bob Paisley, the new man in charge, the arrangement was difficult, and after a while Shankly chose to work out at Everton's Belfield headquarters instead.

He didn't publicly regret his decision to quit, but his unhappiness soon became obvious. He craved the excitement of football, and became a consultant to several League clubs, including John Toshack's Swansea. He was so keen to be involved again that Toshack believed some managers were using him, taking advantage of his eagerness to talk about and analyse football endlessly.

He never lost that legendary enthusiasm. kept up correspondence with former fans, writing his letters personally on a battered old typewriter that now sits in the Anfield museum. And, in 1978, he fulfilled a long-standing promise to join the fans on his beloved Kop.

Throughout his playing and managerial career, Shankly had been a fitness fanatic, and his passion for exercise continued well into retirement. Former Everton captain Mick Lyons has recalled how the one-time boss of Liverpool would organize football matches with local youngsters once the formal training sessions at Belfield were over. "We had a great match today," Shankly once told him. "We won 19–17."

Yet, in September 1981, at the age of 68, Shankly died at Liverpool's Broadgreen Hospital, following two heart attacks. Many believe that without football his heart was broken anyway. But the passionate, wise-cracking motivational genius from the Ayrshire pit village of Glenbuck remains the guiding spirit of Liverpool Football Club.

As the inscription on his Anfield statue says: "He Made the People Happy."

YOUNG, GIFTED AND RED
Shankly's 1970s squad was a mixture of youth and experience.

shake their hands. In the late 1960s he had watched as his great Scottish contemporaries – Jock Stein and Matt Busby – took their clubs to glory on the Continent. Now, under his leadership, Liverpool had become the first English team to win European and domestic honours in a single season.

"I think Europe had become a challenge to Bill," said former club secretary Peter Robinson. "He was obsessed with the Inter Milan game when I first came, and I know he was very hurt in '66 when we lost to Dortmund.

"Although he would never admit it – he used to say it was all about the domestic side and winning the Football League – deep down he really wanted to win a European trophy."

Back Home

But that UEFA Cup final would prove to be Shankly's only triumph abroad. In

THE KIRKBY KID
Phil Thompson forced his way into the first team in the 1973–74 season.

the following season his side were dumped out of the European Cup by a Red Star Belgrade team combining defensive organization, patient passing – and lethal counter-attacks. Leading 2–1 from the home leg, the Yugoslav champions gave an Anfield performance that would become the model for future Liverpool teams in Europe. They absorbed pressure with ease, drew the home side's sting, grabbed the vital away goal, then stroked the ball around as Liverpool became ever more frustrated. Even after Chris Lawler managed to find the net with six minutes left, the visitors never looked like surrendering their advantage. And when they regained their lead in the last minute of time, even the Kop had to applaud a textbook tactical display.

That second round exit left Liverpool concentrating on the domestic front, and attempting to make up ground on a resurgent Leeds United. The

Yorkshiremen had made an astonishing start to the 1973–74 season, going 29 games without defeat to set a new First Division points record. In contrast, Liverpool's opening had been distinctly average, and it wasn't until a strong run of wins in November that they began to regain the previous season's confidence.

There were several reasons. On the field, a mixture of injuries, suspensions and poor form had left the line-up looking far more unsettled. While Clemence, Hughes, Keegan and Callaghan were all ever-presents, Shankly could not make up his mind about the relative attacking merits of Toshack, Boersma and Hall. In defence, Phil Thompson seized his chance when Larry Lloyd limped out of the first team. Then a succession of reserves – including a young Roy Evans – each made a handful of appearances, taking the total number of players used that season to 21.

Off the pitch, there was discord between Shankly and Smith. The manager and his headstrong captain were a combustible mix at the best of times, with the boss once declaring – only half-jokingly – that "Tommy Smith could start a riot in a cemetery". But when he dropped him for an away game at Arsenal, their relationship came under severe strain. Smith walked out on the team, refusing to watch the game from the Highbury stands. Shankly responded immediately by arranging to send him to Stoke on loan, and passing the captaincy to Emlyn Hughes. For a short while it looked like the end of the legendary "Anfield Iron", but then a cartilage injury to Chris Lawler led to Shankly reorganizing his defence, and asking his former skipper to return in the right-back position.

With the row settled, Liverpool entered the new year playing with new purpose and vigour. They remained unbeaten in 12 games and, as Leeds finally began to falter, they made up ground on the runaway leaders. In April they faced Manchester City and Everton, scoring four times without reply, to cut the gap at the top to three points. But then, just as Leeds rediscovered their early form, Liverpool slipped again. They lost three of their last four games and ended the campaign five points behind the men from Elland Road. In his last season before taking over as England manager, Don Revie had reclaimed the championship from his greatest rival.

Still, Shankly had the FA Cup to think about. His team had just reached Wembley thanks to a 3–1 semi-final replay victory over Leicester in which Keegan's form was stunning. Time and again at Villa Park he cut the opposition back line to ribbons, scoring with a blistering volley and helping set up further goals from Toshack and Hall. The 1973–74 season had been the one in which the dynamic little Yorkshireman had become a true star,

PERFECT PARTNERS

"My understanding with Tosh was almost telepathic," said Keegan.

finally claiming his first senior international cap. Now, as he prepared for its Wembley climax, Shankly could not hold back his praise: "We played as well as we have ever played tonight. It was marvellous to watch in such an electric atmosphere. They all played well but Kevin Keegan was just brilliant. He is the finest player in England."

Keegan went on to prove his manager right in the 3–0 Cup final stroll against Newcastle a month later (see page

Steve Heighway scores the second goal for Liverpool.

Ian Callaghan and Kevin Keegan parade the FA Cup around Wembley.

Kevin Keegan pounces on a cross for number three.

If Liverpool needed any extra incentive to lift the FA Cup for the second time in their history it was provided by the opposing centre-forward, Newcastle's England striker Malcolm Macdonald.

"We are going to win the Cup," proclaimed Macdonald after scoring in every round en route to the final. "Wembley is my stage. With that crowd of ours behind us there is not a team in the world who can live with us there."

Such verbal bravado savagely rebounded on Macdonald, as Liverpool captain Emlyn Hughes revealed. "Malcolm was a very good, strong centre-forward who had scored a hat-trick against us in his first home game for Newcastle," said Hughes.

"But in the build-up to the final he did nothing but brag, shouting what he was going to do to us and how he'd terrorize our defence. It was the worst thing he could

have done because it just made us determined that he'd eat his words.

"He was still shouting the odds when the boss Bill Shankly, myself and some of the other lads went on a pre-match TV interview with Newcastle manager Joe Harvey and his players.

"Their lads were immaculately dressed in their Wembley suits and ties. But it was boiling hot and you could see the sweat rolling off them. Just as the interview with Joe finished, Shanks turned to the camera and said: "Boys … they're crapping themselves!" Newcastle heard it, as I'm sure Shanks meant them to, and it struck a psychological blow."

Newcastle's ranks included left-back Alan Kennedy and midfielder Terry McDermott, both of whom would later join Liverpool, and it was the team from Merseyside who gave them a nightmare afternoon.

It was remarkable that Liverpool's domination had failed to reward them by half-time. After the interval it was a different story. Their command and superb passing movements left Liverpool goalkeeper Ray Clemence untroubled with his centre-backs Hughes and Phil Thompson snuffing out any threat from Macdonald and John Tudor.

After an offside verdict denied Alec Lindsay a breakthrough goal, Liverpool

LIVERPOOL 3 NEWCASTLE UNITED 0 WEMBLEY STADIUM, 4 MAY 1974 **REFEREE:** Gordon Kew (Amersham)
Teams **LIVERPOOL:** Clemence; T. Smith, Thompson, Hughes (captain), Lindsay; Hall, Cormack, Callaghan; Keegan, Toshack, Heighway.
NEWCASTLE UNITED: McFaul; Clark, Howard, Moncur (captain), Kennedy; Smith J. (Gibb, 75), McDermott, Cassidy, Hibbitt; Tudor, Macdonald.

"You're nicked!"

"So many Liverpool players were involved. Newcastle were undressed. They were stripped naked." DAVID COLEMAN

seized a 58th-minute lead. Brian Hall made cursory contact with Tommy Smith's cross allowing Kevin Keegan to hit a right-foot shot that Newcastle goalkeeper Ian McFaul touched but had no chance of stopping.

Number two arrived in the 75th minute, drilled in brilliantly by Steve Heighway from John Toshack's headed flick off a Clemence clearance. Two minutes later the virtually anonymous Macdonald, dubbed "Super Mac" by Geordie fans, had the first of his only two shots in the game. It drifted yards wide, prompting a derisory chant of "Super Mouth" from Liverpool supporters, who were ecstatic two minutes from time when the team performed their party piece … an 11-pass move for goal number three.

Clemence launched the move and when

Lindsay flicked the ball to Keegan wide on the left flank he checked before flighting a superb crossfield pass deftly touched first time by Smith, with the outside of his right foot, to Hall.

Hall returned the ball to Smith who then exchanged a one-two with Heighway and the defender's cross from the right arrowed through a crowded goalmouth for Keegan to pounce to score his second of the game.

Newcastle had been mere spectators and BBC commentator David Coleman enthused: "So many Liverpool players were involved. Newcastle were undressed. They weree stripped naked."

When the final whistle sounded Shankly, wearing a raincoat, pink shirt and dark tie emerged beaming from the bench. When two fans bowed at his feet he quipped: "While your down there boys give my shoes a quick polish!"

And Phil Thompson could not resist the jibe: "What's Super Mac got to say now? I'm going to take him home and put him on our mantelpiece for my kid brother Owen to play with!"

Shell-shocked Macdonald admitted: "We never even started to play and we let our fans down. Liverpool turned it on and we turned it off. It's been an experience. You can make a fool of yourself."

108). His performance cemented his reputation as a genuine world-class footballer, and alerted an increasing number of foreign coaches to his talents. In a surprising admission, Keegan later revealed how that one match altered his career: "It did wonders for my confidence at a time when I was quietly considering getting out of the game to try my hand at something else. I had sunk into a mood of feeling that there was surely more to life than football, but my appetite for the game was restored by a match in which nearly everything worked to perfection for me."

The Liverpool fans, gathered in their hundreds of thousands for another triumphant homecoming, were completely unaware that their playing hero had considered quitting. Just as well. They were already in for one of the biggest shocks of their lives.

EXIT SHANKLY

With the new season just five weeks away, journalists and camera crews were summoned to a press conference at Anfield. They thought they were being given the chance to interview Ray Kennedy, the Arsenal star whom Shankly had just captured in a record £200,000 deal, but when club chairman John Smith sat down, he had a much more significant announcement:

"It is with great regret that I have to inform you that Mr Shankly has intimated to me that he wishes to retire from active participation in League football, and that the board has – with extreme reluctance – accepted his decision. I would like to place on record the board's great appreciation for Mr Shankly's magnificent achievements over the

SHANKS FOR THE MEMORIES
*Liverpool's legendary boss says goodbye
after 15 years at Anfield.*

period of his managership. Meanwhile he has agreed to give every assistance to the club for as long as is necessary."

The reporters could not quite believe what they had just heard. When Smith stopped talking, none of them could manage a question, and, in the silence of the room, only the clicks of the photographers' cameras could be heard. After several awkward moments, someone did ask the manager why he was leaving. Shankly, looking tired and drawn, had no ready answer, but, even on his saddest day, he still found a quote to keep the headline writers happy: "It was the most difficult decision I've ever had to make. And when I went in to see the chairman, it was like walking to the electric chair."

The resignation made every front page in Britain – and dominated the sports sections, too. No other story seemed to matter. Even in the *Liverpool Echo*, the news of Kennedy's transfer rated just six paragraphs. But as the newspapers reflected on Shankly's achievements, their readers wanted answers. Why had he gone? Had there been a row with the directors? Had the board tried to persuade him to stay? Was his decision final?

Over the next few days it became clear that there had been no arguments, but the reason for his decision remained a mystery.

Shankly's last match in charge was the 1974 Charity Shield victory against Leeds – an ill-tempered affair in which both Keegan and Billy Bremner were sent off. But nothing stands still in football; as Shankly accepted praise for the past, the new man in the hot seat was planning an even more glorious future.

TOP 10
LEAGUE GOALS 1967-1974

1. ROGER HUNT		57
2. JOHN TOSHACK		36
3. KEVIN KEEGAN		34
4. CHRIS LAWLER		34
5. EMLYN HUGHES		31
6. BOBBY GRAHAM		27
7. PETER THOMPSON		27
8. TOMMY SMITH		25
9. IAN CALLAGHAN		23
10. IAN ST JOHN		23

PLAYER KEVIN **KEEGAN**

Kevin Keegan sat on a dustbin waiting to sign for Liverpool, then proceeded to lift the lid from a host of defences in a brilliant six-year Anfield career.

Following the path trodden four years earlier by goalkeeper Ray Clemence, Keegan came from Scunthorpe United and arrived with Anfield resembling a building site, due to reconstruction of the main stand.

His journey from Lincolnshire to meet Bill Shankly and undergo a medical to conclude his £35,000 transfer also coincided with Liverpool's preparations for the 1971 FA Cup final against Arsenal three days later. Thus, the unknown Doncaster-born 20-year-old from the Fourth Division was far from the centre of attention as he waited for his appointment with the Liverpool manager.

But he certainly wasn't overawed at meeting the great man. Instead of meekly signing as a star-struck youngster, he argued with Shankly for an extra five pounds a week wages! It was evidence of that self-assured streak that swelled Shankly's admiration of Keegan.

"Bill Shankly said that they were offering me £45 a week," Keegan recalled. "I wanted to sign there and then but I remembered my father's advice of not to sell myself cheaply. So I said to Shanks: 'Oh, I thought I'd be getting more than that.'

"At Scunthorpe my basic was £30 plus £8 for a win and £4 for a draw. I told Shanks I thought I was worth £50 a week at Liverpool and said: 'I feel I must better myself.'

"After reminding me of my big opportunity at a great club with such great fans he said: 'OK, son, £50 it is.' He told me that if I played well I'd never have to ask for a rise again. And he kept his promise. In fact, he was like a second father to me."

Shankly was delighted with his acquisition, labelling the modest fee paid to Scunthorpe as "daylight robbery", adding: "Other clubs wanted Kevin but we got him because my good friend Andy Beattie, who was scouting, tipped me off about him. Kevin was one of the

most honest boys of all time. His father Joe had a mining background like me so we understood each other. Kevin was a born winner … all action and all energy."

Keegan had been bought with a view to play in midfield in place of Ian Callaghan, whom Liverpool feared was nearing the end of his Anfield career. It was a plan wrong on both counts. Callaghan played on for a further seven years and just before the start of the 1971–72 season Keegan was pitched into a practice match in the first-team's attack against the reserves, a game the second string usually won.

This time, though, the Keegan-inspired seniors hit seven goals. Four days later Shankly plunged his new recruit into his debut up front alongside John Toshack in the season's opener against Nottingham Forest. Keegan scored, Liverpool won 3–1 and a legend was born.

Keegan became the new sensation of English football, inspiring Liverpool triumphs at home and abroad, starring for and captaining

his country, being elected Footballer of the Year in 1976 and having his own weekly column in the *Daily Express*.

Succeeding the admirable alliance of Roger Hunt and Ian St John, the combination of bustling 5ft 7in Keegan and rangy 6ft 2in Wales striker Toshack proved an uncanny partnership, with Keegan scoring a century of the pair's 195 goals. Only a dubious offside verdict at Arsenal in the final game of their first season in harness denied them the championship, but the following year Keegan missed only two of Liverpool's 54 games in their march to the League title and UEFA Cup double in which he hit 17 goals.

A year later he scored twice at Wembley in Liverpool's crushing 3–0 FA Cup final demolition of Newcastle prior to his "shock and sadness" of Shankly's resignation two months later. When Keegan returned to Wembley in the following August's Charity Shield, he and Leeds United's Billy Bremner were sent off. His massive 11-game ban briefly prompted Keegan to consider quitting the game.

Shankly's successor Bob Paisley helped persuade him otherwise and Keegan was a key man in another championship and UEFA Cup double in 1976. A year later he said a glorious goodbye to Liverpool in their 3–1 conquest of Borussia Moenchengladbach in Rome to win the European Cup for the first time, crowning a season that also landed the championship and runners-up spot in the FA Cup.

It was a fitting farewell before his departure for Hamburg, where he was twice voted European Footballer of the Year, and subsequent stints at Southampton and Newcastle, whom he later managed. He was also boss of Fulham and England before Manchester City. But Keegan's football credo was forged in the heat of the Kop under the burning influence of Shankly.

1976 ● LEAGUE CHAMPIONS

● UEFA CUP WINNERS

1977 ● LEAGUE CHAMPIONS

● EUROPEAN CHAMPIONS

● QUEEN'S SILVER JUBILEE

1978 ● EUROPEAN CHAMPIONS

1979 ● LEAGUE CHAMPIONS

CHAPTER SEVEN *1975–1983*	The Quiet Man

● MARGARET THATCHER ELECTED

1980 ● LEAGUE CHAMPIONS

1981 ● EUROPEAN CHAMPIONS

● LEAGUE CUP WINNERS

● DEATH OF BILL SHANKLY

1982 ● LEAGUE CHAMPIONS

● LEAGUE CUP WINNERS

● FALKLANDS WAR

1983 ● LEAGUE CHAMPIONS

● MILK CUP WINNERS

● BOB PAISLEY RETIRES

● JOE FAGAN BECOMES MANAGER

"AFTER SATURDAY'S DEFEAT AT WEMBLEY WE WONDERED WHAT EFFECT IT WOULD HAVE ON THE PLAYERS. WE NEED NOT HAVE WORRIED BECAUSE, RIGHT FROM THE START, WE DOMINATED THE GAME — AND TURNED IN THE BEST PERFORMANCE IN THE HISTORY OF THE CLUB."

BOB PAISLEY, ROME, 1977

"This one's mine"

IT WAS SHANKLY HIMSELF WHO RECOMMENDED BOB PAISLEY AS HIS SUCCESSOR. HE HAD WORKED WITH HIM SINCE ARRIVING AT ANFIELD, OBSERVING HIS TACTICAL GENIUS, ENCYCLOPAEDIC KNOWLEDGE OF INJURIES AND SHEER COMMONSENSE. HE HAD ALSO WITNESSED AT FIRST HAND HOW THE QUIET GEORDIE WAS EVERY BIT HIS EQUAL WHEN IT CAME TO PLAYER-PSYCHOLOGY.

Shortly after Ray Clemence broke into the first team, Paisley noticed he had trouble with goal-kicks. When questioned about it, the new 'keeper admitted that he hated the wind and that, if he knew it was blowing against him, he would allow the worry to affect his kicking. Paisley's solution was simple but effective. He told the groundstaff to remove the flags that used to flutter from poles high above the old Kemlyn Road Stand. The result: Clemence had no idea which way the wind was blowing, and the one weakness in his game was eradicated.

But despite all his knowledge and qualifications, Paisley was reluctant to step into Shankly's shoes. He was a modest, unassuming man who enjoyed his daily routine of training ground, betting shop and dinner at home with his family. Life in the shadows was sweet, and he had no desire to change it. Pressure, hassle and an intrusive media were the last things he needed.

But the Anfield establishment ganged up on him, finally persuading him to take on the responsibility. Even when he agreed, Paisley saw himself as merely a "buffer" between Shankly and whoever the board decided on as the long-term replacement. He did not plan a revolution, and he left his squad in no doubt about how he felt: "I never wanted this job in the first place and I'm not even sure I can do it. I need all the help I can get from you

WEMBLEY SEND OFF
Keegan and Bremner were banned for 11 matches after their dismissals.

players. There will be no disruptions to the team. Let's just keep playing it the Liverpool way."

But, almost immediately, there was massive disruption. Keegan, who had torn off his shirt in disgust following his Charity Shield dismissal, faced a charge of bringing the game into disrepute. His actions, at a time of increasing football hooliganism, had caused outrage in the media, and one MP had called for him to be kicked out of football for good. When the FA's disciplinary committee handed down an 11-match ban, it seemed obvious that political considerations were at work. And Paisley, deprived of his star player for almost two months, was seething: "People who don't know how to run the country are trying to run football, which they know even less about. If players get this punishment for throwing their jerseys, what is there left for some of the much more offensive things that happen in the game?"

There was more bad news to come when centre-back Larry Lloyd slapped in a transfer request and moved to Coventry. Phil Thompson was ruled out for eight weeks with cartilage damage, then John Toshack suffered a thigh injury that sidelined him for more than a month. Paisley coped with the losses better than expected, rejigging his defence, and bringing in Boersma and Kennedy to lead the front line. The team began well, but by autumn their form was slipping. In one dreadful run between November and February, they won only four League games, losing six and drawing six. They went out of the League Cup after a home defeat by Middlesbrough, then suffered a fourth round FA Cup exit at the hands of Ipswich. Worst of all, their hopes of another European success bit the dust. They had gone into the second round of the Cup-winners' Cup fresh from a record-breaking 12–0 aggregate win over the Norwegian amateurs Stromsgodset Drammen. But then they met their old foes Ferencvaros, whose 1–1 result at Anfield – following a goalless draw in Hungary – was just enough to see them through.

As spring approached there were rumblings about Paisley's suitability for the job. The fans were unhappy at the prospect of a barren season, and there was a growing campaign for Shankly to be given a directorship or formal advisory role. As reports of dressing-room bust-ups hit the newspapers, Paisley's own dealings with the media grew difficult. At one point Keegan went into print to defend his boss against unjustified "sniping". He claimed the backroom atmosphere was fine, and predicted that success would come – with time.

Gradually, things improved. Liverpool put together a strong late run that left them just two points behind the eventual champions, Derby County. Relations with the press thawed, and the arguments surrounding Shankly's future role began to subside. Best of all, the new manager even began to enjoy the job, likening himself to "an apprentice jockey on a Derby horse".

The lack of trophies may have disguised Paisley's first-year achievements, but it was a season in which he introduced players who

TERRY McDERMOTT
Joined the Reds after impressive displays with Newcastle.

would prove crucial to Liverpool's future. From Northampton Town came the unknown Phil Neal – a full-back who would go on to win more medals than any other Liverpool player. Kirkby-born Terry McDermott arrived from Newcastle for £170,000, while the former South Liverpool star Jimmy Case was given his chance after impressive performances in the reserves.

But Paisley's favourite "discovery" was Ray Kennedy – the man Shankly had bought as an out-and-out striker, but who had struggled to live up to his reputation in the Anfield attack. "Ray had really lost his appetite for playing up front but I learned that he had played in midfield as a schoolboy – I think he was surprised I found that out," Paisley later wrote. "That knowledge turned out to be a blessing for both Ray and the club. I had a talk with him and told him we'd try him out in the reserves. The results exceeded our wildest expectations. Ray quickly blossomed into the role, made a first-team place his own, and went on to play for England ... He was many people's choice as English football's player of the seventies."

Paisley's good sense and tactical knowledge were coming to the fore. They were about to make Liverpool the most successful British team in history.

ANOTHER DOUBLE
Two new players made their bow during the 1975–76 season – both destined to become folk-heroes. The first was Joey Jones, a gangly full-back signed from Wrexham, whose determined clenched-fist salutes made him an instant Kop favourite. His success in displacing the cultured Alec Lindsay came as a surprise to many,

RAY KENNEDY
Converted from striker to midfielder after his transfer from Arsenal.

but he quickly won over the doubters with his ferocious tackling, fine distribution and never-say-die spirit.

In attack, Paisley introduced David Fairclough, a flame-haired speed merchant who terrorized opposition defences with his dazzling runs from the half-way line. Although sometimes starting games as deputy for an injured Heighway or Toshack, he was always at his most effective when deployed as 12th man. When he tore apart Everton's defence to score a last-minute goal in the Anfield derby that season, the press gave him the name of "Supersub" – a tag that would last for the rest of his career.

The 1975–76 campaign proved to be another marathon, with Liverpool fighting on four fronts. Failure to get beyond the early rounds of the domestic cups was probably a blessing, as they needed all their strength to compete in a close title race, and among some of the biggest names in Europe. Still, defeat was never nice – particularly when playing the likes of Burnley in the early stages of the League Cup.

In the championship race their main rivals were Queen's Park Rangers, along with an attack-minded Manchester United, who had stormed back from Division Two under Tommy Docherty's charismatic leadership. Liverpool lost at Loftus Road on the opening day, and did not manage to claim top spot until they beat the London side in the Anfield return just before Christmas. The leadership swapped between the three clubs for the next three months, only for United to fall away at Easter. On the final Saturday of the season, Rangers completed their programme with a victory over Leeds, putting them a point above Liverpool, who had a game in hand. That match would take place at Wolves – a team for whom defeat would spell relegation from Division One. And, as if that wasn't tough enough for Paisley's men, the game was scheduled in between the two legs of the UEFA Cup final.

The team had played consistently well in Europe, showing the sort of temperament that was missing in the Shankly years. To the passion, Paisley had added patience. Teams did not have to be steamrollered into

SUPERSUB
David Fairclough played a devastating role in the number 12 shirt.

submission any more. Instead, Liverpool would soak up the pressure and hit them on the break. Scalps on the way to the final included Hibernian, who fell victim to a headed Toshack hat-trick at Anfield in the first round. Next came the Spanish side Real Sociedad, beaten 3–1 on their home ground, then hit for six in their away leg.

In the third round Liverpool came up against Poland's Slask Wroclaw, and what Paisley described as "probably the most difficult match we've ever played in Europe". The reason was the Polish weather – 15 degrees of frost, a biting November wind and an ice-bound surface. The home side may have been better suited to the conditions, but Liverpool managed to overcome them. They won the game 2–1, setting up an Anfield leg in which Case wrapped matters up with his first senior hat-trick.

After seeing off Dynamo Dresden in the following round, they drew a glamorous semi-final tie with Barcelona. The Spanish side – complete with the Reds' old Ajax adversary Johann Cruyff – were one of the most feared on the Continent, and the 70,000 fans who poured into the Nou Camp were expecting them to make light work of the men from Merseyside. But it was a night when Liverpool put on one of their best-ever performances on foreign soil. And Paisley was the man behind it. "Bob laid the rules down before the game," Phil Neal later recalled. "He said that we needed to keep the opposition quiet, and that the way to do that was with plenty of passing. He said that if we denied them a scoring chance in the first half we would feel the opposition fans getting fidgety, and that anxiety would start getting to the Barcelona players. So we went out and played that way – and it worked like a dream."

From the start, Liverpool were composed and assured, with the veteran Ian Callaghan controlling the midfield. Up front, Keegan and Toshack were at their telepathic best, finding each other with nods and flicks that none of the Barcelona defence could anticipate. After 13 minutes they played a one-two that ended with the Welshman eluding his markers and driving a left-footed shot into the opposition net. Liverpool were in front – and their dominance throughout the rest of the game kept their lead intact.

As Paisley had predicted, the home fans became restless throughout the second half. At full-time, substitute Joey Jones saw their anger boil over:

"As soon as the whistle went, all these cushions started coming down from the stands. So I got out of the dug-out and started throwing them back. I was whizzing them like frisbees, and a few of them started bouncing off the Spaniards' heads. Then Bob Paisley grabbed me by the collar and said: 'What do you think you're doing, son?' I told him I wasn't having them throwing cushions at us. And he said: 'They're not throwing them at us – they're throwing them at their own team because we've beaten them.'"

The famous Nou Camp victory set the scene for another electric European night at Anfield. A capacity 55,000 crowd turned out for Barcelona's visit – a game in which the Spaniards often threatened to overturn Liverpool's advantage. Five minutes into the second half Phil Thompson seemed to have settled matters by bundling Toshack's cross over the line ("I'm lethal from two inches," he boasted afterwards). But just 60 seconds later a surging run from Cruyff set up a Barcelona equalizer, and a pulsating fightback.

Despite the Spaniards' best efforts, Liverpool held on for a deserved two-legged victory, and a place in their third European final. This time the opponents were FC Bruges, who – despite their

ADVANTAGE RESTORED
Keegan is mobbed after his vital UEFA Cup equalizer.

lack of pedigree – presented a much sterner test than Barcelona. The opening leg at Anfield was nail-biting and dramatic. Bruges punished some unusually sloppy defending to go two goals up in 12 minutes. The Reds were on the rack, and it took a supreme effort to steady nerves and prevent the Belgians from going further ahead.

At half-time, Paisley rang the changes. Toshack came off, Case went on, and Keegan was given the job of leading the line. Once again, the manager's tactics were inspired. A quarter of an hour after the break, Kennedy clawed a goal back with a powerful drive from the edge of the box. Two minutes later he saw another shot cannon off a post, with Case scoring from the rebound. Three minutes after the restart, Heighway went in search of a winner and was upended in the box. When the referee pointed to the spot, Keegan stepped up to convert.

That narrow, breathless win was still fresh in the memory when Liverpool travelled to Molineux for the climax to their League programme. Excitement on Merseyside was at its height, and an estimated 20,000 fans journeyed to the West Midlands for a match that would decide that season's First Division title and relegation battles. At half-time, it looked as though Wolves might just manage to stay up. But, in the last 15 minutes, Liverpool cancelled out a 1–0 deficit with three expertly taken goals from Keegan, Toshack and Kennedy. The Wanderers fans went home in tears, their team consigned to Second Division football, but Liverpool's Red Army celebrated a ninth title

CHAMPIONS OF CHAMPIONS
The dramatic Molineux win earned the Reds a record ninth title.

Left: *Keegan and Toshack celebrate UEFA Cup victory.*
Right: *Emlyn Hughes holds the trophy aloft.*

success. After surpassing Arsenal's record, their team had become "Champions of Champions".

A fortnight later the Reds faced Bruges in the UEFA Cup final second leg in Belgium. Combining the control of the Continental passing game with the aggression and work-rate that served them so well at home, Paisley's side quelled an opposition determined to cancel out their home lead. Bruges got off to a flyer when Tommy Smith inadvertently handled in the box after 12 minutes. But they lost their 1-0 penalty advantage after just three minutes, when Keegan drilled home a free-kick pass from the edge of the 18-yard area.

The match ended all square, with Liverpool winning 4-3 on aggregate. At the end of only his second year in charge, Paisley had equalled Shankly's greatest achievement – a domestic and European double. "The second half was the longest 45 minutes of my life," the Manager of the Year told reporters afterwards. "There was an awful lot of pride in this game because we came representing England. We did not let the country down and I am very proud of the lads."

He was especially proud of Keegan, the player who – yet again – had inspired the team to some of their greatest victories. The little number seven rounded off

BLUE TO RED
*Ex-Evertonian David Johnson
scored almost a goal every other game.*

another terrific campaign by collecting the Footballer of the Year Award – an honour collected by Ian Callaghan two seasons earlier. But even as he savoured all the acclaim and adulation, Keegan was growing frustrated with life in England. The biggest clubs in Europe were banging at his door – and he was getting ready to open it.

KEVIN'S LAST FLING

It was Real Madrid who made the first serious move. The Spanish giants approached Keegan with a lucrative offer that nearly prised him away from Anfield in the run-up to the 1976-77 season. But after discussions with chairman John Smith, the player reached a compromise with Liverpool. If he would stay at Anfield for one more season – and one more tilt at the European Cup – the club would release him from his contract at the end of it.

With Keegan on borrowed time, and Toshack still prone to regular injuries, Paisley decided it was prudent to take out an insurance policy. A fortnight before the new season began he paid £200,000 for the Ipswich striker David Johnson, a former Everton player who had scored on his League derby debut back in 1971. With so much competition for places in the forward line, Johnson initially struggled to find a role, but he went on to become a key member of future Liverpool sides, averaging almost a goal every other game, and winning England honours.

But that year's team was pure vintage, powering their way to Wembley in the FA Cup and reaching the European Cup final for the first time. In the League, they were unbeaten at Anfield, winning 18 of their 21 home matches. The ever-present Clemence conceded just 33 goals throughout the campaign, with five of them coming in a single freak game at Villa Park. The Reds went down 5-1 in that December fixture – their heaviest defeat since 1963. But for the ever-inventive Kopites, heading back home for the Christmas holidays, the result was an excuse for a new seasonal song:

"Should Aston Villa be forgot,
And never brought to mind..."

And it was soon forgotten. With Ipswich and Manchester City chasing them all the way, Liverpool headed the pack from March until the end of the season. They beat both their closest rivals in April, and further victories over Manchester United and Arsenal meant they needed just one point from their last two games to retain the title. They earned it at home on the final Saturday of the season, with a 0–0 draw against West Ham – Keegan's last competitive game for Liverpool at Anfield.

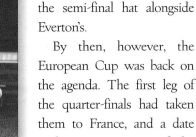

ANFIELD IN ECSTASY
David Fairclough's late goal destroys St. Etienne

It was a strangely muted celebration as the players did their lap of honour, but – as Footballer of the Year Emlyn Hughes admitted – everyone was looking beyond the championship: "This is just the start. We must now pour all our concentration into beating Manchester United in the FA Cup final. Then there's the little matter of the European Cup final four days later. That's the one we want to win above all the others. It's the only piece of silverware missing from the Anfield dressing room."

TREBLE CHANCE

The quest for the two Cups had begun back in September with a simple 7–0 aggregate win over the Irish champions, Crusaders. Turkish side Trabzonspor presented trickier opposition in round two, but, following a 1–0 away defeat, Heighway, Johnson and Keegan each got on the scoresheet in the first 20 minutes at Anfield to provide the Reds with a comfortable 3–1 victory.

With the next round put back until March, Liverpool switched their attention to the domestic knock-out competitions. In the League Cup they fell at the first hurdle, the victims of a 1–0 replay defeat at West Brom. They were taken to a replay in the opening stage of the FA Cup, too. But after Crystal Palace's hard-fought 0–0 draw at Anfield, Liverpool went to Selhurst Park and won by the odd goal in five. Home wins against Carlisle, Oldham and Middlesbrough followed, but then the luck of the draw finally deserted them – as

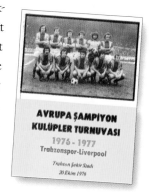

AVRUPA ŞAMPİYON
KULÜPLER TURNUVASI
1976 - 1977
Trabzonspor-Liverpool
Trabzon Şehir Stadı
20 Ekim 1976

their name was pulled out of the semi-final hat alongside Everton's.

By then, however, the European Cup was back on the agenda. The first leg of the quarter-finals had taken them to France, and a date with Europe's team of the moment St Etienne. They were a celebrity side, packed with internationals, and noted for their vibrant, free-flowing style. They were also the dominant force in French football, and had remained unbeaten at home for four years. A Liverpool team minus the injured Keegan held out well in France but couldn't quite manage to keep a clean sheet. Their 1–0 defeat set up a mouth-watering return leg – and an Anfield occasion every bit as dramatic and memorable as the Inter Milan game 12 years previously.

David Fairclough was destined to play the starring role that night. Like every Liverpudlian, he could sense that history was in the making: "You just felt that something extraordinary was going to happen. When our coach was heading towards the Anfield Road before the game, we could just see masses and masses of people ahead of us. And when we got inside the ground I'd never seen so many flags, and I'd never felt such an atmosphere."

The Kop gates were locked an hour before kick-off, and tens of thousands of stranded fans began a mad rush to get into other parts of the ground. Many of those caught up in the crush missed the first act in the night's drama: a goal from Kevin Keegan that levelled the scores with just 60 seconds gone. The Liverpool crowd – who had converted St Etienne's "Allez Les Verts" chant into "Allez Les Rouges" – roared their team on as they went in search of a winner. But after 51 minutes they were left in sickening silence as the Frenchman Bathenay beat Clemence with a superb 30-yard drive.

Because of the away goals rule, Liverpool now had to score twice in order to go through. Ray Kennedy gave them hope when he latched on to a Toshack header to make it 2–1, but, as the game went into its final ten minutes, Liverpool were tiring visibly and finding it increasingly difficult to create chances on goal. It was then that Fairclough entered the fray, sent on to replace Toshack with Paisley's words ringing in his ears: "Just get out there and get a piece of something. See if you can turn this one."

If the fans watching inside the stadium were nervous, the tension for those outside was almost unbearable. Phil Thompson, lying in a hospital bed with knee damage, was one of the countless Liverpudlians with their ears glued to the live match coverage. With six minutes of the game remaining, he was tuned into Liverpool's commercial station, Radio City. The increasingly hysterical commentator made such an impact that – 25 years on – Thompson still recalls his every word: "I can remember what he said exactly. He said: 'Liverpool look as if they may have lost it now; it looks as though the game has gone away from them. Here's Ray Kennedy with the ball. He passes it forward. He passes it forward to David Fairclough. And David Fairclough is going on. And he's going on ... AND HE'S SCORED! ... HE'S SCORED!'"

Thompson's screams caused panic among the nurses who thought he had aggravated his injury. But the noise was nothing compared to the roars inside Anfield, where 55,000 people celebrated the most dramatic goal they had ever seen. On the pitch Fairclough leapt for joy, only to be smothered within seconds by his ecstatic team-mates. As he emerged from the melee, Keegan stood with his arms outstretched, and said what everyone in the stadium was thinking: "Supersub – you've done it again!"

There was enough emotion packed into that one night to last a whole season. But it was far from over. In the next round Liverpool overcame Swiss side FC Zurich to set up the biggest game in their history – the European Cup final against German champions Borussia Moenchengladbach (see page 122). And just a week later they recorded a 3–0 replay victory over Everton to secure an FA Cup final date with Manchester United.

TWO OUT OF THREE AIN'T BAD

Just four days separated those crucial Wembley and Rome finals. But before the Wembley game, the FA announced that if a replay was needed, it would have to take place at the end of June.

Paisley was appalled at the possibility of an already-lengthy season stretching on for another five weeks. Desperate to avoid a Wembley stalemate, he altered his team formation, opting for a three-man attack instead of his favourite 4-4-2 formation. "That FA decision swayed me into playing David Johnson up front with Kevin Keegan and Steve Heighway because I couldn't bear the thought of a replay," he later wrote. "And I regretted not playing Ian Callaghan as a fourth man in midfield, because I'm sure we would not have lost if I had used what I knew to be our most effective formation."

Liverpool went into the first match as favourites, having beaten Tommy Docherty's men in the League only three weeks earlier, but the United they met this time were a more spirited bunch. Liverpool, playing in white, had the best of the early play, but – despite their trademark precision passing – failed to show the ruthlessness that was needed in front of goal. United absorbed their pressure and, with Steve Coppell and Gordon Hill on the wings, always looked likely to mount dangerous counter-attacks.

Five minutes into the second half, United pulled ahead thanks to a low, angled shot from Stuart Pearson. Two minutes later, Jimmy Case collected a Joey Jones pass with his back to goal. Two United defenders were closing in on the midfielder when he flicked the ball into the air, swivelled and rifled an unstoppable half-volley into the opposition net.

Having finally discovered their edge up front, it began to look like Liverpool's day. The Merseyside fans, gathered behind the goal where Case had scored, took the equalizer as a cue to begin singing about their forthcoming visit to Italy. But just three minutes after their side drew level, they found themselves behind again – this time the result of a fluke

TOP 10	
LEAGUE APP'S 1975–1983	
1. PHIL NEAL	336
2. PHIL THOMPSON	258
3. RAY KENNEDY	250
4. RAY CLEMENCE	248
5. KENNY DALGLISH	244
6. TERRY McDERMOTT	216
7. GRAEME SOUNESS	210
8. ALAN HANSEN	195
9. JIMMY CASE	182
10. ALAN KENNEDY	169

FA CUP FINAL 1977
Johnson outjumps Brian Greenhoff, but United won the game 2–1.

Lou Macari shot that hit Jimmy Greenhoff on the back and deflected past Clemence.

Liverpool threw everything at United in the last half-hour. With Callaghan on for Johnson, the old passing movements returned and they started to find a way through the opposition back four. There were goalmouth scrambles, balls were cleared from the line, and Ray Kennedy hit the woodwork with a fierce shot. But the United defence were disciplined and resolute, out to avenge their Wembley defeat against Southampton a year earlier, and determined to stop their Merseyside rivals from making history with a unique treble.

Docherty's men succeeded, leaving Liverpool to reflect on a game that they really should have won within the first 45 minutes. The players looked tired and dejected as they left the field, and all their followers were concerned about the effects this defeat would have on the Rome game. But by the time their train got back to Lime Street, Paisley noted that their "depression had turned to defiance". It was Ray Clemence who summed up their feelings best: "We know we can play better than that, and we will. So God help Moenchengladbach on Wednesday night."

But there was to be no divine intervention for the Germans. In Rome,

A LEGEND BEGINS
Paisley and Peter Robinson welcome Kenny Dalglish to Anfield.

Liverpool turned in what Paisley described as "the best performance in the history of the club". They returned to a city where the miles of bunting for the Queen's Silver Jubilee had been torn down and replaced with an endless sea of red and white. An unforgettable homecoming – the biggest since 1965 – was followed by a testimonial for the team's self-styled "Roy of the Rovers", Tommy Smith. With Anfield packed, and the biggest prize in European football on show, the curtain finally came down on their most incredible season ever.

It was the most satisfying moment of Paisley's career. He had just been named Manger of the Year for the second successive season, and even the imminent loss of Keegan to West Germany's SV Hamburg could not prevent him from looking forward with confidence: "I hope I'm not being boastful when I say I think that this is only the beginning. There is no team in the world that we need fear. Obviously we will miss Kevin, but we have plans for a replacement who could bring a new dimension to our play."

KENNY'S FROM HEAVEN

The banner on the Kop said it all. There, among the thousands of red-and-white chequered flags brought back from Rome, was a message to the player on whose shoulders the future rested: "Kenny's Worth Every Penny."

Paisley had just paid a club record £440,000 to bring Kenny Dalglish from Celtic to Anfield. The 26-year-old Scot had started his Liverpool League career with a goal in a 1–1 draw at Middlesbrough. Now in the first home match of the 1977–78 season he was on target again, helping to fire the Reds to a 2–0 win against Newcastle. He went on to score six times in his first seven games, becoming an instant idol of the Kop and dispelling the memory of Keegan's departure. Keegan did, in fact, make a return trip to Anfield that season as his Hamburg side took on Liverpool in the new European Super Cup. He and his colleagues held out for a 1–1 draw in Germany, but back on Merseyside they were thrashed 6–0, with Dalglish among those on the scoresheet.

Thompson, Hughes and Case salute the fans.

Liverpool and their fans ran the gamut of emotions during five days in May 1977, from the misery of an FA Cup final defeat by Manchester United to the heady triumph of a European Cup final victory over Borussia Moenchengladbach in Rome's Olympic Stadium.

The 2–1 defeat by United at Wembley ended the Treble dream of Bob Paisley's already crowned League champions. But Paisley and his players, along with 26,000 supporters, buried their disappointment and headed in upbeat mood for their date with destiny in the Eternal City.

It proved to be an occasion long since weaved into the fabric of Anfield legend, Liverpool responding with a superb performance befitting the Queen's Silver Jubilee year and one that ultimately overwhelmed their classy West German foes.

Paisley made one change from the Wembley team, Ian Callaghan replacing David Johnson, who was named among the substitutes. John Toshack's Achilles injury meant that Alan Waddle was also on the bench.

Liverpool quickly dictated the course of the contest and an indication that fortune was to smile on them, rather than scowl as it had at Wembley, came when Rainer Bonhof's 20-yard shot, against the run of play, beat Ray Clemence but thudded off the England

'keeper's right post after 22 minutes.

Six minutes later Liverpool broke the deadlock after Callaghan robbed Bonhof to send Steve Heighway marauding down the right flank. As Terry McDermott found space Heighway slipped a superb pass into the midfielder's path and his brilliant right-foot shot flashed across the advancing Wolfgang Kneib into the net.

There was general satisfaction in the Liverpool camp at half time with their lead and the fact that they had kept a tight rein on Borussia's top scorer Jupp Heynckes.

Neither had they given much scope to Ulrich Stielike, the 22-year-old midfielder about to join Real Madrid for £400,000, while the hugely admired Berti Vogts, rated

LIVERPOOL 3 BORUSSIA MOENCHENGLADBACH 1 ROME, 25 MAY 1977 **REFEREE**: Robert Wurtz (France)
Teams **LIVERPOOL:** Clemence, Neal, Jones, Smith, Kennedy, Hughes, Keegan, Case, Heighway, Callaghan, McDermott. Substitutes unused: Fairclough, McDonnell, Waddle, Johnson, Lindsay. **BORUSSIA MOENCHENGLADBACH:** Kneib, Vogts, Klinkhammer, Wittkamp, Bonhof, Wohlers (Hannes), Simonsen, Wimmer (Kulik), Stielike, Schaefer, Heynckes. Substitutes unused: Heindenreich, Koppel, Kleff.

Ray Kennedy, Terry McDermott and Jimmy Case savour the moment.

Europe's top man marker, was being led a merry dance by Kevin Keegan on the England star's farewell appearance before his £500,000 departure to Hamburg.

Yet Borussia, reacting to manager Udo Lattek's interval pep talk, launched a full-scale assault and equalized in the 51st minute when their fleetfooted Danish raider Allan Simonsen cut in from the left and drove a blistering shot beyond Clemence high into the far corner of the net.

For the first time on that sultry evening the Borussia fans made themselves heard and Clemence rescued Liverpool when he prevented the Germans going ahead by stopping a Stielike shot with his knees, following a Simonsen cross. "Because of

what it meant that was probably the best save I ever made," said Clemence.

It was also the springboard for Liverpool to recapture control. Three minutes later, Heighway's corner from the left was met by Tommy Smith and his header sailed past Kneib for a storybook goal on his 600th appearance for the club he joined as a 14-year-old. "I'm changing my name to Roy of the Rovers," Smith joked.

Clemence had yet more work to do, saving bravely on the edge of his box as Heynckes and Simonsen challenged him for Stielike's cross, before Liverpool secured Europe's greatest prize for the first time with eight minutes left.

Keegan set off on yet another run and

this time the tormented Vogts sent him crashing. French referee Robert Wurtz, having rejected two earlier strong penalty appeals, this time had no doubt and that ever-reliable spot-kick taker Phil Neal duly beat Kneib to spark a Red Roman carnival on and off the pitch.

At the final whistle the entire Liverpool bench leapt in delight. "I've had some great moments in football, but nothing compares with this," exclaimed Paisley, who had become the first English-born manager to lift the European Cup.

The dream had been fulfilled. Beaming captain Emlyn Hughes thrust the trophy into the balmy Roman air. Liverpool were champions of Europe at last.

But, despite his finishing power, Liverpool's League form could not match up to the previous year's. Paisley's warning that "everyone will be out to topple the European champions" proved right, as even the most mediocre sides raised their game on visits to Anfield. Birmingham came to the one-time fortress and won 3–2; Aston Villa went away 2–1 to the good; Everton, Ipswich and even Bristol City all managed to draw. Reds coach Ronnie Moran has recalled how opposing teams greeted such results:

"I've watched players from other clubs go absolutely berserk after winning a League match against us. I've seen a chairman break out champagne for nothing more than a routine victory. I asked him: 'What's the point of celebrating like that over one result? The end of the season is a long way off.' He replied: 'Ah, but we've beaten Liverpool,' as if they deserved a trophy for that alone."

One team who were not overawed that season were Nottingham Forest, newly promoted, and boasting ex-Liverpool centre-half Larry Lloyd at the heart of their defence. Under Brian Clough's leadership, Forest set the First Division alight, racing into an early lead at the top and making it impossible for the challengers to dislodge them. They also lifted the League Cup to add to their championship success and, as with Division One, it was Liverpool who came runners-up.

Defeat in the final was a severe disappointment to the Reds, who had still not won the trophy in more than a decade of trying. They dominated the game at Wembley but found themselves denied time and again by Chris Woods, an 18-year-old reserve 'keeper who had replaced the ineligible Peter Shilton. Woods gave another outstanding performance in the Old Trafford replay. But the following day's headlines were all about the controversial goal that

GRAEME SOUNESS
*The future skipper combined aggression
with skill and cunning.*

TALL, DARK AND HANSEN
*The Scot became one of
Liverpool's finest-ever defenders.*

settled the match – a Forest penalty, awarded after Phil Thompson fouled striker John O'Hare at least a yard outside the 18-yard box.

One player who might have made a crucial difference in that final was Graeme Souness, a polished, uncompromising midfielder whom Paisley had recently signed from Middlesbrough. Like Shilton, he was ruled ineligible because he had played in the competition with his previous club. But when it came to Europe, there were no restrictions. And Souness would go on to play a pivotal role in Liverpool's European Cup defence.

Joining him in the line-up that season was Alan Hansen, a Scottish Under-21 international, newly arrived from Partick Thistle. Tall, slim and elegant, Hansen had made an immediate impression while deputizing, in turn, for the injured Hughes and Thompson. As the season went on, Hansen began to claim a regular place. He was balanced and composed in defence, but could be destructive when carrying the ball forward. According to Paisley, he was "the most skilful centre-half I've ever seen in British football".

Although not playing together in all the qualifying rounds, Hansen, Dalglish and Souness formed the spine of the team that lifted Europe's greatest football prize for the second year running. On the way to the final against Belgian champions FC Bruges, Liverpool had beaten Dynamo Dresden, Portugal's Benfica, and the previous year's vanquished finalists, Borussia Moenchengladbach. The Germans, desperate to wipe out memories of Rome, went to Anfield guarding a 2–1 lead from the first leg. But, in front of a raucous 51,000 crowd, Liverpool gave their performance of the season, winning 3–0 thanks to goals from Kennedy, Dalglish and Case.

The final was played at Wembley, on a night when virtually everyone in the 90,000 crowd appeared to be wearing red

Top: *Dalglish strikes the 1978 European Cup final winner.*
Bottom: *The team kept the trophy for the second year running.*

and white. It never came near to the Rome game as a spectacle, and any neutrals in the ground would have been bored rigid by the Belgians' ultra-negative tactics. But it will always be remembered for one piece of Dalglish magic in the 65th minute. Collecting a sublime through-pass from Souness on the edge of the Bruges penalty area, the striker appeared to make time stand still: "At the angle he was to goal, and the position in which he received the ball, many players would have snatched at the chance," said Paisley. "But Kenny's ice-cool football brain delayed the shot until the Bruges 'keeper had committed himself – then Kenny tucked the ball away."

The game ended 1–0 and Liverpool collected the European Cup for the second year running – the first British club to do so. The Wembley triumph had helped to establish the likes of Hansen and Souness as key players for the future, and just a few weeks later some

of the favourite faces from the past were on their way. Among them was Joey Jones, who had lost his place through injury, and was now Wrexham-bound again. Tommy Smith wound up his extended Anfield career and moved on to join former clubmate John Toshack, who had taken over the managerial reins at Swansea. And, following a Liverpool career spanning nearly two decades, it was finally time for Ian Callaghan to bow out. The ever-popular midfielder left after making an incredible 856 senior appearances for the Reds, and cementing his reputation as the club's finest-ever servant.

DOMESTIC DOMINANCE

There would be no new European or domestic cups to add to the trophy cabinet over the next two years, but in that time Liverpool's dominance of the League was total. Paisley used only 18 players throughout the 84 games, achieving a consistency of style that few, if any, clubs have ever matched. Phil Neal, who played in every one of those games, sometimes felt the manager had virtually made himself redundant: "He had developed a team that, at one stage, I felt could possibly run itself," he recalled. "Bob had so many leaders within the team – particularly the 1978–79 season when we scored 85 goals and conceded only 16 in the League."

That goals-against figure remains an all-time record, along with the team's 28 clean sheets and their final tally of 68 points (equivalent to 97 under the three-points-for-a-win system). The line-up was amazingly consistent. There was Clemence in goal, then Neal and Alan Kennedy at full-back, with Hansen partnering Thompson at the centre of defence. In midfield, Ray Kennedy was an ever-present, while Case, Souness and McDermott missed just 11 games between the three of them. Dalglish – the 1979 Footballer of the Year – played every game in attack, usually assisted by either Heighway or Johnson.

They gave notice of their awesome ability by opening the campaign with six straight wins. One of them – a 7–0 drubbing of Tottenham – is fondly remembered as one of the most complete performances Anfield has ever witnessed. In a game overflowing with magical moments, the undoubted highlight was a move originating with McDermott deep in his own half, and ending with the same player planting a perfect header into the Spurs net.

From then on it was goals all the way. They hit six

past Norwich, five past Derby, and four each against Manchester City and Bolton. Meanwhile the defence was watertight, with Clemence – another ever-present – picking the ball out of his net at Anfield just four times all year. "That season was sensational, and I am tempted to say that the team was the best I ever played in," Souness reflected some time later. "It was not a case of winning games, but a question of how many we were going to win by. We were knocking the ball about so well and enjoying so much possession that it was almost boring."

So invincible was the new-look team that another of the club's favourite stalwarts decided it was time to move on. Emlyn Hughes had managed only 16 appearances in the 1978–79 season, and he could see that his days as a first-team regular were behind him. But the departure of the former captain was entirely amicable, and his transfer to Wolves underlined his outstanding value to the club. He had arrived from Blackpool as a £65,000 teenager. Twelve years and seven trophies later, he was being sold for £90,000.

Otherwise, it was business as usual in the new campaign. Interest in the European Cup ended at the first hurdle, due to defeat by the Soviet Champions Dynamo Tbilisi. Nottingham Forest – who had put them out of Europe the previous season – killed off the Reds' League Cup hopes with a 2–1 aggregate victory in the semi-final. A Charity Shield win against Arsenal had given the fans a happy day out at Wembley, but defeat by the Gunners in a twice-replayed FA Cup semi-final destroyed their hopes of returning in May.

But those results again left Liverpool free to concentrate on the League – and a record-breaking 12th championship success. They achieved it thanks to more mean defensive displays, and by continuing their rampant form in front of goal. David Johnson enjoyed his most productive season, scoring 21 goals in 37 League starts. Dalglish weighed in with another 16, while McDermott added 11 and Ray Kennedy nine. In all, the team hit the target 81 times in 42 League games, and added 27 more goals in the various cup competitions.

But Paisley did not want any of his players to grow

complacent. As the season drew to a close, he spent £350,000 on a young striker named Ian Rush.

A NEW TROPHY FOR THE CABINET

The Welshman was one of 23 players used in the 1980–81 season – and that figure may explain why Liverpool finished in their lowest position for a decade. They ended up fifth in the League, trailing new champions Aston Villa, plus Ipswich, Arsenal and West Bromwich Albion. It was the season in which they became the draw specialists, with 17 of their matches ending level. With 62 goals, the free-scoring period had also come to an end. And for Rush it was a miserable year indeed. He made nine appearances in all competitions, failing to find the target in every one of them. He also had a blazing row with the manager – and looked like he was on his way out of Anfield by the summer.

GOAL RUSH
The Welshman became the most prolific striker in Liverpool's history.

Falling behind in the League, and dumped out of the FA Cup by Everton, the team concentrated their domestic efforts on the one trophy that had eluded them. They began their League Cup challenge with a 5–1 aggregate victory over Bradford. They beat Swindon 5–0 in the third round, then overcame Portsmouth and Birmingham in the following stages, before winning a two-legged semi-final against Manchester City to book their place at Wembley.

Their opponents that day were the attractive, ball-playing West Ham, a team buoyed by a large support from the East End, plus a great many London "neutrals". For the most part, the Hammers fans were silent as Liverpool grabbed a goal through Alan Kennedy and looked thoroughly in control. But, with the match drifting towards injury time, they suddenly exploded into life. Liverpool conceded a penalty, and the Londoners drew level with virtually the last kick of the game.

The Villa Park replay brought the Reds supporters out in force. Packed into the huge uncovered Holt End, they saw their team slip behind due to an early Paul Goddard goal. But after coming so close for so many years,

Liverpool were determined not to lose out in this competition again. They piled on the pressure throughout the game, getting their rewards with a Dalglish equalizer and an unlikely winner from Hansen. Two decades after first entering the competition, Liverpool had won the League Cup. For the next few years it would become their own personal property.

PARIS IN THE SPRINGTIME

The early 1980s were a traumatic period for Merseyside. Factory closures, the decline of the docks and the effects of the recession all combined to send the local economy into freefall. The riots that engulfed Liverpool's inner-city that summer were not the result of racial problems, as was first suspected. The underlying causes were economic. Between the mid-1970s and 1981 the area had lost almost a third of its manufacturing industry. Unemployment was nudging 20 per cent and, in areas like Toxteth, one in three adults was out of a job.

With less money around, Liverpool's gates inevitably began to suffer. From a mid-1970s average of 47,000, attendances at Anfield dropped by almost a quarter. Towards the end of the unsuccessful 1980–81 League campaign crowds declined even further. For one game against Manchester City just 24,462 summoned the interest – and cash – to turn up.

Even the European Cup lost some of its pulling power. Only 20,000 paid to watch Liverpool take on Finland's Oulu Palloseura in the first round and, despite being hyped as another Battle of Britain, the home tie against Alex Ferguson's Aberdeen attracted a disappointing 36,000 – with a significant number of them travelling down from Scotland. At least there was entertainment value for the fans who turned up for those home games. Liverpool put ten past the Finnish amateurs after being held to a surprising 1–1 away draw. Against Aberdeen, the Reds had built up a slender 1–0 lead at Pittodrie. But at Anfield they put on one of their performances of the season, scoring four times without reply. It was, Ferguson later admitted, an "annihilation" that taught him the value of passing and keeping possession.

In the third round there was another treat: a resounding 5–1 win against the Bulgarian champions CSKA Sofia, made possible by a spectacular display of sharpshooting that yielded a Souness hat-trick. By now the spectator

A LONG TIME COMING
Dalglish helped land the first League Cup – and brought a smile to the face of his skipper.

TOP 10
HAT-TRICKS 1975–1983

1.	IAN RUSH	4
2.	KENNY DALGLISH	2
3.	JOHN TOSHACK	2
4.	JIMMY CASE	1
5.	DAVID FAIRCLOUGH	1
6.	DAVID JOHNSON	1
7.	TERRY McDERMOTT	1
8.	GRAEME SOUNESS	1

interest was reviving, and more than 44,000 were on hand for the semi-final visit of Bayern Munich. But, despite the Kop's best vocal encouragement, Liverpool were unable to break down a strong, disciplined defence, and the first leg ended all square at 0–0.

They needed to draw on all their European experience to get the desired result in Germany but, in the end, the night belonged to two Liverpool rookies. Reserve Colin Irwin gave such an assured performance in defence that injured skipper Phil Thompson – the man he replaced – nominated him as man of the match. Up front, Howard Gayle came off the bench in place of a limping Dalglish – and then proceeded to terrorize the German back line with his speed and dribbling. The only way the Munich players could deal with the 22-year-old Liverpudlian was by subjecting him to a barrage of fouls. Seeing the youngster's temper beginning to fray late in the game, Paisley decided to substitute the substitute – replacing him with Jimmy Case. But by then Gayle had done his job, and the German defence were deeply unsettled.

With seven minutes left Liverpool grabbed an away goal thanks to a cool strike from Ray Kennedy. But after crack centre-forward Karl-Heinz Rummenigge levelled four minutes later, Bayern subjected Clemence's goal to the most intense pressure imaginable – raining in crosses, shots and headers that almost brought them a dramatic late winner. In the end, though, Liverpool held out, moving Paisley to describe it afterwards as one of the club's greatest performances in Europe.

GAY PAREE, GAY PAREE
Alan Kennedy's goal clinches victory at the Parc des Princes stadium.

The scene was now set for a third European Cup final, this time in the Parc des Princes stadium against six-times winners Real Madrid. Thousands of fans scraped together the money for what promised to be an epic clash between the dominant teams of the past and present. But all those expecting a classic in Paris were in for a severe disappointment. The pride of England and Spain played out a drab, bruising contest in which negative tactics and cynical tackles were all too common. Goalmouth action was virtually non-existent, and as the game went into its last ten minutes the prospect of extra time – or even a penalty shoot-out – grew increasingly likely.

Then came a sudden rush of blood to the head of Alan Kennedy, the full-back who had only just returned to the side after breaking a wrist. Chesting down a throw-in on the left, Kennedy charged towards Real's 18-yard area. Seeing his team-mate beat off one challenge, centre-forward David Johnson ran into space and screamed for the ball at the far post. But the man nicknamed "Barney Rubble" simply bulldozed on, looking up from eight yards out and unleashing a vicious shot into the Spaniards' net from the tightest of angles.

Then he carried on running. Past the goal. Through the rows of photographers. Over the perimeter boards. And on towards the 12,000 ecstatic Liverpudlians gathered at that end. Johnson, the first player to catch up, flung his arms around Kennedy and told him he was "a greedy sod" for failing to pass. But the striker was just as delirious as the fans. He had been a substitute for Rome '77, and an injury victim at Wembley '78. Now he was finishing the full 90 minutes of a European Cup final – and emerging as a winner.

It was a special night, too, for captain Phil Thompson – a man so desperate to keep his hands on the trophy that he later took it home, out to his local pub, and then to bed. And, for boss Bob Paisley, it completed a hat-trick unequalled before or since: "I'm so proud to be the manager of the first British club to win

Journalists found out about Kevin Keegan's eagerly awaited replacement in August 1977. "Where do you think that Dalglish feller's going?" was the question Bob Paisley fired at them.

Clearly he did not need an answer. The much-vaunted Celtic player was obviously Anfield-bound, and the impact of Paisley's revelation was massive.

Speculation about a new arrival had been rife all summer. Birmingham's Trevor Francis, Arsenal's Liam Brady and Cardiff's Peter Sayer were all mooted as transfer targets. It transpired, however, that Paisley was single-minded on the matter and declared: "There's only one player for a passing team like ours. Dalglish is coming to us. He's also got a great appearance record because you want your key men playing in most of the games. This club's been built on marathon men."

The following Thursday, Dalglish duly put pen to paper to become a Liverpool player – a £440,000 deal that Paisley's close friendship with Celtic boss Jock Stein helped to secure. It was, as chairman John Smith said, "The best piece of football business ever." Liverpool had captured Dalglish – with £60,000 still in the bank from the sale of Keegan.

"There was something very appealing about Liverpool FC," said Dalglish. "I was there briefly as a 15-year-old when Bill Shankly was manager, and I knew it was similar to Celtic. When the time came for me to leave Parkhead there was only one place I wanted to go and that was Liverpool. I also knew they'd give me the chance of success in Europe which I was yearning for."

Dalglish was the second of Paisley's majestic Scottish signings in eight months – following Alan Hansen and preceding Graeme Souness – and he fulfilled his dream the following May when his goal against Bruges at Wembley kept the European Cup at Anfield.

It was the first in a litany of prizes as a Liverpool player and manager, including eight championships, three European Cup, two FA Cup and four League Cup triumphs. He made

European Cup Winner.

515 senior appearances, scoring 172 goals, won a record 102 Scotland caps and is their 30-goal top scorer with Denis Law.

Dalglish's subtlety and sophistication changed Liverpool's style. He had sublime craft and vision, yet was blessed with a physique to withstand the fierce buffeting of defenders. "I just hoped that after my early trials and tribulations in management someone on high would smile on me and guide my hand," Paisley recalled.

"My plea was answered when we got Kenny. What a player! He's the greatest I've ever seen play for this club and probably the strongest, taking into account the stick he gets. I only wish I could have had Kenny and Kevin in the same team."

Amazingly, Dalglish's broad Glaswegian tones and Paisley's Durham accent made it difficult for the two men to converse, but they had perfect communication in the language of football as they tore up the game's record books.

They also had mutual respect. "If anyone in football owes Bob a greater debt than me, I'd like to meet him," said Dalglish. "He brought me to Liverpool as a player, then pointed me in the right direction as a manager." There is

Kenny Dalglish at Wembley 1983.

no doubt, either, that Kenny Dalglish pointed Liverpool in the direction of unprecedented success.

"My plea was answered when we got Kenny. What a player! He's the greatest I've ever seen play for this club and probably the strongest, taking into account the stick he gets."

BOB PAISLEY

THIS ONE'S ON ME
After Paris, Thompson took the cup to his local pub in Kirkby.

the European Cup three times," he said. "It was a triumph for our character once again."

PAISLEY'S CLEAR-OUT

Of the players who helped Paisley to that third success, only two had served under Shankly. He could look at the team who conquered Europe with selfish pride: it was, undoubtedly, the side that Bob built. But the manager had no room for sentiment and was, if anything, more ruthless than his predecessor when it came to off-loading former favourites who had gone beyond their peak. As the supporters basked in the afterglow of Paris, the manager planned a ruthless cull of the Anfield squad.

But the first change was forced on him. Just a month after collecting his third European Cup Winners' medal, 'keeper Ray Clemence announced that

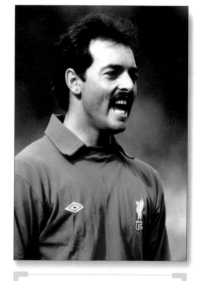

CLOWN PRINCE
Grobbelaar was an eccentric, but brilliant, goalkeeper.

he wanted a move. Paisley, who considered him the best goalkeeper he had ever seen, tried to persuade him to stay. But Clemence, unsettled by the arrival of the pushy Zimbabwean international Bruce Grobbelaar, and finding it difficult to keep himself motivated after 14 years at Anfield, was determined to seek out a new challenge. That summer, he agreed to join Tottenham for £300,000.

With such a vital cog gone, many managers would have opted for continuity elsewhere. But throughout the 1981–82 season no area of the team was immune from Paisley's radical shake-up. There were big-name departures, such as Ray Kennedy's transfer to Swansea and Jimmy Case's move to Brighton. Long-time stalwarts, like David Johnson, found it increasingly hard to command a regular first-team place. And for Phil Thompson, the days as club skipper came to an end. In one of the most cold-eyed decisions of all, Paisley passed the captaincy on to Graeme Souness.

There were plenty of new faces for the Kop to become familiar with. In goal there was Grobbelaar, an extrovert former soldier who had seen action in the African bush. In at the back came Preston's Mark Lawrenson, a record £900,000 signing whose tackling skills were unequalled anywhere in the First Division. The midfield sported an almost entirely new look, with both Ronnie Whelan and Sammy Lee breaking through from the reserves, and Craig Johnston – a dynamic Kevin Keegan lookalike – arriving in a high-profile transfer from Middlesbrough. And, claiming a regular place up front was Ian Rush, the striker who finally began justifying his lethal goalscoring reputation.

Paris had proved to be the turning point for the Welshman. He was so angry and upset at being left off the subs' bench that he called for a showdown meeting with Paisley. When he asked why he had been omitted from the squad, the manager was brutal: "You don't score goals so you're not worth your place." Rush demanded a transfer and stormed out of the door. But Paisley remained calm and gave one last parting shot: "You'll have to pay your way by scoring goals."

Years later, Rush admitted that the manager had won their psychological battle "hands down". Paisley wanted him to be more selfish on the pitch, and believed he could only get the best out of him by making him angry. It worked in spades. Rush became a sensation in front of goal in his first full season, finishing as top scorer with 30 in all competitions. He also developed a deadly partnership with Dalglish that powered Liverpool towards another domestic double.

The League Cup – by now sponsored and rebranded as the Milk Cup – was the first silverware to arrive. Defence of the trophy began with a 5–0 win over Exeter in front of a miserable 11,478 house at Anfield. But it ended before 100,000 at Wembley, gathered to witness a clash with Tottenham. London's Fancy Dans, complete with Clemence in goal, looked as though they had the trophy wrapped up after Steve Archibald fired them into a first-half lead. But with just two minutes left, man of the match Ronnie Whelan struck a decisive equalizer.

Some classic Paisley psychology helped Liverpool go into extra-time with a distinct advantage. As the two sides collapsed on to the turf waiting for the referee to signal the restart, Liverpool's boss raced on to the pitch and ordered his players to get to their feet. He could see Spurs were shattered, and wanted them to believe their opponents were still fresh and raring to go. Like most Paisley theories, this one proved correct. Liverpool ran the Londoners ragged in the 30-minute additional period, with Whelan adding a second thanks to an unstoppable shot, and Rush adding a third goal from close range. So the Cup remained with Liverpool – only this time it was Souness who received the trophy.

Two months later the same player was presented with the League championship trophy. It was an unlikely title success, following a disastrous opening spell in which the Reds won only three of 11 games. The low point came on Boxing Day when

IRISH GEM
Whelan's Wembley goals won the Milk Cup.

a 3–1 home defeat by Manchester City left them lying 12th in the table. But then Rush and Dalglish clicked, the midfield began to gel, and Grobbelaar eliminated the errors that had plagued his early performances. They set off on an astonishing 22-game run that yielded 19 wins and just one defeat. When Spurs went to Anfield on 15 May the home side needed just three more points to finish top. Clemence – given a rapturous reception by the Kop – did his best to deny them. But goals from Lawrenson, Whelan and Dalglish delivered a 3–1 victory – and a 13th League title.

It had been another exhilarating campaign, but there were low points along the way. Defeat at Second Division Chelsea had sent Liverpool out of the FA Cup. Bulgaria's CSKA Sofia gained early European Cup revenge by getting the better of them in the third round. And, after flying to Tokyo for their first World Club championship, the Reds suffered an embarrassing 3–0 loss to the flamboyant Brazilians of Flamengo.

But those disappointments were nothing compared to the sadness that greeted the death of Bill Shankly on 29 September 1981. Four days after the former manager's fatal heart attack, a capacity 48,000 crowd crammed into Anfield to pay their respects before the League game against John Toshack's Swansea. It was a highly charged afternoon when heartbroken fans waved banners in honour of their old hero, and chanted his name from the terraces. But perhaps the most poignant sight was the grief-stricken Toshack lining up for the minute's silence, then stripping off his Swansea track-suit to stand, head bowed, in his old Liverpool shirt.

BYE-BYE, BOB

Liverpool went into the new season knowing it would be Bob Paisley's last in charge. He had spent 42 years at Anfield, was approaching retirement

TOP 10 LEAGUE GOALS 1975–1983	
1. KENNY DALGLISH	96
2. DAVID JOHNSON	62
3. TERRY McDERMOTT	52
4. RAY KENNEDY	46
5. IAN RUSH	41
6. PHIL NEAL	35
7. DAVID FAIRCLOUGH	34
8. GRAEME SOUNESS	31
9. JOHN TOSHACK	26
10. KEVIN KEEGAN	24

BILL SHANKLY'S STATUE, ANFIELD
Shanks died in 1981 but his memory is still honoured at the place he loved.

age, and felt ready for a rest after proving himself the most successful manager in Europe. Some critics thought he should have gone as soon as he made the announcement. They feared he would become a "lame duck" boss, losing interest in the team, and influence over the players, during the long season ahead.

But they didn't know him. Paisley was determined to go out on a high note, and he attacked his final year in charge with the same enthusiasm and attention to detail that had informed his entire managerial career. After the previous season's clear-out there was little wheeler-dealing left to do. He would sell Terry McDermott to his old club Newcastle, and spend £450,000 on the Middlesbrough striker David Hodgson. But otherwise he let his existing squad build on the understanding they had already developed. Sure enough, they became a blisteringly efficient winning machine.

It was the year that Dalglish and Rush tore First Division defences to shreds. Like Keegan and Toshack before them, they developed an instinctive understanding that no one could anticipate, and a speed of execution that few could match. One of the most familiar Anfield sights was Dalglish holding the ball up inside the opposition half, turning his back to goal, then twisting to release an inch-perfect pass into the path of his partner. The lightning-fast Rush would skin his marker, round the 'keeper, then slot the ball into the net. It was a move they honed to perfection, and one that brought hat-tricks for Rush against Coventry and Notts County. But never

was it more devastating than at Goodison Park on 6 November 1982 – the day Liverpool destroyed their Merseyside rivals 5–0, with Rush hitting four.

The duo's combined total of 42 League goals helped the club clinch a 14th championship – nine points ahead of second-placed Watford, and with a month of the season to spare. Elsewhere, it was a familiar story. Jimmy Case broke Liverpool hearts by grabbing Brighton's winner at Anfield in the fifth round of the FA Cup. And in Europe, Poland's Widzew Lodz denied the Reds a place in the semi-finals after a 4–3 aggregate win.

But for Paisley there was one last trip to Wembley – the ground that had become known as "Anfield South" because of the frequency of Liverpool's appearances there. The occasion was the 1983 Milk Cup final against Manchester United, a glamour tie that more than upstaged its FA Cup counterpart that season. Liverpool won the trophy for the third successive year, thanks to a 2–1 win and goals from Whelan and Alan Kennedy. But when it was time for Souness to be presented with the trophy he declined – insisting, instead, that his manager be the one to collect it.

It was a gesture of respect to the man who had presided over the most astonishing run of success in English football history: six League championships, three European Cups and three League Cups, plus a UEFA Cup, a European Super Cup and five Charity Shields. Bob Paisley retired after Liverpool's last League game on 14 May 1983. Who on earth could replace him?

BOB'S FINAL CUP
The 1983 Milk Cup was Paisley's last Wembley triumph.

The conqueror in a flat cap. The man with the Midas touch. Or, as Kevin Keegan so memorably called him, the legend with no ego.

All these descriptions are highly appropriate to the persona of Bob Paisley, the most successful manager in English football history. There is another very fitting epithet for him … the reluctant genius.

When the dust settled on Bill Shankly's shock decision to quit Liverpool in the summer of 1974, the club turned to his long-serving assistant Bob Paisley to pick up the baton. But Paisley, as happy being unobtrusive back stage as Shankly had been to bask in the front stage spotlight, initially rejected the overtures of chairman John Smith and secretary Peter Robinson.

"I couldn't believe Bill had packed it in," Paisley recalled. "I tried to persuade him to stay, to have a break, go on a cruise and then come back. But he was adamant. I'd never even thought of being manager."

After persistent pleading by the club – "We went down on our hands and knees," revealed Robinson – Paisley, at 55, finally agreed to take the job. "I thought that if I accepted it would prevent the whole backroom set up being disturbed," he said. "But I looked on myself as a buffer until they appointed a new manager and I told the players that."

Some "buffer" he proved to be. In his nine seasons in command he led Liverpool to 19 trophies, including a trio of European Cup triumphs and six League championships, surely the most concentrated glut of silverware any club will ever collect. Yet Paisley was a man of modesty and humility, shunning personal publicity whenever possible.

His knowledge of injuries, which had its roots in his playing days when he took a physiotherapy postal course, was uncanny. In this respect Paisley was a crucial link between

the dressing room and Shankly, who at best was uneasy with unfit players and at worst liable to pour scorn on them or even ignore them.

But as manager in his own right Paisley's qualities as a tactician and a footballing judge flourished. "In ten minutes watching a match he could detail the strengths and weaknesses of both teams," observed his backroom aide Tom Saunders, later a Liverpool director.

The happy boss.

Ian Callaghan, the only first-team player to span Shankly's reign from the old Second Division to European Cup glory under Paisley, recalls: "Shanks was the greatest motivator in the world, but Bob was the finest tactician. With his Durham accent he wasn't the easiest to understand. But he got his points across briefly and succinctly. He'd say things like: 'Their No. 4 hits a good long one.' That meant you had to try to stop their right half getting the ball because his long passing was good."

Paisley's signings were also inspired. Has any manager ever bettered Paisley's "treble

Scotch" acquisitions of Kenny Dalglish, Alan Hansen and Graeme Souness? Has there ever been a shrewder re-invention of a player than Paisley's transformation of Ray Kennedy from striker to left midfielder?

Yet the before becoming Manager of the Millennium, Paisley had almost left Liverpool twice. In 1950, he was ready to walk out after being omitted from the FA Cup final team against Arsenal. Only a heart-to-heart talk with friend and team-mate Albert Stubbins persuaded him to stay.

Four years later, his playing days ending, he was ready to return to his bricklaying trade or open a fruit and vegetable shop when he received a surprise invitation to join Anfield's backroom staff. Paisley also feared for his Liverpool future when Shankly arrived in December 1959. But, while Shankly cleared out 24 players, he retained the entire training staff – and Paisley and Joe Fagan would eventually pioneer the famous Boot Room.

One abiding image of Paisley is of him sitting quietly and tee-totally in the Holiday Inn St Peters amidst the tumultuous celebrations after Liverpool's 1977 European Cup final victory.

"I think the Pope and I are the only two people in Rome sober tonight," Paisley quipped after becoming the first English-born manager to win Europe's most prestigious trophy. "I like a drink, but tonight I'm drinking in the occasion. I want to savour every marvellous moment of this.

"The last time I was in Rome I drove in on a tank in 1944. We were winners then and we're winners again this time, thankfully, in football."

The man with no ego, had carved his name in glory. That night, he wrote in his match diary:

"After Saturday's defeat at Wembley we wondered what effect it would have on the players. We need not have worried, because, right from the start, we dominated the game – and turned in the best performance in the history of the club."

1984 • EUROPEAN CHAMPIONS

• LEAGUE CHAMPIONS

• MILK CUP WINNERS

1985 • HEYSEL STADIUM DISASTER

• DALGLISH APPOINTED MANAGER

1986 • LEAGUE CHAMPIONS

• FA CUP WINNERS

CHAPTER EIGHT *1984–1991*	Triumphs and Tragedies

1987 • SCREEN SPORT SUPER CUP WINNERS

• ALDRIDGE, BARNES AND BEARDSLEY SIGN

1988 • LEAGUE CHAMPIONS

• FA CUP FINAL DEFEAT BY WIMBLEDON

1989 • HILLSBOROUGH DISASTER

• FA CUP WINNERS

• BERLIN WALL FALLS, ROMANIAN REVOLUTION

1990 • LEAGUE CHAMPIONS

• NELSON MANDELA FREED

1991 • DALGLISH RESIGNS

• GRAEME SOUNESS APPOINTED MANAGER

• GULF WAR

•

"IAN RUSH WAS THE PREDATOR SUPREME.
HIS GREATEST ATTRIBUTES WERE HIS PACE,
FIRST TOUCH, AND THE SORT OF TELEPATHIC
UNDERSTANDING OF WHERE TO BE THAT
ALL GREAT STRIKERS HAVE."

THE FOOTBALL LEAGUE: "100 LEAGUE LEGENDS"

Liverpool fans at Wembley, 1988

THE ANSWER WAS STARING EVERYONE IN THE FACE. AS PAISLEY'S LONG-SERVING NUMBER TWO, JOE FAGAN KNEW THE CLUB INSIDE OUT. HE HAD BEEN A STALWART OF THE BOOT ROOM FOR MORE THAN TWO DECADES, COULD PINPOINT EVERY STRENGTH AND WEAKNESS IN THE TEAM, AND, CRUCIALLY, HAD THE RESPECT AND SUPPORT OF THE PLAYERS.

"He and Bob had been so close for so many years that we hardly noticed the difference," wrote skipper Graeme Souness. "We were using the same hotels, the same training methods and things ticked along very much the same. Joe's approach is similar and, if anything, he made the game even simpler than Bob."

With a squad of players at their peak, simplicity and continuity were all the club needed. Liverpool stormed to a hat-trick of League championships and ended the 1983–84 season with more honours than they had ever collected in a single campaign. The "promote from within" policy had worked when Shankly quit. Now, with Paisley in retirement, it was proving a resounding success once more.

Not that it looked that way at the beginning of the season. After being beaten by Manchester United in the Charity Shield clash, Liverpool made a slow start in the League, drawing at home to newly promoted Wolves, and allowing Sunderland to sneak an Anfield victory shortly afterwards. Goals were a problem throughout the opening period as the team found the net just 12 times in ten games. But then, at the end of October, Luton Town came to Anfield and found themselves on the end of a 6–0 thrashing. Ian Rush grabbed five of them – becoming the first Liverpool player to go nap in a League game since John Evans in 1954. The Welshman's amazing achievement sent the team to the top of the table, and paved the way for the most prolific season of his career.

Ron Atkinson's Manchester United were Liverpool's

SMOKIN' JOE
Fagan took over as boss after 15 years on the backroom staff.

closest challengers for most of the campaign, along with Nottingham Forest and Southampton. But, in the end, none of them could catch a team whose form remained remarkably consistent, despite two major injury blows. Deprived of Ronnie Whelan for much of the opening half of the season, Fagan drafted in reserve Steve Nicol – a young Scot whose all-round abilities quickly made him indispensable. Then, faced with the temporary loss of Dalglish, the manager introduced Republic of Ireland international striker Michael Robinson, a £200,000 close-season buy from Brighton.

But those two casualties aside, Fagan was lucky with his injury list. Five players – Grobbelaar, Kennedy, Hansen, Lawrenson and Lee – played all 42 games, while Neal and Rush missed just one apiece. His side did suffer the odd hiccup – such as the 4–0 drubbing by Coventry at Highfield Road. But they made up for that reverse when Bobby Gould's team visited Anfield with a week of the season left. The 5–0 victory – with Rush scoring four – virtually clinched the title. When it was secured, with a 0–0 draw at Notts County five days later, Liverpool became the first club to claim three successive championships since Arsenal in the 1930s.

By then, they had also made history by lifting the Milk Cup yet again. It had been a rocky road, with the team easily disposing of Brentford, but needing replays to overcome Fulham, Birmingham and Sheffield Wednesday. There was another shock in the two-legged semi-final when little Walsall came from behind twice to earn a 2–2 draw at Anfield. But then Liverpool went to the West Midlands and settled the tie with a comfortable 2–0 win.

However, off the field, tragedy was narrowly averted. As the travelling Liverpool fans celebrated Ronnie Whelan's second goal, a wall at the front of the Laundry End collapsed, sending hundreds of them tumbling down the steps and on to the pitch. TV cameras showed some supporters holding their bloodied faces as stewards and emergency services tried to evacuate the terracing. Liverpool players also went to help, and Souness was pictured carrying a little boy to safety after he had been caught up in the crush. After several anxious minutes, it became clear that none of the injuries was particularly serious. Police restored order behind the goal, and the referee – who had led the players off to the dressing room – was confident enough to allow play to restart. But the episode served as a grim warning about the state of some football grounds, and the dangers posed by old, crumbling terraces. The fans had escaped. This time.

MERSEYSIDE UNITED

Victory over Walsall set up a final the whole of Merseyside had been praying for: Liverpool v. Everton at Wembley. For Reds fans it was a chance to display their superiority on the biggest and most glamorous stage. For Everton, newly resurgent under Howard Kendall, it was an opportunity to emerge from their neighbours' shadow after 14 miserable, trophyless years.

In truth, it needed a mouth-watering final to ignite the fans' interest that year. The continuing recession had bitten ever deeper into attendance levels, and, as the least prestigious competition, the Milk Cup had suffered most. Only 11,638 had turned up for the fourth round replay against Birmingham that season. And when Brentford came to Merseyside, already 4–1 down from the first leg, a mere 9,902 passed through the Anfield turnstiles.

Predictably, the prospect of the first-ever Wembley Merseyside derby

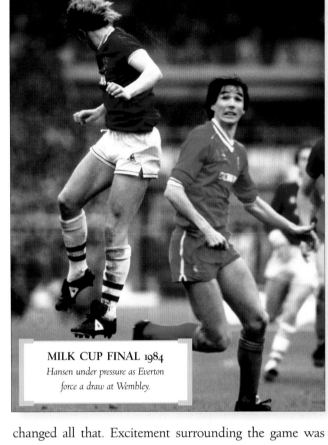

MILK CUP FINAL 1984
Hansen under pressure as Everton force a draw at Wembley.

changed all that. Excitement surrounding the game was intense, and even a ticket allocation of 35,000 per club wasn't great enough to meet the demand. The final was to be played on Sunday, 25 March, and from the Saturday morning onwards the motorways heading south were packed with Liverpool and Everton fans, the rival supporters in many cases belonging to the same families. Thousands shared the journey, and traffic police rubbed their eyes as they saw red and blue scarves trailing from the same vehicles.

But by 3 pm on matchday the friendliness had given way to the usual rivalry. On an afternoon of driving rain, Everton had the best of the first-half play, showing aggression and confidence, and having a strong penalty appeal turned down after

TOP 10		
LEAGUE APP'S 1984–1991		
1.	BRUCE GROBBELAAR	243
2.	RONNIE WHELAN	228
3.	STEVE NICOL	215
4.	IAN RUSH	207
5.	ALAN HANSEN	197
6.	STEVE McMAHON	189
7.	JAN MOLBY	157
8.	GARY GILLESPIE	156
9.	JOHN BARNES	140
10.	PETER BEARDSLEY	131

TOP 10
LEAGUE GOALS 1984–1991

1.	IAN RUSH	107
2.	JOHN BARNES	61
3.	JOHN ALDRIDGE	50
4.	PETER BEARDSLEY	46
5.	JAN MOLBY	34
6.	STEVE NICOL	29
7.	STEVE McMAHON	28
8.	RONNIE WHELAN	27
9.	JOHN WARK	26
10.	PAUL WALSH	25

Alan Hansen apparently handled in his own 18-yard box. The Blues had three more clear-cut chances before the interval, and, even though Liverpool showed more enterprise in the second half, they couldn't find a way past Everton's solid centre-back partnership of Kevin Ratcliffe and Derek Mountfield.

One goal at either end would probably have settled matters, but when Rush sent in a powerful volley midway through the half, Welsh international 'keeper Neville Southall was equal to it. And when a swerving cross left Grobbelaar floundering just five minutes before the end, Graeme Sharp elected to head the ball back to one of his team-mates, rather than direct his effort at an empty net. So the game ended all square with the two teams completing a joint lap of honour, and Wembley Stadium echoing to the combined chant of "Merseyside, Merseyside, Merseyside". The friendly spirit had resumed – for another 72 hours at least.

On the Wednesday night came the Maine Road replay – a game played before 52,000 supporters, making just as much noise as the 100,000 who had gathered at Wembley. Everton again started brightly, and almost took the lead

TREBLE SCOTCH
Hansen, Dalglish and Souness celebrate the 1984 Milk Cup victory.

after 12 minutes when Grobbelaar scrambled across his line to stop a powerful drive from Peter Reid. But ten minutes later came a precision move involving Neal, Lee, Johnston and Dalglish. Eventually the ball fell to Souness, who evaded Ratcliffe's tackle before unleashing a blistering left-footer past Southall.

Everton put up a spirited fight and came near to equalizing several times before the final whistle blew. But Liverpool played with more conviction than they did in the first game and were worth their win, even without a goal from Rush, who had scored in every previous round. There was consolation for Kendall's team when they went back to Wembley two months later and won the FA Cup, completing Merseyside's first clean sweep of domestic honours since 1966. But, as far as the Reds were concerned, there was still much more to play for.

ALL ROADS LEAD (BACK) TO ROME

After two seasons of disappointment, Liverpool were determined to get back among Europe's élite. They began their quest in imperious style, beating BK Odense 1–0 in Denmark, then hitting five without reply in the home leg. But when the Spanish champions Athletic Bilbao earned a goalless draw at Anfield, few observers rated Liverpool's chances of going any further. It took a brilliant team performance – and an Ian Rush header – to silence the critics and book a passage to the third round.

Potuguese champions Benfica were the next opponents – beaten 1–0 at Anfield, and slaughtered 4–1 before 70,000 fans at the Stadium of Light. Then, in the semi-final, came Dinamo Bucharest, a team who marred Liverpool's 1–0 Anfield victory with a disgraceful series of over-the-top tackles and reckless fouls. Back in Romania they were even more brutal. They subjected their visitors to kicks, trips and elbows from the kick-off. Souness, who had been caught up in a violent tussle in the Anfield game, was subjected to the worst treatment. By full-time his socks were torn to shreds, his shin pads split and his legs bruised from top to bottom. But by then he didn't care. He had set up a superb volleyed goal for Rush, inspired his team to a stirring 2–1 win, and helped secure their place in another European Cup final.

That game would be held at Italy's Olympic Stadium, home of AS Roma. And Liverpool's opponents would be... AS Roma. Back in 1977, when the Reds first lifted the trophy, Liverpudlians had made the Italian capital their own. But this time, facing the pride of Rome, they were going into the lions' den. The 20,000 who made the journey from Merseyside entered a city in a frenzy. Banners predicting victory were draped from every apartment block in sight, and most Italians couldn't understand why their opponents were even bothering to turn up. In their minds the Cup was already won. A best-selling scarf outside the stadium bore the legend: "Roma – European Champions 1984."

The fevered atmosphere on the terraces communicated itself to the dressing room. But, as Alan Kennedy later revealed, the Liverpool players found their own way of handling the pressure:

"I can remember Craig Johnston saying: 'Hey, we look a little bit nervous, so how about singing a song as we go out?' So we actually sang the Chris Rea track 'I Don't Know What It Is, But I Love It' as we walked past the Roma dressing room, and they just couldn't believe it. And suddenly we felt ten feet tall going out on to that pitch, singing, confident. I think it showed in the first 15 minutes, because we played the better football – and then we scored a goal through Phil Neal."

That opener was the result of a classic piece of opportunism – it followed a clumsy clearance that cannoned off Rush into Neal's path just six yards out from goal. But it gave Liverpool a valuable advantage and, as the game headed towards the interval, Roma were struggling to find a way back. But then, right on the stroke of half-time, Roberto Pruzzo grabbed a headed equalizer that sent the Italian fans into delirium. If ever Liverpool needed to keep their legendary composure, it was then.

That's just what they did. But their achievement in earning a 1–1 draw led to an even greater test of nerve: a penalty shoot-out before 70,000 fans – and a worldwide TV audience of millions. Fagan knew the pressure his players were under. As he came on to the pitch he told them: "You've done great, you couldn't have done better. I'm proud of you whatever happens." All that remained was for him to name the five penalty-takers: Neal,

ROMA V. LIVERPOOL EUROPEAN CUP FINAL 1984
*Singing eased the players' tension, while Neal's goal
and Grobbelaar's antics helped win the Cup.*

Souness, Rush, Nicol and Kennedy.

Although Kennedy was chosen to take the first spot-kick, Nicol insisted on assuming the responsibility. He looked confident when he stepped up – but devastated when he sent his shot over the bar. Souness converted the second, before Roma's Bruno Conti placed his shot high and wide to make the scores level again. The Italian 'keeper Franco Tancredi – who had saved half of the last 16 penalties against him – had no chance as Neal and Rush struck perfectly placed spot-kicks. But Grobbelaar, pulling faces, and pretending his legs had turned to jelly, seemed to play havoc with Francesco Graziani's nerves. A split-second after the Italian international made contact, it was clear his drive was heading for the crossbar.

As Liverpool's 'keeper ran from his line in celebration all eyes switched to Kennedy. He was an unlikely match-winner, but after securing the European Cup in Paris he now had the chance to do it a second time: "The pressure was on me, but I was quietly confident," he said. "I knew I would do my best, and that if I got it on target I would score." And so he did – with a left-footed shot that sent Tancredi the wrong way, and brought Europe's premier prize back to Anfield for a fourth time.

It was an incredible end to an incredible season. Joe Fagan had won a treble at the first time of asking, earning himself the Manager of the Year accolade. Ian Rush was named Footballer of the Year and the PFA Player of the Year, and – with 49 goals for club and country – became the recipient of Europe's coveted Golden Boot. Liverpool had ridden the loss of Paisley, and, just a year after his departure, it seemed like the good times

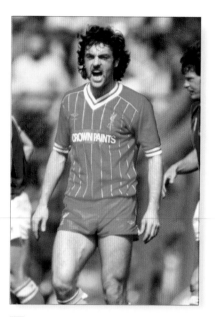

JOHN WARK
The midfield marksman outgunned Rush in his first season.

would go on forever. But the bubble was about to burst in the most extreme and tragic fashion.

HEYSEL HORROR

Fagan went into his second campaign minus the services of Souness, who had moved to the Italian club Sampdoria for £500,000. He replaced him with fellow Scottish international John Wark, who had impressed the Liverpool boss with his habit of scoring from midfield while with Division One rivals Ipswich. Wark never displayed the former captain's commanding influence, but he did prove to be extremely effective in front of goal. His surging runs through the middle brought a new dimension to the Liverpool attack. And, in his first year with the club, he outstripped Rush by hitting the net 27 times in all competitions.

But his form was one of the few bright spots in a thoroughly miserable 1984–85 season. Liverpool's four-year Milk Cup stranglehold finally ended with a third round exit at Tottenham. They finished the League title race a full 13 points behind eventual champions Everton. And, in the FA Cup, they lost a semi-final replay to their increasingly bitter North-west rivals, Manchester United.

Add to that a Wembley Charity Shield defeat by their Merseyside neighbours, plus a loss to Argentina's Independiente in the World Club Championship, and it was clear that hopes of another successful season were rapidly turning to dust.

At least the European Cup offered salvation. In contrast to their domestic form, Liverpool had played with style and confidence in the tournament, dispatching Polish champions Lech

JUVENTUS V. LIVERPOOL, EUROPEAN CUP FINAL 1985
The lack of segregation made trouble on the Heysel terraces inevitable.

Poznan, Portugal's Benfica, FK Austria Memphis and the Greek title holders, Panathinaikos. By the time they reached the final they had scored 18 goals in the competition, and conceded just four. They were 90 minutes away from a fifth triumph in Europe's premier competition – with only Italy's Serie A giants Juventus standing in their way.

The venue was Belgium's Heysel stadium, an ageing, faded arena in the heart of Brussels. Liverpool officials had expressed concern about its suitability in the weeks leading up to the game. But any worries about safety, and the apparent lack of fan segregation, were brushed aside by both UEFA and the Belgian football authorities. As far as they were concerned, the ground was fine: the 30th European Cup final would go ahead as planned on Wednesday, 29 May 1985.

The decision would prove fatal. Supporters arrived in Brussels to find a dilapidated stadium, shambolic security and inadequate crowd arrangements. Many Liverpool fans walked through the turnstiles without being asked to show their tickets. Once inside they felt the terracing crumbling beneath their feet, and the crush barriers begin to give way against their massed weight. Most surprising of all, they saw that a section of their terrace had been given over to Italian fans. All that separated them was a length of flimsy wire-mesh fence.

With no stewards to enforce an alcohol ban, the atmosphere between the English and Italians grew nasty. And, with no police to keep them apart, the rival fans at either side of the wire began trading insults and blows. Around half an hour before kick-off, a length of fencing was torn down and Liverpool followers pushed their way

HEYSEL 1985
Belgian police survey the aftermath of the tragedy that claimed 39 lives.

into the Juventus section. In their desperation to get to safety the Italians fled, causing a huge crush that led to the collapse of a wall at the front of the terrace. Millions watching on television heard the bang that accompanied that collapse. Minutes later they watched the first of the 39 dead bodies being carried away on stretchers.

Amazingly the final went ahead. Although most fans inside the stadium were unaware of the extent of the tragedy, UEFA officials feared there would be more trouble if the match was abandoned. The Liverpool players, numbed by what had just unfolded in front of their eyes, reluctantly agreed. But, for most of those on the pitch, the 1-0 defeat passed by in a blur.

The Heysel disaster brought a proud, unblemished European record to a sickening halt. Under-strength policing, poor distribution of tickets and a decrepit stadium, along with a charge from a minority of Liverpool "fans", all played a part in the disaster. As Belgian investigators began the task of identifying the ring-leaders, both the club and the Merseyside Police offered their help and support. In the bout of soul-searching that followed, many true supporters swore they would never attend another match. Some players, like Grobbelaar, seriously considered quitting. And a distraught Joe Fagan confirmed that he'd had enough.

Spurred on by politicians throughout Europe, UEFA slapped an indefinite ban on all English clubs taking part in Continental competition. They also ruled that Liverpool should serve a further three years of exclusion once it was lifted. The club accepted its punishment. But with its reputation sullied, and its finances potentially crippled, the future had never looked more uncertain.

KENNY THE GAFFER
The new player-manager spent half his first season in the dug-out.

Joe Fagan picked up a broom, proceeded to sweep Notts County's visitors' dressing room and declared: "I never rated Manchester United a threat." The date was 12 May 1984 and his team's goalless draw had just secured the League championship and won the battle with United, who suffered a late collapse to finish fourth.

It was the second triumph of Fagan's first season as manager in succession to the trophy-strewn Bob Paisley. The Milk Cup had earlier been secured, and less than three weeks after that Meadow Lane title clincher, Fagan's side famously conquered Roma in a dramatic penalty shoot-out in their own stadium to bring the European Cup to Anfield for the fourth time.

That made 63-year-old Smokin' Joe – so called because of his penchant for cigarettes – the first manager in the entire history of English football to land a Treble, a fact that seemed to be air-brushed out of the record books amidst the media furore over Sir Alex Ferguson leading United to three trophies 15 years later.

The photograph of Fagan relaxing in a poolside deckchair in Rome, flanked by the European Cup and two uniformed carabiniere, has been committed to Anfield legend. It also captured the man, a down-to-earth, hard-headed professional yet one with a capacity to be slightly laid-back. His realism shone through when he accepted the challenge of following Paisley, with whom he had founded Anfield's famous Boot Room. "Nobody can follow Bob. If you thought like that, it would drive you mad," said Fagan. "I'm my own man, I'll do my best and do it my way."

His way was very much Liverpool's way even though he had rejected Anfield overtures to sign as a promising young centre-half, explaining: "For some reason local boys at Everton and Liverpool tended to be made scapegoats if the team wasn't doing well, so after playing for Earlstown Bohemians I joined Manchester City in 1938."

His League debut was delayed until January 1947, but he became City captain, making 158 senior appearances and scoring twice. He moved to Nelson in 1951 followed

Joe Fagan

"Joe blew his top about once a year but that was enough. When he did nobody would dare look him in the eyes". GRAEME SOUNESS

by a brief three-match spell at Bradford Park Avenue. In 1953 he became Rochdale trainer, working under future Everton manager Harry Catterick, whose fulsome recommendation secured Fagan a job on Liverpool's training staff. That was in 1958, some 18 months before Shankly's arrival signalled the Anfield "revolution".

Fagan acquired a massive font of knowledge in his rise through the backroom ranks and was the automatic successor when Paisley ended his incredible reign in 1983. "There's a man following me called Fagan – and he doesn't need the help of the Artful Dodger to pick up anything that glitters," Paisley told a London dinner.

Fagan swiftly bolstered his squad, signing Gary Gillespie and Michael Robinson in the first few weeks as manager, and later recruiting John Wark, Paul Walsh, Jan Molby

and Kevin MacDonald.

They joined a dressing room that already had the utmost respect for Fagan, who once even dropped the great Kenny Dalglish! "As players we were desperate for Joe to succeed because we knew how much he'd contributed," said his captain Graeme Souness. "Joe blew his top about once a year but that was enough. When he did nobody would dare look him in the eyes."

Sadly, Fagan's eyes were moist with tears in May 1985 when, having informed the club of his retirement months earlier, his final match in charge proved to be the tragic mayhem of Heysel.

In the summer of 2001, shortly after witnessing Liverpool achieve another Treble under Gérard Houllier, Fagan died at the age of 80, assured of a permanent place in the pantheon of Anfield greats.

BACK FROM THE BRINK

In the midst of those worries the Anfield directors put one of their boldest plans into action. They had decided, on the eve of the ill-fated Heysel game, to offer the manager's job to Kenny Dalglish, breaking with the Boot Room tradition that had served them so well for so long. The appointment came as a surprise to many, and Dalglish provided a further shock when he announced that he would also remain on the playing staff. Still, he had earned unlimited respect from the fans over the years, and most were prepared to put their faith in him. His appointment of Bob Paisley as an "unofficial adviser" only added to their confidence.

GREAT DANE
Jan Molby developed into one of the best passers of the 1980s.

Dalglish was quick to make changes. Within weeks of the start of his new regime, both Steve Nicol and the young Irishman Jim Beglin became the regular full-backs. Jan Molby, a Danish midfielder who had been bought to help plug the Souness gap, was given a sweeper role, operating behind the back four. Craig Johnston, who had been out of favour under Fagan, became an automatic choice. And into the centre of the park stepped the ex-Everton and Aston Villa hard man, Steve McMahon. But even those who found themselves marginalized – like Alan Kennedy and Phil Neal – had to accept that Dalglish only made changes with the good of the club in mind. For half the season he even dropped himself – preferring the exciting ball skills of Paul Walsh.

His team began the new season well enough, but soon found themselves overshadowed by a Manchester United side that won all ten opening games. Liverpool made up ground

KENNY'S IN HEAVEN
Dalglish celebrates his last-day-of-the-season winner at Stamford Bridge.

when United faltered, but they still lagged behind Everton, who grabbed a notable 2–0 win at Anfield in February. It wasn't just the press who wrote off the Reds' chances after that defeat. The view was shared by new skipper Alan Hansen, who even told his manager that it was "the most limited Liverpool team" he had ever played in.

But the captain was about to be proved spectacularly wrong. Liverpool went on to claim 31 points from their next 11 matches, with a rejuvenated attack hitting six past Oxford, five against Coventry and Birmingham, and four against Queens Park Rangers. The performances were superb, with Molby spraying inch-perfect passes around the park, Rush back to his lethal best, and Dalglish himself prising open the tightest defences. Kevin MacDonald, a Scot signed from Leicester City back in 1984, was another star. He earned his call-up when McMahon was injured, and was effective enough to keep his place until the final game. Although MacDonald's style of play would never make him a crowd favourite, his team-mates were quick to appreciate his work-rate and passing ability. As Hansen wrote later: "I would say that at the tail end of the 1985–86 season, he was far and away our most influential player."

The magnificent late run put the Reds within touching distance of the title. But, to get their hands on the trophy, they still needed a victory at Stamford Bridge on the last day of the season. "Liverpool will win the championship over my dead body," declared Chelsea chairman Ken Bates in pre-match interviews. But, not for the first time, that type of psychology backfired. A super-motivated Liverpool took to the field, with Dalglish – preferring to let his feet do the talking – grabbing the only goal of the game. As Bates went home with his lips sealed, the Liverpool fans celebrated an unprecedented 16th League title success.

RUSH AT THE DOUBLE

A week later they were back in London to see their team walk on to the pitch at Wembley. Dalglish, in his first season in charge, was on the threshold of achieving the only League/FA Cup Double in Liverpool's history. And Everton were the one team blocking his way.

They were the strongest side Goodison had produced in years. Since their 1984 Milk Cup defeat, they had gone on to win the FA Cup, the League championship and the European Cup Winners' Cup. Peter Reid, Trevor Steven and the ex-Liverpool player Kevin Sheedy had formed one of the most effective midfield partnerships in the country. And, with Gary Lineker up front, Everton had the only striker in Britain who could match Rush's speed and finishing skills.

On an afternoon of blistering heat it was the England centre-forward who struck first, brushing off a challenge from Hansen, then following up a shot that Grobbelaar could only parry. He spurned a chance to volley home a second goal before the interval, and both Sheedy and Steven went close with shots just after the break. Liverpool seemed unable to find either rhythm or understanding. Their frustrations became apparent when Grobbelaar and Beglin almost traded blows following a defensive mix-up.

WIZARD FROM OZ
Craig Johnston fires Liverpool into the lead in the first all-Merseyside FA Cup final.

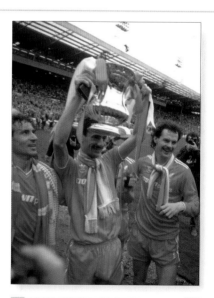

RUSH THE DESTROYER
The striker tastes Wembley victory with Craig Johnston and Kevin McDonald.

But suddenly everything changed. With nearly an hour gone Rush ran on to a perfectly weighted pass from Molby to round the Everton 'keeper Bobby Mimms and slot the ball into an empty net. Six minutes later he found Molby on the left, then saw the big Dane's cross fall to Johnston, who rifled the ball home from just eight yards out.

The red half of Wembley erupted. As Everton wilted in the sunshine, the Liverpool fans watched MacDonald and Molby stroke the ball around the midfield, Johnston cover every blade of grass, and Rush threaten with each forward run. With six minutes left, their day was complete. Ronnie Whelan chased a ball down the right flank, then chipped it into Rush's path. The Welshman's drive was so powerful it broke the TV camera placed at the back of Mimms' goal.

Liverpool had achieved the Double, and everyone associated with the club experienced a mixture of joy and relief. Twelve months after Heysel, the players had hauled themselves back to the summit of English football, and had begun to restore pride in their city. The supporters, far from deserting the team, had started to return, pushing the average Anfield gate to its highest for five seasons. And Dalglish, possibly Liverpool's finest-ever player, had also proved to be a formidable boss. After just 12 months at the helm, he was named Manager of the Year.

THE ENTERTAINERS

But he was still largely reliant on the players he had inherited, and it was only a matter of time before he put together a team he could truly call his own. A barren 1986–87 campaign probably hastened the process, but so

During Liverpool's tortuous 1980 FA Cup semi-final struggle with Arsenal, which ran to four meetings, two periods of extra-time and spanned almost three weeks, an 18-year-old Welsh striker completed a £330,000 transfer from Chester that was overshadowed by the club's Cup marathon.

But while Liverpool ultimately lost to Arsenal they were huge winners in securing their own marathon man in Ian Rush, a legendary, long-distance goalscorer whose deeds in a two-part Anfield career made him a Kop icon.

The fee paid by manager Bob Paisley was then a British record for a teenager and one that Rush admitted "scared me to death" as he reflected on his move from £50-a-week life in the Third Division to the glamour of a club about to retain the League championship.

"I'd already turned down Liverpool once when they came in for a me a couple of months earlier because I honestly didn't think I was good enough," said Rush. But eagle-eyed Liverpool chief scout Geoff Twentyman knew a glittering prospect when he saw one and his assessment was shared by Paisley and his managerial aide Tom Saunders.

Manchester City's Malcolm Allison and Tony Book were amongst others on Rush's trail, but Liverpool won the race to sign the boyhood Evertonian, who displayed a scoring instinct from his earliest days.

At the age of 11 he hit 72 goals for Deeside Primary Schools to ensure they won all 33 of that season's matches, and his deadly finishing skills alerted former Manchester City and Wales full-back Cliff Sear, in his role as Chester's youth team boss.

"I saw Ian playing for Flint Under-14s and I was struck right away by how razor sharp he was," Sear recalled. "He could hit the ball with either foot, had great pace and was bursting

with confidence. He stuck out like a sore thumb!" Chester signed him first as a schoolboy and then on apprentice forms. As a six-feet plus full-time professional he had made only 38 senior appearances, scoring 17 goals, when he joined Liverpool on 28 April 1980, a year to the day from his Chester debut.

But he had to show patience and

Ian Rush

persistence before earning a regular Liverpool place. A year in the reserves, during which he won the first batch of 73 Wales caps, saw him make only nine senior appearances without scoring and at the start of 1981–82 a frank exchange with Paisley put the lean and hungry marksman on the road to greatness.

"I knocked on the manager's door, went in and blurted out: 'Why am I not in the side? What's happening?' Bob told me that I wasn't putting the ball in the net and I was concentrating too much on playing possession football and laying the ball off. That really riled me and it ended up with me saying I'd better leave Liverpool! But shortly after that everything changed." Paisley sent on Rush as a second-half substitute for David Johnson in the European

Cup return with Oulu Palloseura at Anfield … and he broke his duck within four minutes. Two more goals in the League Cup clash with Exeter then a First Division brace against Leeds showed Rush had turned on the tap.

It became a torrent. Rush formed a breathtaking partnership with Kenny Dalglish that would help him amass a club record 346 goals from 660 senior appearances in two spells at Liverpool, split by a year at Juventus in 1987–88.

He returned to resume his habit of scoring goals and collecting medals, his overall haul comprising five championships, a European Cup, three FA Cups and five League Cups. His 44 FA Cup goals is the biggest individual total since the 19th century, his five Cup final goals is an all-time record and he shares the 49-goal League Cup record with Geoff Hurst.

Rush hit a record 28 goals for Wales, an all-time high Mersey derby haul of 25 and his remarkable total of 47 first-team goals in 1983–84 is the highest ever by a Liverpool player in a season. That same year, he was voted Footballer of the Year and PFA Player of the Year.

He scored five in a game against Luton, hit four goals in a match three times and collected 16 hat-tricks to become Liverpool's talismanic hero. The 1987 League Cup final defeat by Arsenal ended their 144-game run of never losing when Rush scored.

To the adoring fans he was simply Rushie, but his team-mates called him Tosh. "It was because, even though I wasn't the best in the air, I headed a goal against Benfica that John Toshack would have been proud of!" he explained.

Rush's magnificent Liverpool career earned him an MBE and it ended as club captain in the 1996 FA Cup final against Manchester United before he joined Leeds and, later, Newcastle and Wrexham. After gaining a FIFA coaching badge he launched the Ian Rush Finishing School. "Bob Paisley taught me not to be frightened to miss," said the man who terrorized defences across Europe.

did a series of injuries and departures. Among those whose Liverpool careers effectively ended that season were Jim Beglin and Kevin MacDonald, who both suffered broken legs. Sammy Lee, who had struggled for a first-team place under Dalglish, decided to move on to Queens Park Rangers. And John Wark emerged from a succession of injuries to return to his old club, Ipswich.

But the biggest gap was left by Ian Rush, whose £3.2 million switch to Juventus shattered Liverpool's transfer record. The Italians had made their move shortly after his demolition of Everton in the Cup final – but the two clubs agreed to defer the deal for a year. Rush signed off in style, hitting 30 League goals, and scoring in the 2–1 defeat by Arsenal in the final of the Littlewoods Cup, as the League Cup was now called. He also continued to torment Everton, grabbing the equalizer in the 1–1 Charity Shield clash, scoring the goal that put them out of the FA Cup, and getting on the scoresheet twice in a 3–1 League win at Anfield. To cap it all, he appeared in both legs of the Screen Sport Super Cup final – and scored five times as Liverpool beat their neighbours 7–2 on aggregate.

His departure could have been disastrous, but instead it proved to be a catalyst. John Aldridge, a Scouse Rush-lookalike, had been bought as his replacement towards the end of the 1986–87 season, for £750,000. But throughout the summer and autumn the manager plotted radical changes to the way his side would look and play.

With the money from Juventus burning a hole in his pocket, Dalglish splashed out £900,000 on Watford's John Barnes, a dazzling Jamaican-born forward whose curled free-kick against Liverpool the previous year had been a candidate for Goal of the Season. But that strike was nothing to the one that

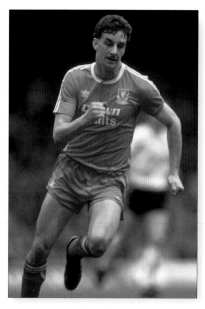

JOHN ALDRIDGE
Rush's replacement was every bit as deadly in front of goal.

had made his name – a mesmerizing run and shot past the Brazilian defence, which still ranks among England's best-ever goals.

Four weeks after capturing Barnes, the manager smashed the all-British transfer record by bringing Peter Beardsley to Anfield from Newcastle. The little Geordie striker had been setting the First Division alight with his sublime skills, following a starring role for England at the 1986 World Cup in Mexico. Fast, tricky, strong and packing a ferocious shot, he was the most sought-after player in the land – even at an asking price of £1.8 million. But still the spending spree wasn't over. Two months into the new season, Dalglish spent the remainder of the cash on Aldridge's former Oxford United team-mate Ray Houghton, a livewire Irish international midfielder, who could open up defences – and score as many as he created.

The four new boys helped form a team brimming with flair and imagination. At the season's half-way mark they passed the 50-goal barrier. They also went 29 games unbeaten, equalling a record set by Leeds United 14 years earlier. Inspired by the entertainment on offer, the Liverpool fans flocked back in ever-increasing numbers. But the 40,000 who turned up every fortnight were treated to results as well as exhibitions: "There was an invincibility about us when we went out to play at Anfield," Houghton recalled. "You felt that, with the brand of football we were playing, we just couldn't get beaten. In most games we weren't going out wondering whether we were going to win. It was a question of how many we would win by."

Beardsley fulfilled his promise in spades, grabbing 15 League goals and taking a hand in many others. Barnes'

JOHN BARNES
"Digger" was voted Footballer of the Year in his first Anfield season.

cavalier performances filled stadiums up and down the country, and earned him the double accolade of Footballer of the Year and PFA Player of the Year. Meanwhile, Aldridge erased the pain of Rush's transfer, hitting 29 goals in all competitions, and winning Europe's Golden Boot. "John usually knew where I was going to put the ball before I did," said Barnes. "I would just try to get it in the box, and, more often than not, he could tell whether it was going to the near post or the far post. He could anticipate what was going to happen, get ahead of the defenders and score."

Dalglish's dream-team won the championship by April – the first side to clinch the title before the Littlewoods Cup final had been played. They lost only two games, scored 87 goals, and ended with 90 points from 40 matches. Their finest performance was the 5–0 Anfield destruction of Nottingham Forest, with two goals from Aldridge, and others from Beardsley, Houghton and centre-back Gary Gillespie. Amid the superlatives bandied about that night, there was this observation from England legend Tom Finney: "It was the finest exhibition I've seen the whole time I've played and watched the game. You couldn't see it bettered anywhere – not even in Brazil. The moves they put together were fantastic."

His praise was echoed throughout the media. During the long years of Liverpool's success reporters had – often unjustly – portrayed the team as a "machine". But now everyone applauded the invention and style that left even the strongest opponents looking ordinary. "We had such a great squad

PETER BEARDSLEY
The Geordie helped make Liverpool the most entertaining team in Britain.

of players," said Houghton, "that Kenny could have fielded two sides in the First Division. And they probably would have finished first and second." No one could deny that Dalglish had assembled a team of world-beaters. And only a fool would have bet against them securing another Double.

But that fool would have won handsomely. In one of the greatest Wembley shocks of all time, Liverpool lost the FA Cup final to Wimbledon – a team long regarded as something of a joke by football's purists. Twelve years earlier, the club wasn't even in the Football League. But, with financial backing from a wealthy local businessman, the Plough Lane men had fought their way to the top flight, thanks to raw aggression, "route one" tactics and fierce team spirit.

It was an unattractive combination, but one that brought Liverpool's spectacular season to a humiliating end. Spurred on by a mere 10,000 followers, Wimbledon defended desperately from the outset, relying on their 6 ft 4 in 'keeper Dave Beasant to make a string of superb saves. But with 36 minutes gone, Beardsley chipped the ball past him after shrugging off an illegal challenge from defender Andy Thorne. For a few seconds, a Liverpool victory seemed inevitable. But then everyone realized that the referee had blown for a free-kick rather than letting the advantage be played.

The disallowed goal proved to be the turning point. A minute later, Wimbledon went ahead through Lawrie Sanchez. With half an hour left, Beasant saved a penalty from Aldridge. And, from then on, a packed Dons defence held out in the face of

THE DOUBLE DENIED
Beasant's penalty save from Aldridge in the 1988 FA Cup final.

sustained Liverpool pressure. It was an amazing achievement, but – while not denying Wimbledon their place in history – it's worth remembering the referee's own post-match quote: "I suppose there was every opportunity to play the advantage, and perhaps, in hindsight, I should have done."

It was a sad end to an exhilarating season, but one that soon faded in the memory. By the time Liverpool played in their next FA Cup final, the players, fans and officials saw football through a changed perspective. Mere defeat on the pitch was nothing compared to a tragedy on the terraces.

THE DARKEST DAY

Liverpool's 1988–89 campaign contained enough talking points to fill a book on its own – including a nail-biting championship race decided by a last-gasp Arsenal goal in front of a disbelieving Kop. It also featured the prodigal's homecoming – the joyful return of Ian Rush after just one season in Italy. But even the most dramatic sporting moments get overshadowed by news events. And this was the season when Liverpool found themselves at the centre of the world's biggest story.

HILLSBOROUGH DISASTER 1989
Thousands of fans spill onto the pitch to escape the chaos in Leppings Lane.

It unfolded before millions of TV viewers at Hillsborough stadium, Sheffield, venue for the club's FA Cup semi-final with Nottingham Forest. Followers of Liverpool – a club with an average gate of 39,000 – had been allocated the Leppings Lane end of the ground. Forest, who attracted home crowds of just over 20,000, were given the "Kop" end – a terrace with a capacity twice as large as Leppings Lane.

At around 2.30 pm there was a crush involving Liverpool fans attempting to get into the ground in time for the kick-off. A quarter of an hour later the crowd had swelled to 5,000, making entry to the turnstiles impossible. Senior police officers, watching the scene on CCTV monitors, decided something needed to be done about the mounting chaos. But instead of ordering the kick-off to be put back, a decision was taken to open a single large steel door in the perimeter wall.

The result was a stampede of fans through the gangway leading to Pens Three and Four of Leppings Lane – two central enclosures that were already full to capacity. When the teams came on to the pitch at 2.54 pm, the excitement created a forward surge that caused a suffocating crush. Those arriving late were unaware of the pressure building up at the front. For those who had taken their places early, there was no escape – their faces and bodies were pressed against the steel fencing designed to stop pitch invasions.

Within minutes of the kick-off, a Liverpool attack created yet another surge. By then the crush had become so unbearable that desperate fans were begging to be lifted to the seating area above the terrace. At 3.06 pm a few managed to force their way through a narrow space on to the pitch. But, with the police ignoring pleas to help relieve the pressure, some ran towards the Liverpool players screaming. One by one they delivered the terrifying news: "People are dying back there."

Suddenly, the enormity of the problems dawned. A policeman ran on to the field, ordering the referee to stop the game. Bodies were lifted forward and laid out on the cinder track. And, as the players were led to their dressing rooms, the BBC cut to presenter Des Lynam by the pitch-side: "There are people in tears here. There has been no violence from the Liverpool fans. They say they got the wrong end of the ground, the gates were opened and the tickets were not inspected. They are blaming the authorities for opening the gates."

In the minutes of mayhem that followed, those fans tore off advertising boards to construct makeshift stretchers. St John Ambulance officers rushed to administer first aid and the kiss of life. Scores of distressed supporters walked around gasping for breath. On the pitch, dozens of children, teenagers, men and women lay dead or dying. A total of 94 Liverpool fans lost their lives on 15 April 1989. Lee Nichol, 14, died two days later. Tony Bland, 17 at the time of the disaster, remained in a coma for nearly four years before his life-support system was finally switched off.

Merseyside was engulfed in feelings of shock, grief, anger and disgust. Shock at the sheer scale of the tragedy. Grief for those who died, and for their bereft families and friends. Anger at the authorities who had planned the crowd arrangements – and at the police for their loss of control. Disgust at those sections of the media who were determined, despite all the evidence, to pin the blame on the fans themselves. The cruelty of that coverage – particularly to the victims' relatives at a time when they were over-whelmed with grief – is still hard to fathom, and even more difficult to forgive. Despite its belated apologies, *The Sun* has still to recover its Merseyside sales.

Although the tragedy had occurred in Sheffield, it was Anfield that quickly became the focus of the city's mourning. By the end of the night the Shankly Gates were festooned with flowers. When dawn broke, thousands of fans had made their way to the ground to pay their respects, and to share their sense of shock and loss. The club opened its doors to the public, and the Kop goalmouth soon became a shrine, carpeted with bouquets, scarves, poems and poignant messages. Kenny Dalglish asked the players to attend the ground that Sunday, as a show of support. Ray Houghton later described the scene in his season's diary:

THE FLOWERS OF HILLSBOROUGH 1989
A small, private message and a huge, public display of grief.

"It is difficult to explain the atmosphere at Anfield. It was like nothing I had ever experienced before – a mixture of grief, confusion and calm. All the players were there and we went on to the pitch and saw some fans. No one was really talking, just nodding, shaking hands. It was quiet, so quiet. The pitch area is usually a cauldron of noise when fans come face to face with players, but this wasn't a day for celebrating. The goal had become a tribute to the dead. Flowers decorated the six-yard box, and other colours had been tied to the posts and crossbar. We just stared, and then a lone voice from somewhere on the Kop shouted: 'Don't worry, we all loved you.' And suddenly every one of us either burst into tears or held their head in their hands."

For the next fortnight, the manager and his players formed an intense bond with the fans, attending memorial masses, visiting the injured in hospital and comforting the bereaved in their homes. The club made arrangements for at least one player to be present at each funeral, though some – including Hansen, Dalglish and Barnes – attended many more. Several first-team members pulled out of international duty, preferring to join in the mourning. Their wives, led by Marina Dalglish, staffed the Anfield hospitality suites, offering tea, conversation and counselling to any victims' relatives who wanted to call in. Even former players rushed to Merseyside to provide what help and comfort they could. John Toshack flew in from Spain. Craig Johnston, who had quit the game the previous year, travelled back from his home in Australia.

An estimated quarter of a million people passed

THOUSANDS OF FANS HAD MADE THEIR WAY TO THE GROUND TO PAY THEIR **RESPECTS**, AND TO **SHARE** THEIR SENSE OF **SHOCK** AND **LOSS**. THE KOP GOALMOUTH SOON BECAME A **SHRINE**, CARPETED WITH **BOUQUETS**, **SCARVES**, **POEMS** AND **POIGNANT** MESSAGES.

through the Anfield gates in the days after the disaster. The following Saturday, at 3.06 pm, the stadium was packed for a special minute's silence, with Steve Nicol joining the supporters on the Kop, and his team-mates standing with their heads bowed in the centre circle. But the sadness and sorrow wasn't confined to Liverpool, for this was a tragedy that all football fans knew, instinctively, could have happened to them. They observed their own minute's silences, organized cash collections, and sent messages of support from every part of the country. Europe, too, felt the loss. Bayern Munich and Napoli, playing in the semi-finals of the UEFA Cup, each made donations of £17,000 to the victims' families. Germany's Borussia Dortmund offered the gate receipts from an exhibition match against Moscow Dynamo. And in Italy, the San Siro stadium witnessed one of the most moving displays of fan solidarity ever: 70,000 followers of AC Milan and Real Madrid combining to sing the Liverpool anthem "You'll Never Walk Alone".

The tragedy affected the Anfield staff in different ways. Local-born players like John Aldridge and Steve McMahon found the immediate grief hard to bear. Others like Dalglish showed rock-like dignity at the time, but suffered longer-term emotional effects. Liverpool had always enjoyed a special relationship with their supporters, particularly since Bill Shankly's arrival, but in the aftermath of the Hillsborough Disaster any lingering "them and us" feelings were swept away. The annual Anfield memorial service and the "eternal flame" shrine to those who died are permanent reminders of how the club, the players, the fans – and the city – mourned as one.

FOOTBALL RESUMES

For those not directly affected by the tragedy, normal life began to return. On 30 April, Liverpool played a fund-raising friendly against Celtic before a 60,000 crowd in Glasgow. Dalglish recalled himself to the team, and even managed to score as the Reds ran out 4–0 winners against his old club. Three days later they faced Everton in an emotion-charged League derby. Under normal circumstances, a 0–0 draw would have satisfied no one at Goodison Park. But, after what Merseyside had just been through, it seemed the most appropriate result for the 45,000 packed into the ground.

By then the Anfield officials had resolved their dilemma over whether to stay in the FA Cup. It had caused much debate and soul-searching, but, in the end, it was the fans who made it clear they wanted the club to go on. So, three weeks after Hillsborough, Liverpool again met Forest in a rearranged semi-final clash at Old Trafford. Another minute's silence, another deafening roar – and then a performance of determination, skill and controlled aggression. Liverpool won the game 3–1 thanks to an own goal, and two strikes from Aldridge. They had made it to the last stage of the FA Cup for the second successive year – and this time they would face Everton, in what soon became known as "Merseyside's Memorial Final".

And of all the days the two clubs have faced each other, 20 May 1989 remains one of the most memorable. A month earlier, a chain of red and blue scarves had connected Anfield and Goodison – and on Cup final day the unprecedented show of unity continued. The supporters stood together, sang together and paid their respects together. Then, as the sun beat down, they watched the most thrilling Wembley final for years.

Aldridge, making up for the previous season's penalty miss, put his side ahead after just four minutes. As the game went into injury time it looked like it would be the

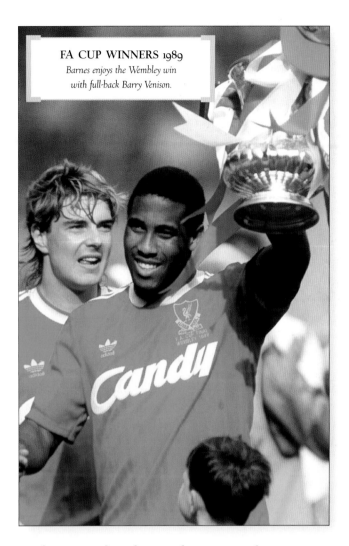

FA CUP WINNERS 1989
Barnes enjoys the Wembley win with full-back Barry Venison.

match winner, but then, with just seconds remaining, Blues' substitute Stuart McCall followed up a Dave Watson shot to equalize. At the start of extra-time, Dalglish sent on Rush in Aldridge's place. He had been on the field only five minutes when his shot beat the opposition 'keeper Neville Southall – restoring Liverpool's lead, and breaking Dixie Dean's long-standing record of 19 derby goals. Incredibly, Everton came back again, as McCall chested down a Hansen clearance before volleying an equalizer. But just two minutes later, Barnes sent in a low cross – and Rush stooped to head the winner.

It was Ronnie Whelan, handed the captaincy during one of Hansen's injury bouts, who lifted the trophy, letting loose a tide of emotions among the Liverpool fans. Nothing could ever make up for the tragedy that some had just lived through, but there was a widespread feeling, throughout the whole of football, that Wembley had provided the right result.

ALDO'S REVENGE
The striker made up for his 1988 penalty miss by scoring against Everton.

MATCH LIVERPOOL 9 CRYSTAL PALACE 0

Peter Beardsley takes aim during the 9–0 demolition.

This was the record-setting evening when Liverpool's one over the eight left their fans in ecstasy – and reduced John Aldridge to tears as he bade an emotional farewell to the Kop. It was his last appearance before his £1.1 million move to Spain's Real Sociedad, and the Republic of Ireland striker made his exit in a style straight from the pages of comic-strip fiction.

Newly promoted Palace were handed a harsh lesson in life at the top. Their manager, Liverpool-born and boyhood Anfield supporter Steve Coppell, could only grimace as his side were engulfed by a red tide. The rout began after only eight minutes, thanks to a curled effort from Footballer of the Year Steve Nicol. After 16 minutes, Steve McMahon lofted a shot over Palace 'keeper Perry Suckling, and the Liverpool advantage was doubled.

Seconds before the interval Barnes sent Beardsley through and, as Palace defenders converged on the England raider, the ball broke to Rush who made it 3–0. The second half was only 11 minutes old when Liverpool added another through Gary Gillespie's near-post diving header after Barnes had nodded on Beardsley's corner.

Palace then paid a high price for Geoff Thomas' 63rd-minute foul on Rush. From the free-kick Whelan found Beardsley who, after a one-two with Rush, drilled in goal number five. Referee Keren Barratt's penalty award to Liverpool five minutes later, for a Jeff Hopkins trip on Whelan, prompted the Kop to chant: "Aldo, Aldo."

Dalglish responded to the public clamour by sending on the former Oxford and Newport star in place of Beardsley, with his first task to take the penalty at the Kop end. Aldridge, Liverpool's top scorer for the previous two seasons, kept a cool head after being flung into the emotional furnace and beat Suckling from the spot to make it 6–0.

"I knew I was leaving and I wanted to take that penalty," said Aldridge. "The only penalty I failed with for Liverpool was in the FA Cup final the previous year, and even though

LIVERPOOL 9 CRYSTAL PALACE 0

ANFIELD, FIRST DIVISION, 12 SEPTEMBER 1989 **REFEREE:** Keren Barratt (Coventry).
TEAMS **LIVERPOOL:** Grobbelaar, Hysen, Burrows, Nicol, Whelan, Hansen, Beardsley (Aldridge, 68), Gillespie, Rush, Barnes, McMahon (Molby, 79).
CRYSTAL PALACE: Suckling, Pemberton, Burke, Gray, Hopkins, O'Reilly, McGoldrick, Thomas, Bright, Wright, Pardew. Substitutes: Shaw, Dyer.

Steve Nicol started and finished the rout.

emotions were running high I was determined to say goodbye by putting that one away against Palace. I had my usual split second glance at the 'keeper then put the kick to his left and into the net. It was a wonderful moment."

Two minutes later Palace were awarded a penalty for Nicol's challenge on Alan Pardew. But, in keeping with their night of torment, Thomas blazed his kick high over under-employed Bruce Grobbelaar's bar.

Liverpool made it seven in the 79th minute, through a Barnes free-kick that flew high into the net. And when his corner was headed in by Glenn Hysen after 82 minutes, the scoreline surpassed Liverpool's seven-goal demolition of Tottenham 11 years earlier.

Nicol, the player who started the barrage, finished it two minutes from time by scoring his second and Liverpool's ninth. It secured the club's biggest top-flight win and equalled their biggest margin of League victory … a 10–1 Second Division defeat of Rotherham Town in February 1896.

It was the first time eight Liverpool players had scored in a League game. Only Ronnie Whelan, David Burrows, Alan Hansen and substitute Jan Molby failed to get on the scoresheet.

But the night belonged to Aldridge who said goodbye by removing his No. 12 jersey, socks and boots and hurling them into the Kop, where he once stood as a boy idolizing Roger Hunt. "I've had to brush away a few tears and my heart goes out to the fans. They're something really special," said the man who scored 63 goals in 104 Liverpool outings.

ARSENAL HANGOVER

Liverpool began the following season still coming to terms with how the previous one had ended. Six days after the Cup final they had faced Arsenal at Anfield. The Reds had gone 25 games unbeaten, and were three points ahead of their north London rivals, with a superior goal difference. When the first half ended goalless, it would have been almost impossible to get odds on Arsenal winning by the necessary two clear goals to claim the title. Even when they scored with a controversial indirect free-kick, there were few who believed the Liverpool defence would crack again. But then, with the Kop baying for the final whistle, Arsenal's Michael Thomas latched on to a through-ball from Alan Smith, ran into the Liverpool box and stroked the ball past Grobbelaar. The championship had been decided by virtually the last kick of the last match. And Liverpool's Double dream lay in tatters.

There was only one way to respond: following a summer of head-shaking and teeth-clenching, Dalglish's team set out to bring the title back to Anfield. But it soon emerged that they would be doing it without Aldridge, top scorer for the previous two seasons, and the man who had done more than anyone to fill the temporary gap left by Rush. It was the Welshman's return that caused his departure. Unable to give a starting place to both strikers, Dalglish felt compelled to accept an offer from Spain's Real Sociedad. A month into the new campaign Aldridge made his last appearance in a Liverpool shirt, coming on as a substitute to score a penalty in the 9-0 massacre of Crystal Palace (see pages 151–2).

That game helped kick-start

NIGHTMARE ENDING
Michael Thomas beats Grobbelaar, and wins the title for Arsenal.

Liverpool's season after a hesitant opening in which they had won two and drawn two. Within a fortnight they were at the top of the table, and showing the sort of form that had electrified the First Division a couple of seasons earlier. The defence had a new look, thanks to the introduction of Swedish international centre-back Glenn Hysen, who had been bought from the Italian club Fiorentina. Whelan, McMahon and Molby continued to hold the midfield together, while, up front, Beardsley and Rush formed an effective partnership that produced 41 goals in all competitions.

But the star of the 1989–90 season was John Barnes, playing at his peak and terrorizing defences wherever he went. Despite often attracting the attention of two markers, Barnes always managed to shake them off, going deep, switching wings, employing bursts of speed and power that left all others standing. His runs, shooting ability and skill from set pieces brought him 28 goals that season – and he more than deserved to inherit the Footballer of the Year mantle from Steve Nicol.

For a time it looked as though Liverpool might be on course for the Double once more. They began their FA Cup defence with a record 8-0 thrashing of Swansea City in a third round home replay. They then overcame Norwich, Southampton and QPR before drawing Crystal Palace in the semi-final. After what had happened earlier in the season, the Reds looked certainties to get to Wembley. But at Villa Park, Palace showed they had learned the lessons from their Anfield humiliation. Despite conceding goals from Rush, McMahon and Barnes, they ended up winning the game 4-3.

TOP 10 HAT-TRICKS 1984–1991	
1. IAN RUSH	6
2. JOHN WARK	4
3. PAUL WALSH	3
4. JOHN ALDRIDGE	3
5. RONNIE WHELAN	2
6. STEVE McMAHON	2
7. GARY GILLESPIE	1
8. STEVE NICOL	1
9. RONNIE ROSENTHAL	1
10. JOHN BARNES	1
10. PETER BEARDSLEY	1
10. JAN MOLBY	1
10. STEVE STAUNTON	1
ALL COMPETITIONS	

THE **STAR** OF THE 1989–90 SEASON WAS **JOHN BARNES**, PLAYING AT HIS **PEAK** AND **TERRORIZING** DEFENCES. HE MORE THAN **DESERVED** TO INHERIT THE **FOOTBALLER OF THE YEAR** MANTLE FROM **STEVE NICOL**

Still, there was the League to play for, and this time it was Aston Villa and Arsenal – again – providing the main competition. Liverpool had gained some revenge against George Graham's side by claiming a 1–0 victory in the Charity Shield back in August. Two months later the Gunners hit back, dumping the Reds out of the Littlewoods Cup in a third round tie at Highbury. Now, in the final few weeks of the season, they were slugging it out again. Only this time Liverpool's manager had a secret weapon.

His name was Ronny Rosenthal, an Israeli international signed on loan from Belgium's Standard Liège. A powerful, marauding winger with the confidence to shoot from any angle, Rosenthal enlivened a Liverpool attack

CHEERS, BOSS
Dalglish, Roy Evans ... and more
silverware for the trophy cabinet.

that had begun to look weary in the final run-in. He made a couple of appearances as a substitute, then marked his full debut by scoring a hat-trick in a 4–0 away win at Charlton. He played in eight games in all, hitting seven goals and giving Liverpool the final push towards their 18th League championship.

By the time they played their last home game that title was already secured. Liverpool strode to a single-goal victory over Derby County, and Dalglish gave the Kop an extra treat, coming on as a substitute in the final few minutes before the trophy was presented. As a player, it was his last-ever senior game for Liverpool. And, unbeknown to everyone, his managerial reign was also coming to an end.

1992 FA CUP WINNERS

BILL CLINTON BECOMES 42ND PRESIDENT OF THE UNITED STATES

1993 ROBBIE FOWLER DEBUT

1994 FA CUP DEFEAT BY BRISTOL CITY

SOUNESS LEAVES

CHAPTER NINE
1991–1998

Paradise Lost

ROY EVANS APPOINTED MANAGER

KOP TERRACES DEMOLISHED

1995 COCA-COLA CUP WINNERS

BOSMAN RULING

1996 WEMBLEY DEFEAT BY MANCHESTER UNITED

DEATH OF BOB PAISLEY

1997 BARNES LEAVES

PAISLEY GATEWAY OPENED

MICHAEL OWEN DEBUT

1998 EVANS AND GÉRARD HOULLIER MADE JOINT MANAGERS

"I WOULD LIKE TO PAY TRIBUTE TO ALL ROY HAS DONE FOR THE CLUB OVER 35 YEARS. I OFFERED HIM ANOTHER POSITION BUT HE HAS CHOSEN TO TAKE A BREAK."

DAVID MOORES PAYS TRIBUTE TO ROY EVANS

Farewell to the standing Kop

IN FOOTBALL, THE DECADES RARELY BEGIN ON TIME. LIVERPOOL'S FIFTIES SLUMP REALLY BEGAN IN 1948. SHANKLY'S GREAT SIXTIES SIDE SPENT THEIR FIRST TWO YEARS TRYING TO WIN PROMOTION. AS FOR HIS ALL-CONQUERING SEVENTIES TEAM, IT WAS 1973 BEFORE THEY ACTUALLY LANDED A TROPHY. SO IT WAS WITH THE NINETIES. MANY TRACE THE ROOTS OF THAT ERA'S DECLINE TO 22 FEBRUARY 1991: THE DAY KENNY DALGLISH WALKED AWAY FROM ANFIELD.

"It was with very real regret that we learned of his decision to resign as team manager," said club chairman Noel White. "I would like to assure our supporters that we did everything in our power to change his mind, and to continue to do the job which he has done with such conspicuous success during the last five years or so. However he has made it clear – and I know he would tell you this himself – that he was determined to give up active participation in professional football, and he has also assured us that we could do nothing to alter his decision to resign."

How had it happened? Why did a man who lived and breathed football decide to leave it all behind? What made him depart a club where he was so idolized? Why choose a moment when his team were top of the League, and in the middle of an epic series of FA Cup replays with Everton?

His face and body language provided the answer. Slumped next to White at that Anfield press conference, Dalglish looked stressed and exhausted. For long periods he stared at the floor, unwilling to look at the journalists and photographers. When he did speak his answers were short and his voice quiet. No, he had not been offered

FEELING THE STRAIN
The events at Hillsborough had a lasting effect on Dalglish.

another job. Yes his decision was final. Although he offered no immediate explanation, those close to him could guess the cause. Dalglish later confirmed their suspicions, admitting that the strain and distress of the Hillsborough disaster had made him feel like his "head would explode".

Remembering the magnificent way he'd conducted himself in the aftermath of that tragedy, most people sympathized. He was drained, and needed to put his own emotional well-being before the good of the club. But, still, his decision caused dismay. Many fans – and the majority of the players – hoped that Alan Hansen would become his successor. But the veteran club captain was suffering from long-term knee damage, and wanted out of football. When he announced his own retirement, just a fortnight later, it seemed like the golden era of success was coming to an end.

By then Liverpool had slipped from top spot after losing two successive League games. Everton, who'd shared a thrilling 4–4 FA Cup tie two days before Dalglish's departure, had also dumped them out of the tournament by winning the second replay. The back-line had been rocky all season, with neither Gillespie nor

Hysen commanding the box in the way Hansen had done for so long. Barnes and Rush were getting the goals up front, but too often found their efforts were being cancelled out by defensive errors. In one game at Elland Road, Liverpool allowed Leeds to rub-out a four-goal lead – only to grab a fifth in the dying stages.

For the best part of two months, Ronnie Moran held the fort as caretaker-manager. But in that time Liverpool effectively slipped out of the title race, dropping points and losing touch with the eventual champions, Arsenal. Then, with just five games remaining, the board announced a permanent replacement for Dalglish. Anfield was in for nearly three years of turbulence.

SOUNESS TAKES OVER

The appointment of Graeme Souness was greeted with almost universal approval. As a player, he was a living legend: the ultimate competitor who combined awesome power with skill, subtlety and cunning. He'd captained a Liverpool team who had conquered Europe, proved himself among the giants of Italy's Serie A, then gone on to transform Glasgow Rangers as player-manager. Under his guidance, the Ibrox club had emerged from Celtic's shadow, attracted international stars, and begun a stranglehold on the Scottish Premier League that would last for almost a decade.

PHIL BOERSMA
The seventies striker returned to Anfield as assistant to Souness.

THE PRODIGAL'S RETURN
Souness with Molby, Grobbelaar and Mark Wright.

Life was always going to be harder in England, but Souness prided himself on taking challenges head-on. He breezed into Anfield brimming with confidence, announced his intention to get the club back where they belonged, and immediately made it clear he would do things his way. Firstly, he insisted that Liverpool appoint Rangers colleague Phil Boersma as his assistant – despite the knowledge and experience already available in the Boot Room. He also took charge of the players' diets, supervised a change in training techniques, and moved all the club's coaching and medical facilities from Anfield to Melwood.

After watching the side finish as runners-up, Souness began a radical rebuilding programme. The close-season signings of Derby's Mark Wright and Dean Saunders – for a combined fee of £5.1 million – marked the start of Liverpool's busiest-ever period in the transfer market. For the next two years barely a month went by without the manager selling a player or reaching for the cheque-book. He also showed a keen eye for up-and-coming youngsters – giving debut opportunities to future internationals like Steve McManaman, Jamie Redknapp and Robbie Fowler.

Souness won deserved praise for his youth development policy, but his treatment of older players caused unrest in the dressing room and on the terraces. For years Liverpool had only sold their senior stars once they began to wane. But in transfer-listing Beardsley, McMahon, Houghton and Steve Staunton, the manager was off-loading players who were still at their peak. John Barnes survived the cull. But later, in his autobiography, he claimed the manager got rid of too many, too soon: "Souness didn't intentionally change Liverpool's style, but the process of dispensing with five players immersed in the Liverpool way and bringing in others, whether home-grown or recruited, inevitably meant an alteration of the playing pattern.

"It was a problem bedding in so many at once. When Kenny brought me and Peter Beardsley into the Liverpool side, it was a relatively straightforward blending process. There were only two of us to assimilate into the team. Souness over-reached himself. It can take a season for one player to settle in, let alone five or six. The policy of progression was broken. Had Souness adopted a more sensible, cautious approach, the older players would have been phased out as the others matured. During his 33 months in charge, Souness sold 18 players and bought 15. Liverpool were in a permanent state of flux."

And it showed. He used 26 players throughout the 1991–92 season, and Liverpool ended sixth – their worst finish in Division One for 27 years. They won just 16 of their 42 League games, and their miserable total of 47 goals was their second lowest since joining the top flight. Equally difficult to stomach was a fourth-round exit in the Rumbelows-sponsored League Cup – at the hands of Peterborough.

Competing in the UEFA Cup following their post-Heysel ban, the team showed some early promise by beating the French side Auxerre 3–0 at Anfield, sensationally overcoming a 2–0 deficit from the first leg. But in the next

ROB JONES
The former Crewe full-back made an impressive start.

round Genoa cruelly exposed their weaknesses, following up a 2–0 home advantage with a comfortable 2–1 win at Anfield. It was only the fourth time the Reds had lost a European tie at home in a quarter of a century. However, an enforced six-year absence had left them bereft of continental experience. And those who watched the Italians cruise to victory realized it would be a long time before Liverpool could rejoin Europe's elite.

Souness was frustrated and under pressure. Throughout the season he'd splashed out nearly £9 million, landing – among others – Rangers winger Mark Walters, Hungarian international Istvan Kozma and the Arsenal midfielder Michael Thomas. But, aside from McManaman and the ex-Crewe Alexandra full-back Rob Jones, none of his new faces lived up to their promise. In addition, the Melwood treatment room was at bursting point – as first Barnes, then Molby, Rush, Wright and Whelan all hobbled out of the team injured.

Serious problems began to develop off the field, too. A medical check-up revealed the 38-year-old manager was suffering from heart disease, and, just hours after watching his team's FA Cup semi-final against Portsmouth, he announced that he needed emergency bypass surgery. Happily, the treatment proved to be a complete success and Souness, flanked by his doctors, even managed to walk out onto the Wembley pitch less than a month later. But, by then, he was involved in more controversy. While recovering in hospital, he'd agreed to do a paid exclusive with *The Sun* – a paper still widely reviled on Merseyside because of its Hillsborough coverage. When it ran the interview on the third anniversary of the disaster, the manager's decision seemed to be even more ill-judged. He later made a

MARK WALTERS
A £1.25 million capture from Glasgow Rangers.

FA CUP FINAL 1992
*Souness is flanked by his doctors as Ronnie Moran
leads the team out at Wembley (right).*

[AT LEAST **SOUNESS** FINISHED THE SEASON
WITH A **TROPHY**. LIVERPOOL **WON**
THE FINAL 2-0 AGAINST A **SUNDERLAND**
SIDE WHO OFFERED **LITTLE** RESISTANCE.]

AS GOOD AS IT GOT
*The win over Sunderland was the high
point of Souness' managerial spell.*

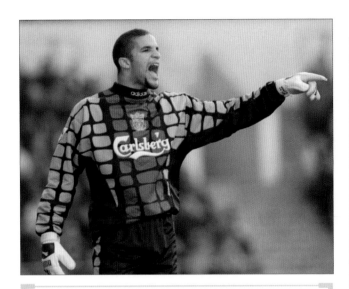

DAVID JAMES
The ex-Watford 'keeper made strong claims for an England place.

public apology, and donated his fee to Liverpool's Alder Hey Children's Hospital. But his relationship with a large section of fans had been seriously damaged.

At least he finished the season with a trophy. Liverpool won the final 2–0 against a Sunderland side who offered little resistance. Steve McManaman, switching from left to right flank in the second half, tore their defence to shreds and provided the pass for Thomas to open the scoring shortly after the restart. On 67 minutes the ex-Arsenal man touched a ball from Saunders into the path of Rush – who then stroked home a record fifth goal in FA Cup finals.

The volatile season had ended on a high note, but anyone hoping for a period of calm and consolidation was to be disappointed. Within a matter of weeks the Anfield door was revolving again, as Hysen returned to Sweden, Houghton left for Aston Villa and full-back Barry Venison was sold to Newcastle. In the other direction came Watford's giant young 'keeper David James, and Tottenham's £2.5 million midfielder Paul Stewart. Clearly, Souness's heart problems had not dented his determination to run things

his way. That summer, a behind-the-scenes row became public, as he dismissed reserve team coach, Phil Thompson.

FROM BAD TO WORSE

Liverpool's Centenary Season coincided with the birth of the Premiership – but neither landmark provided any cause for celebration. Throughout the campaign an increasingly disgruntled Anfield crowd watched their team deteriorate as Alex Ferguson's Manchester United emerged from their shadow. Again they finished in sixth place, though this time they leaked 55 goals, and wound up a full 25 points behind their great rivals. Their European Cup Winners' Cup quest finished abruptly, with a 6–2 aggregate loss to Spartak Moscow. And hopes of holding on to the FA Cup ended on a wretched January night at Anfield, as Second Division Bolton strode to a 2–0 Third Round victory.

Some critics rated that result the most humiliating since the defeat by non-League Worcester City back in the fifties. A seething Souness delivered a public rebuke to the team, openly questioning the commitment of some his most experienced players. And, as the press speculated about the boss' own future, club chairman David Moores felt compelled to deliver a message to the

NEIL RUDDOCK
His commitment, skill and aerial power made him a Kop favourite.

supporters: "Being half-way down the Premier League and out of three major Cup competitions is totally unacceptable. The Board have chosen to stay calm, to support the manager and team and do everything we can to overcome the present difficulties."

Moores continued to resist the growing pressure to sack Souness. Instead, he and the Board opted for a close-season reshuffle that saw Roy Evans being promoted to the position of assistant manager. As a coach who provided a link with the Shankly and Paisley eras, Evans was seen as a stabilizing force. But whatever his restraining influence, he couldn't prevent the chopping and changing that had become such a defining feature of the Souness reign.

> LIVERPOOL WERE TRAILING PREMIERSHIP LEADERS MANCHESTER UNITED BY 20 POINTS. TIME WAS RUNNING OUT FOR SOUNESS, AND ONLY A SUCCESSFUL FA CUP RUN OFFERED A CHANCE OF SURVIVAL.

By now he wasn't just selling players he'd inherited – he was getting rid of some of his own signings. Saunders lasted just over a year before being transferred to Aston Villa. Wright and Stewart spent most of their time on the bench, while Danish defender Torben Piechnik languished in the reserves. Still, more recruits kept coming: among them England striker Nigel Clough, a £2.7 million capture from Notts Forest, and Neil Ruddock, a £2.5 million buy from Spurs. In perhaps his most controversial deal, Souness sold the promising youngsters David Burrows and Mike Marsh to West Ham, taking hard-man Julian Dicks in exchange. Dicks had built up a spectacularly bad disciplinary record, attracting dozens of cautions and eight red cards during his career. He was a folk hero around Upton Park, but the Anfield crowd – brought up on free-flowing football and fair play – found his signing hard to accept.

Amid all the transfer activity, the injury list had gone beyond a joke. Just three months into the 1993–94 season, 23 players were unfit for the first team. Unsurprisingly, those who did get a place in such an ever-changing side found it difficult to strike up an understanding. By the turn of the year Liverpool were out of the Coca Cola Cup – after losing a penalty shoot-out to Wimbledon – and trailing Premiership leaders Manchester United by 20 points. Time was running out for Souness, and only a successful FA Cup run offered a last chance of survival.

It was First Division Bristol City who removed it. Their 1–0 third round replay victory sent an Anfield crowd home in despair, and the Liverpool directors into emergency session. Three days later, David Moores

DEAN SAUNDERS
An FA Cup winner in his short Liverpool career.

announced that the club and manager had parted company: "For all of us at Anfield, and for Graeme himself, this is a very sad day," he told reporters. "We have understood the difficulties he has faced over nearly three seasons with an unprecedented number of injuries, and the need to bring young players forward much more quickly than is usual at Anfield.

"However, Liverpool Football Club is all about winning things and being a source of pride to our fans. It has no other purpose. With the single exception of winning the FA Cup in Graeme's first season, the results in the League and the other domestic competitions – and in Europe – have been well below what is expected by the club and supporters."

Souness' appointment had been a brave and exciting experiment but, ultimately, a failure. When it came to finding his successor the club returned to the time-honoured method.

ROY TAKES OVER

Roy Evans' accession to the boss' chair surprised nobody. He'd been seen as a manager-in-waiting ever since Shankly persuaded him to give up his playing career at the age of 25, and join the coaching staff instead. Many believed he should have taken over when Dalglish quit; others even

TOP 10 LEAGUE APP'S 1991-1998	
1. JOHN BARNES	164
2. DAVID JAMES	163
3. JAMIE REDKNAPP	149
4. ROBBIE FOWLER	140
5. ROB JONES	136
6. STEVE MCMANAMAN	136
7. MARK WRIGHT	135
8. IAN RUSH	130
9. NEIL RUDDOCK	113
10. MICHAEL THOMAS	96

MATCH THE KOP'S LAST STAND

A brilliant goal against Leeds and a match-winning strike against Bayern Munich had brought Norwich City's Jeremy Goss his fair share of publicity in the 1993–94 season. However, his winner at Anfield earned him a place in history.

Goss and company became the ultimate party-poopers, denying Liverpool the victory that everyone had expected in their final match before a standing Kop. The Liverpool fans still played their part in making 30 April 1994 a day to remember. The players, alas, did not.

The supporters had not wholly approved of the Kop's demolition, but Liverpool, like every Premier League club, were bound by the recommendations of Lord Taylor. His report, following the Hillsborough disaster, called for all-seater stadia. So, plans for a new 12,000-capacity stand were drawn up, and the Kop, as people knew it, had to go.

On that final day, over 16,000 Kopites in a capacity 44,000 crowd, came to celebrate the past and revel in the memories. They brought their scarves, flags and banners, filled every corner of the terrace, and punctured the air with the songs and chants that had made them famous.

Heroes of the past – Albert Stubbins, Billy Liddell, Ian Callaghan, Tommy Smith, Steve Heighway, David Johnson, Phil Thompson, Craig Johnston, David Fairclough and Kenny Dalglish – were saluted before kick-off. Then Joe Fagan escorted Jessie Paisley and Nessie Shankly onto the pitch to a roar so loud it almost raised the roof of all four stands.

Remarkably, neither the array of stars nor the incessant prompting from a magnificent, colourful Kop, could inspire Liverpool to victory in a match beamed to 13 countries. Such a poor performance did not befit this

John Barnes takes on the Canaries.

The last Kop.

"Over 16,000 Kopites in a capacity 44,000 crowd, came to celebrate the past and revel in the memories."

occasion, and the only saving grace was that Goss' 36th-minute volley was not followed by more Norwich goals.

However, this defeat was not going to spoil the party. Gerry Marsden led the crowd through "You'll Never Walk Alone" – the hit song he covered in the mid-1960s, and which, with Bill Shankly's encouragement, became the Kop's anthem. They sang it repeatedly after the game finished. And when the last Kopites left, at 6 pm, the curtain came down on a football institution.

The Spion Kop: 1906–1994.

THE BOOT ROOM BOY TAKES OVER
Evans had served under five different managers before being appointed boss.

thought he was ready when Fagan retired.

"The pride I feel is almost indescribable," he anounced. "I am a Liverpool lad. I stood on the Kop as a youngster, and I understand the expectations of all our supporters."

Unfortunately he couldn't give his fellow Kopites the send-off they wanted. The old terrace was pulled down at the end of the season to comply with all-seater regulations following the Hillsborough disaster. Liverpool lost their last home game (see page 164) and finished the season in eighth place. They were out of Europe and – as far as the bookmakers were concerned – out of the running for the following year's Premiership crown.

But there were reasons to be optimistic. Evans had assembled a back-room team steeped in Liverpool tradition – Doug Livermore, who played under Shankly, Ronnie Moran,

ROBBIE FOWLER
Also known as "God".

with his unrivalled experience, and Sammy Lee, from Fagan's Treble-winning side. Seventies star Steve Heighway was grooming a succession of youngsters for the first team, and seeing former pupils like McManaman challenge for England honours. Robbie Fowler (see page 167), another Heighway protégé, had also broken into the senior team – demonstrating his explosive talent by hitting all five goals in the Coca Cola Cup demolition of Fulham.

Some critics doubted Evans' capacity to take tough decisions, but he quickly weeded out those he believed fell short of Liverpool standards. Dicks and Piechnik were sold, Clough and Thomas axed, and the talented, but wayward, youngster Don Hutchison shipped out. Those who stayed regained their fitness and form in time for the 1994-95 campaign. Molby shed weight and rediscovered his passing

[MCMANAMAN'S opening **GOAL** was one of the **BEST** WEMBLEY
HAD EVER **WITNESSED** – A **FIERCE** SHOT FOLLOWING
A **MESMERIZING** RUN FROM THE **HALF-WAY** line.]

touch; an equally slimline Barnes dropped back into midfield, putting in performances that earned him an England recall. Upfront, McManaman was given a free role, finding space and skipping past defences. And Fowler began the new season as he'd left off, showing a Rush-like instinct in front of goal, and scoring three against Arsenal in the space of four minutes and 33 seconds – the fastest Liverpool hat-trick on record.

That 3–0 win helped propel them to the top of the table – a position that had seemed impossible just a few

TOP 10	
LEAGUE GOALS 1991-1998	
1. ROBBIE FOWLER	84
2. IAN RUSH	45
3. STAN COLLYMORE	26
4. STEVE MCMANAMAN	23
5. JOHN BARNES	22
6. JAMIE REDKNAPP	15
7. NEIL RUDDOCK	11
8. MARK WALTERS	11
9. NIGEL CLOUGH	7
10. DON HUTCHISON	7

months previously. But sadly it wasn't to last. Despite new arrivals John Scales and Phil Babb shoring up the defence, Liverpool's form became inconsistent, and they soon fell behind Manchester United and Blackburn in the championship race. In the end it was Blackburn – under the guidance of a rested and rejuvenated Kenny Dalglish – who claimed the crown on a dramatic last day of the season at Anfield. His players were in despair when Jamie Redknapp grabbed Liverpool's last-minute winner. But, just seconds after the final whistle, they learned that

PLAYER ROBBIE FOWLER

They called him God because, in their eyes, he could do no wrong. Robbie Fowler was respected by his team-mates and worshipped by Liverpool fans. Just when opposing defences were sick to death of Ian Rush rattling in goals for the Reds, along came the kid from Toxteth, whose predatory instincts were every bit as deadly.

Like Rush, Fowler was a goal-machine and generally accepted as the most natural British finisher of his generation. With a blast, a tap or a deft chip, usually despatched from a devastatingly accurate left foot, he could find the net from all angles. Indeed, he rates his cracking left-foot shot in the 1996 FA Cup semi-final against Aston Villa as the finest goal of his Anfield career.

The youngest player to score 100 Liverpool goals, Fowler was the prime example of a local lad made good. Each time he pulled on the famous red shirt he was fulfilling the dream of thousands of Scousers. And despite the adulation and riches which came his way, he never forgot his humble origins. To the Kop, he was one of their own.

Fowler never quite courted controversy, but it tended to seek him out. A series of events, both on and off the field, probably earned him as many negative headlines as his scoring exploits had earned him positive ones. However, they only served to cement his popularity with his adoring public.

Supporters were saddened when, in search of regular first team football, he felt obliged to leave Liverpool for Leeds in November 2001. But they can always console themselves in the knowledge that it was their team which benefited for so long from his talent, instead of the other one across Stanley Park.

Influenced by his dad, who played at

Robbie Fowler

"Each time Robbie pulled on the famous red shirt he was fulfilling the dream of thousands of Scousers. To the Kop, he was one of their own."

amateur level, Fowler had begun playing with a football when he was just three. He grew up an Evertonian, idolizing Trevor Steven and even playing for the Blues' youth team as a 14-year-old. Anfield scout Jim Aspinall is probably the man who prevented Fowler from ending up at Goodison Park, inviting him to train a few nights a week with Liverpool. Kenny Dalglish was in charge when he signed schoolboy forms with the Reds, and the manager would sometimes drop the impressionable Fowler off at home after training.

Guided by Steve Heighway, the youngster caught the eye of new boss Graeme Souness. He scored on his senior debut, then hit five in the League Cup tie against Fulham at Anfield – becoming only the fourth player to go nap in Liverpool's history. In the 1994–95 campaign, Fowler struck more than 30 goals and was named the PFA Young Player of the

Year. Another prolific season followed – as did his call up for England.

Fowler missed the 1998 World Cup with a serious knee injury. By the time he returned to fitness, Gérard Houllier had joined Liverpool and a new era was dawning. He was injured again in the 1999–2000 season, and, with Michael Owen and Emile Heskey emerging as the club's first-choice strikers, Fowler's starts became restricted.

Despite limited appearances, he had a huge hand in the 2000–01 Treble-winning season, hitting a stunning volley in the Worthington Cup final, and producing a piece of brilliance off the bench that helped secure the UEFA Cup. With Jamie Redknapp sidelined, it was Fowler – as vice-captain – who lifted all three trophies in Liverpool's most successful campaign since the 1980s. But sadly, within a matter of months, he had gone.

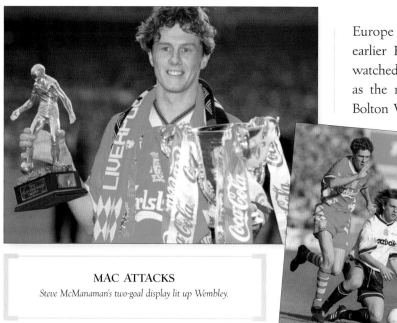

Europe had already been secured. Two months earlier Evans had led his team out at Wembley, then watched as Steve McManaman confirmed his reputation as the most exciting young talent in the Premiership. Bolton Wanderers were the opponents in the Coca Cola Cup final – a First Division team who had humbled Liverpool at Anfield just two seasons earlier. But this time, McManaman was the difference, collecting passes from Barnes and Redknapp, before gliding effortlessly past the Wanderers defenders. His opening goal was one of the best Wembley had ever witnessed – a fierce shot following a mesmerizing run from the half-way line. His second was an almost carbon-copy – and proved to be the decisive strike as Liverpool ran out 2–1 winners.

MAC ATTACKS

Steve McManaman's two-goal display lit up Wembley.

United had lost at West Ham – and blown their chance to finish top. Kenny beamed, the Rovers fans went wild – and, for once, even the Kop celebrated another team's success.

The Reds had finished fourth, but their route back to

So, silverware was back in the Anfield cabinet, attendances were up, and Europe beckoned.

VICTORY IS SWEET

The Coca Cola win gave Evans an early taste of success.

In his first full season, Evans had put together a team who'd halted Liverpool's League decline. A couple more signings, and they would be seen as title challengers again.

THE UNDER-ACHIEVERS

His transfer targets were guaranteed to generate excitement. Bolton's Jason McAteer was a Birkenhead boy with LFC in his blood; a star of Ireland's 1994 World Cup squad, and the player who'd demonstrated his skill and passion during Wanderers' defeat by Liverpool at Wembley. Stan Collymore was a goalscoring genius – a striker who'd powered Notts Forest to promotion and a UEFA Cup place, hitting the target 41 times in 64 League starts.

STAN'S OUR MAN
Collymore arrived in a record £8.5 million deal.

Evans smashed the English transfer record to land him. On the first day of the new season Collymore repaid some of the £8.5 million fee, scoring with a superb curled shot in the 1–0 win over Sheffield Wednesday. He was injured in the following game, but bounced back a fortnight later to hit a 30-yard screamer that helped beat Blackburn 3–0. Not to be outdone, Fowler promptly went out and grabbed four in the 5–2 rout of Bolton.

For much of the 1995–96 season, Evans' team played like the Liverpool of old. They were mean at the back and lethal up front. Their game flowed, they kept possession, strung endless passes together, and played the most attractive football in the Premiership. Had it not been for a disastrous November, when they failed to win a single game and fell to sixth spot, many observers thought they could have won the title race. As it was, they battled their way back to within two points of the leaders, only to suffer a late dip in form as Alex Ferguson's men sailed away at the top.

UEFA Cup defeat by Danish side Brondby, and a Coca Cola Cup exit at Newcastle's hands had dampened press talk of a Liverpool revival. But in the FA Cup they continued to show their best form, effortlessly swatting Rochdale and Shrewsbury in the early rounds, and comfortably overcoming Charlton, Leeds and Aston Villa on the last steps to Wembley. If ever there was a moment for Liverpool to re-assert themselves as kings of the North-west, it came in May 1996, the day they faced Premiership champions, Manchester United. But they missed it. In a

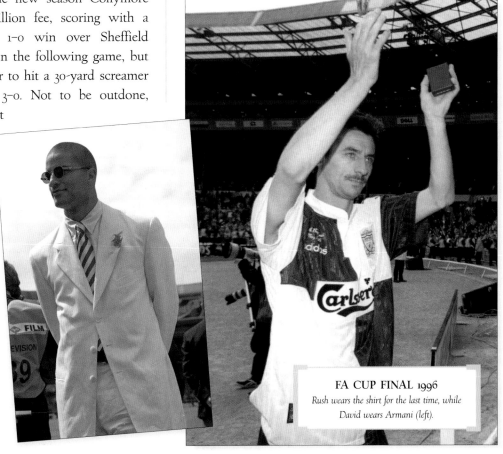

FA CUP FINAL 1996
Rush wears the shirt for the last time, while David wears Armani (left).

dull final, notable only for its lack of goalscoring opportunities – and Ian Rush's last appearance for Liverpool – Eric Cantona settled matters with an 86th-minute strike. The FA Cup went to Manchester, and United's supporters celebrated their second Double of the decade.

The defeat was galling enough, but events surrounding that match were to have a long-term effect on the team's reputation and morale. At a time when the media was growing obsessed with footballers' pay-packets, the Liverpool players walked out for the pre-match pitch inspection clad in expensive cream Armani suits and designer sunglasses. The newspapers went wild, claiming they paid more attention to their image than their play. David James' good-looks had already brought him modelling assignments; the likes of Redknapp, Babb and McAteer had become schoolgirl pin-ups; Collymore dated celebrity girlfriends. Now they were accused of flaunting their wealth, living the high life and neglecting what they were paid to do. The damaging myth of the "Spice Boys" was born.

"The 'Spice Boys' criticism was purely down to the players not being successful," John Barnes later wrote.

JAMIE REDKNAPP
A brilliant career blighted by injuries.

"The press thought the reason Liverpool were not winning trophies was because the players were going out modelling all the time. Ryan Giggs and David Beckham model clothes and they have won the European Cup. The press hyped up this 'Spice Boy' abuse to explain why Liverpool weren't doing well. It made good headlines but it was unfair. Apart from Gazza, I cannot think of a footballer who trains harder than Jason McAteer. He did some shampoo modelling and was slammed for it. All the players tagged as 'Spice Boys' loathed it. Accusations of not caring about Liverpool, of being obsessed only with money, women and modelling were far from the truth."

But the allegations persisted, and the mud began to stick. As the increasingly successful Ferguson won a reputation for iron-fist discipline at Old Trafford, there was a growing perception that Evans' Anfield regime was lax. Collymore didn't help matters by refusing to move from his home in the Midlands, publicly criticizing his manager, then refusing to turn out for the reserve team. No other players shared his destructive attitude. But, like him, far too many failed to fulfill their potential on the pitch.

They ended the 1996–97 season in fourth place, out of

OUT OF EUROPE...
Defeat by Paris St Germain cost the Reds a place in the Cup Winners' Cup final.

...OUT OF ANFIELD
Barnes left for Newcastle after a glorious decade with Liverpool.

BRIEF ENCOUNTER

Evans and Gérard Houllier were made joint managers in the summer of 1998.

contention for the new, financially-lucrative Champions League. Their hopes of taking the Cup Winners' Cup had also foundered at the semi-final stage, as a series of goalkeeping errors by James gifted the tie to Paris St Germain. By then, the newspapers were routinely referring to the Liverpool players as "underachievers", and even the most loyal Anfield supporters began to wonder if Evans really was the man to motivate them.

But the Board gave him cash as well as support. That summer he embarked on a £10 million re-building programme, bringing in Wimbledon's Oyvind Leonhardsen and the German international striker Karl Heinz-Riedle, whose goals had won the European Cup for Borussia Dortmund. After 61 League games, and 26 Premiership goals, Collymore was sold to Aston Villa. And, following an illustrious ten-year career Anfield, John Barnes was given a free transfer to Newcastle.

His departure marked a significant change in Liverpool's tactics. Evans replaced him with England international Paul Ince, whose hard-tackling, ball-winning style was in direct contrast to the thoughtful, possession-minded play that had dominated the midfield for so long. Ince, a £4.5 million capture from Inter

ST MICHAEL

Owen broke into the first team while only 17.

Milan, also had a history of disciplinary problems, although his reputation for bravery and commitment – earned during his glory days at Old Trafford – made him a popular choice as the new club captain.

Despite the new additions, Liverpool ended yet another season without a trophy. On the field their form veered from brilliant to abysmal. In the dug-out, Evans and his backroom team could ony bite their tongues in frustration: "It's the same old story, and it's driving me round the bend," said the manager after a UEFA Cup defeat by Strasbourg. "I'm the man in charge. I make the decisions. But I can't go out there and kick the ball for them."

In the Premiership, they improved just one place to finish third. They were again out of the running for the Champions League, and – without the teenage goalscoring phenomenon Michael Owen (see page 184) – they would have had difficulty qualifying for Europe at all. The 17-year-old hit 21 League goals during the campaign, including four in the Anfield clash with Notts Forest. He made his international debut in February 1998, then rounded off a glittering season with a spectacular goal for England against Argentina in the World Cup finals.

But even Owen's devastating form couldn't mask the team's failings, and the Liverpool board demanded an improvement. That summer, they made a move for ex-French national coach, Gérard Houllier, who, as Technical Director, had helped guide his nation to World Cup success. Much to their delight, the articulate and highly regarded Houllier agreed to their offer. And on 16 July 1998, he and Evans were unveiled as the new "joint managers" of Liverpool FC.

MANAGER ROY EVANS

Evans in sole charge...

Roy Quentin Echlin Evans was not just the people's choice to succeed Graeme Souness – he was also the obvious one. In fact, to do so was his destiny.

Twenty years earlier, Liverpool's then chairman, John Smith, had predicted his eventual rise to one of the most sought-after yet stressful jobs in football. Evans was just 25 then, having hung up his boots after just 11 first-team appearances, and relishing his new role as reserve team coach. By the time of his appointment as manager, the likeable lad from Bootle had worked alongside some of Liverpool's most legendary

figures, and acquired a wealth of knowledge along the way.

Originally a Bill Shankly pupil, Evans subsequently became a trusted aide to Bob Paisley, Joe Fagan and Kenny Dalglish, before being appointed as assistant manager to Graeme Souness. He had already proved himself as a coach by guiding Liverpool's reserve team to a succession of Central League titles in 11 seasons. Then, in January 1994, it was time to step out of the shadows and into the big time.

Following the years of turbulence under Souness, the new boss achieved dressing room unity. Within little more than a year, he brought in new faces like Scales and Babb.

He also introduced the wing-back system and gave McManaman a free-role in attack – a tactic that would led to a devastating Wembley performance, and a Coca Cola Cup victory over Bolton in 1995. To say Evans was proud of this victory was an understatement. In fact he treasured the trophy so much, he even slept with it when he got it back to his hotel room.

With the likes of Barnes, McAteer, Redknapp and Fowler in the ranks, Evans had every reason to believe that more silverware would come. For much of the 1995–96 season Liverpool regained the simplicity that was their 1980s hallmark. They were the cleanest and most attractive side in the

...as joint manager.

League. When it came to possession and passing, no one could touch them. But they lacked resilience and mental strength, qualities which their increasingly successful Old Trafford rivals had in abundance. The defeat by United in the 1996 FA Cup final seemed to underline the difference between the two teams. Neither played well, but United had made a habit of winning, even when they were below par.

The result heralded a wholesale change: the easing out of Barnes, a more aggressive playing style, and the acquisition of big-money signings like Ince and Collymore. When these, too, failed to deliver, Evans faced accusations that he was too soft. However, the critics who

"With the likes of Barnes, McAteer, Redknapp and Fowler in the ranks, Evans had every reason to believe that more silverware would come."

compared him unfavourably with Liverpool's past managers never acknowledged the changing times. How would Shankly and Paisley have coped with freedom of contract, millionaire wages and the growing power of agents?

Still, the lack of progress on the field was a concern, and the club's directors decided to strengthen the management team at the start of the 1998–99 season. They hoped that Gérard Houllier's European touch, coupled with Evans' Anfield experience, would prove a

winning formula. But when obvious problems arose, and the pressure on him increased, the dignified Evans chose to end his long association with the club he had served so loyally.

"Today is a sad day for me personally," said chairman David Moores as he announced the departure. "I would like to pay tribute to all Roy has done for the club over 35 years. I offered him another position, but he has chosen to take a break. I could talk for hours about Roy and my respect for him."

1998 GÉRARD HOULLIER APPOINTED SOLE MANAGER

PHIL THOMPSON APPOINTED ASSISTANT

SHANKLY STATUE UNVEILED

STEVEN GERRARD DEBUT

1999 ANFIELD ACADEMY OPENS

CHAPTER TEN *1998–2002*	**Le Boss**

SAMI HYYPIA SIGNED

2000 EMILE HESKEY ARRIVES FOR £11 MILLION

2001 TREBLE WINNERS

CHARITY SHIELD WINNERS

EUROPEAN SUPER CUP WINNERS

OWEN – EUROPEAN FOOTBALLER OF THE YEAR

GÉRARD HOULLIER'S HEART SURGERY

2002 PLANS FOR NEW ANFIELD UNVEILED

OWEN AND HESKEY PLAY IN 2002 WORLD CUP

2003 WORTHINGTON CUP WINNERS

STEVEN GERRARD APPOINTED CLUB CAPTAIN

2004 THE REDS QUALIFY FOR THE CHAMPIONS LEAGUE

GÉRARD HOULLIER LEAVES

"THE OBJECTIVE IS TO GET BACK TO WINNING WAYS. THAT CAN ONLY BE ACHIEVED WITH MORE EFFORT, MORE CONCENTRATION, BETTER DISCIPLINE AND THE TOTAL COMMITMENT OF THE PLAYERS."

GÉRARD HOULLIER

THE MANAGERIAL EXPERIMENT LASTED UNTIL NOVEMBER. IN THAT TIME THE TEAM LOST FOUR PREMIERSHIP MATCHES; INCE AND MCMANAMAN WERE SENT OFF IN A UEFA CUP VICTORY OVER VALENCIA; AND, IN ONE OF THE MOST DISMAL ANFIELD PERFORMANCES OF MODERN TIMES, LIVERPOOL WENT OUT OF THE LEAGUE CUP, NOW RENAMED THE WORTHINGTON CUP, LOSING 3–1 TO TOTTENHAM.

It was a humiliating surrender that sent a meagre crowd home demoralized. Less than 24 hours later, Roy Evans cut his links with the club and handed full control of the team to Gérard Houllier.

"I went into partnership with my eyes open and hoping it could work," Evans said. "But it hasn't worked: results have not gone our way. I feel I have done the job with honesty and integrity, and, although some people would say otherwise, I dispute that my record is one of failure. Fourth, third, fourth and third cannot be termed a failure. At any other club it would be a success, but not at Liverpool."

There was much sympathy for Evans but, as a lifelong Liverpudlian, he knew that his fellow supporters measured success in silverware. The talented players he had assembled had delivered only one trophy in four years. Worse, the team – and the club – appeared to be going backwards. The game had changed. Entry to the Champions League had given competing clubs huge financial muscle, and the upper hand in attracting the best players from abroad. The mass influx of foreigners had raised the levels of skill, strength and professionalism required to win the Premiership. Their wage levels, and freedom of contract, had given them more power than ever before.

Liverpool needed to respond, and no one recognized that more than Houllier. As a successful international coach he could pinpoint the physical and tactical

GÉRARD HOULLIER
Took over the reins in the 1998–99 season.

weaknesses in the team. He could identify what was wrong with the training methods, players' diets and match preparation. And, crucially, he wasn't afraid to challenge certain Anfield traditions: "It's not that they were complacent here," he later said. "It was just: 'We were winning and it worked. We were just doing five-a-side and it worked.' Like in life, if you don't question and try to update your methods you will be left behind. The passion of this game is that it is traditional, it is orthodox. But at the same time you have to be adventurous; you have to do something which is more forward thinking. That's how you progress. Here, it was: 'This is the way we play, this is the way we train, this is the way we travel.'"

The Board may have welcomed a manager who wasn't weighed down with baggage from Liverpool's past. But when it came to his assistant, they plumped for a man synonymous with the glories of an earlier era. "I think most people will recognize that this is one of the greatest days of my life," said former captain Phil Thompson. "Things need to be turned around and nothing will give me greater joy than to help bring success back to the club I love. I have a burning passion for Liverpool and I hope to transfer this to the training pitch and to matches."

The quiet visionary, aided by the fierce partisan, was an unlikely but appealing combination. The supporters watched approvingly as Houllier instilled a new professionalism into his squad: he banned mobile phones from the training ground, discouraged the drinking culture and insisted on high standards of behaviour on and off the field. Players who accepted the new codes of discipline were helped and encouraged. Those who kicked against them were told they could leave.

Liverpool ended the season in seventh spot. Before the closing game, Jason McAteer had gone to Blackburn, and the highly versatile Steve Harkness had rejoined Graeme Souness at Benfica. In the summer, Houllier presided over a major clear-out that saw the disaffected Ince moving to Middlesbrough, Norwegian defender Bjorn Tore Kvarme switching to St Etienne, and the gifted, but erratic, goalkeeper David James starting a new career with Aston Villa.

Liverpool netted around £9 million from those sales. But, when McManaman moved to Real Madrid, the club didn't collect a penny. The £15 million-rated winger took advantage of the so-called Bosman ruling, which entitled players to a free transfer once their current contract was up. The rule, established in a European court case involving the Belgian player Jean-Marc Bosman, had opened the way for players to command huge signing-on fees and salaries: in McManaman's case, a reputed £60,000 a week. Liverpool were undoubtedly

MORE WORK NEEDED

Houllier watched his side fall to seventh spot in his first season.

HOW MUCH?

McManaman was worth £15 million, but Liverpool didn't collect a penny.

the losers in the deal, but would use the Bosman ruling to their own advantage in the months ahead.

As a confirmed believer in the rotation system, Houllier wanted a bigger squad. Drawing on his vast international experience and contacts, he set about rebuilding Liverpool with a mixture of local talent and foreign imports. He laid out £4 million on the Dutch international 'keeper Sander Westerveld, paid his old club Lens £3.5 million for the Czech raider Vladimir Smicer, and spent £8 million prising the German midfielder Dietmar Hamann away from Newcastle. Convinced of the need for four strikers, he supplemented his Fowler-Owen partnership by signing Bayer Leverkusen's Erik Meijer, and Marseille's exciting Guinea-born international Titi Camara.

But his most impressive deal involved the defence. Faced with an exorbitant asking price for Tottenham's Sol Campbell, Houllier went after the giant young Finn Sami Hyypia, who had been enjoying a largely anonymous career with Dutch side Willem II. Still with money to spare following that £2.6 million transfer, he took advantage of Blackburn's relegation by making a successful bid for their Swiss international Stéphane Henchoz. For a combined fee of just £6 million, the Liverpool boss had formed the strongest centre-back partnership in the Premiership.

In his first full season in

charge the team conceded just 30 goals. Injuries and inconsistency were an early feature, but they then put together a terrific run that brought just two League defeats in 27 matches. Had it not been for a loss at Bradford on the very last day, they would have qualified for a Champions League spot. As it was, they finished fourth, booking a place in the UEFA Cup and moving Houllier to declare that his rebuilding project was "ahead of schedule".

The signs of progress were everywhere. The internationals, like Hyypia and Hamann, exuded authority, while local youngsters, such as Bootle's Jamie Carragher and Chester-born Danny Murphy, showed huge potential. Owen and Fowler were both recovering their fitness after a series of injuries. And the brilliant Anfield Academy graduate Steven Gerrard was attracting England's attention at the tender age of 19. For all the talk of a "foreign legion", the first-team squad contained as much home-grown talent as it ever had.

But, if Liverpool were to get back among the honours, yet more strengthening was needed. In March 2000, Houllier broke the club transfer record by paying £11 million for the Leicester City striker Emile Heskey. Three months later he made a £5.5 million bid for Middlesbrough's left-sided midfielder Christian Ziege. Then, in a move that infuriated Everton fans, he spent £6 million on England international Nick Barmby. As the transfer bills mounted, Houllier also found some notable bargains. Taking advantage of the Bosman ruling, he picked up the accomplished Bayern Munich full-back Markus Babbel on a free transfer. He then surprised

STEVIE WONDER
Gerrard made his debut at 18, and England caps soon followed.

RECORD BREAKER
Houllier spent £11 million to prise Emile Heskey from Leicester.

everyone by offering a new lease of life to the 35-year-old former Scottish captain, Gary McAllister.

As the 2000–01 season dawned, the new squad had good reason to be confident. But, as they formed their familiar pre-match "huddle" on the opening day at Anfield, no one could have predicted the dramas that lay ahead.

ONLY 63 GAMES TO GO...

For such an extraordinary season, it was a decidedly ordinary start. In the League the team gathered just 27 points out of a possible 51, dropping to sixth place in the Premiership by mid-December. They were getting the goals but, far too often, failing to hold on to their lead. At Southampton, they threw away a 3–0 advantage to come away with just a single point. At Elland Road, Leeds striker Mark Viduka blew away their 2–0 lead by firing four past Westerveld.

The Reds got their season on track with two superb wins in the space of six days. On 17 December they travelled to Old Trafford to face a Manchester United team which had already opened up an eight-point gap at the top. The vast 67,000 home crowd thought another win was assured – until Danny Murphy curled home an exquisite free-kick to take the points back to Merseyside. The following Saturday it was the turn of second-placed Arsenal. With their confidence high, Liverpool put on one of their most dazzling displays of the season, hammering the Gunners 4–0, with goals from Gerrard, Owen, Barmby and Fowler.

By then, UEFA Cup excitement was growing. Barmby had been the hero

[THE VAST 67,000 OLD TRAFFORD CROWD THOUGHT A WIN WAS ASSURED – UNTIL DANNY MURPHY CURLED HOME AN EXQUISITE FREE-KICK TO TAKE THE POINTS BACK TO MERSEYSIDE.]

of the early rounds, scoring the single away goal that sank Rapid Bucharest, then helping the team record a 3–2 victory over Slovan Liberec in the Czech Republic. Playing in Athens, before an intimidating, and increasingly hysterical, Olympiakos crowd, Barmby was again the key man, grabbing the first goal in a hard-fought 2–2 draw. Back at Anfield, he set up Heskey's opening goal, then rounded off a brilliant individual display by netting the second. Liverpool were through to round four – and looking forward to a date with their 1980s foes, Roma.

A two-month gap between the European ties left them free to concentrate on the domestic competitions. With a packed programme ahead, Houllier decided to bolster the squad with two more quality internationals. First to arrive was Igor Biscan, a powerfully built

NICK BARMBY
His brilliant Cup form helped Liverpool progress in Europe.

Croatian midfielder bought from Dinamo Zagreb for £5.5 million. Then, in January 2001, the manager captured Barcelona's world-class striker Jari Litmanen on a free transfer. Back in his native Finland, Litmanen was a legend whose face even adorned the country's postage stamps. He had made more than 60 appearances for his country, inspired Ajax to a hat-trick of Dutch championship successes, and helped the Amsterdam side win the 1995 European Cup. Despite his obvious talents he had struggled to find a regular first-team place after switching to Spain. But now, thanks to the Bosman ruling, he was joining the club he had supported since boyhood.

He made his debut in the Worthington Cup semi-final against Crystal Palace. In the early stages of the tournament Liverpool had been rampant, sweeping aside Chelsea and

TOP 10
LEAGUE APPS 1998-2004

1.	JAMIE CARRAGHER	214
2.	MICHAEL OWEN	214
3.	SAMI HYYPIA	183
4.	STEVEN GERRARD	170
5.	DANNY MURPHY	169
6.	EMILE HESKEY	150
7.	DIETMAR HAMANN	144
8.	STEPHANE HENCHOZ	135
9.	PATRIK BERGER	125
10.	VLADIMIR SMICER	111

Fulham, and running up a record 8-0 away victory at Stoke. But, at Selhurst Park, they were hesitant, allowing Palace to build a 2-1 advantage, and encouraging their striker Clinton Morrison to taunt the Reds' forwards publicly before the return leg. It was a bad mistake. Back at Anfield a deadly Liverpool hit five, and Morrison capped a blank Palace performance by missing a golden chance to pull one back – right in front of the Kop.

Houllier's team – for all the new faces, differing nationalities and constant rotation – had begun to gel. At the beginning of February a capacity Anfield crowd saw them beat West Ham 3-0 to go third in the Premiership. Manchester United had virtually clinched the title, but Liverpool were in a Champions League spot, making solid progress in the FA and UEFA Cups, and through to their first domestic final in six years. No English club had ever won three knock-out tournaments in one season. But an increasingly confident Houllier declared that nothing was beyond his young side: "If we aim for the moon, maybe we'll land among the stars."

WE'RE ALL GOING TO...CARDIFF?

The first test came in south Wales, home of Cardiff's new Millennium Stadium. The breathtaking 76,000-seat arena had taken over from Wembley as the temporary stage for all England's domestic finals. And the Worthington Cup climax featuring Liverpool and Birmingham City was its curtain-raiser.

The high two-tiered stands around the stadium helped stoke one of the loudest and most intense Cup final atmospheres of modern times, with Birmingham's supporters eager to see their team add to their one major honour and the travelling Kopites desperate for a return to the glory days. In the preceding weeks the Liverpool fans had read a constant stream of stories surrounding captain Robbie Fowler: his history of problems off the field, claims of his unhappiness with the rotation system, and rumours of multi-million-pound bids from

Premiership rivals. For a while it seemed as though he wouldn't feature. But, following an injury to Michael Owen, the man the Kop called "God" was included in attack.

And it was a day he will remember. With 29 minutes gone, Heskey headed Westerveld's long clearance into

> "I GOT GOOSE PIMPLES WHEN I WAS FLYING THROUGH THE AIR, AND WHEN I KEPT THE SHOT OUT IT WAS THE BEST FEELING IN THE WORLD."
> SANDER WESTERVELD

WORTHINGTON CUP FINAL, 2001
Westerveld makes the crucial save, and Fowler lifts the season's first trophy.

Fowler's path. He looked up, spotted the 'keeper off his line, and fired a spectacular left-foot volley into the net from 20 yards out. "It was a wonderful strike," Phil Thompson said later. "Only Robbie could score a goal like that on such a big occasion." But it wasn't enough. After Gerrard limped off with second-half cramp, Birmingham put Liverpool under relentless pressure. Three minutes into injury time Henchoz brought down City's Martin O'Connor in the 18-yard area – then watched Darren Purse equalize from the spot.

Half an hour later, the score remained at 1–1 and the referee signalled a penalty shoot-out – the first in a final in the competition's history. Kicking towards the Liverpool end, Birmingham fluffed their opening chance, allowing the Reds to build up a 3–2 lead with strikes from McAllister, Barmby and Ziege. Parity was restored when Hamann blasted his effort straight at the 'keeper, and, when Fowler converted with a cool chip, the contest ended level at 4–4. It meant sudden death: if one side scored and the other missed, that would be it. Jamie Carragher made no mistake with his kick. But then 20-year-old Andrew Johnson sent a weak effort to Westerveld's left – and the Liverpool 'keeper dived to save.

"I'm sure most of our supporters were really nervous, but I can honestly say I wasn't," said the Dutchman afterwards. 'I got goose pimples when I was flying through the air, and

RAPTURE IN ROME
Owen grabbed both goals in the Olympic stadium.

THINK TWICE...
Referee Garcia-Aranda changes his mind about awarding a penalty to Roma.

when I kept the shot out it was the best feeling in the world." It felt pretty good for everyone else, too. After a six-year absence, silverware had returned to the Anfield trophy cabinet.

THE GHOSTS OF EUROPE PAST

The games began to come thick and fast. Just a week before their Cardiff triumph, Liverpool had booked their FA Cup quarter-final place with a stirring 4–2 win over Manchester City, and that victory was sandwiched between the two UEFA Cup clashes with Roma. The Italian giants, six points clear at the top of Serie A, and boasting top-drawer internationals like Batistuta, Totti and Delvecchio, were everyone's favourites to win the home tie. Before boarding the plane, even Houllier seemed nervous: "They are the best side left in the tournament and one of the best sides in Europe right now. I feel our team is not as strong as Roma's but, over two games, you never know."

He needn't have worried. On a momentous night in the Olympic Stadium, Liverpool put on a performance that recalled the glories of '77 and '84. Hamann and McAllister dominated the midfield; Hyypia and Henchoz smothered every Roma attack; while, up front, a fit-again Owen confirmed his status as one of the world's top strikers. Pouncing on a casual back-pass just after the interval, he sidestepped a challenge and fired in from an acute angle. With less

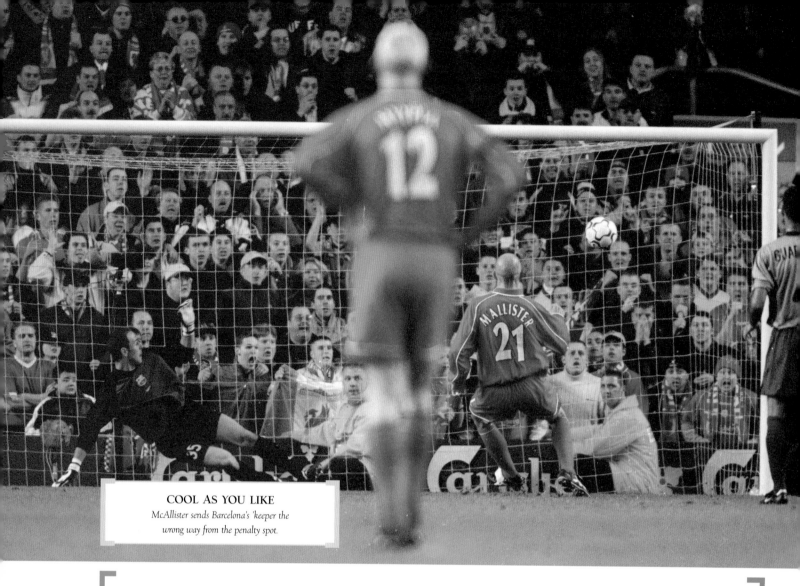

COOL AS YOU LIKE
McAllister sends Barcelona's 'keeper the wrong way from the penalty spot.

[A **QUARTER** OF A **CENTURY** AFTER LIVERPOOL'S **LEGENDARY** WIN AT THE NOU CAMP, THE **NEW-LOOK** REDS **SILENCED** THE **CATALAN** CROWD ONCE MORE.]

than 20 minutes remaining, he added his second – a perfectly placed near-post header from McAllister's cross.

Some newspapers claimed the Italians hadn't taken the UEFA Cup seriously. But they brought their strongest squad for the return at Anfield – and showed a determination and commitment that put Liverpool on the back foot from the kick-off. The ground was throbbing. The club had declared it a Bob Paisley "tribute night", and the Kop was festooned with banners celebrating the memory of Liverpool's most successful manager. When the referee awarded a penalty for an offence against Heskey it looked like a party atmosphere would take over. But then Owen

TOP 10
LEAGUE GOALS 1998-2004

1.	MICHAEL OWEN	117
2.	EMILE HESKEY	39
3.	ROBBIE FOWLER	37
4.	DANNY MURPHY	25
5.	PATRIK BERGER	21
6.	STEVEN GERRARD	20
7.	SAMI HYYPIA	15
8.	JAMIE REDKNAPP	15
9.	STEVE MCMANAMAN	15
10.	PAUL INCE	14

planted a feeble kick straight at the 'keeper – and a tiring Roma were given a fresh lease of life.

With 70 minutes gone, Guigou hit a 25-yard screamer that cancelled out some of his team's 2–0 deficit. Then, with the game edging towards the final whistle, a Roma cross hit Babbel on the elbow. The Kop held its breath as the referee appeared to point to the spot. But just seconds later the Spanish official walked away from the 18-yard area and signalled for a corner. The Italians went wild. In the minute of mayhem that followed, they had four players cautioned. Tomassi, the most vehement protester, later saw his yellow card turn red, as his frustration led to a series of cynical fouls. Roma's anger made them lose focus. They failed to threaten Liverpool's goalmouth again, and by the end of the tie it was the home fans who were celebrating. The Reds had gone through – by the skin of their teeth.

The fourth round tie with Porto was a much simpler affair: a goalless away draw followed by a clinical 2–0 victory at Anfield. On a night when Gerrard staked his most powerful claim to the Young Player of the Year Award, Owen was also at his best in attack. His headed goal, following a clean strike by Murphy, wrapped up the contest by half-time. And, at the end of 90 minutes, the overall team performance had Houllier purring: "We had a strategy, developed it and grew in confidence after our goals. There are teams that will now be wary of meeting Liverpool."

Were Barcelona one of them? Not judging by their statements before the semi-final. The Spanish giants had airily dismissed Liverpool as a negative side, a shadow of the teams who had dominated European football in the late 1970s and early 1980s. In public, at least, they were relishing the Merseysiders' visit. So were the 90,000 fans who turned out to see the likes of Rivaldo, Kluivert and Overmars display their talents – and convert their dominance into goals.

But it didn't happen. A quarter of a century after Liverpool's legendary win at the Nou Camp, the new-look Reds silenced the Catalan crowd once more. Houllier's 4-5-1 formation soaked up everything the home side could throw at it, and a neutered Barcelona attack had little option but to fire in hopeful long-range shots. By the end of the 90 minutes, Westerveld had hardly

TOP 10	
HAT-TRICKS 1998-2004	
1. MICHAEL OWEN	10
2. ROBBIE FOWLER	4
3. PATRIK BERGER	1
4. EMILE HESKEY	1

THREE OF THE BEST
Owen's hat-trick ensured Premiership victory over Newcastle.

broken sweat. His defence, along with Houllier's game-plan, had strangled one of the world's most lethal strike-forces.

The stage was set for Anfield's biggest European occasion in years – a night to stir memories of Inter Milan and St Etienne; a chance to ease the awful legacy of Heysel, and the years of failure and frustration that had followed. And it was a night when Liverpool did not disappoint. From the moment McAllister calmly side-footed his 44th-minute penalty into the net, his defensive team-mates closed down the Spanish attack once again. Westerveld, completely failing to clear a Petit through-ball, caused one moment of second-half panic, but Kluivert, having a game he would want to forget, reacted too late, and let the ball roll harmlessly out of play.

The game ended 1–0, and the emotional full-time scenes will be long remembered. Scarves, tears, a bow from Houllier, and a Kop banner that summed up everyone's thoughts: "LFC: Unparalleled history, glorious future."

GREAT SCOT

McAllister's goal had underlined his pivotal role in the run-in to Liverpool's marathon season. Just three nights earlier he had starred in an unforgettable Goodison derby that shattered Everton's season and got the Reds' Champions League ambitions back on track. Until the final minute, it had all the hallmarks of a typically dramatic but frustrating contest. Liverpool had twice thrown away a lead, Fowler's penalty had struck a post, and Biscan had received a red card for a reckless tackle. But then, with just seconds left on the clock, Liverpool won a free-kick

Tuesday, 30 June 1998 was the day that changed Michael Owen's life. He had already made his name in England after ending his first full season as the Premiership's joint top scorer. But it was at the Stade Geoffroy Guichard in St Etienne that Owen earned global recognition with an unforgettable World Cup goal against Argentina.

It was his temperament as much as his talent – he also converted a penalty in the ill-fated shoot-out – which impressed observers. Suddenly this 18-year-old had left an indelible mark on the world game. Not bad for someone who, just two years earlier, had been earning only £170 a month as an Anfield apprentice!

So fast that he once ran 100m in 10.9 seconds; a promising schoolboy boxer; skilled in golf and snooker (and the proud possessor of a *Blue Peter* badge), it's easy to imagine him succeeding in whatever sport he chose to specialize.

Owen and goals have always gone together. He has been a clinical finisher ever since lacing on his first pair of football boots at the age of seven. In the early 1990s, he broke Ian Rush's record for Deeside Primary School with 97 goals.

Owen was schooled by his father, Terry, a former Everton professional. And the youngster, who idolized Gary Lineker, dreamed of following in the footsteps of both men by carving out a career at Goodison Park. But, after a spell at the FA's School of Excellence at Lilleshall, he opted for an Anfield future. His goals helped Liverpool win the 1996 FA Youth Cup, and on his 17th birthday he signed professional terms.

He made his senior debut as a substitute at Selhurst Park in May 1997, and, needless to say, got on the score sheet. He then

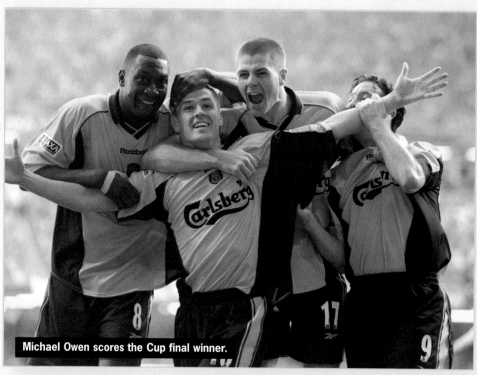

Michael Owen scores the Cup final winner.

In 2001 Owen scored 37 times in 57 games throughout the year. They included the dramatic late double in the FA Cup final against Arsenal, and a famous hat-trick in England's 5-1 World Cup demolition of Germany.

rapidly turned into the saviour of an underachieving Liverpool side, became the youngest England international of the century, received the Young Player of the Year award, and scored his World Cup wonder goal ... all within a timespan of 13 months.

A damaged hamstring in April, 1999 raised doubts about his future fitness. But, typically, despite subsequent injuries, Owen always bounced back to defy the doubters. Indeed, in 2001 he scored no less than 37 times in 57 games throughout the year. His tally included the dramatic late double in the FA Cup final against Arsenal, and a famous hat-trick in England's 5–1 World Cup demolition of Germany in Munich.

Those exploits earned him the coveted Ballon D'Or, and made him the only serving Liverpool player in history to be European Footballer of the Year. There was further pride

in April 2002 when, at the age of 22 years, 124 days, he became the second-youngest skipper in England's history against Paraguay. As captain, he scored twice in the European Championship win over Slovakia to celebrate his 50th cap – at the age of 23 years 7 months, he is the youngest ever to reach a half-century.

Owen bagged four in a 6–0 demolition of West Bromwich in April 2003, equalling the club's record Premiership away win and taking him past 100 League goals in 185 appearances. His headed equaliser in the 1–1 UEFA Cup draw at Olimpija Ljubljana in September 2003 edged him past the 20-goal European club record he had shared with Ian Rush, a total Owen increased to 22 later in the campaign. In all, Michael Owen has scored 158 goals in 297 appearances for Liverpool and looks certain to get many more.

midway inside the Everton half. And, with the most impudent, outrageous effort of his career, McAllister curled the ball into the net from an incredible 44 yards.

That victory meant more than just three points. It instilled a sense of belief in both the players and the fans, and made anything seem possible. From that moment, the team played with an air of invincibility, and it was McAllister who was at its heart. Three days after the Barcelona triumph, he was on target in a 3–1 home win over Tottenham. The following weekend he scored Liverpool's second in a 2–0 victory at Coventry. Seventy-two hours later the Reds won at Bradford – and the Scotsman was on the scoresheet for the fifth successive game.

Ominously for Liverpool's rivals, Michael Owen also scored in that match. He followed it with a hat-trick in a League win against Newcastle, then two more in a home draw with Chelsea. Liverpool were now back in third spot. With 60 games of the season gone, they faced two cup finals and a Premiership clash that would determine their European future.

According to Houllier, they were "playing for immortality". And the man dubbed "the baby-faced assassin" was on their side.

St Michael

Cardiff, 12 May 2001: temperatures soared into the 80s and the hopes of Liverpool fans rose even higher. "What We Achieve In Life Echoes Through Eternity," proclaimed one banner; "At Gérard's Command – Unleash Hell," read another. The script lines from the Oscar-winning movie *Gladiator* were designed to inspire, as were the reminders of the Reds' Millennium Stadium triumph three months earlier: "We always win in Wales," sang the travelling Kopites.

But their confidence was about to be shaken. Arsenal dominated this FA Cup final from the off, pegging their

opponents into their own half and forcing desperate clearances from the Liverpool back four. In midfield, Patrick Vieira reigned supreme. If team-mate Thierry Henry had taken only half his chances, the game would have been dead by half-time.

To be fair, the Frenchman almost did get on the scoresheet after 17 minutes. He saw his powerful goal-bound shot stopped by the arm of Henchoz, then watched in disbelief as his penalty appeals were waved away. Out of 73,000 people, the referee and his assistant appeared to be the only two who didn't witness the Liverpool defender make contact. No goal, no caution, not even a corner kick.

PICK THAT ONE OUT
The goal that finished off Arsenal in Cardiff.

But the relief was merely temporary. Arsenal's attacks came in waves, while Liverpool's strike-force of Heskey and Owen looked impotent. When Freddie Ljungberg skipped past Westerveld to fire in the opener, the only surprise was that it had taken 70 minutes. But finally the Londoners had made their pressure count – and no one could doubt that they deserved it.

It was time for rotation. McAllister, who had spent much of the game cowering under a towel, protecting his bald pate from the sun, had been exposed to its full glare on the pitch. Houllier then sent on Fowler to add more punch to the attack, and a fresh-legged Berger replaced the weary Murphy.

The substitutions gave Liverpool an improved shape and a late injection of life, but the game still looked beyond them. Then, with just eight minutes left, McAllister's free-kick spread panic in the Arsenal box. Centre-back Martin Keown strained to reach the cross. The ball skimmed off the top of his head. Babbel nodded it into Owen's path. And the little striker fired an instinctive volley past 'keeper David Seaman.

Never has a match changed more swiftly. Arsenal, who had oozed confidence and authority, suddenly

With four European Cups to their credit, the name of Liverpool still figured among the elite of the Continent. However, since their last European final at the Heysel Stadium, the Reds' foreign excursions had not been worthy of their illustrious history.

Really, a club of Liverpool's stature should have been familiar with the Champions League format long before Gérard Houllier guided them to the quarter-finals in 2001–02. And apart from a 1997 Cup Winners' Cup semi-final appearance, they had not even had a sniff of success in the other European tournaments.

That's why a victory over Alaves in the UEFA Cup final was so important. It would propel Liverpool back to the forefront of European football, earn them a crack at the prestigious Super Cup, and a chance to pit themselves against the Continent's best once more.

The clash at Dortmund's Westfalenstadion was their 62nd game of a marathon campaign. It was a season in which they had been labelled negative, despite already racking up 118 goals. On this night in Germany they would make their critics look even more foolish. They would put five past Alaves, in what was to be one of the most exhilarating matches of all time.

The Reds' fans were up for it. The 20,000 who travelled to Germany had just seen their team win the FA Cup in the most dramatic manner, and now nothing seemed beyond them. From early in the day, Dortmund's main square had been awash with red, white and, yes, blue, as Liverpool and Alaves supporters stood united, swapping shirts, scarves, songs and stories.

Just four minutes after the kick-off before the Merseyside contingent were on their feet, celebrating Markus Babbel's headed opener. Any thoughts that Houllier's side would erect a defensive barrier disappeared when Steven Gerrard ran onto Michael Owen's pass to double Liverpool's lead after 17 minutes.

That was that, everyone thought. And it might have been had the Spaniards not thrown on striker Ivan Alonso for defender Dan Eggen. Within five minutes the substitute had reduced the arrears, heading home a cross from wing-back Cosmin Contra, a constant torment.

However, five minutes before the break, Gary McAllister restored the Reds' two-goal advantage by converting a penalty following a foul on Owen. Again, that should have been game over. But Alaves stunned Liverpool with two Javi Moreno goals inside five minutes, shortly after the re-start.

Mysteriously, and fatally, Moreno was substituted at the time when Alaves were on the ascendancy, and Houllier replaced Emile Heskey with Robbie Fowler. The double change turned the tide in the Reds' favour, and Fowler appeared to have settled matters with a stunning individual goal in the 73rd minute.

But, incredibly, with just a minute left on the clock, Alaves hit back with a Jordi Cruyff header, forcing extra-time and a "golden goal" decider.

The sudden death period brought chances at both ends, plus sendings off for Magno and Antonio Karmona. And it was from the free-kick awarded for Karmona's foul on Vladimir Smicer that Liverpool's victory came. Set-piece specialist McAllister flighted the ball

Houllier and his players paraded their latest piece of silverware around the pitch: the historic Treble had been achieved.

beautifully into the Alaves penalty area – then watched in delight as Delfi Geli glanced inadvertently into his own net.

It was over. There was no chance to come back. On the field McAllister was buried under his team-mates; in the stands, strangers hugged and danced. Minutes later Houllier and his players paraded their latest piece of silverware around the pitch: the historic Treble had been achieved. "Our fans have been the driving force behind our tremendous season," said the Anfield boss. "I don't think we could have done it without their magnificent support. Today we have given them something back."

looked ragged. Liverpool, previously so cautious, threatened Seaman's goal with every move. Two minutes from time, Owen hunted down Berger's long ball from defence, sped past Lee Dixon and evaded a lunging tackle from Tony Adams. He was deep inside the Arsenal box, but had been forced to take the ball wide to the left. Surely this naturally right-sided striker couldn't score with his weaker foot? From such an impossible angle? Against England's undisputed number one? Yes! Yes!! Yes!!!

What followed passed in a blur: Owen performing a cartwheel; Henry sinking to his knees; the entire Liverpool bench erupting on to the pitch. The celebrations in the stands still hadn't subsided by the time the final whistle blew. And then there were more images to cherish: Fowler calling on an injured Jamie Redknapp to

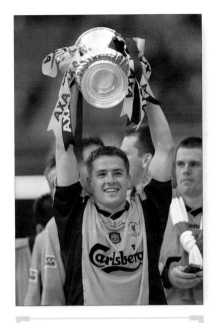

THE BOY DONE GOOD
Owen lifts the FA Cup.

help lift the trophy; Carragher sporting a red top-hat; the full squad leading 20,000 Liverpool fans in a rousing rendition of "You'll Never Walk Alone".

Twelve years after Arsenal had stolen the League championship with a last-gasp Anfield winner, Liverpool had got their revenge. It was a measure of the new team's fighting spirit, and a vindication of Houllier's tactics. It was also a personal triumph for Michael Owen. "I can't believe what's just happened," he told reporters in the tunnel. "I'll go to bed every night dreaming about those goals."

Yet the amazing season still hadn't finished. Five days later the team lifted the UEFA Cup following the most exciting European final of recent times (see page 186). Then, with a unique treble of knock-out trophies in the

2001 TREBLE PARADE
An estimated half a million people welcomed the team home.

cabinet, they booked their place in the Champions League with a 4–0 win at Charlton.

Half a million people welcomed them back to Merseyside the day after that last Premiership game. The triumphal open-topped bus tour recalled the halcyon days of the 1970s and 1980s, and confirmed Houllier's place among Liverpool's legends. More than four decades had passed since a single-minded Scot breezed into Anfield and stirred a sleeping giant. Now an equally focused Frenchman had restored the club's flagging spirits and wounded pride. "Are you Shankly in disguise?" sang an adoring band of supporters at the city's Pier Head. They knew a saviour when they saw one.

THE FAMOUS FIVE

The manager showed his confidence in the squad with a marked lack of activity in the close-season transfer market. Apart from paying £4 million to bring Monaco's John Arne Riise to Anfield, Houllier spent most of the summer securing the futures of existing players. By the time the new campaign got under way, Gerrard, Hamann, Henchoz and Carragher had all signed contracts tying them to Anfield until 2005. Owen – by now rated in the £50 million bracket – was also close to a deal that would keep him in a Liverpool shirt for another four years.

But there was a growing question mark over Fowler. He had been linked with moves to rival clubs all summer, and his involvement in a training-ground bust-up with Phil Thompson sent the rumour machine into overdrive.

FOWLER'S DELIGHT
"I always dreamt of doing this," said the striker.

ANOTHER ONE FOR CHARITY
Sami Hyypia lifts the Shield following victory over Manchester United.

Not that those stories unsettled his team-mates. As an axed Fowler watched the Charity Shield clash with Manchester United from the Millennium Stadium stands, Liverpool turned their early dominance into goals. McAllister struck a psychological blow, converting a penalty after less than 60 seconds. A quarter of an hour later, Owen doubled the advantage, pouncing on a defensive error and steering a close-range shot past Fabien Barthez. The Premiership champions came back strongly, and grabbed a goal through Dutch striker Ruud van Nistelrooy, but Liverpool's tightly-organized defence held out. They recorded their third successive win over United, and claimed their fourth trophy of 2001.

And, within a fortnight, they collected another. Facing European champions Bayern Munich, the Reds brought the Super Cup to Anfield with a highly impressive 3–2 victory. Riise, playing on his old ground, opened the scoring after 22 minutes; Heskey and Owen, who terrorized the Bayern defence throughout, both claimed goals either side of the interval. The win in Monaco was another landmark for Liverpool, as they became the only English team to lift five trophies in a single calendar year. It also gave the players a massive confidence boost as they prepared for their debut in the Champions League.

A place in the group stage had been secured with a qualifying round stroll against Finland's FC Haka. Liverpool won the away leg 5–0, with Owen claiming a hat-trick, and both Hyypia and Litmanen getting a rapturous reception from

JOHN ARNE RIISE
I wanna know-ow-ow how you scored that goal.

their countrymen. Back at Anfield, though, the biggest cheers were for Fowler. Restored to the team after apologizing to Thompson, he marked his return by getting on target in a comfortable 4–1 win.

Houllier's hard line with Fowler showed his commitment to the highest standards both on and off the pitch. Despite the recent successes, the manager demanded further improvement and wouldn't allow anything to stand in his way. There was no place for sentiment. Westerveld – whose penalty-saving heroics had helped win the Worthington Cup – found himself out of the team for good after his mistakes led to a Premiership defeat at Bolton. Within days Houllier had recruited Poland's number one Jerzy Dudek and brought in the England Under-21 'keeper Chris Kirkland as cover.

The Bolton reverse was typical of Liverpool's early-season problems. There was also a shock 3–1 loss at home to Aston Villa, and an embarrassing Worthington Cup exit at the hands of Grimsby. Houllier found his options

limited. Barmby and Berger were both long-term casualties, and Owen had been sidelined with hamstring problems. Even worse, the ultra-dependable Markus Babbel was stricken with a debilitating virus that would keep him out of action for a year.

But, once again, the players displayed their fighting qualities, winning the Goodison derby, then stringing together further victories over Spurs and Newcastle. As Leeds visited Anfield in mid-October, the fans were again talking about their title prospects. But then came dramatic news about their manager – and the fate of the Premiership suddenly seemed irrelevant.

IT'S MORE IMPORTANT THAN THAT

It was at half-time in the Leeds match that Houllier began complaining of chest pains. A swift examination by the club doctor led to further hospital tests and emergency open-heart surgery. Doctors had discovered an "acute dissection of the aorta", a condition affecting the largest artery of the body. Without surgery, they were sure it would lead to internal bleeding and death. Houllier gave them permission to operate – and the ten hours of life-saving treatment began.

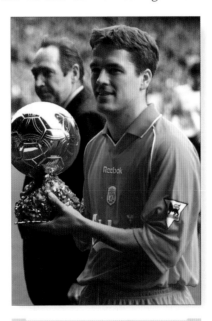

ULTIMATE ACCOLADE
Owen is named European Footballer of the Year.

The surgery proved a complete success, but it was clear that Liverpool's inspirational manager would be back later rather than sooner. "A return to the club is the furthest thing from our mind at the moment," said Liverpool's chief executive Rick Parry. "What has happened has put football into perspective." It was true. Houllier's sudden illness had given the club, its players and fans a severe jolt – and a reminder that football really wasn't more than a matter of life and death, as his most famous predecessor once claimed. Houllier faced months of recuperation. Many were afraid the team might lose its way without him, but no one wanted him to endanger his long-term health by rushing back too soon.

MANAGER GÉRARD **HOULLIER**

Fans welcome Gérard Houllier back from illness.

"When I came I was described as a revolutionary with a guillotine. Actually I prefer to convince people rather than dictate. But if I can't convince then I have to dictate."
GÉRARD HOULLIER

Well, since when was Anfield a democracy anyway? After ending a decade of gloom, winning five trophies in a single year, and twice guiding the team into the Champions League, Gérard Houllier earned the right to do things his way. He had won the faith of Liverpool fans everywhere. "In Ged We Trust," declares the Kopites' banner.

Their idol once stood among them. As a young teacher in the late sixties, Houllier spent a year at the city's Alsop secondary school, and soon fell in love with the style of football played at Anfield. His first match on the terraces came in 1969, when the Reds ran up a record 10–0 European win over Dundalk. "The Kop was very unusual – you wouldn't find that in France or anywhere else 30 years ago," he later recalled. "The noise, the singing, the moving. It was swaying all the time; you could only see half of the game! It was quite an atmosphere."

Football was already in his blood. His father was the director of a French amateur club and, on his return home, Houllier took an interest in how the players were coached and prepared. He later became a coach himself, and between 1976 and 1982, guided Noeux-les-Mines from the Fifth to the Second Division of the French League. At FC Lens, he boosted his reputation by helping them to a UEFA Cup place. And, as coach of Paris St Germain, he inspired the team to the French title.

Houllier was known for his scientific approach to the game, placing emphasis not just on skill, but on tactics, preparation and mental attitude. It was the sort of approach required by the French FA who, in 1988, offered him a job assisting Michel Platini as coach of the national team. He subsequently took over from Platini, but decided to quit

True red.

Bringing the silverware back to Anfield.

when France failed to qualify for the 1994 World Cup finals. However, working as Technical Director, he became instrumental in developing the team that won the tournament four years later.

After that success Houllier let it be known that he wanted a return to club football. He considered offers from Sheffield Wednesday and Celtic, but, following talks with Liverpool official Peter Robinson, decided on the controversial managerial job-share at Anfield. Houllier was genuinely upset when that arrangement failed to work out, but, as soon as Roy Evans left him in sole charge, he began the radical shake-up that eventually brought the honours rolling back.

To Houllier, football was not so much his business as his life. Sleep was an occupational hazard and a waste of precious hours which could be devoted to work.

To Houllier, football was not so much his business as his life. Sleep was an occupational hazard and a waste of precious hours which could be devoted to work. Even when incapacitated after emergency surgery, he remained in constant touch with the club, giving advice to Phil Thompson on tactics, and even helping organize transfer deals.

Some people feared that a full-time return to the game would kill him; those close to him knew that football would keep him alive.

An engaging, intelligent man, Houllier – to quote Liverpudlians – gave them their pride back. Forward thinking and progressive, he dragged the club out of its time-warp, while respecting the philosophy laid down by Shankly. Through his methods, Liverpool initially registered progress in every season of his reign, moving from seventh place to fourth, to third and then second in 2002. Then the team missed out on fourth place in 2003, but made it to the Champions League qualifiers a year later. And, for the fans, there'll always be the memory of that Treble.

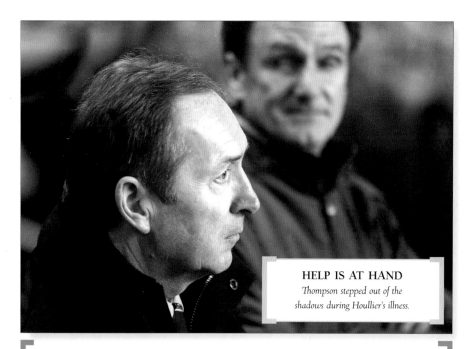

HELP IS AT HAND
Thompson stepped out of the shadows during Houllier's illness.

> IN HIS FIRST SIX GAMES AS BOSS, THOMPSON HAD GUIDED LIVERPOOL A STAGE CLOSER TO THE EUROPEAN CUP, AND TO THE VERY SUMMIT OF THE PREMIERSHIP.

So the reins were temporarily passed to Phil Thompson, the assistant manager who had given Houllier his total loyalty since the day the Frenchman took sole charge of team affairs. The one-time skipper began with a Champions League victory at Dynamo Kiev, followed by an away draw with Portugal's Boavista, and a 2–0 home win over Borussia Dortmund. In the League he oversaw victories over Leicester and Charlton. Then, with the Kop displaying a spectacular mosaic of the French national flag, the Reds overwhelmed Manchester United 3–1. In his first six games as boss, Thompson had guided Liverpool a stage closer to the European Cup, and to the very summit of the Premiership.

"The biggest pressure has been carrying on Gérard's good work," he told

UP TO THE TASK
The team won five of their first six matches under Thompson.

reporters. "I didn't want to let him down, and I wanted to give him something to come back to. It's been difficult, but it's been great as well because the results have been positive. The results have given Gérard a lift, too, because the well-being of this club means so much to him.'

Sadly, the results didn't last. A 3–1 home defeat by Barcelona dented the team's Champions League ambitions. Arsenal exacted some FA Cup revenge with a fourth-round knockout. And a poor League run saw Liverpool drop to fifth spot by mid-January. The fans also had to bow to the inevitable and wave goodbye to Fowler. His long-predicted transfer finally materialized at the end of November when Leeds tabled an £11 million bid. The move came just a month after he had scored a hat-trick against Leicester, and ended a glorious Anfield career that had yielded 171 goals in 330 games.

But the Reds' attack still boasted Owen, the prolific striker who had just been crowned European Footballer of the Year. And he was soon joined by Nicolas Anelka, the former Arsenal hitman keen to resurrect a career that had stalled with Paris St Germain. Anelka had worked with Houllier as a youngster in France, and it was the manager who interrupted his convalescence to help arrange the loan deal. Given the player's trouble-some reputation, many fans considered him a risk. But his pace, touch and workrate delighted the sceptics – and his equalizer in the Anfield derby was enough to win over the remaining doubters.

Their winter blip behind them, Liverpool were climbing the table again. Danny Murphy's strike at Old Trafford had lifted them into third place. Emile Heskey's five goals in three games helped them make up further ground on the leaders. Then a 2–1 victory at Middlesbrough saw them jump to second. The title race was becoming the most exciting for years with Arsenal, Manchester United and Liverpool all vying for top spot. For the Reds of Anfield, European success also beckoned. There could not be a better time for their manager to make his return.

ALLEZ, HOULLIER

It happened before the Champions League tie with Roma – a night to rank among Anfield's best. As the players took to the field, Houllier emerged from the tunnel to view the Kop's "Allez" mosaic, and to accept their rapturous and emotional welcome. After draws in Italy and Barcelona, and in the two games with Galatasaray, his team needed to win by at least two goals to go through. They also faced a Roma side desperate to avenge their controversial UEFA Cup exit at Liverpool's hands the previous year. But from the moment Houllier took his long-awaited bow, the result

THE ITALIAN JOB
Heskey's header secured the win against Roma.

never felt in doubt. "It was a special atmosphere that only this ground can produce," Thompson later declared. "This was St Etienne – Part Two."

Jari Litmanen, in for the injured Owen, started the ball rolling with a coolly taken penalty after seven minutes. A rampant Liverpool then flooded forward, with both Gerrard and Riise going agonizingly close before the interval. In the second half the Italian champions stirred and threatened a fightback. But on 63 minutes Murphy floated a free-kick into the Roma box, and Heskey rose above a sea of defenders to head home the second. Liverpool went through to the last eight in the Champions League, the players went off to a deafening ovation, and both Houllier and Thompson were visibly moved as thousands stayed behind to chant their names.

But that emotional evening turned out to be the season's high point. As Europe's top tournament reached the knock-out stage, Liverpool took a 1–0 advantage to Bayer Leverkusen, only for their dreams to be shattered by a 4–2 defeat in Germany. On the domestic front their brilliant late run twice took them to the top of the League, but Arsenal – in even more devastating form – won their games in hand to lift the title.

So to the last day of the season, a 5–0 thrashing of Ipswich, the highest points total for more than a decade, and automatic qualification for the Champions League. Once, a runners-up spot would have caused furrowed brows around Anfield, but, among the 44,000 who packed the ground every other week, there were few complaints. Those fans had witnessed another extraordinary chapter in the life of Liverpool FC: a season in which the club lost its manager for five months, yet showed the spirit, character and resilience that have won friends and admirers the world over.

Houllier, now firmly back at the helm, was busy in the transfer market during the World Cup summer of 2002. Senegal sprang a sensation in the opening game of the finals in Japan and South Korea by toppling reigning

WELCOME BACK, BOSS
The Kop's mosaic brought a tear to Houllier's eye.

champions France in Seoul and two of the players who helped that African nation make history by reaching the quarter-finals were soon Anfield-bound from their French clubs.

Forward El Hadji Diouf was signed for £10 million from Lens and Salif Diao, his international midfield team-mate, cost £5 million from Sedan. Houllier also signed midfielder Bruno Cheyrou for £3.7 million from Lille.

Another midfield player, Alou Diarra, joined on a Bosman free from Bayern Munich but was sent out on loan to Le Havre, and French goalkeeper Patrice Luzi was signed on a free from Monaco as back-up for Jerzy Dudek and Chris Kirkland.

These arrivals followed several departures from the club including the inspirational Scotland veteran Gary McAllister, who took up the challenge of managing Coventry City.

Others to leave were Nick Barmby, on an initial £2.75 million appearance-linked move to Leeds, Stephen Wright, who joined Sunderland for £3 million, and Jari Litmanen, on a free transfer to Ajax. Additionally, Houllier opted against the £12 million Anelka from Paris St Germain. After five months on loan at Anfield, the controversial striker ended up at Manchester City.

Houllier's revamping of his squad, following their second-place finish the previous season, stoked Kop ambitions for the new 2002–03 campaign. This, many believed, would be the season when all those years of championship yearning would end and the first League title since 1990 would land at Anfield.

Until November those dreams took wing as Liverpool swept to the Premiership summit. They brushed off a

THREE OF THE BEST
Michael Owen plants the ball beyond the reach of Manchester City keeper Peter Schmeichel for the first of his hat-trick of goals at Maine Road.

disappointing 1–0 Community Shield defeat by Double winners Arsenal at Cardiff's Millennium Stadium to launch a long, unbeaten League run.

Despite home goalkeeper Peter Enckelman saving a Michael Owen penalty with his outstretched leg, they opened with a 1–0 win at Aston Villa, thanks to a goal early in the second half from John Arne Riise. When the curtain went up at Anfield, it took Diouf, playing alongside Owen, just three minutes of his home debut to score against Southampton.

The Senegalese raider added another in the second half with a Danny Murphy penalty steering Liverpool to a 3–0 win. It extended the club's record of never losing a match when the England midfielder had scored and ensured their best Premiership start for eight years.

They then embarked on a series of three consecutive 2–2 draws – at Blackburn and home to Newcastle and Birmingham. That Liverpool had been ahead in all three games deepened their frustration and the two Anfield results were particularly galling for Houllier and his squad as they had squandered a two-goal lead in both.

Houllier responded by shaking up the side for the trip to the Reebok Stadium to face Bolton. Out went calf casualty Stephane Henchoz, Riise, Diouf and even Owen. In came Diao – lining up in defence for his first League start – Bruno Cheyrou for his first Premiership start, Emile Heskey and Milan Baros, the Czech Republic striker who had cost £3.3 million from Banik Ostrava in 2001.

It was Baros's first taste of League action in England and he responded with two great goals, taking his total to eight in his last three appearances, having scored four for the club's reserve side and two for his country the

> WHEN THE CURTAIN WENT UP AT ANFIELD, IT TOOK DIOUF, PLAYING ALONGSIDE OWEN, JUST THREE MINUTES OF HIS HOME DEBUT TO SCORE AGAINST SOUTHAMPTON.

previous weekend. However, it needed a late strike from Heskey to secure all three points for Liverpool and avoid a fourth consecutive 2–2 draw.

Owen again sat on the bench for Liverpool's next engagement – a 2–0 defeat at Valencia in their opening Champions League game – but was back when they resumed winning ways with a 2–0 defeat of West Bromwich and he rifled a hat-trick at Maine Road as Manchester City's 23-match unbeaten home record fell.

That 3–0 win was sandwiched between a 1–1 home draw with Basle and a 5–0 hammering of Spartak Moscow in the Champions League, the team's biggest European win for more than four years. Successive 1–0 wins over Chelsea at home and Leeds away, thanks to Diao's first League goal, took Liverpool to the top of the Premiership. Wins over Tottenham and West Ham kept them there until, inexplicably, their League form nosedived.

A 1–0 reverse at Boro on November 9 ended a 14-game unbeaten League run. Then followed a goalless home draw with Sunderland, who hardly crossed the halfway line, signalling the third-worst League sequence in the club's history — 11 games without a win.

It was January before they tasted another Premiership victory, Emile Heskey's only goal of the game giving them a 1–0 win at Southampton, and their title hopes were in ruins. Although Owen scored four and reached his century of League goals in a 6–0 rout of West Bromwich – equalling Liverpool's biggest away win in the Premiership – Anelka came back to haunt Liverpool in their penultimate match of the season.

The French striker scored both goals in Manchester City's 2–1 win at Anfield which meant that Liverpool's last game, at Chelsea, became a shoot-out for fourth place and the accompanying Champions League qualifying

spot. Sadly for Liverpool, the London club came out on top 2–1, pushing Houllier's side into fifth place.

So a League season that promised much ended on a downbeat note, as had the FA Cup and European quests. First Division Crystal Palace scored a shock 2–0 Anfield win in a fourth-round FA Cup replay and, despite Owen's hat-trick in Moscow for a 3–1 win over Spartak, a 1–0 home defeat by Valencia and a 3–3 draw in Basle ended Liverpool's Champions League hopes.

A switch to the UEFA Cup brought a 2–0 aggregate win over Vitesse Arnhem and a 3–0 knock-out of

SPUD GUN
Danny Murphy scores the winner against Aston Villa in the 4–3 Worthington Cup quarter-final win.

Auxerre, only for Liverpool to tumble out on a 3–1 aggregate to Celtic, who won an atmospheric Anfield quarter-final second leg 2–0. Liverpool's disappointment was eased by their Worthington Cup final triumph over Manchester United which showed that the side was still in the business of lifting trophies.

During the summer of 2003, Houllier signed players he felt would bolster both the attacking and defensive sides of his squad, paying Fulham £3.5 million for Republic of Ireland right-back Steve Finnan and recruiting Australian raider Harry Kewell in a £5 million move from Leeds. French teenagers Anthony Le Tallec, a midfielder, and striker Florent Sinama-Pongolle, also arrived for a joint fee of £6 million.

Moving out of Anfield were Abel Xavier, released to join Galatasaray, Patrik Berger, freed to sign for Portsmouth, and Markus Babbel, who joined Blackburn on a one-year loan. Gregory Vignal, too, moved out on loan, first to Rennes then to Espanyol.

But neither Finnan nor Kewell did full justice to their talents during their first season. Injury restricted Finnan to appearances in little more than half of Liverpool's matches, while Kewell, despite scoring 11 goals including characteristically spectacular strikes (notably against Levski Sofia and his former club Leeds), felt unfulfilled.

Steven Gerrard opens the scoring.

On a memorable March day in Wales in 2003, Liverpool's blended two sweet experiences: winning silverware and toppling fierce rivals Manchester United.

Despite Sir Alex Ferguson's side arriving at Cardiff's Millennium Stadium for the Worthington Cup Final as favourites to lift the trophy, it was Gérard Houllier's team who upset the odds to achieve more Anfield glory in the League Cup, the competition which has appeared in so many guises. They really put the lid on their foes from the opposite end of the East Lancashire Road by winning 2–0 under the stadium's closed roof.

Liverpool's journey to triumph began the previous November when they were paired with Southampton at Anfield in the third round. In their previous outing, four days earlier, they had beaten West Ham 2–0 at home in the Premiership with a brace of goals from Michael Owen.

Fulfilling his promise to give other players a taste of senior action Houllier made ten changes for the cup tie; Vladimir Smicer was the only player retained in the starting line-up.

Steven Gerrard, rested for the West Ham game, returned for his first stint as captain in place of absent Sami Hyypia – a taste of things to come – and 19-year-old local boy

Jon Otsemobor made his debut at right-back. It was also Markus Babbel's first competitive appearance for 15 months after his brave battle against a debilitating illness.

Southampton showed from early in the game that they meant business and Chris Kirkland, stepping into Liverpool's goal for Jerzy Dudek, earned the accolade of Man of the Match for a series of fine saves to keep them at bay.

The contest was still goalless when Liverpool won a 44th-minute free-kick. Patrik Berger, famed for his set-piece skills, let fly and the ball flashed into the net off visiting defender Michael Svensson. Southampton

equalised through Agustin Delgado early in the second half but two minutes later El Hadji Diouf regained Liverpool's lead and, on the hour, Milan Baros stamped their ticket to round four with a goal to clinch a 3–1 win.

Next up for Liverpool were Ipswich Town. They came to Anfield from the depths of Division One, but they proved stubborn opponents. Houllier utilised his squad, making eight changes from the previous game – a 2–1 home defeat by Manchester United – including debuts for Neil Mellor, who started, and John Welsh, who came on as a substitute.

They were rocked when Tommy Miller shot the East Anglian outsiders ahead inside the first quarter of an hour, a lead they maintained until nine minutes after the interval when Mark Venus felled Mellor and El Hadji Diouf equalised from the penalty spot. Ipswich, though, battled on without further breaches right through to the end of extra time before Liverpool won by the slimmest of margins – 5–4 on penalties. Ipswich's Jamie Clapham was the only errant taker out of ten when his kick hit the bar and flew over.

Liverpool had to travel to Aston Villa in the quarter-final on a night when patience was a virtue for fans and players alike. The kick-off was delayed by 80 minutes through ticket collection chaos and the match was four minutes into stoppage time, just before 11.00pm, when Danny Murphy rifled his second goal of the game to give Liverpool a thrilling 4–3 win.

In a see-saw contest, Villa, who had taken a first-half lead, came back from 1–3 down to equalise after Murphy's leveller and further Liverpool goals from Milan Baros and Gerrard. The dramatic victory set up a tense, two-leg semi-final collision with First Division promotion-chasers Sheffield United.

Liverpool lost 2–1 in the first game at Bramall Lane where their goal came from Mellor – his first at senior level – to mark his return to his native city. Two late goals from United's Michael Tonge ensured it would be a tough second leg. Although Diouf put Liverpool ahead on the night in the eighth minute, and so level overall, the outcome was still on a knife edge as the duel stretched into

extra time. To the Kop's relief, Owen swooped in the 107th minute for a 3–2 aggregate win to book a Cardiff collision with Manchester United and Liverpool's record ninth appearance in the final.

Houllier and his squad struck a psychological blow long before a ball was kicked in the final. They won the toss to wear their red strip, the traditional colours Liverpool wore when they beat United in the 1983 League Cup Final and the 2001 Charity Shield. It was a lucky omen, hinting at victory for Liverpool – and it was gloriously fulfilled.

Goalkeeper Dudek atoned for two fateful errors in the 2–1 Premiership defeat at Anfield the previous December by distinguishing himself under fire in Cardiff, denying Ruud van Nistelrooy on three occasions, as well as Juan Veron and Paul Scholes – and even when he was beaten, Stephane Henchoz cleared another Veron effort off the line.

Such defiance protected the lead Liverpool had snatched six minutes before the break when Murphy and John Arne Riise linked on the left to find Gerrard – and his 30-yard blast struck David Beckham's foot and looped over Fabien Barthez into the net.

Four minutes from the end, with United unable to pierce Liverpool's defences, the game was won. Dietmar Hamann intercepted the ball from Mikael Silvestre and played it into Owen's path. He raced away and planted a shot beyond Barthez to clinch victory and Liverpool's record seventh triumph in the competition they first won in 1981.

"When you win against Manchester United you need the whole team to play well – and that's what they did," enthused Gérard Houllier, after holding aloft his sixth trophy as manager. "I felt for the fans when they had to wait so long to get in at Villa in the semi-final and I was proud for them today. There is a great communion between the fans and the players."

Four minutes from time, with United unable to pierce Liverpool's defences, the game was won.

Michael Owen leads the celebrations.

"The manager bought me for a reason and as far as I'm concerned I haven't lived up to it," was the Aussie's honest verdict. "Nobody can do anything about it except me. I just haven't played like I should but I'm working to put it right." Kewell and Finnan (as a substitute) made their debuts in the season's curtain-raiser when Liverpool, without banned Steven Gerrard, came face to face with Roman Abramovich's Chelsea revolution.

Juan Veron put the visitors ahead and, although Michael Owen equalised with a twice-taken, second-half penalty, Jimmy Floyd Hasselbaink struck the winner three minutes from time to inflict Liverpool's first home defeat on the opening weekend since 1962.

Goalless draws at Aston Villa and at home to Tottenham left Houllier's side without a win in their opening three games – and five in all after successive defeats at the end of the previous season.

> THEIR RESPONSE NEXT TIME OUT WAS THE SWEETEST OF ALL: A 3-0 WIN AT CITY RIVALS EVERTON. THE PLAYERS POWERED INTO THE MERSEY DERBY RECORD BOOKS.

Their response next time out was the sweetest of all: an emphatic 3-0 win at city rivals Everton. Houllier named an unchanged side for only the third time in 99 Premiership games – which included Igor Biscan for injured Stephane Henchoz – and his players powered into the Mersey derby record books.

A goal in each half for Michael Owen, and Kewell's first for the club, secured a record fourth consecutive victory at Goodison and stretched their unbeaten derby run to eight matches. A 3-1 win at Blackburn a week later was marred by two serious injuries. Jamie Carragher's right leg was broken after a clumsy lunge by Lucas Neill, who was sent off, while Milan Baros suffered a broken ankle after a fair challenge, ironically from on-loan Anfield defender Babbel.

Both Carragher and Baros were ruled out until the New Year and Houllier declared: "I'd have forgone the three points to have these two players still available." With John Arne Riise and Emile Heskey coming in for the injured duo, Liverpool followed a 2-1 win over Leicester with a 1-1 draw at Olimpija Ljubljana to open their UEFA Cup campaign.

Owen's sixth goal in four games also took him into the club records. His headed equaliser was his 21st

European strike, overtaking the 20-goal tally he had previously shared with Ian Rush.

Although Owen scored again – from a penalty – next time out it was not enough to prevent a 3-2 defeat at Charlton. On returning to Anfield to meet prospective champions Arsenal there was agony for Owen.

Despite taking the lead through Kewell's first home goal, Liverpool crashed 2-1 through a Sami Hyypia own goal and a superb, swerving shot from Robert Pires. It left Liverpool in eighth place, nine points adrift of Arsene Wenger's team. Compounding Anfield woes was a leg injury to Owen. He was to appear in only four of the next 17 games, and was also hit by ankle and thigh problems.

Houllier switched the captaincy from Hyypia to Gerrard before the UEFA return with Ljubljana, which resulted in a 4-1 aggregate win, but they suffered a third consecutive Premiership defeat, losing 1-0 at Portsmouth, before ending that gloomy run with a 3-1 home win over Leeds.

Two headers by Emile Heskey, who also had a penalty saved, helped Liverpool to an entertaining 4-3 Carling Cup win at Blackburn, although their hopes in that competition ended in the next round with a 3-2 home defeat by Bolton.

HEADS YOU WIN
Vladimir Smicer scores the one of the Reds' three headed goals in the home win against Bolton.

Liverpool made progress in Europe with a 2–1 aggregate win over Steaua Bucharest but their League form continued to stutter as they ended the calendar year with only one win from four games.

A tricky FA Cup hurdle at Third Division Yeovil was successfully negotiated with goals from Heskey and a Danny Murphy penalty prior to Liverpool's first League win at Chelsea since 1989, through the game's only goal from Bruno Cheyrou. A 1–0 home win over Aston Villa was followed by a 2–1 defeat at Tottenham and a 1–1 draw at embattled Wolves.

Cheyrou stole the headlines again with both goals in a 2–1 FA Cup win over Newcastle in an atmospheric Anfield duel. Home success over Manchester City in February gave them their first win in five Premiership games, sufficient to move them into fourth place ahead of Newcastle by a single-goal advantage.

IT'S A KNOCK-OUT

Bruno Cheyrou celebrates scoring his second in the 2–1 FA Cup win over Newcastle.

Their FA Cup hopes perished 1–0 in a Fratton Park replay after vastly depleted Portsmouth had drawn 1–1 at Anfield. The UEFA Cup stayed on Liverpool's horizon after a 6–2 aggregate conquest of Levski Sofia – but not for long. Olympique Marseille drew 1–1 at Anfield in the fourth round first leg, Didier Drogba equalising Milan Baros's opener with the first French club goal scored on Liverpool's home soil since St Etienne 27 years earlier.

A hotly disputed penalty awarded against sent-off Igor Biscan for pulling back Steve Marlet set Marseille *en route* to a 3–2 victory in the return after Heskey had put Liverpool ahead. Their 2–1 defeat on the night was only Houllier's fourth reverse in 27 European away games since taking sole charge.

It reduced Liverpool's season to a quest to finish in fourth spot, with its ticket into the qualifiers for the lucrative Champions League. Those ambitions had been hampered by a 2–0 defeat at Southampton, where Owen had a penalty saved by Antti Niemi. But successive home wins, 3–0 over Portsmouth and 1–0 against Wolves, through Hyypia's towering stoppage time header, took them back to fourth.

A goalless draw at Leicester and a 4–0 home demolition of Blackburn – their biggest win of the season – kept them on course before Thierry Henry's brilliant hat-trick sent them plunging to a 4–2 Good Friday defeat at Arsenal. It was followed by a dismal 1–0 home defeat by fellow Euro-hopefuls Charlton, their first Anfield win since 1954.

Fulham kept Kop nerves jangling by earning a goalless Anfield draw and, although Liverpool stayed fourth, Newcastle, with games in hand, and resurgent Aston Villa were threatening in their slipstream. Houllier's recall of Murphy at Manchester United paid a golden dividend when his 63rd-minute penalty won the game – a week after Gerrard had become the third Liverpool player to fail from the spot during the season.

It was Murphy's third winner in four visits to Old Trafford and the team followed up with a 2–0 home win over Middlesbrough. Their penultimate outing, to Birmingham, saw them produce one of their finest displays of the season, Owen, Heskey and the superb Gerrard making it an emphatic 3–0 triumph.

Newcastle's draws with Wolves and Southampton the following midweek secured Liverpool's Champions League qualifying ticket even before Sir Bobby Robson's side went to Anfield in the final game, a 1–1 draw leaving the clubs fourth and fifth respectively. Owen's second-half equaliser was his 118th League goal, equalling the total of the legendary Kenny Dalglish.

By "mutual consent", manager Gérard Houllier left the club in May 2004, having successfully brought Liverpool to the point once more where the elite clubs of Europe were again within the Reds' sights. He was succeeded by former Valencia coach Rafael Benitez.

PLAYER STEVEN GERRARD

Gerrard celebrates his goal against Leeds in March 2003.

Gérard Houllier used one word to capture the crucial importance of Steven Gerrard to his Liverpool side. "Irreplaceable" was the adjective that sprang instantly to the manager's lips when he pondered the talents of his captain and inspirational midfielder.

Dynamic is another label that fits the style and unquenchable spirit of the Huyton-born star who became, at 23, leader of his club and country, a pivotal player for both Houllier and England coach Sven-Goran Eriksson.

Indeed, Gerrard's involvement in all areas of the field, curtailing an opposition raid one moment and sparking an attacking response the next, has become such a personal trademark that, as one Kop fan observed on the Radio Merseyside Football Phone-In:

"The only thing Stevie doesn't do is get on the end of his own crosses… and he'll probably do that soon!"

The 2003 04 season was unforgettable for Gerrard. His football life was transformed from despair to pride in the span of a few months as he matured as a player for both Liverpool and England. His anguish at losing to Chelsea in the season's last game in May 2003, which denied Liverpool a Champions League place, led to him being sent off.

Gerrard's fate brought the right response. He used his dismissal to beneficial effect and vastly improved his on field discipline. Underlining that is the fact that his first yellow card of the following season did not come until Liverpool's 47th match, the Easter Monday home duel with Charlton.

Gerrard's reward came in October. In a surprise move by Houllier, he made Gerrard the new club captain, taking over from Finnish defender Sami Hyypia for the 3 0 home UEFA Cup win over Olimpija Ljubljana.

The following March he was honoured further, when Eriksson made him England captain, in the absence of David Beckham, in the 1 0 defeat by Sweden in Gothenburg. "I remember when I first met Steven," recalled Eriksson. "If I compare the man now to the young boy, then he has progressed enormously. He deserves to be captain."

Eriksson's choice pleased another former England captain, Bryan Robson, who said back in the summer of 2003: "When Beckham isn't there, Gerrard is my choice. He is now the key player for England."

He became the 12th Liverpool player to

be named England captain — an illustrious line that began with Ephraim Longworth in 1921 but, ironically, it was the first time in Gerrard's 23 international appearances that he had been on the losing side.

Clearly he is tailor made for the job, and is eager for his international career to flourish after the misery of missing out on the 2002 World Cup Finals through a groin injury.

"I was really proud to wear the England arm band and I think the Liverpool captaincy has taken my game to the next level," Gerrard reflected. "It gave me a great boost and it's something I'd always wanted, even if I didn't expect it to happen at 23."

It fulfilled part of a fantasy for home grown Gerrard which was fired in 1990 when, aged nine, he stood on the Kop and saw Alan Hansen lift the League Championship trophy. His dream of following in his footsteps as captain has been realised. The title remains a burning ambition. "As captain I feel the responsibilty to make sure the club is doing well. I want to be challenging for the title every year. There's no reason at all why we can't be challenging with the top teams."

Gerrard's commitment to the club was underlined when he signed a new, four year contract in November 2003, declaring: "I've been here since I was eight years old and there has not been a single moment when I have wanted to play for someone else. I want to win a lot more trophies with the club. I want to get them back into the Champions League and I want to stay here for as long as possible."

Houllier gladly concurred with that, saying: "You would have to cut off both my arms and my legs before I let go of Steven Gerrard because I would have them both wrapped around him. I want him to be not only player of the year in England but he has every chance in future to be European and World player of the year as well."

Steven Gerrard, the world is your stage…

"I think the Liverpool captaincy has taken my game to the next level, and it's something I've always wanted."

MODERN-DAY ANFIELD

This famous panorama could be consigned to history if the new 60,000-seat Anfield, to be built in nearby Stanley Park, gets the go-ahead for 2006.

RESULTS

1892–93

LANCASHIRE LEAGUE

DATE	OPPOSITION	VENUE	SCORE	ATT.	GOALSCORERS
03/09	Higher Walton	H	8–0	200	Smith (2), McQue (2), Cameron (2), McVean, McBride
24/09	Bury	H	4–0	4,000	Miller (2), McVean, Cameron
01/10	West Manchester	H	3–1	3,000	Wyllie, Smith, Miller
22/10	Higher Walton	A	5–0	150	Miller (3), Wyllie (2)
05/11	Blackpool	A	0–3	3,000	
12/11	Fleetwood R	A	4–1	2,000	McVean (2), Miller, Smith
26/11	Rossendale Utd	A	2–0	1,500	Miller, McBride
03/12	Fleetwood R	H	7–0	1,000	Miller (5), McVean, M.McQueen
17/12	Blackpool	H	0–2	4,000	
24/12	South Shore	A	1–0	2,000	Wyllie
31/12	Heywood Central	H	6–2	1,000	Wyllie (2), McVean (2), M.McQueen, Miller
02/01	Fairfield	A	4–1	3,000	Miller, Wyllie, H.McQueen, Cameron
07/01	Heywood Central	A	2–1	1,000	Wyllie, McBride
14/01	West Manchester	A	0–0	2,000	
11/02	Bury	A	0–3	8,000	
18/02	Nelson	A	3–2	1,500	Miller (2), McVean
25/02	Southport Central	H	2–0	1,500	McBride, M.McQueen
04/03	Nelson	H	3–0	2,000	M.McQueen (2), H.McQueen
16/03	Fairfield	H	5–0	2,000	Miller (2), McLean, Wyllie, H.McQueen
18/03	South Shore	H	4–1	2,000	Wyllie, Miller (2), McVean
25/03	Rossendale Utd	H	2–1	1,200	Smith, Wyllie
15/04	Southport C	A	1–1	1,500	Miller

Lanc League Position 1st   P 22 Pts 36

LANCASHIRE CUP

DATE	OPPOSITION	VENUE	SCORE	ATT.	GOALSCORERS
17/09	Southport C*	H	2–0	4,000	Wyllie, Smith
08/10	West Manchester*	A	3–1	5,000	Miller (2), Kelvin
28/01	Darwen	H	1–0	8,000	McVean
11/03	Bootle	A	1–2	5,000	H.McQueen

* QUALIFYING ROUNDS

FA CUP QUALIFYING ROUNDS

DATE	OPPOSITION	VENUE	SCORE	ATT.	GOALSCORERS
15/10	Nantwich	A	4–0	700	Miller (3), Wyllie
29/10	Newtown	H	9–0	4,000	Wyllie (3), McVean (2), McCartney, H.McQueen, Cameron, Townsend (o.g.)
19/11	Northwich V	A	1–2	1,000	Wyllie

1893–94

FOOTBALL LEAGUE DIVISION TWO

DATE	OPPOSITION	VENUE	SCORE	ATT.	GOALSCORERS
02/09	Middlesbrough I	A	2–0	2,000	McVean, McQue
09/09	Lincoln C	H	4–0	5,000	McBride (2), Gordon, McVean
16/09	Ardwick	A	1–0	6,000	Stott
23/09	Small Heath	H	3–1	8,000	Stott (2), D.Henderson
30/09	Notts Co	A	1–1	6,000	H.McQueen
07/10	Middlesbrough I	H	6–0	6,000	McLean, Stott (3), D.Henderson, H.McQueen
14/10	Small Heath	A	4–3	8,000	Gordon, Stott, D.Henderson, H.McQueen
21/10	Burton Swifts	A	1–1	3,000	McVean
28/10	Woolwich Arsenal	A	5–1	7,000	McLean, M.McQueen, McCartney, Stott, Bradshaw
04/11	Newcastle Utd	H	5–1	8,000	Stott, Gordon (2), Bradshaw, Dick
11/11	Walsall Twn S	D	1–1	5,000	Bradshaw
18/11	Notts Co	H	2–1	8,000	Gordon, D.Henderson
25/11	Newcastle Utd	A	0–0	2,000	
02/12	Ardwick	H	3–0	4,000	Stott, H.McQueen, D.Henderson
09/12	Walsall Twn S	H	3–0	5,000	McVean (3)
28/12	Crewe A	A	5–0	4,000	Gordon, Bradshaw, H.McQueen, McVean, D.Henderson
30/12	Grimsby T	A	2–0	3,000	Bradshaw, D.Henderson
01/01	Woolwich Arsenal	H	2–0	5,000	McBride, McVean
06/01	Rotherham T	A	4–1	500	Stott (2), D.Henderson, H.McQueen
13/01	Rotherham T	H	5–1	4,000	H.McQueen, Bradshaw (2), D.Henderson (2)
03/02	Northwich V	H	4–0	3,000	McLean (pen), Stott (2), Bradshaw
03/03	Burton Swifts	H	3–1	8,000	Worgan (2), McLean (pen)
17/03	Lincoln C	A	1–1	4,000	Givens
24/03	Crewe A	H	2–0	3,000	Dick, H.McQueen
28/03	Northwich V	A	3–2	3,000	Givens, H.McQueen, McLean
31/03	Grimsby T	A	1–0	4,000	Givens
07/04	Burslem P Vale	A	2–2	5,000	McVean, M.McQueen
14/04	Burslem P Vale	H	2–1	5,000	Hannah, McQue

Div Two Position 1st   P 28 Pts 50

TEST MATCH FOR PROMOTION

DATE	OPPOSITION	VENUE	SCORE	ATT.	GOALSCORERS
28/04	Newton Heath	H	2–0	5,000	Gordon, Bradshaw

FA CUP

DATE	OPPOSITION	VENUE	SCORE	ATT.	GOALSCORERS
27/01	Grimsby T	H	3–0	8,000	Bradshaw (2), McQue
10/02	Preston NE	H	3–2	18,000	D.Henderson (2), McVean
24/02	Bolton W	A	0–3	20,000	

1894–95

FOOTBALL LEAGUE DIVISION ONE

DATE	OPPOSITION	VENUE	SCORE	ATT.	GOALSCORERS
01/09	Blackburn R	A	1–1	12,000	Bradshaw
03/09	Burnley	A	3–3	10,000	Gordon, Bradshaw, H.McQueen
08/09	Aston Villa	H	1–2	20,000	Bradshaw
13/09	Bolton W	H	1–2	6,000	Ross
15/09	West Brom A	A	0–5	6,000	
22/09	Blackburn R	H	2–2	14,000	McVean, H.McQueen
29/09	Wolves	A	1–3	4,000	Ross (pen)

06/10	Sheffield Utd	H	2–2	12,000	Kerr, Bradshaw
13/10	Everton	A	0–3	44,000	
20/10	Stoke C	H	2–0	8,000	Ross (2)
27/10	Aston Villa	A	0–5	5,000	
03/11	Burnley	H	0–3	8,000	
10/11	Stoke C	A	1–3	5,000	Kerr
17/11	Everton	H	2–2	30,000	D.Hannah, Ross (pen)
24/11	Sunderland	A	2–3	8,000	McVean, D.Hannah
01/12	Wolves	H	3–3	7,000	Bradshaw (2), McVean
08/12	Sheffield Utd	A	2–2	8,000	Bradshaw (2)
15/12	Small Heath	H	7–0	7,000	Bradshaw (2), D.Hannah
25/12	Bolton W	A	0–1	8,000	
29/12	Small Heath	A	0–3	5,000	
01/01	West Brom A	H	4–0	12,000	Bradshaw (2), Ross, D.Hannah
05/01	The Wednesday	A	0–5	10,000	
09/01	Derby Co	A	1–0	6,000	Ross
12/01	Nottingham F	H	5–0	5,000	McVean (2), Ross, McQue, D.Hannah
02/03	Derby Co	H	5–1	12,000	Bradshaw, Kerr, Ross (2), D.Hannah
25/03	Sunderland	H	2–3	20,000	Ross, Becton
30/03	The Wednesday	H	4–2	6,000	Bradshaw (2), Becton (2)
06/04	Nottingham F	A	0–4	4,000	
12/04	Preston NE	A	2–2	10,000	Ross, Becton
20/04	Preston NE	H	2–5	20,000	Bradshaw (2)

Div One Position 16th   P 30 Pts 22

TEST MATCH (AT BLACKBURN)

DATE	OPPOSITION	VENUE	SCORE	ATT.	GOALSCORERS
27/04	Bury		0–1	5,000	

FA CUP

DATE	OPPOSITION	VENUE	SCORE	ATT.	GOALSCORERS
12/02	Barnsley St P	A	2–1*	4,000	McVean, Ross
11/02	Barnsley St P	A	4–0	4,000	Bradshaw, Drummond, McVean, H.McQueen
16/02	Nottingham F	H	0–2	5,000	

* MATCH COUNTED AS 1–1 DRAW AFTER BARNSLEY PROTEST

1895–96

FOOTBALL LEAGUE DIVISION TWO

DATE	OPPOSITION	VENUE	SCORE	ATT.	GOALSCORERS
07/09	Notts Co	H	3–2	7,000	Ross, McQue, Bradshaw
14/09	Newcastle Utd	H	5–1	8,000	Ross (3), Becton, Bradshaw
21/09	Loughborough T	A	4–2	3,500	Ross, Allan, D.Hannah (2)
28/09	Burslem P Vale	H	5–1	5,000	Allan (4), D.Hannah
30/09	Burton Wand	H	4–1	3,000	Bradshaw (2), Becton (2)
05/10	Newcastle Utd	A	0–1	12,000	
07/10	Crewe A	A	6–1	3,000	Allan (2), Ross (2), Geary (2)
12/10	Newton Heath	H	7–1	10,000	Becton (2), Bradshaw (2), Geary (2), Ross
19/10	Grimsby T	A	0–1	5,000	
21/10	Burslem P Vale	A	4–5	1,000	Becton (3), Geary
26/10	Notts Co	A	3–0	8,000	Bradshaw, Geary, Ross
02/11	Newton Heath	A	2–5	10,000	Becton, Ross
09/11	Leicester Fosse	H	3–1	7,000	Geary (2), Wilkie
16/11	Woolwich Arsenal	A	2–0	10,000	Bradshaw, Geary
23/11	Darwen	H	0–0	3,000	
30/11	Leicester Fosse	A	0–2	8,000	
07/12	Loughborough T	H	1–0	1,000	Becton
14/12	Darwen	A	4–0	2,000	McQue, Becton, Geary, McVean
21/12	Lincoln C	A	1–0	3,000	Allan
01/01	Manchester C	H	3–1	20,000	Ross (2), McVean
04/01	Rotherham	A	5–0	2,000	Allan (3), Ross, Bradshaw
11/01	Woolwich Arsenal	H	3–0	5,000	Ross (2), McQue
25/01	Lincoln C	H	6–1	4,000	Ross (2), Bull, Geary, Becton, Allan
18/02	Rotherham	H	10–1	2,000	Allan (4), McVean (3), Ross (2), Becton
22/02	Grimsby T	H	3–1	10,000	Allan (2), Becton
29/02	Burton Swifts	A	7–0	1,500	McCartney, Ross (3), Becton (3)
07/03	Burton Wand	A	1–2	2,000	Allan
21/03	Burton Swifts	H	6–1	4,000	Bradshaw (2), Allan (2), Ross, McQue
28/03	Crewe A	H	7–1	3,000	Allan (3), McVean (2), McQue, Becton
03/04	Manchester C	A	1–1	25,000	Allan

Div Two Position 1st   P 30 Pts 46

TEST MATCHES

DATE	OPPOSITION	VENUE	SCORE	ATT.	GOALSCORERS
18/04	Small Heath	H	4–0	20,000	Allan (2), McCartney, Bradshaw
20/04	Small Heath	A	0–0	20,000	
25/04	West Brom A	H	2–0	20,000	Bradshaw, Allan
27/04	West Brom A	A	0–2	6,000	

FA CUP

DATE	OPPOSITION	VENUE	SCORE	ATT.	GOALSCORERS
01/02	Millwall	H	4–1	10,000	Ross, Becton, Allan, Bradshaw
15/02	Wolves	A	0–2	15,000	

1896–97

FOOTBALL LEAGUE DIVISION ONE

DATE	OPPOSITION	VENUE	SCORE	ATT.	GOALSCORERS
01/09	The Wednesday	A	2–1	2,000	Allan (2)
05/09	Blackburn R	A	0–1	7,000	
07/09	Bolton W	H	0–2	15,000	
12/09	Derby Co	H	2–0	20,000	Methven (o.g.), Bradshaw
19/09	Bury	A	2–1	7,000	McVean, Allan
26/09	West Brom A	H	0–0	14,000	
03/10	Everton	A	1–2	45,000	Ross
10/10	Nottingham F	H	3–0	10,000	Michael, McVean, Bradshaw
17/10	Sunderland	A	3–4	6,000	Goldie, Gow (o.g.) Allan
19/10	Sheffield Utd	A	1–1	6,000	Bradshaw
24/10	Blackburn R	H	4–0	10,000	Allan (2), Ross, Michael
31/10	West Brom A	A	1–0	5,000	Allan

(1896–97 continued)

DATE	OPPOSITION	VENUE	SCORE	ATT.	GOALSCORERS
07/11	Sunderland	H	3–0	10,000	D.Hannah (2), McVean
14/11	Preston NE	A	1–1	10,000	Michael
21/11	Everton	H	0–0	30,000	
28/11	Nottingham F	A	0–2	6,000	
12/12	Bury	H	3–1	7,000	Allan (2), McVean
19/12	Derby Co	A	2–3	10,000	Michael, Neill
25/12	Aston Villa	H	3–3	15,000	Becton (2; 1 pen), Allan
26/12	Burnley	A	1–4	9,000	Becton
01/01	Bolton W	A	4–1	20,000	Allan (2), Geary, McCartney
02/01	Sheffield Utd	H	0–0	15,000	
09/01	Wolves	A	2–1	2,000	Allan, Geary
16/01	Stoke C	H	1–0	10,000	Allan
16/02	Stoke C	A	1–6	7,000	Allan
04/03	Wolves	H	3–0	4,000	Becton, Bradshaw, Allan
13/03	Aston Villa	A	0–0	18,000	
27/03	Burnley	H	1–2	12,000	Neill
03/04	The Wednesday	H	2–2	6,000	Michael, Becton (pen)
10/04	Preston NE	H	0–0	12,000	

Div One Position 5th   P 30 Pts 33

FA CUP

DATE	OPPOSITION	VENUE	SCORE	ATT.	GOALSCORERS
30/01	Burton Swifts	H	4–3	4,000	Hannah, Allan, Cleghorn, Ross
13/02	West Brom A	A	2–1	16,147	McVean, Neill
27/02	Nottingham F	H	1–1	15,000	Becton
03/03	Nottingham F	A	1–0	10,000	Allan
20/03	Aston Villa	N	0–3	30,000	(at Bramall Lane)

1897–98

FOOTBALL LEAGUE DIVISION ONE

DATE	OPPOSITION	VENUE	SCORE	ATT.	GOALSCORERS
04/09	Stoke C	A	2–2	5,000	Becton, Walker
11/09	Preston NE	H	0–0	20,000	
18/09	The Wednesday	A	2–4	8,000	Walker, Becton
25/09	Everton	H	3–1	30,000	Cunliffe, McQue, Becton
02/10	Preston NE	A	1–1	8,000	McCartney
09/10	Stoke C	H	4–0	12,000	Cunliffe (2), Bradshaw, Becton
16/10	Everton	A	0–3	40,000	
23/10	Derby Co	H	4–2	12,000	McQue, Cunliffe, Marshall (2)
30/10	Aston Villa	A	1–3	25,000	Bradshaw
06/11	Nottingham F	H	1–2	10,000	Cunliffe
13/11	West Brom A	A	1–2	10,000	Becton
20/11	Wolves	H	1–0	12,000	Finnerhan
27/11	Nottingham F	A	3–2	8,000	McCowie, Lumsden (2)
11/12	Wolves	A	1–2	8,000	Bradshaw
18/12	Blackburn R	H	0–1	5,000	
25/12	Bolton W	A	2–0	8,000	Cunliffe, McCowie
27/12	Sunderland	H	0–2	30,000	
29/12	Sheffield Utd	A	2–1	8,000	McCowie, Hartley
01/01	West Brom A	H	1–1	12,000	McCartney
08/01	Blackburn R	A	1–2	6,000	Ball (o.g.)
22/01	Sunderland	A	0–1	9,000	
05/02	Sheffield Utd	H	0–4	18,000	
12/03	Notts Co	H	2–0	8,000	Becton, Cox
19/03	Bolton W	H	1–1	7,000	Bradshaw
26/03	Bury	A	2–0	2,000	McCowie, Becton
31/03	Bury	H	2–2	3,000	Geary, McCowie
02/04	Notts Co	A	2–3	8,000	McCowie, Becton
11/04	The Wednesday	H	4–0	7,000	Morgan, Becton (2), Robertson
12/04	Derby Co	A	1–3	3,500	Walker
16/04	Aston Villa	H	4–0	20,000	Robertson, Walker, Morgan, Becton

Div One Position 9th   P 30 Pts 28

FA CUP

DATE	OPPOSITION	VENUE	SCORE	ATT.	GOALSCORERS
29/01	Hucknall St J	H	2–0	8,000	Becton, McQue
12/02	Newton Heath	A	0–0	12,000	
16/02	Newton Heath	H	2–1	6,000	Wilkie, Cunliffe
26/02	Derby Co	A	1–1	20,000	Bradshaw
02/03	Derby Co	H	1–5	15,000	Becton (pen)

1898–99

FOOTBALL LEAGUE DIVISION ONE

DATE	OPPOSITION	VENUE	SCORE	ATT.	GOALSCORERS
03/09	The Wednesday	H	4–0	18,000	Morgan, Robertson, Walker, W.Goldie
10/09	Sunderland	A	0–1	30,000	
17/09	Wolves	H	1–0	15,000	Cox
24/09	Everton	A	2–1	45,000	McCowie (2; 1 pen)
01/10	Notts Co	H	0–0	12,000	
08/10	Stoke C	A	1–2	8,000	Cox
15/10	Aston Villa	H	0–3	20,000	
22/10	Burnley	A	1–2	10,000	Morgan
29/10	Sheffield Utd	H	2–1	10,000	McCowie (pen), Allan
05/11	Newcastle Utd	A	0–3	20,000	
12/11	Preston NE	H	3–1	12,000	Morgan (2), Allan
19/11	Bury	A	0–3	6,000	
26/11	Nottingham F	H	3–0	12,000	McCowie, Morgan, Walker
03/12	Bolton W	H	2–0	12,000	Morgan, McCowie
10/12	Derby Co	A	0–1	6,000	
17/12	West Brom A	H	2–2	18,000	Walker, Morgan
24/12	Blackburn R	A	3–1	6,000	Robertson (2), Cox
26/12	West Brom A	A	1–0	10,000	Morgan
27/12	Notts Co	H	1–1	16,000	Allan
31/12	The Wednesday	A	3–0	4,000	Massey (o.g.), Walker, Allan (pen)
02/01	Sheffield Utd	H	2–0	12,000	Walker, Cox
07/01	Sunderland	H	0–0	20,000	
14/01	Wolves	A	0–0	7,000	
21/01	Everton	H	2–0	30,000	Walker, Robertson
04/02	Stoke C	H	1–0	8,000	W.Goldie
18/02	Burnley	H	2–0	12,000	Allan, Robertson
11/03	Preston NE	A	2–1	9,000	Morgan, Allan
25/03	Nottingham F	H	0–1	14,000	
01/04	Bolton W	A	1–2	15,000	Morgan
03/04	Newcastle Utd	H	3–2	12,000	Cox, Walker, Allan
08/04	Derby C	H	4–0	15,000	Raisbeck, Walker (3)
20/04	Bury	H	1–0	10,000	Walker
22/04	Blackburn R	H	2–0	20,000	Allan, Robertson
29/04	Aston Villa	A	0–5	41,357	

Div One Position 2nd   P 34 Pts 43

FA CUP

DATE	OPPOSITION	VENUE	SCORE	ATT.	GOALSCORERS
28/01	Blackburn R	H	2–0	14,000	Cox, Allan
11/02	Newcastle Utd	H	3–1	7,000	Morgan, Raisbeck, Higgins (o.g.)
25/02	West Brom A	A	2–0	17,124	Morgan, Robertson
18/03	Sheffield Utd	N	2–2	35,000	Allan, Morgan (at Nottingham)
23/03	Sheffield Utd	N	4–4	20,000	Walkler, Allan, Boyle (o.g.), Cox (at Bolton)
27/03	Sheffield Utd	N	1–0	30,000	Allan (at Fallowfield; abandoned)
30/03	Sheffield Utd	N	0–1	20,000	(at Derby)

1899–00

FOOTBALL LEAGUE DIVISION ONE

DATE	OPPOSITION	VENUE	SCORE	ATT.	GOALSCORERS
02/09	Stoke C	A	2–3	10,000	Hunter Raisbeck
09/09	Sunderland	H	0–2	10,000	
16/09	West Brom A	H	0–2	10,000	
23/09	Everton	H	1–2	30,000	Robertson
30/09	Blackburn R	A	0–2	7,000	
05/10	Notts Co	A	1–2	10,000	Cox
07/10	Derby Co	H	0–2	12,000	
14/10	Bury	A	1–2	6,000	Walker
21/10	Notts Co	H	3–1	10,000	Raisbeck, Robertson, Walker
28/10	Manchester C	A	1–0	20,000	Robertson
04/11	Sheffield Utd	H	2–2	20,000	Hunter, Robertson
11/11	Newcastle Utd	H	1–1	8,000	Walker
18/11	Aston Villa	H	3–3	20,000	Morgan, Walker, Raisbeck
25/11	Wolves	H	1–1	12,000	Walker
02/12	Burnley	A	1–2	5,000	Walker
09/12	Preston NE	H	1–0	7,000	Walker
16/12	Nottingham F	A	0–1	12,000	
23/12	Glossop NE	H	5–2	5,000	S.Hunter (3) Satterwaite (2)
25/12	Derby Co	A	2–3	10,000	S.Hunter, Robertson
30/12	Stoke C	H	0–0	5,000	
06/01	Sunderland	A	0–1	3,000	
13/01	Blackburn R	H	2–0	6,000	Morgan (2)
20/01	Everton	A	1–3	30,000	Raybould (after 30 seconds!)
03/02	Blackburn R	H	3–1	6,000	Cox (2) Robertson
03/03	Manchester C	H	5–2	20,000	Raybould (2, 1pen), Walker, Satterwaite, Cox
10/03	Sheffield Utd	A	2–1	15,000	Raybould, Satterwaite
17/03	Newcastle Utd	A	2–0	18,000	Robertson, Walker
24/03	Aston Villa	A	0–1	15,000	
31/03	Wolves	A	1–0	7,000	Robertson
07/04	Burnley	H	0–1	10,000	
09/04	Bury	H	2–0	5,000	Raybould (2)
14/04	Preston NE	A	3–1	5,000	Satterwaite, Raybould, Cox
21/04	Nottingham F	H	1–0	10,000	Robertson (pen)
28/04	Glossop NE	A	2–1	2,000	W.Goldie, Walker

Div One Position 10th   P 34 Pts 33

FA CUP

DATE	OPPOSITION	VENUE	SCORE	ATT.	GOALSCORERS
27/01	Stoke C	A	0–0	8,000	
01/02	Stoke C (R)	H	1–0	10,000	Hunter
17/02	West Brom A	H	1–1	15,000	Cox
21/02	West Brom A (R)	A	1–2	13,000	Robertson

1900–01

FOOTBALL LEAGUE DIVISION ONE

DATE	OPPOSITION	VENUE	SCORE	ATT.	GOAL SCORERS
01/09	Blackburn Rovers	H	3–0	20,000	T.Robertson, Satterthwaite, Raybould
08/09	Stoke City	A	2–1	10,000	T.Robertson, Raybould
15/09	West Brom A	H	5–0	18,000	Goldie, Walker, Raybould (2), T.Robertson
22/09	Everton	A	1–1	50,000	Raybould
29/09	Sunderland	H	1–2	20,000	Wilson
06/10	Derby County	A	3–2	8,000	T.Robertson (2) Walker
13/10	Bolton W	H	2–1	12,000	Cox, Satterthwaite
20/10	Notts Co	A	0–3	18,000	
27/10	Preston N E	H	3–2	12,000	McGuigan, Cox, Raybould
03/11	Wolves	A	1–2	12,000	Walker
10/11	Aston Villa	H	5–1	18,000	Raybould (2), McGuigan, Walker (2)
17/11	The Wednesday	A	2–3	10,000	Raybould, Raisbeck
24/11	Newcastle Utd	A	1–1	17,000	Cox
01/12	Sheffield Utd	H	1–2	15,000	Satterthwaite
08/12	Manchester C	A	4–3	20,000	Raybould, Cox, T Robertson, McGuigan
15/12	Bury	H	1–0	14,000	Cox
22/12	Nottingham F	A	0–0	6,000	
25/12	Derby Co	H	0–0	18,000	
29/12	Blackburn Rovers	A	1–3	8,000	Raybould
01/01	Stoke City	H	3–1	15,000	T Robertson, Cox, McGuigan
19/01	Everton	H	1–2	18,000	Cox
16/02	Bolton W	A	0–1	8,000	

ORIGINALLY TO BE PLAYED ON 02/02 BUT POSTPONED DUE TO STATE FUNERAL OF QUEEN VICTORIA

DATE	OPPOSITION	VENUE	SCORE	ATT.	GOAL SCORERS
23/02	Sunderland	H	1–0	11,249	Cox
02/03	Preston NE	A	2–2	1,500	Satterthwaite, Raybould
09/03	Wolves	H	1–0	12,000	Raybould
16/03	Aston Villa	A	2–0	14,000	McGuigan, S.Hunter
23/03	The Wednesday	H	1–1	12,000	Raybould
30/03	Newcastle Utd	H	3–0	10,000	S.Hunter (2) Raybould
08/04	Notts Co	H	1–0	15,000	Raybould
13/04	Manchester City	A	3–1	14,000	T Robertson (2) Cox
20/04	Bury	A	0–0	8,000	
22/04	Sheffield Utd	H	2–0	12,000	Raybould, Satterthwaite
27/04	Nottingham F	H	2–0	20,000	Cox, Goldie
29/04	West Brom A	A	1–0	4,000	Walker

Div One Postion 1st   P34 Pts 45

1900–01 (CONTINUED)

FA CUP

DATE	OPPOSITION	VENUE	SCORE	ATT.	GOALSCORERS
05/01	West Ham Utd	A	1–0	6,000	Raybould

FAC SUPPLEMENTARY ROUND

DATE	OPPOSITION	VENUE	SCORE	ATT.	GOALSCORERS
09/02	Notts Co	A	0–2	15,000	

1901–02

FOOTBALL LEAGUE DIVISION ONE

DATE	OPPOSITION	VENUE	SCORE	ATT.	GOALSCORERS
02/09	Small Heath	A	0–0	10,000	
07/09	Stoke C	A	0–1	10,000	
14/09	Everton	H	2–2	30,000	White, Raybould
21/09	Sunderland	A	1–1	16,000	Cox
28/09	Small Heath	H	3–1	20,000	Raybould (2), T Robertson (pen)
05/10	Derby Co	A	1–1	8,000	T Robertson
12/10	The Wednesday	H	1–2	15,000	T Robertson
19/10	Notts Co	A	2–2	10,000	S Hunter, Cox
26/10	Bolton W	H	1–1	16,000	McGuigan
02/11	Manchester City	A	3–2	20,000	T Robertson, Satterthwaite, Cox
09/11	Wolves	H	4–1	16,000	Satterthwaite, T Robertson (pen), McGuigan (2)
23/11	Newcastle Utd	A	0–1	18,000	
30/11	Aston Villa	H	1–0	18,000	Raybould
07/12	Sheffield Utd	A	1–2	12,000	Raybould
14/12	Nottingham F	H	0–2	12,000	
26/12	Sunderland	H	0–1	20,000	
28/12	Blackburn R	H	1–0	12,000	McGuigan
04/01	Stoke C	H	7–0	10,000	McGuigan (5) Raybould (2)
11/01	Everton	A	0–4	25,000	
01/02	Bury	A	0–0	7,000	
15/02	Notts Co	H	0–1	10,000	
22/02	Bolton W	A	0–1	10,000	
01/03	Manchester C	H	4–0	20,000	Cox, Raybould (3)
08/03	Wolves	A	1–3	6,000	Raybould
15/03	Grimsby T	A	1–1	6,000	Goddard
22/03	Newcastle Utd	H	0–1	12,000	
29/03	Aston Villa	A	1–0	20,000	Fleming
01/04	The Wednesday	A	1–1	15,000	Raybould
05/04	Sheffield Utd	H	1–0	5,000	Raybould
12/04	Nottingham F	H	1–1	12,000	Goddard
14/04	Derby Co	H	0–2	12,000	
19/04	Bury	H	1–0	12,000	Raybould
21/04	Grimsby T	H	2–2	12,000	Raybould (2)
26/04	Blackburn R	A	1–1	2,000	Walker

Div One Position 11th   P34   Pts 32

FA CUP

DATE	OPPOSITION	VENUE	SCORE	ATT.	GOALSCORERS
25/01	Everton	H	2–2	25,000	T Robertson (pen), Hunter
30/01	Everton	A	2–0	20,000	Raisbeck, Hunter
08/02	Southampton	A	1–4	20,000	Fleming

1902–03

FOOTBALL LEAGUE DIVISION ONE

DATE	OPPOSITION	VENUE	SCORE	ATT.	GOAL SCORERS
06/09	Blackburn R	H	5–2	20,000	Raybould (2), Cox (2), Livingstone
13/09	Sunderland	A	1–2	20,000	Raybould (pen)
20/09	Stoke C	H	1–1	20,000	Roose (o.g.)
27/09	Everton	A	1–3	40,000	Raybould (pen)
04/10	The Wednesday	H	4–2	17,000	Raybould (2, 1 pen), Livingstone, Goddard
11/10	West Brom A	A	2–1	20,000	Raybould (2)
18/10	Notts Co	H	0–2	16,000	
25/10	Bolton W	A	1–1	8,000	Raybould
01/11	Middlesbrough	H	5–0	15,000	Raybould (3) Chadwick, Cox
08/11	Newcastle United	A	2–1	5,000	Raybould, Goddard
15/11	Wolves	H	4–1	15,000	Livingstone, Cox, Goddard, Raybould
22/11	Derby Co	A	1–2	10,000	Chadwick
29/11	Sheffield Utd	A	0–2	7,000	
06/12	Grimsby T	H	9–2	5,000	Livingstone, Raybould (4, 1 pen), Chadwick (2), Goddard (2)
13/12	Aston Villa	A	2–1	20,000	Goddard, Raybould
20/12	Nottingham F	H	2–1	16,000	Goddard, Cox
25/12	Bolton W	H	5–1	20,000	Wilson (2), Raybould (pen), Chadwick, Cox
27/12	Bury	A	1–3	11,000	Raybould
01/01	West Brom A	H	0–2	25,000	
03/01	Blackburn R	A	1–3	5,000	Green
17/01	Stoke C	A	0–1	5,000	
31/01	The Wednesday	A	1–3	15,000	Goddard
14/02	Notts Co	A	2–1	7,000	Goddard (2)
28/02	Middlesbrough	A	2–0	15,000	Raybould, Chadwick
07/03	Newcastle Utd	H	3–0	15,000	Raybould (2) Raisbeck
23/03	Derby Co	H	3–1	8,000	Goldie, Raybould , Cox
28/03	Sheffield Utd	H	2–4	15,000	Cox, Raybould
30/03	Sunderland	H	1–1	3,000	Raybould
04/04	Grimsby T	A	1–3	6,000	Chadwick
10/04	Everton	H	0–0	28,000	
11/04	Aston Villa	H	2–1	15,000	Goddard, Raybould
18/04	Nottingham F	A	0–1	3,000	
25/04	Bury	H	2–0	10,000	Raybould (2)
27/04	Wolves	A	2–0	8,000	Raybould, Cox

Div One Position 5th   P34   Pts 38

FA CUP

DATE	OPPOSITION	VENUE	SCORE	ATT.	GOAL SCORERS
07/02	Manchester Utd	A	1–2	15,000	Raybould

1903–04

FOOTBALL LEAGUE DIVISION ONE

DATE	OPPOSITION	VENUE	SCORE	ATT.	GOAL SCORERS
05/09	Nottingham F	A	1–2	12,000	Smith
12/09	The Wednesday	H	1–3	18,000	Cox
19/09	Sunderland	A	1–2	17,000	Dunlop
26/09	West Brom A	H	1–3	18,000	Cox
01/10	Notts Co	A	2–4	10,000	Cox, Fleming (pen)
03/10	Small Heath	A	2–1	10,000	Parkinson, Fleming (pen)
10/10	Everton	H	2–2	30,000	Morris (2)
17/10	Stoke C	A	2–5	8,000	Cox, Fleming
24/10	Derby Co	H	3–1	13,000	Goddard, Morris, Parkinson
31/10	Manchester C	A	2–3	30,000	Goddard, Parkinson
07/11	Notts Co	H	2–1	10,000	Hughes, Prescott (o.g.)
14/11	Sheffield Utd	H	1–2	12,000	Goddard (pen)
21/11	Newcastle Utd	H	1–0	5,000	Morris
28/11	Aston Villa	A	1–2	12,000	Parkinson
12/12	Wolves	H	1–2	15,000	Parkinson
19/12	Bury	A	2–2	5,000	Cox (2)
25/12	Derby Co	A	0–2	16,000	
26/12	Blackburn R	H	1–2	20,000	Buck
28/12	Wolves	A	2–4	10,000	Parkinson, Raisbeck
02/01	Nottingham F	H	0–0	14,000	
09/01	The Wednesday	A	1–2	13,000	Raybould
16/01	Sunderland	H	2–1	20,000	Cox, Raybould
23/01	West Brom A	A	2–2	12,000	Hughes, Carlin
30/01	Small Heath	H	0–2	15,000	
13/02	Stoke C	H	0–0	10,000	
22/02	Middlesbrough	H	1–0	15,000	Robinson
27/02	Manchester C	H	2–2	15,000	Robinson, Raybould
12/03	Sheffield Utd	A	3–0	20,000	Robinson, Goddard, J.Hewitt
19/03	Newcastle Utd	A	1–1	20,000	Goddard
26/03	Aston Villa	H	1–1	14,000	Robinson
01/04	Everton	A	2–5	40,000	Robinson, Parry
02/04	Middlesbrough	A	0–1	12,000	
16/04	Bury	H	3–0	10,000	West (pen), Cox, Fleming
23/04	Blackburn R	A	3–2	4,000	Raybould, Cox, Goddard

Div One Position 17th   P34   Pts 26

FA CUP

DATE	OPPOSITION	VENUE	SCORE	ATT.	GOAL SCORERS
06/02	Blackburn R	A	1–3	16,990	Raybould

1904–05

FOOTBALL LEAGUE DIVISION TWO

DATE	OPPOSITION	VENUE	SCORE	ATT.	GOAL SCORERS
01/09	Burton Utd	H	2–0	10,000	Robinson (2)
03/09	Glossop NE	H	2–2	12,000	Goddard, Hewitt
10/09	Chesterfield	A	1–1	5,000	Goddard
17/09	Bradford C	A	4–1	15,000	Morris, Parry, Cox (2)
24/09	Lincoln C	A	2–0	6,000	Raybould (2)
01/10	Leicester F	H	4–0	12,000	Robinson (4)
08/10	Barnsley	A	2–0	5,000	Robinson (pen), Carlin
15/10	West Brom A	H	3–2	15,000	Robinson, Parkinson (2)
22/10	Burnley	A	2–0	9,000	Robinson, Cox
29/10	Grimsby Town	H	5–0	12,000	Chorlton (2), Raybould (2), Robinson
05/11	Blackpool	A	3–0	8,000	Parkinson, Robinson (2)
12/11	Burslem P Vale	H	2–1	5,000	Mullineux (o.g.), Raybould
19/11	Gainsborough T	A	2–1	4,000	Raybould, Parkinson (pen)
03/12	Bolton W	A	0–2	30,000	
17/12	Bristol C	H	3–1	12,000	Raisbeck, Parkinson
24/12	Manchester Utd	A	1–3	40,000	Parkinson
26/12	Barnsley	H	2–1	25,000	Robinson, Raybould
31/12	Glossop NE	A	2–0	9,000	Parkinson, Goddard
07/01	Chesterfield	H	6–1	10,000	Robinson, Raisbeck, Goddard, Parry, Raybould (2)
21/01	Lincoln C	H	1–1	7,000	Robinson
28/01	Leicester F	A	3–0	12,000	Robinson, West, Goddard
11/02	West Brom A	A	2–0	9,000	Raybould, Parkinson
25/02	Grimsby T	A	1–0	6,000	Parkinson
04/03	Blackpool	H	5–0	6,000	Parkinson (3), Robinson, Goddard
07/03	Bradford C	A	4–2	10,000	Parkinson (2; 1 pen), Raybould, Robinson
11/03	Doncaster R	H	4–1	5,000	Robinson (2), Cox, Dunlop
18/03	Gainsborough T	H	6–1	14,000	Parkinson (2), Raybould (3), Goddard
25/03	Burton Utd	A	1–2	3,000	Cox
01/04	Bolton W	H	1–1	25,000	Chorlton (pen)
08/04	Burslem P Vale	A	8–1	13,000	Parkinson (3), Robinson (2), Cox (2), Raybould
15/04	Bristol C	A	1–0	5,000	Cox
21/04	Doncaster R	H	1–0	20,000	Raybould
22/04	Manchester Utd	H	4–0	28,000	Cox, Raybould (3)
29/04	Burnley	H	3–0	10,000	Parkinson, Robinson, Cox

Div Two Position 1st   P34   Pts 58

FA CUP

DATE	OPPOSITION	VENUE	SCORE	ATT.	GOALSCORERS
04/02	Everton	H	1–1	28,000	Parkinson
08/02	Everton	A	1–2	40,000	Goddard

1905–06

FOOTBALL LEAGUE DIVISION ONE

DATE	OPPOSITION	VENUE	SCORE	ATT.	GOAL SCORERS
02/09	Woolwich Arsenal	A	1–3	20,000	Robinson
09/09	Blackburn R	H	1–3	15,000	Cox
11/09	Aston Villa	A	0–5	15,000	
16/09	Sunderland	A	2–1	20,000	Raybould (2)
23/09	Birmingham	H	2–0	20,000	Robinson, Hewitt
30/09	Everton	A	2–4	40,000	Hewitt (2)
07/10	Derby Co	H	4–1	20,000	Cox (2), Robinson, Goddard
14/10	The Wednesday	H	2–3	15,000	Robinson, Hewitt
21/10	Nottingham F	A	4–1	15,000	Hewitt, Cox, Raybould, Robinson
28/10	Manchester C	A	1–0	25,000	Hewitt
04/11	Bury	H	3–1	14,000	Carlin, Robinson (2)
11/11	Middlesbrough	H	5–1	18,000	Hewitt (3), Carlin(2)
18/11	Preston NE	H	1–1	15,000	Hewitt
25/11	Newcastle Utd	A	3–2	30,000	West (2 pens), Raybould
02/12	Aston Villa	H	3–0	25,000	Cox, Hewitt, Spence (o.g.)
09/12	Wolves	H	4–0	10,000	Hewitt (2), Raybould, Goddard
16/12	Sheffield Utd	A	2–1	15,000	Parry, Cox
23/12	Notts Co	H	2–0	10,000	Robinson, Hewitt
25/12	Bolton W	H	2–2	25,000	Hewitt, Goddard

26/12	Stoke C	A	1–2	20,000	Hewitt
30/12	Woolwich Arsenal	H	3–0	15,000	Raisbeck, Goddard, Raybould
01/01	Stoke C	H	3–1	25,000	Raybould (2), Hewitt
06/01	Blackburn R	A	0–0	10,000	
20/01	Sunderland	H	2–0	12,000	Hewitt, Carlin
27/01	Birmingham C	A	0–1	15,000	
10/02	Derby Co	A	3–0	3,000	Hewitt, Raybould, Robinson
17/02	The Wednesday	H	2–1	20,000	Cox (2)
03/03	Manchester C	H	0–1	25,000	
14/03	Nottingham F	A	2–1	6,000	Hewitt (2)
17/03	Middlesbrough	H	6–1	18,000	Parkinson, Carlin (2), Hewitt, Cox, Goddard
21/03	Notts Co	A	0–3	8,000	
24/03	Preston NE	A	2–1	20,000	Chorlton, Hewitt
02/04	Bury	A	0–0	10,000	
09/04	Newcastle Utd	H	3–0	10,000	Parkinson (2), Raybould
13/04	Everton	A	1–1	33,000	West (pen)
14/04	Wolves	A	2–0	10,000	Hewitt, Goddard
16/04	Bolton W	A	2–3	25,000	Parkinson (2)
21/04	Sheffield Utd	H	3–1	10,000	Parkinson (2), Robinson

Div One Position 1st P34 Pts 51

FA CUP

DATE	OPPOSITION	VENUE	SCORE	ATT.	GOALSCORERS
13/01	Leicester Fosse	H	2–1	12,000	Raybould, Goddard
03/02	Barnsley	A	1–0	10,000	West
24/02	Brentford	H	2–0	20,000	Hewitt, Goddard
10/03	Southampton	H	3–0	20,000	Raybould (3)
31/03	Everton (SF)	N	0–2	37,000	(at Villa Park)

1906–07

FOOTBALL LEAGUE DIVISION ONE

DATE	OPPOSITION	VENUE	SCORE	ATT.	GOALSCORERS
01/09	Stoke C	H	1–0	30,000	Hewitt
08/09	Blackburn R	A	1–1	18,000	Cox
10/09	Bury	H	2–2	10,000	Raybould, Hewitt
15/09	Sunderland	H	1–2	30,000	Hewitt
22/09	Birmingham	A	1–2	10,000	Cox
29/09	Everton	H	1–2	40,000	Parkinson
06/10	Woolwich Arsenal	A	1–2	25,000	McPherson
13/10	The Wednesday	H	1–2	15,000	Raybould
20/10	Bury	A	3–1	10,000	Robinson, Raybould (2)
27/10	Manchester C	H	5–4	20,000	Robinson (3), Raybould, McPherson
03/11	Middlesbrough	A	1–0	18,000	Raybould
10/11	Preston NE	H	6–1	15,000	Raisbeck (2), Raybould (2), McPherson (2)
17/11	Newcastle Utd	A	0–2	35,000	
24/11	Aston Villa	H	5–2	25,000	Robinson (2), Raybould, Goddard, Raisbeck (pen)
01/12	Derby Co	A	1–0	10,000	Hewitt
08/12	Bristol C	A	1–3	14,000	Robinson
15/12	Notts Co	H	5–1	5,000	Robinson, McPherson, Raybould (2), Raisbeck (pen)
22/12	Sheffield Utd	A	0–1	14,000	
25/12	Manchester Utd	H	0–0	20,000	
26/12	Bolton W	H	0–2	25,000	
01/01	Bolton W	A	0–3	20,000	
05/01	Blackburn R	H	0–2	18,000	
19/01	Sunderland	A	5–5	20,000	Parkinson (3), Raybould, Cox
26/01	Birmingham	H	2–0	15,000	Parkinson, McPherson
09/02	Woolwich Arsenal	H	4–0	25,000	Parkinson (2), McPherson, Cox
16/02	The Wednesday	A	3–2	12,000	McPherson, Raybould, Cox
02/03	Manchester C	A	0–1	20,000	
11/03	Stoke C	A	1–1	3,000	Hewitt
16/03	Preston NE	A	1–3	10,000	Cox
23/03	Newcastle Utd	H	4–1	25,000	Goddard, Cox, Bradley, Hewitt
29/03	Everton	A	0–0	45,000	
30/03	Aston Villa	A	0–4	26,000	
01/04	Mancheter Utd	A	0–1	20,000	
06/04	Derby Co	H	2–0	6,000	Hewitt (2)
13/04	Bristol City	H	2–4	10,000	McPherson, Raybould
17/04	Middlesbrough	H	2–4	10,000	Goddard, Blanthorne
20/04	Notts Co	A	0–2	1,000	
27/04	Sheffield Utd	H	2–2	10,000	Raybould, McPherson

Div One Position 15th P38 Pts 33

FA CUP

DATE	OPPOSITION	VENUE	SCORE	ATT.	GOALSCORERS
12/01	Birmingham C	H	2–1	20,000	Raybould (2)
02/02	Oldham A	A	1–0	21,500	McPherson
23/02	Bradford C	H	1–0	18,000	Cox
09/03	The Wednesday	A	0–1	30,000	

1907–08

FOOTBALL LEAGUE DIVISION ONE

DATE	OPPOSITION	VENUE	SCORE	ATT.	GOALSCORERS
02/09	Nottingham F	A	1–3	10,000	C.Hewitt
07/09	Manchester Utd	A	0–4	20,000	
14/09	Blackburn City	H	2–0	20,000	Goddard (2)
16/09	Sheffield Utd	H	0–0	7,000	
21/09	Bolton W	A	4–0	15,000	Bradley, J.Hewitt (2), Robinson
28/09	Birmingham C	A	3–4	20,000	J.Hewitt, Robinson, Goddard
05/10	Everton	A	4–2	40,000	J.Hewitt, Raisbeck, Cox, C.Hewitt
12/10	Sunderland	H	1–0	20,000	Fitzpatrick
19/10	Woolwich Arsenal	A	1–2	25,000	J.Hewitt
26/10	The Wednesday	H	3–0	20,000	Fitzpatrick, J.Hewitt, C.Hewitt
02/11	Bristol C	A	0–2	12,000	
09/11	Notts Co	H	6–0	18,000	McPherson, C.Hewitt, J.Hewitt (3), Robinson
16/11	Manchester C	A	1–1	25,000	McPherson
23/11	Preston NE	H	1–2	14,000	C.Hewitt
07/12	Aston Villa	H	5–0	18,000	Robinson (2),Parkinson (2), Goddard
14/12	Newcastle Utd	H	1–5	20,000	Parkinson
21/12	Middlesbrough	A	1–3	14,000	Parkinson
25/12	Chelsea	H	1–4	25,000	J.Hewitt
28/12	Sheffield Utd	A	3–0	5,000	J.Hewitt, Saul, Robinson
01/01	Nottingham F	H	0–0	20,000	
18/01	Bolton W	H	1–0	20,000	Parkinson

25/01	Birmingham C	A	1–1	15,000	J.Hewitt
08/02	Sunderland	A	0–1	30,000	
15/02	Woolwich Arsenal	H	4–1	25,000	J.Hewitt (3), Bradley
29/02	Bristol C	H	3–1	15,000	J.Hewitt (2), Bradley
07/03	Notts Co	A	2–2	10,000	Parkinson, Raisbeck (pen)
09/03	The Wednesday	A	2–1	5,000	Robinson, J.Hewitt
14/03	Manchester C	H	0–1	10,000	
21/03	Preston NE	A	0–3	15,000	
25/03	Manchester Utd	H	7–4	10,000	J.Hewitt (2), McPeherson (3), Robinson (2)
28/03	Bury	A	1–3	8,000	C.Hewitt
04/04	Aston Villa	A	1–5	18,000	Orr
06/04	Blackburn Rovers	A	3–1	8,000	Orr, J.Hewitt, Cox
11/04	Newcastle Utd	A	1–3	30,000	Orr
17/04	Everton	H	0–0	35,000	
18/04	Middlesbrough	H	0–1	10,000	
20/04	Chelsea	A	2–0	35,000	Chorlton, Parkinson
27/04	Bury	H	2–1	10,000	Orr (2)

Div One Position 8th P38 Pts 38

FA CUP

DATE	OPPOSITION	VENUE	SCORE	ATT.	GOALSCORERS
11/01	Derby Co	H	4–2	15,000	Cox, Gorman, Bradley, Parkinson
01/02	Brighton & HA	H	1–1	36,000	Cox
05/02	Brighton & HA	A	3–0	10,000	Bradley (2), Cox
22/02	Newcastle Utd	A	1–3	45,987	Saul

1908–09

FOOTBALL LEAGUE DIVISION ONE

DATE	OPPOSITION	VENUE	SCORE	ATT.	GOALSCORERS
01/09	Aston Villa	H	3–2	14,000	Hewitt, Chorlton (pen), Robinson
05/09	Chelsea	H	2–1	20,000	Orr
12/09	Blackburn R	A	0–1	25,000	
14/09	Sheffield Utd	A	2–0	13,000	Orr (2)
19/09	Bradford C	H	4–0	25,000	Orr, Parkinson, Hewitt (2)
26/09	Manchester Utd	A	2–3	25,000	Cox, Raisbeck (pen)
01/10	Nottingham F	A	1–5	10,000	Bowyer
03/10	Everton	A	0–1	40,000	
10/10	Leicester F	A	2–3	12,000	Orr (2)
17/10	Woolwich Arsenal	H	2–2	18,000	Orr, Hewitt
24/10	Notts Co	A	2–1	15,000	Parkinson, Orr
31/10	Newcastle Utd	H	2–1	20,000	Orr, Cox
07/11	Bristol City	A	0–1	10,000	
14/11	Preston NE	H	2–1	18,000	Hewitt, Robinson
21/11	Middlesbrough	A	0–1	15,000	
28/11	Chelsea	A	1–3	12,000	Bowyer
05/12	The Wednesday	H	3–2	10,000	Hewitt, Bowyer, Orr
12/12	Bury	A	1–2	10,000	Hewitt
19/12	Sheffield Utd	H	2–1	10,000	Orr (2)
25/12	Aston Villa	A	1–1	20,000	Orr
26/12	Nottingham F	H	1–1	25,000	Orr
01/01	Sunderland	A	4–1	18,000	Hewitt (3), Goddard
02/01	Chelsea	A	0–3	25,000	
09/01	Blackburn R	H	1–1	20,000	Robinson
23/01	Bradford C	A	2–0	20,000	Hewitt, Orr
30/01	Manchester Utd	H	3–1	20,000	Goddard, Chorlton (pen), Hewitt
13/02	Leicester C	H	4–1	10,000	Bradley, Goddard (2), Bowyer
20/02	Woolwich Arsenal	A	0–5	15,000	
27/02	Notts Co	H	1–1	12,000	Robinson
13/03	Bristol C	H	1–2	5,000	Chorlton (pen)
20/03	Preston NE	A	0–2	15,000	
27/03	Middlesbrough	H	1–2	12,000	Harrop
03/04	Manchester C	A	0–4	18,000	
09/04	Everton	A	0–5	45,000	
10/04	The Wednesday	A	1–2	20,000	Robinson
12/04	Sunderland	H	3–0	20,000	Orr (pen), Parkinson, Raisbeck
17/04	Bury	H	2–2	15,000	Orr (2)
30/04	Newcastle Utd	A	1–0	30,000	Orr

Div One Position 16th P38 P36

FA CUP

DATE	OPPOSITION	VENUE	SCORE	ATT.	GOALSCORERS
16/01	Lincoln C	H	5–1	8,000	Orr (3), Hewitt, Parkinson
06/02	Norwich	H	2–3	25,000	Cox, Robinson

1909–10

FOOTBALL LEAGUE DIVISION ONE

DATE	OPPOSITION	VENUE	SCORE	ATT.	GOALSCORERS
04/09	Chelsea	A	1–2	25,000	Hewitt
06/09	Bolton W	A	2–1	20,000	Parkinson (2)
11/09	Blackburn R	H	3–1	25,000	Stewart, McDonald, Parkinson
18/09	Nottingham F	A	4–1	15,000	Parkinson (3), Orr
25/09	Sunderland	H	1–4	30,000	Hewitt
02/10	Everton	A	3–2	45,000	Goddard, Stewart, Parkinson
09/10	Manchester Utd	H	3–2	30,000	Parkinson (2), Stewart
16/10	Bolton W	H	2–1	25,000	Bowyer, Stewart
23/10	The Wednesday	H	3–1	30,000	Stewart, Parkinson (2)
30/10	Bristol C	H	1–0	8,000	Robinson
06/11	Bury	H	2–2	25,000	Parkinson, Goddard
13/11	Tottenham H	A	0–1	25,000	
20/11	Preston NE	H	2–0	20,000	Goddard, Stewart
27/11	Notts Co	A	1–3	5,000	Harrop
04/12	Newcastle Utd	H	6–5	22,000	Stewart, Parkinson (2), Orr (2), Goddard
11/12	Middlesbrough	H	0–0	25,000	
18/12	Aston Villa	A	1–3	18,000	Parkinson (pen)
25/12	Bolton W	H	3–0	25,000	Parkinson (pen), Goddard, Orr
27/12	Woolwich Arsenal	H	1–1	15,000	Parkinson
28/12	Sheffield Utd	A	2–4	15,000	Goode, McDonald
01/01	Woolwich Arsenal	A	5–1	25,000	Parkinson (3, 1 pen), Bowyer (2)
08/01	Chelsea	H	5–1	25,000	Stewart (3), Parkinson (2)
22/01	Blackburn R	H	1–1	25,000	Stewart
12/02	Everton	H	0–1	40,000	
19/02	Manchester Utd	A	4–3	45,000	Goddard (2), Stewart (2)
26/02	Bradford C	H	1–0	15,000	Goddard

1909–10 (CONTINUED)

DATE	OPPOSITION	VENUE	SCORE	ATT.	GOALSCORERS
05/03	The Wednesday	A	0–3	12,000	
12/03	Bristol C	H	0–1	20,000	
19/03	Bury	A	2–1	10,000	Bowyer, Goddard
25/03	Sheffield Utd	H	0–0	30,000	
26/03	Tottenham H	H	2–0	20,000	Parkinson, Stewart
28/03	Sunderland	A	1–2	20,000	Stewart
02/04	Preston NE	A	0–2	4,000	
09/04	Notts Co	H	2–1	15,000	Stewart, Parkinson
16/04	Newcastle Utd	A	3–1	20,000	Goddard (2,1 pen), Stewart
20/04	Nottingham F	A	7–3	5,000	Parkinson (4), Bowyer (2), Stewart
23/04	Middlesbrough	A	2–2	8,000	Parkinson, Goddard
30/04	Aston Villa	H	2–0	30,000	Orr, Parkinson

Div One Position 2nd P38 Pts 48

FA CUP

DATE	OPPOSITION	VENUE	SCORE	ATT.	GOALSCORERS
15/01	Bristol City	A	0–2	10,000	

1910–11

FOOTBALL LEAGUE DIVISION ONE

DATE	OPPOSITION	VENUE	SCORE	ATT.	GOAL SCORERS
03/09	Bradford C	H	1–2	20,000	Stewart
10/09	Blackburn R	A	2–1	20,000	Parkinson (2)
17/09	Nottingham F	H	2–3	23,000	Brough, Orr
19/09	Sheffield Utd	A	0–2	8,000	
24/09	Manchester C	A	2–1	20,000	Gilligan, Parkinson
01/10	Everton	H	0–2	40,000	
08/10	The Wednesday	A	0–1	10,000	
15/10	Bristol C	H	4–0	15,000	Brough, Harrop, Parkinson (2)
22/10	Newcastle Utd	A	1–6	20,000	Peake
29/10	Tottenham H	H	1–2	20,000	Brough
05/11	Middlesbrough	A	2–2	20,000	Goddard, Bowyer
12/11	Preston NE	H	3–0	8,000	Orr, Parkinson, Bowyer
19/11	Notts Co	A	0–1	10,000	
26/11	Manchester Utd	H	3–2	12,000	Goddard (pen), Parkinson, Stewart
03/12	Oldham A	A	1–3	8,000	Goddard
10/12	Bury	A	0–3	6,000	
17/12	Sheffield Utd	H	2–0	10,000	Parkinson, Stewart
24/12	Aston Villa	A	1–1	16,000	Stewart
26/12	Sunderland	H	1–2	35,000	Goddard (pen)
27/12	Everton	A	1–0	51,000	Parkinson
31/12	Bradford C	A	3–1	17,000	Bowyer, Parkinson (2)
02/01	Sunderland	A	0–4	12,000	
07/01	Blackburn R	H	2–2	6,000	Parkinson, Goddard
21/01	Nottingham F	A	0–2	12,000	
28/01	Manchester C	H	1–1	16,000	Bowyer
11/02	The Wednesday	H	3–0	12,000	Parkinson (3)
18/02	Bristol C	A	1–1	6,000	Parkinson
27/02	Newcastle Utd	H	3–0	8,000	Gilligan (2), Parkinson
04/03	Tottenham H	A	0–1	20,000	
11/03	Middlesbrough	H	3–0	20,000	Parkinson, Gilligan, Goddard
18/03	Preston NE	A	1–2	2,000	Orr
25/03	Notts Co	H	2–1	10,000	Goddard (2)
01/04	Manchester Utd	A	0–2	12,000	
08/04	Oldham A	H	1–0	13,000	Gilligan
14/04	Woolwich Arsenal	A	0–0	15,000	
15/04	Bury	H	2–0	15,000	Peake (2)
17/04	Woolwich Arsenal	H	1–1	20,000	Parkinson (benefit game for Sam Hardy)
29/04	Aston Villa	H	3–1	25,000	Orr (2), McDonald

Div One Position 13th P38 Pts 37

FA CUP

DATE	OPPOSITION	VENUE	SCORE	ATT.	GOALSCORERS
14/01	Gainsborough T	H	3–2	15,000	Bowyer (2), Goddard
04/02	Everton	A	1–2	50,000	Parkinson

1911–12

FOOTBALL LEAGUE DIVISION ONE

DATE	OPPOSITION	VENUE	SCORE	ATT.	GOALSCORERS
02/09	Woolwich Arsenal	A	2–2	12,000	McConnell, Gilligan
04/09	Bolton W	A	1–2	15,000	Parkinson
09/09	Manchester C	H	2–2	25,000	Parkinson, Orr
16/09	Everton	A	1–2	40,000	Parkinson
23/09	West Brom A	A	1–2	18,000	Parkinson
30/09	Sunderland	A	2–1	12,000	McDonald, Robinson
07/10	Blackburn R	H	1–2	30,000	Harrop
14/10	The Wednesday	A	2–2	12,000	Gilligan, Parkinson
21/10	Bury	H	1–1	10,000	Gilligan
28/10	Middlesbrough	A	2–3	13,720	Uren, Gilligan
04/11	Notts Co	H	3–0	15,000	Bovill (2), Goddard
11/11	Tottenham H	A	0–2	20,000	
18/11	Manchester Utd	H	3–2	15,000	Parkinson, Bovill (2)
25/11	Preston NE	H	0–1	10,000	
02/12	Aston Villa	A	0–5	16,000	
09/12	Newcastle Utd	H	0–1	20,000	
16/12	Sheffield Utd	A	1–3	12,000	Parkinson
23/12	Oldham A	H	1–0	10,000	Gilligan
25/12	Bolton W	H	1–0	25,000	Parkinson
30/12	Woolwich Arsenal	H	4–1	16,000	Parkinson (2), Bovil (2)
01/01	Bradford C	H	1–0	40,000	Uren
06/01	Manchester C	A	3–2	15,000	Parkinson, Bovill, W.Stuart
20/01	Everton	H	1–3	35,000	Gilligan
27/01	West Brom A	A	0–1	15,000	
10/02	Blackburn R	A	0–1	15,000	
17/02	The Wednesday	H	1–1	15,000	Robinson
24/02	Bury	A	2–2	8,000	Gracie, Stewart
02/03	Middlesbrough	H	1–1	25,000	Miller
09/03	Notts Co	A	0–0	15,000	
16/03	Tottenham H	H	1–2	20,000	Lacey
23/03	Manchester Utd	A	1–1	12,000	Parkinson
30/03	Preston NE	A	1–2	9,000	Gilligan
05/04	Sunderland	H	2–1	30,000	Lowe, Gilligan
06/04	Aston Villa	H	1–2	30,000	Gilligan

08/03	Bradford C	A	2–0	10,000	Speakman, Gilligan
13/04	Newcastle Utd	A	1–1	15,000	Stewart
20/04	Sheffield Utd	A	2–0	25,000	Stewart, Goddard (pen)
27/04	Oldham A	A	1–0	8,000	Gilligan

Div One Position 17th P38 Pts 34

FA CUP

DATE	OPPOSITION	VENUE	SCORE	ATT.	GOALSCORERS
13/01	Leyton Orient	H	1–0	33,000	Parkinson
03/02	Fulham	A	0–3	30,000	

1912–13

FOOTBALL LEAGUE DIVISION ONE

DATE	OPPOSITION	VENUE	SCORE	ATT.	GOAL SCORERS
04/09	Oldham A	H	2–0	20,000	Tosswill, Miller
07/09	Woolwich Arsenal	H	3–0	30,000	Peart (o.g.), Goddard (2)
09/09	Chelsea	A	2–1	16,000	Goddard, Gracie
14/09	Bradford C	A	0–2	20,000	
21/09	Manchester C	H	1–2	25,000	Lacey
28/09	West Brom A	A	1–3	20,000	Miller
05/10	Everton	H	0–2	46,000	
12/10	The Wednesday	A	0–1	20,000	
14/10	Sheffield Utd	A	1–4	3,000	Metcalfe
19/10	Blackburn R	H	4–1	20,000	Metcalfe (2), Ferguson, Goddard (pen)
26/10	Derby Co	A	2–4	6,000	Metcalfe (2)
02/11	Tottenham H	H	4–1	20,000	Mackinlay, Goddard, Parkinson (2)
09/11	Middlesbrough	A	4–3	11,973	Miller, Metcalfe (2), Parkinson
16/11	Notts Co	H	0–0	15,000	
23/11	Manchester Utd	A	1–3	14,000	Mackinlay
30/11	Aston Villa	H	2–0	30,000	Mackinlay, Miles (o.g.)
07/12	Sunderland	A	0–7	14,000	
14/12	Bolton W	A	1–1	12,000	Mackinlay
21/12	Sheffield Utd	H	2–2	20,000	Parkinson, Metcalfe
26/12	Newcastle Utd	H	2–1	35,000	Miller (2)
28/12	Woolwich Arsenal	H	1–1	15,000	Peake
01/01	Newcastle Utd	A	0–0	20,000	
04/01	Bradford C	H	2–1	20,000	Parkinson, Mackinlay
18/01	Manchester C	A	1–4	20,000	Stewart
25/01	West Brom A	H	2–1	20,000	Miller (2)
08/02	Everton	A	2–0	40,000	Parkinson (2)
10/02	Oldham A	A	1–3	25,000	Metcalfe
15/02	The Wednesday	H	2–1	25,000	Metcalfe, Miller
01/03	Derby Co	A	2–1	18,000	Welfare, Lacey
08/03	Tottenham H	A	0–1	15,000	
10/03	Blackburn R	H	1–5	4,000	Mackinlay
15/03	Middlesbrough	H	4–2	15,000	Peake, Lowe, Metcalfe, Parkinson (pen)
22/03	Notts Co	A	0–3	7,000	
24/03	Chelsea	H	1–2	25,000	Lacey
29/03	Manchester Utd	H	0–2	12,000	
05/04	Aston Villa	A	3–1	25,000	Goddard, Parkinson, Metcalfe
12/04	Sunderland	H	2–5	28,000	Metcalfe (2)
19/04	Bolton W	H	5–2	28,000	Metcalfe, Parkinson (3), Goddard

Div One Position 12th P38 Pts 37

FA CUP

DATE	OPPOSITION	VENUE	SCORE	ATT.	GOALSCORERS
15/01	Bristol C	H	3–0	15,000	Goddard (pen), Peake, Lacey
01/02	Woolwich Arsenal	A	4–1	8,653	Metcalfe (3), Lacey
22/02	Newcastle Utd	H	1–1	37,903	Lacey
26/02	Newcastle Utd	A	0–1	45,000	

1913–14

FOOTBALL LEAGUE DIVISION ONE

DATE	OPPOSITION	VENUE	SCORE	ATT.	GOALSCORERS
01/09	Derby Co	A	1–1	7,000	Miller
06/09	Blackburn R	A	2–6	30,000	Miller (2)
13/09	Sunderland	H	1–3	25,000	Gracie
20/09	Everton	A	2–1	40,000	Lacey (2)
27/09	West Brom A	H	0–0	25,000	
04/10	The Wednesday	A	1–4	25,000	Crawford (pen)
11/10	Bolton W	H	2–1	15,000	Miller (2)
18/10	Chelsea	A	0–3	40,000	
25/10	Oldham A	H	0–3	25,000	
01/11	Manchester Utd	A	0–3	20,000	
08/11	Burnley	H	1–1	18,000	Lacey
15/11	Preston NE	A	1–0	12,000	Mackinlay
22/11	Newcastle Utd	H	0–0	20,000	
29/11	Tottenham H	H	2–1	25,000	Dawson, Miller
06/12	Aston Villa	A	1–2	15,000	Sheldon (pen)
13/12	Middlesbrough	A	2–1	25,000	Miller, Gracie
20/12	Sheffield Utd	A	1–0	10,000	Miller
25/12	Manchester C	H	4–2	30,000	Lacey, Sheldon (2), Gracie
26/12	Manchester C	A	0–1	25,000	
27/12	Blackburn R	H	3–3	30,000	Dawson, Miller, Lacey
01/01	Bradford C	H	0–1	35,000	
03/01	Sunderland	A	2–1	15,000	Sheldon, Parkinson
17/01	Everton	H	1–2	35,000	Metcalfe
24/01	West Brom A	A	1–0	10,000	McDougall
07/02	The Wednesday	H	1–2	20,000	Lacey
14/02	Bolton W	A	1–2	20,000	Miller
28/02	Oldham A	A	2–2	12,000	Nicholl, Metcalfe
14/03	Burnley	A	2–5	16,000	Banks, Nicholl
18/03	Chelsea	H	3–0	12,000	Banks (2), Miller
21/03	Preston NE	H	3–1	25,000	Miller (2), Nicholl
01/04	Newcastle Utd	A	1–8	18,000	Sheldon, Miller (pen)
04/04	Tottenham H	A	0–0	25,000	
10/04	Derby Co	H	1–0	30,000	Banks
11/04	Aston Villa	H	0–1	40,000	
13/04	Bradford C	A	0–1	20,000	
15/04	Manchester Utd	H	1–2	25,000	Dawson
18/04	Middlesbrough	H	0–4	15,000	
27/04	Sheffield Utd	H	2–1	7,000	Miller (2)

Div One Position 16th P38 Pts 35

FA CUP

DATE	OPPOSITION	VENUE	SCORE	ATT.	GOALSCORERS
10/01	Barnsley	H	1–1	33,000	Lacey
15/01	Barnsley	A	1–0	23,999	Lacey
31/01	Gillingham	H	2–0	42,045	Lacey, Ferguson
21/02	West Ham Utd	A	1–1	15,000	Miller
25/02	West Ham Utd	H	5–1	43,729	Lacey (2), Miller (2), Metcalfe
07/03	QPR	H	2–1	43,000	Sheldon, Miller
S FINAL: 28/03					
Aston Villa			2–0	27,474	Nicholl (2)
FINAL: 25/04					
Burnley			0–1	72,778	

SEMI–FINAL PLAYED AT WHITE HART LANE, FINAL PLAYED AT CRYSTAL PALACE

1914–15

FOOTBALL LEAGUE DIVISION ONE

DATE	OPPOSITION	VENUE	SCORE	ATT.	GOALSCORERS
02/09	Bolton W	H	4–3	15,000	Sheldon, Lacey, Metcalfe, Nicholl
05/09	Notts C	H	1–1	15,000	Metcalfe
12/09	Sunderland	A	2–2	12,000	Sheldon (pen), Metcalfe
19/09	The Wednesday	H	2–1	25,000	Miller (2)
21/09	Blackburn R	A	2–4	15,000	Metcalfe, Nicholl
26/09	West Brom A	A	0–4	15,000	
03/10	Everton	H	0–5	32,000	
10/10	Chelsea	A	1–3	30,000	Pagnam
17/10	Bradford C	H	2–1	20,000	Miller (2)
24/10	Burnley	A	0–3	18,000	
31/10	Tottenham H	H	7–2	20,000	Pagnam (4), Sheldon (2), Banks
07/11	Newcastle Utd	A	0–0	25,000	
14/11	Middlesbrough	H	1–1	25,000	Pagnam
21/11	Sheffield Utd	A	1–2	6,000	Pagnam
28/11	Aston Villa	H	3–6	15,000	Nicholl (2), Miller
05/12	Manchester C	H	1–1	8,000	Nicholl
12/12	Bradford Pk Av	A	0–1	8,000	
19/12	Oldham A	H	1–2	10,000	Pagnam
25/12	Bolton W	A	1–0	15,000	Lacey
26/12	Manchester Utd	H	1–1	25,000	Pagnam
02/01	Notts Co	A	1–3	8,000	Miller
16/01	Sunderland	H	2–1	17,000	Miller, Pagnam
23/01	The Wednesday	A	1–2	12,000	Pagnam
06/02	Everton	A	3–1	30,000	Sheldon, Nicholl, Pagnam
13/02	Chelsea	H	3–3	14,000	Pagnam (3)
27/02	Burnley	H	3–0	22,000	Sheldon (pen), Nicholl (2)
06/03	Tottenham H	A	1–1	12,000	Sheldon
10/03	Bradford C	A	0–2	5,000	Metcalfe, Pagnam
13/03	Manchester C	A	3–2	20,000	Pagnam, Metcalfe, Miller
20/03	Middlesbrough	A	0–3	6,000	
24/03	West Brom A	H	3–1	20,000	Pagnam (2), Mackinlay
29/03	Newcastle Utd	H	2–2	3,000	Miller, Pagnam
02/04	Manchester Utd	A	0–2	12,000	
03/04	Aston Villa	A	2–6	12,000	Sheldon (pen), Miller
05/04	Blackburn R	H	3–0	30,000	Miller, Nicholl, Sheldon
12/04	Sheffield Utd	H	2–1	4,000	Pagnam, Sheldon (pen)
17/04	Bradford Pk Av	H	2–1	20,000	Pagnam, Banks
24/04	Oldham A	A	2–0	5,000	Pagnam (2)

Div One Position 13th   P38 Pts 37

FA CUP

DATE	OPPOSITION	VENUE	SCORE	ATT.	GOALSCORERS
09/01	Stockport Co	H	3–0	10,000	Pagnam (2), Metcalfe
30/01	Sheffield Utd	A	0–1	25,000	

FOOTBALL LEAGUE 1915/16–1918/19

CANCELLED DUE TO FIRST WORLD WAR

1919–20

FOOTBALL LEAGUE DIVISION ONE

DATE	OPPOSITION	VENUE	SCORE	ATT.	GOALSCORERS
30/08	Bradford C	A	3–1	25,000	Lewis, Chambers, Pearson
01/09	Arsenal	H	2–3	12,000	Chambers, Pagnam
06/09	Bradford C	H	2–1	30,000	Pagnam, Mackinlay
08/09	Arsenal	A	0–1	25,000	
13/09	Aston Villa	H	2–1	28,000	Pagnam, Mackinlay
20/09	Aston Villa	A	1–0	30,000	Forshaw
27/09	Newcastle Utd	H	1–1	40,000	Pagnam
04/10	Newcastle Utd	A	0–3	40,000	
11/10	Chelsea	A	0–1	40,000	
18/10	Chelsea	H	0–1	40,000	
25/10	Burnley	A	2–1	15,000	Chambers (2)
01/11	Burnley	H	0–1	30,000	
08/11	Bradford Park Ave	A	2–1	15,000	Chambers, Lacey
15/11	Bradford Park Ave	H	3–3	30,000	Forshaw (2), Pearson
22/11	Preston NE	A	1–2	14,000	Chambers
29/11	Preston NE	H	1–2	12,000	Lewis
06/12	Middlesbrough	A	2–3	20,000	Lewis, Pearson
13/12	Middlesbrough	H	1–0	30,000	Chambers
20/12	Everton	A	0–0	40,000	
25/12	Sunderland	H	3–2	30,000	Lacey, Hobson (o.g.), T.Miller
26/12	Manchester Utd	A	0–0	45,000	
27/12	Everton	H	3–1	49,662	Lewis, T.Miller (2)
01/01	Manchester Utd	H	0–0	30,000	
03/01	Sheffield Utd	A	2–3	25,000	T.Miller (2)
17/01	Sheffield Utd	H	2–0	35,000	T.Miller, Lewis
24/01	Bolton W	A	3–0	20,000	Lacey, T.Miller, Bromilow
04/02	Bolton W	H	2–0	30,000	Lewis (2)
07/02	Blackburn R	A	2–0	20,000	T.Miller (2)
14/02	Blackburn R	H	3–0	30,000	Chambers (2), Bamber
26/02	Notts Co	A	0–1	12,000	
28/02	Notts Co	H	3–0	30,000	Pearson, Sheldon, T.Miller
10/03	The Wednesday	H	1–0	15,000	Chambers
13/03	The Wednesday	A	2–2	20,000	Forshaw, Mackinlay
20/03	Manchester C	H	1–0	35,000	Chambers
27/03	Manchester C	A	1–2	40,000	Chambers (pen)
02/04	Oldham A	H	1–1	23,000	T.Miller
03/04	Derby C	H	3–0	28,000	Forshaw (3)

DATE	OPPOSITION	VENUE	SCORE	ATT.	GOALSCORERS
05/04	Oldham A	H	2–2	30,000	Chambers (2)
10/04	Derby C	A	0–3	14,000	
17/04	West Brom A	H	0–0	40,000	
24/04	West Brom A	A	1–1	40,000	Mackinlay
01/05	Sunderland	A	1–0	30,000	Chambers

Div One Position 4th   P42 Pts 48

FA CUP

DATE	OPPOSITION	VENUE	SCORE	ATT.	GOALSCORERS
10/01	South Shields	A	1–1	10,000	Lewis
14/01	South Shields	H	2–0	40,000	Lewis, Sheldon
31/01	Luton T	A	2–0	12,640	Lacey (2)
21/02	Birmingham C	H	2–0	50,000	Sheldon, T.Miller
06/03	Huddersfield T	A	1–2	44,248	T.Miller

1920–21

FOOTBALL LEAGUE DIVISION ONE

DATE	OPPOSITION	VENUE	SCORE	ATT.	GOALSCORERS
28/08	Manchester C	H	4–2	45,000	Mackinlay, T.Miller (2), W.Wadsworth
01/09	West Brom A	A	1–1	30,000	T.Miller
04/09	Manchester C	A	2–3	40,000	Chambers, W.Wadsworth
06/09	West Brom A	H	0–0	35,000	
11/09	Oldham A	H	5–2	30,000	Johnson (2), Chambers, Sheldon, Bamber
18/09	Oldham A	A	0–0	20,000	
25/09	Preston NE	H	6–0	40,000	Chambers, H.Wadsworth, Johnson (3), Forshaw
02/10	Preston NE	A	3–2	28,000	Chambers, Forshaw, H.Wadsworth
09/10	Sheffield Utd	H	2–2	40,000	Mackinlay, Johnson
16/10	Sheffield Utd	A	1–0	20,000	Chambers
23/10	Everton	H	1–0	50,000	Forshaw
30/10	Everton	A	3–0	55,000	Johnson, Chambers (2)
06/11	Bradford Pk Av	H	0–1	35,000	
13/11	Bradford Pk Av	A	3–1	12,000	Chambers, Forshaw (2)
20/11	Newcastle Utd	A	0–2	50,000	
27/11	Newcastle Utd	H	0–1	40,000	
04/12	Burnley	H	0–0	35,000	
11/12	Burnley	A	0–1	30,000	
18/12	Aston Villa	H	4–1	35,000	Johnson (2),Lewis, Mackinlay (pen)
25/12	Chelsea	A	1–1	45,000	Johnson
27/12	Chelsea	H	2–1	50,000	W.Wadsworth, Chambers
01/01	Aston Villa	A	2–0	30,000	Johnson, Chambers
15/01	Sunderland	H	0–0	30,000	
22/01	Sunderland	A	1–2	18,000	Chambers
05/02	Manchester Utd	A	1–1	30,000	Chambers
09/02	Manchester Utd	H	2–0	35,000	Lewis, Chambers
12/02	Bradford C	A	2–1	35,000	Chambers (2)
19/02	Bradford C	A	0–0	28,000	
26/02	Huddersfield T	H	4–1	35,000	W.Wadsworth, Chambers (2), Forshaw
05/03	Huddersfield T	A	2–1	18,000	Chambers, Johnson
12/03	Middlesbrough	H	0–0	40,000	
19/03	Middlesbrough	A	1–0	25,000	Chambers (pen)
25/03	Tottenham H	H	1–1	40,000	Forshaw
26/03	Blackburn R	A	1–1	25,000	Forshaw
28/03	Tottenham H	A	0–1	35,000	
02/04	Blackburn R	H	2–0	35,000	Chambers, H.Wadsworth
09/04	Derby C	A	0–0	10,000	
16/09	Derby C	H	1–1	28,000	Chambers
23/04	Bolton W	A	0–1	25,000	
30/04	Bolton W	H	2–3	30,000	Johnson, Lacey
02/05	Arsenal	A	0–0	17,000	
07/05	Arsenal	H	3–0	27,000	Chambers, Forshaw, W.Wadsworth

Div One Position 4th   P42 Pts 51

FA CUP

DATE	OPPOSITION	VENUE	SCORE	ATT.	GOALSCORERS
08/01	Manchester Utd	H	1–1	36,000	Chambers
12/01	Manchester Utd	A	2–1	29,189	Lacey, Chambers
29/01	Newcastle Utd	A	0–1	61,400	

1921–22

FOOTBALL LEAGUE DIVISION ONE

DATE	OPPOSITION	VENUE	SCORE	ATT.	GOALSCORERS
27/08	Sunderland	A	0–3	40,000	
31/08	Manchester C	H	3–2	27,000	Forshaw, Matthews (2)
03/09	Sunderland	H	2–1	40,000	Matthews, Forshaw
07/09	Manchester C	A	1–1	25,000	Chambers
10/09	Sheffield Utd	A	1–0	30,000	Bromilow
17/09	Sheffield Utd	H	1–1	30,000	Chambers
24/09	Chelsea	A	1–1	35,000	Matthews
01/10	Chelsea	H	1–1	35,000	Forshaw
08/10	Preston NE	A	1–1	20,000	Beadles
15/10	Preston NE	H	4–0	38,000	Chambers, Forshaw, Lucas (pen), Beadles
22/10	Tottenham H	A	1–0	31,593	Beadles
29/10	Tottenham H	H	1–1	40,000	Lewis
05/11	Everton	A	1–1	52,000	Shone
12/11	Everton	H	1–1	50,000	Forshaw
19/11	Middlesbrough	H	4–0	35,000	Shone (3), Lucas (pen)
26/11	Middlesbrough	A	1–3	24,000	Shone
03/12	Aston Villa	A	1–1	30,000	Chambers
10/12	Aston Villa	H	2–0	40,000	Shone, Forshaw
17/12	Manchester Utd	H	2–1	40,000	Lacey, Chambers
24/12	Manchester Utd	A	0–0	30,000	
26/12	Newcastle Utd	H	1–0	40,000	Chambers
27/12	Huddersfield T	H	2–0	40,000	Chambers (2)
31/12	Bradford C	A	0–0	18,000	
02/01	Newcastle Utd	A	1–1	50,000	Forshaw
14/01	Bradford C	H	2–1	15,000	Chambers, Forshaw
21/01	Huddersfield T	A	1–0	20,000	Chambers
04/02	Birmingham C	A	2–0	15,000	Chambers (2)
11/02	Birmingham C	H	1–0	30,000	Forshaw
25/02	Arsenal	H	4–0	40,000	Forshaw (3), Turnbull (o.g.)
04/03	Blackburn R	A	0–0	35,000	
11/03	Blackburn R	H	2–0	35,000	Mackinlay, Forshaw
18/03	Bolton W	H	0–2	30,000	
22/03	Arsenal	A	0–1	12,000	

1921–22 (CONTINUED)

25/03	Bolton W	A	3–1	30,000	Forshaw (2), Chambers
01/04	Oldham A	H	2–0	30,000	Chambers, Gilhespy
08/04	Oldham A	A	0–4	12,000	
14/04	Burnley	A	1–1	30,000	Chambers
15/04	Cardiff C	H	5–1	50,000	Bromilow, Chambers (3), McNab
17/04	Burnley	H	2–1	50,000	Chambers, Forshaw
22/04	Cardiff C	A	0–2	30,000	
29/04	West Brom A	H	1–2	45,000	Beadles
06/05	West Brom A	A	4–1	15,000	Forshaw, Beadles (2), McNab

Div One Position 1st   P42   Pts 57

FA CUP
DATE	OPPOSITION	VENUE	SCORE	ATT.	GOALSCORERS
07/01	Sunderland	A	1–1	30,000	Forshaw
11/01	Sunderland	H	5–0	46,000	Forshaw (2), Chambers (2), W Wadsworth
28/01	West Brom A	H	0–1	50,000	

CHARITY SHIELD
DATE	OPPOSITION	VENUE	SCORE	ATT.	GOALSCORERS
10/05	Huddersfield T	N	0–1	29,000	(at Old Trafford)

1922–23

FOOTBALL LEAGUE DIVISION ONE
DATE	OPPOSITION	VENUE	SCORE	ATT.	GOALSCORERS
26/08	Arsenal	H	5–2	40,962	Johnson (3), Bromilow, Chambers
30/08	Sunderland	A	0–1	36,000	
02/09	Arsenal	A	0–1	20,000	
06/09	Sunderland	H	5–1	30,000	Forshaw, Chambers (2), Johnson, Mackinlay
09/09	Preston NE	A	3–1	34,000	W Wadsworth, Johnson, Chambers
16/09	Preston NE	H	5–2	36,000	Chambers, Forshaw (3), Bromilow
23/09	Burnley	H	3–0	45,000	Chambers, Forshaw (2)
30/09	Burnley	A	0–2	25,000	
07/10	Everton	H	5–1	54,368	Chambers (3), McNab, Bromilow
14/10	Everton	A	1–0	52,000	Johnson
21/10	Cardiff C	H	3–1	35,000	Gilhespy, Forshaw, W Wadsworth
28/10	Cardiff C	A	0–3	40,000	
04/11	Tottenham H	A	4–2	45,000	Chambers (2), Forshaw, Gilhespy
11/11	Tottenham H	H	0–0	30,000	
18/11	Aston Villa	A	3–0	32,000	Mackinlay, Chambers, Johnson
25/11	Aston Villa	H	1–0	40,000	Chambers
02/12	Newcastle Utd	A	0–2	30,000	
09/12	Newcastle Utd	H	1–0	35,000	Chambers
16/12	Nottingham F	H	2–1	25,000	Johnson, Mackinlay
23/12	Nottingham F	A	3–1	20,000	Johnson, Forshaw (2)
25/12	Oldham A	A	2–0	20,166	Mackinlay, Johnson
26/12	Oldham A	H	2–1	40,000	Mackinlay, Forshaw
30/12	Chelsea	A	0–0	40,000	
06/01	Chelsea	H	1–0	25,000	Lacey
20/01	Middlesbrough	A	2–0	25,000	Chambers, Johnson
27/01	Middlesbrough	H	2–0	40,000	Chambers, Johnson
07/02	West Brom A	A	2–0	28,000	Forshaw, Johnson
10/02	West Brom A	H	0–0	18,000	
17/02	Blackburn R	H	3–0	25,000	Forshaw (3)
03/03	Bolton W	H	3–0	25,000	Forshaw, Johnson, Hopkin
12/03	Blackburn R	A	0–1	30,000	
17/03	Manchester C	A	0–1	40,000	
24/03	Manchester C	H	2–0	25,000	Chambers, Forshaw
30/03	Sheffield Utd	H	2–1	40,000	Chambers (2)
31/03	Birmingham C	A	1–0	30,000	Chambers
02/04	Sheffield Utd	A	1–4	40,000	Forshaw
07/04	Birmingham C	H	0–0	30,000	
14/04	Huddersfield T	H	0–0	17,000	
18/04	Bolton W	A	1–1	25,000	Forshaw
21/04	Huddersfield T	A	1–1	45,000	Chambers
28/04	Stoke C	A	0–0	20,000	
05/05	Stoke C	H	1–0	30,000	Chambers

Div One Position 1st   P42   Pts 60

FA CUP
DATE	OPPOSITION	VENUE	SCORE	ATT.	GOALSCORERS
13/01	Arsenal	H	0–0	37,000	
17/01	Arsenal	A	4–1	40,000	Chambers (2), Johnson, Mackinlay (pen)
03/02	Wolves	A	2–0	40,079	Johnson, Forshaw
24/02	Sheffield Utd	H	1–2	51,859	Chambers

1923–24

FOOTBALL LEAGUE DIVISION ONE
DATE	OPPOSITION	VENUE	SCORE	ATT.	GOALSCORERS
25/08	West Brom A	A	0–2	25,000	
29/08	Birmingham C	H	6–2	16,000	Walsh (2), Forshaw, Chambers (3)
01/09	West Brom A	H	0–0	40,000	
05/09	Birmingham C	A	1–2	25,000	Walsh
08/09	Preston NE	A	1–0	20,000	Walsh
15/09	Preston NE	H	3–1	35,000	Chambers, Walsh (2)
22/09	Burnley	A	0–2	18,000	
29/09	Burnley	H	1–0	40,000	Forshaw
06/10	Everton	A	0–1	51,000	
13/10	Everton	H	1–2	50,000	Walsh
20/10	Nottingham F	H	4–2	30,000	Mackinlay (2,1 pen), Walsh (2)
27/10	Nottingham F	A	1–0	15,000	Walsh
03/11	Huddersfield T	H	1–1	30,000	Chambers
10/11	Huddersfield T	A	1–3	15,000	Chambers
17/11	Aston Villa	A	0–0	25,000	
24/11	Aston Villa	H	0–1	20,000	
01/12	Sheffield Utd	A	1–1	20,000	Chambers
08/12	Sheffield Utd	H	2–3	40,000	Chambers, Forshaw
15/12	Cardiff C	H	0–2	35,000	
22/12	Cardiff C	A	0–2	30,000	
25/12	Newcastle Utd	H	0–1	35,000	
26/12	Newcastle Utd	A	1–2	25,000	Keetley
29/12	West Ham Utd	H	2–0	30,000	Walsh (2)
01/01	Chelsea	H	3–1	30,000	Shone, Walsh, Keetley
05/01	West Ham Utd	A	0–1	25,000	

19/01	Manchester C	A	1–0	20,000	Chambers
26/01	Manchester C	H	0–0	20 000	
09/02	Bolton W	H	3–1	30 000	Chambers, Forshaw, Mackinlay (pen)
16/02	Sunderland	A	0–0	20,000	
01/03	Arsenal	A	1–3	35,000	Chambers
12/03	Bolton W	A	1–4	10,000	Walsh
15/03	Blackburn R	H	0–0	30,000	
19/03	Sunderland	H	4–2	30,000	Chamber, Mackinlay (2), Shone
22/03	Blackburn R	A	0–0	15,000	
29/03	Tottenham H	H	1–0	20,000	Chambers
02/04	Arsenal	H	0–0	30,000	
05/04	Tottenham H	A	1–1	22,470	Shone
12/04	Middlesbrough	H	3–1	20,000	Mackinlay, Walsh (2)
18/04	Chelsea	A	1–2	38,000	Baker (o.g.)
19/04	Middlesbrough	A	1–1	15,000	Shone
26/04	Notts Co	H	1–0	15,000	Forshaw
03/05	Notts Co	A	2–1	8,000	Cornwall (o.g.), Shone

Div One Position 12th   P42   Pts 41

FA CUP
DATE	OPPOSITION	VENUE	SCORE	ATT.	GOALSCORERS
12/01	Bradford C	H	2–1	25,000	Chambers (2)
02/02	Bolton W	A	4–1	51,596	Walsh (3), Chambers
23/02	Southampton	A	0–0	18, 671	
27/02	Southampton	H	2–0	49,000	Chambers, Forshaw
08/03	Newcastle Utd	A	0–1	56,595	

1924–25

FOOTBALL LEAGUE DIVISION ONE
DATE	OPPOSITION	VENUE	SCORE	ATT.	GOALSCORERS
30/08	Aston Villa	H	2–4	42,000	Mackinlay, Shone
06/09	Arsenal	A	0–2	30,000	
13/09	Manchester C	H	5–3	30,000	Mackinlay, Forshaw, Shone (2), Johnson
15/09	Blackburn R	A	1–3	25,000	Mackinlay
20/09	Bury	A	0–0	25,000	
27/09	Nottingham F	H	3–0	33,000	Rawlings (2), Shone
04/10	Everton	A	1–0	53,000	Rawlings
11/10	Newcastle Utd	A	0–0	30,000	
15/10	Blackburn R	H	0–0	20,000	
18/10	Sheffield Utd	H	4–1	35,000	Forshaw (4)
25/10	Sunderland	H	3–1	40,000	Rawlings (2), Chambers
08/11	Preston NE	A	3–1	25,000	Rawlings, Forshaw (2)
12/11	Huddersfield T	H	2–3	25,000	Forshaw, McNab
15/11	Burnley	A	1–2	20,000	Forshaw
22/11	Leeds Utd	H	1–0	25,000	Forshaw
29/11	Birmingham	A	2–5	25,000	Chambers, Forshaw
06/12	West Brom A	H	1–1	25,000	Forshaw
13/12	Tottenham H	A	1–1	25,604	Forshaw
15/12	Cardiff C	A	3–1	25,000	Forshaw (2), Shone
20/12	Bolton W	H	0–0	15,000	
25/12	Notts Co	A	2–1	10,000	Forshaw (2)
26/12	Notts Co	H	1–0	46,187	Chambers
03/01	Arsenal	H	2–1	24,000	Forshaw, Chambers
17/01	Manchester C	A	0–5	30,000	
21/01	Aston Villa	H	4–1	30,000	Shone, Walsh (2), Chambers
24/01	Bury	H	4–0	30,000	Shone (2), Rawlings, Walsh
04/02	Nottingham F	A	1–0	20,000	McNab
07/02	Everton	H	3–1	54,000	Shone, Hopkin, Chambers
14/02	Newcastle Utd	H	1–1	33,000	Forshaw
28/02	Sunderland	A	0–3	18,000	
14/03	Preston NE	A	0–4	12,000	
16/03	Sheffield Utd	A	1–0	30,000	Shone
21/03	Burnley	H	3–0	25,000	Baron (2) Shone
28/03	Leeds Utd	A	1–4	25,000	T.Scott
04/04	Birmingham C	H	1–1	28,000	Baron
10/04	West Ham Utd	H	2–0	30,000	Chambers, Shone
11/04	West Brom A	A	0–0	25, 000	
13/04	West Ham Utd	A	1–0	25,000	Mackinlay
18/04	Tottenham H	H	1–0	12,000	Baron
25/04	Bolton W	A	0–2	25,000	
29/04	Cardiff C	H	1–2	20,000	Baron
02/05	Huddersfield Town	A	1–1	16,000	T.Wilson (o.g.)

Div One Position 4th   P42   Pts 50

FA CUP
DATE	OPPOSITION	VENUE	SCORE	ATT.	GOALSCORERS
10/01	Leeds Utd	H	3–0	39,000	Shone (2), Hopkin
31/01	Bristol C	A	1–0	29,362	Rawlings
21/02	Birmingham C	H	2–1	44,000	Rawlings, Shone
07/03	Southampton	A	0–1	21,501	

1925–26

FOOTBALL LEAGUE DIVISION ONE
DATE	OPPOSITION	VENUE	SCORE	ATT.	GOALSCORERS
29/08	Leicester C	A	1–3	27,000	Mackinlay
02/09	Notts Co	H	2–0	26,000	Flint (o.g.), Forshaw
05/09	West Ham Utd	H	0–0	30,000	
12/09	Arsenal	A	1–1	35,000	Walsh
19/09	Manchester Utd	H	5–0	18,000	Forshaw (3), Chambers, Rawlings
26/09	Everton	H	5–1	55,000	Forshaw (3), Walsh, Chambers
01/10	Notts Co	A	2–1	15,000	Bromilow, Walsh
03/10	Burnley	A	1–2	15,000	Chambers
10/10	Leeds Utd	H	1–1	27,000	Baron
17/10	Manchester C	H	2–1	35,000	Chambers, Forshaw
24/10	Tottenham H	H	1–3	34,477	Forshaw
31/10	Sunderland	H	2–2	40,000	Chambers, Forshaw
14/11	West Brom A	H	2–0	30,000	Oxley (2)
21/11	Birmingham	A	0–2	12,000	
25/11	Huddersfield T	A	0–0	6,000	
28/11	Bury	A	0–1	30,000	
05/12	Blackburn R	A	1–1	5,000	Chambers
12/12	Cardiff C	H	0–0	30,000	
19/12	Sheffield Utd	A	1–3	20,000	Forshaw
25/12	Newcastle Utd	H	6–3	35,000	Chambers (3), Oxley, Forshaw, Pratt

26/12	Newcastle Utd	A	0–3	50,000	
01/01	Aston Villa	H	3–1	30,000	Forshaw (2), Oxley
02/01	Leicester C	H	0–3	35,000	
16/01	West Ham Utd	A	2–1	15,000	Mackinlay, T.Scott
23/01	Arsenal	H	3–0	40,000	Forshaw (2), Oxley
06/02	Everton	A	3–3	45,000	Oxley, Forshaw (2)
13/02	Burnley	H	3–2	35,000	Chambers, Forshaw (2)
20/02	Leeds Utd	A	1–1	40,000	Forshaw
27/02	Manchester C	A	1–1	35,000	Forshaw
06/03	Tottenham H	H	0–0	25,000	
10/03	Manchester Utd	A	3–3	30,000	Forshaw, Hodgson (2)
13/03	Sunderland	A	2–3	16,000	Chambers, Baron
20/03	Huddersfield T	H	1–2	35,000	Forshaw
27/03	West Brom A	A	3–0	10,500	Hodgson, Forshaw (2, 1 pen)
02/04	Bolton W	A	1–0	30,000	Chambers
03/04	Birmingham C	H	2–2	35,000	Hodgson, Hunter (o.g.)
05/04	Bolton W	H	2–2	30,000	Chambers, Hopkin
06/04	Aston Villa	A	0–3	15,000	
10/04	Bury	A	1–0	30,000	Chambers
17/04	Blackburn R	H	2–2	20,000	Chambers, Forshaw
24/04	Cardiff C	A	2–2	10,000	Chambers (2)
01/05	Sheffield Utd	H	2–2	15,000	Reid (2)

Div One Position 7th P42 Pts 44

FA CUP

DATE	OPPOSITION	VENUE	SCORE	ATT.	GOALSCORERS
09/01	Southampton	A	0–0	18,031	
13/01	Southampton	H	1–0	42,000	Forshaw
30/01	Fulham	A	1–3	36,381	Forshaw

1926–27

FOOTBALL LEAGUE DIVISION ONE

DATE	OPPOSITION	VENUE	SCORE	ATT.	GOALSCORERS
28/08	Manchester Utd	H	4–2	40,000	Forshaw (3), Hodgson
30/08	Aston Villa	A	1–1	25,000	Forshaw
04/09	Derby Co	A	1–2	21,526	Edmed
08/09	Aston Villa	H	2–1	27,000	Forshaw, Chambers
11/09	Sheffield Utd	H	5–1	40,000	Hodgson (3), Forshaw (2, 1 pen)
18/09	Arsenal	A	0–2	35,000	
25/09	Everton	A	0–1	38,000	
02/10	Leeds Utd	H	2–4	30,000	Forshaw, Hodgson
09/10	Newcastle Utd	A	0–1	30,000	
16/10	The Wednesday	A	2–3	20,000	Reid (2)
23/10	Leicester C	H	1–0	35,000	Chambers
30/10	Blackburn R	A	1–2	20,000	Chambers
06/11	Huddersfield T	H	2–3	33,000	Forshaw (2)
13/11	Sunderland	A	1–2	9,186	Forshaw
20/11	West Brom A	H	2–1	20,000	Hodgson, Chambers
27/11	Bury	A	2–0	25,000	Hodgson, Chambers
04/12	Birmingham C	H	2–1	35,000	Forshaw (2)
11/12	Tottenham H	A	2–1	27,839	Edmed, Chambers
18/12	West Ham Utd	H	0–0	28,000	
25/12	Burnley	A	0–4	32,000	
27/12	Burnley	H	2–2	45,000	Chambers (2)
28/12	Bolton W	H	3–2	20,000	Hodgson, Chambers (2)
01/01	Bolton W	A	1–2	32,223	Edmed
15/01	Manchester Utd	A	1–0	35,000	Forshaw
22/01	Derby Co	H	3–2	25,000	Hodgson (3)
05/02	Arsenal	H	3–0	30,000	Chambers, Reid, Cope (o.g.)
07/02	Sheffield Utd	A	4–1	30,000	Reid (2), Chambers, T.Scott
12/02	Everton	H	1–0	52,677	Chambers
23/02	Leeds Utd	A	0–0	14,000	
26/02	Newcastle Utd	H	1–2	34,000	Reid
05/03	The Wednesday	H	3–0	32,000	Chambers (2), Mackinlay
12/03	Leicester C	A	2–3	25,000	Reid (2)
19/03	Blackburn R	H	2–2	27,000	Chambers, Reid
26/03	Huddersfield T	A	0–1	5,000	
02/04	Sunderland	H	1–2	33,000	Chambers
09/04	West Brom A	A	1–0	12,000	Edmed
15/04	Cardiff C	H	5–0	35,037	Reid (2), Edmed, Hodgson, Lucas (pen)
16/04	Bury	H	2–2	25,000	Hodgson (2)
18/04	Cardiff C	A	0–2	12,000	
23/04	Birmingham C	A	0–3	10,000	
30/04	Tottenham H	H	1–0	20,000	Edmed
07/05	West Ham Utd	A	3–3	25,000	Devlin, Hodgson (2)

Div One Position 9th P42 Pts 43

FA CUP

DATE	OPPOSITION	VENUE	SCORE	ATT.	GOALSCORERS
08/01	Bournemouth	A	1–1	13,243	Hodgson
12/01	Bournemouth	H	4–1	36,800	Hopkin, Chambers (3)
29/01	Southport	H	3–1	51,600	Hodgson, Chambers, Edmed
19/02	Arsenal	A	0–2	43,000	

1927–28

FOOTBALL LEAGUE DIVISION ONE

DATE	OPPOSITION	VENUE	SCORE	ATT.	GOAL SCORERS
27/08	Sheffield Utd	A	1–1	25,000	Devlin
31/08	Bury	H	5–1	30,000	Devlin (4), Hodgson
03/09	Aston Villa	H	0–0	35,000	
10/09	Sunderland	A	1–2	29,479	Hodgson
17/09	Derby Co	H	5–2	35,000	McNab, Devlin (2), Hodgson, Edmed
19/09	Bury	A	2–5	10,940	Crown (o.g.), Devlin
24/09	Manchester Utd	A	1–3	35,000	Edmed
01/10	Portsmouth	H	8–2	30,000	Devlin (4), Hodgson (3), Pither
08/10	Leicester C	A	1–1	30,000	Hodgson
15/10	Everton	A	1–1	56,000	Edmed
22/10	Bolton W	A	1–2	30,000	Edmed
29/10	Blackburn R	H	4–2	28,000	Reid (2), Devlin, Hodgson
05/11	Cardiff C	H	1–1	15,000	Devlin
12/11	The Wednesday	H	5–2	35,000	Hodgson (2), Reid (3)
19/11	Middlesbrough	A	1–1	18,741	Chambers
26/11	Huddersfield T	H	4–2	35,000	Edmed, Bromilow, Hodgson (2)
03/12	Newcastle Utd	A	1–1	40,000	Hodgson

10/12	Birmingham C	H	2–3	30,000	Hodgson (2)
17/12	Tottenham H	A	1–3	28,000	Jackson
24/12	Manchester Utd	H	2–0	35,000	T.Scott, Chambers
27/12	Arsenal	A	0–2	35,000	
31/12	Sheffield Utd	H	2–1	30,000	Chambers, Reid
02/01	Burnley	H	2–2	30,000	Edmed, Reid
07/01	Aston Villa	A	4–3	45,000	Edmed (2), Reid, Hopkin
21/01	Sunderland	H	2–5	35,000	Hopkin, Reid
04/02	West Ham Utd	H	1–3	35,000	Edmed (pen)
11/02	Portsmouth	A	0–1	17,000	
15/02	Derby Co	H	3–2	9,069	Race, Edmed (2)
25/02	Everton	H	3–3	56,447	Hopkin, Bromilow, Hodgson
03/03	Bolton W	H	4–2	30,000	Hodgson, Reid (2), Edmed
07/03	Arsenal	H	3–6	40,000	Hodgson (2), Race
10/03	Blackburn R	H	1–2	10,000	Edmed (pen)
17/03	Cardiff C	H	1–2	35,000	Reid
24/03	The Wednesday	A	0–4	25,000	
31/03	Middlesbrough	H	1–1	26,840	Hodgson
06/04	Burnley	A	2–2	22,000	Walsh, Reid
07/04	Huddersfield T	H	4–2	25,000	Reid, Hodgson, Edmed, Walsh
14/04	Newcastle Utd	H	0–0	33,000	
21/04	Birmingham C	A	0–2	18,000	
25/04	Leicester C	H	1–1	30,000	Reid
28/04	Tottenham H	H	2–0	30,000	Bromilow, Hodgson
05/05	Manchester Utd	A	1–6	31,000	Hodgson

Div One Position 16th P42 Pts 39

FA CUP

DATE	OPPOSITION	VENUE	SCORE	ATT.	GOALSCORERS
14/01	Darlington	H	1–0	28,500	Chambers
28/01	Cardiff C	A	1–2	20,000	Edmed (pen)

1928–29

FOOTBALL LEAGUE DIVISION ONE

DATE	OPPOSITION	VENUE	SCORE	ATT.	GOALSCORERS
25/08	Bury	H	3–0	40,000	Miller (2), Whitehurst
01/09	Aston Villa	A	1–3	35,000	McDougall
05/09	Sheffield Utd	H	1–2	30,000	Edmed
08/09	Leicester C	H	6–3	25,000	Edmed, Done, McDougall, Reid, Hodgson (2)
10/09	Sheffield Utd	A	3–1	20,000	Edmed (2), Reid
15/09	Manchester Utd	A	2–2	18,000	Hodgson, Edmed
22/09	Leeds Utd	H	1–1	40,000	McDougall
29/09	Everton	A	0–1	60,000	
06/10	West Ham Utd	A	1–1	35,000	McDougall
13/10	Newcastle Utd	H	2–1	35,000	Hodgson, McDougall
20/10	Huddersfield T	A	2–3	30,000	Edmed (2)
27/10	Arsenal	A	4–4	50,000	Edmed, Hodgson (3)
03/11	Birmingham C	H	1–2	35,000	Clarke
10/11	Portsmouth	H	1–0	25,000	Salisbury
17/11	Bolton W	H	3–0	30,000	Hodgson (2), Edmed
24/11	The Wednesday	A	2–3	15,000	McDougall, Bromilow
01/12	Derby Co	H	3–0	30,000	Hodgson, McDougall, Clarke
08/12	Sunderland	A	1–2	16,000	Done
15/12	Blackburn R	H	1–1	35,000	Hodgson
22/12	Manchester C	A	3–2	20,000	Hodgson (2), Race
25/12	Burnley	A	2–3	35,000.	Edmed, Clarke
26/12	Burnley	H	8–0	45,000	Clarke (2), Edmed (2), Hodgson (3), Salisbury
29/12	Bury	A	2–2	25,000	Hodgson (2)
05/01	Aston Villa	H	4–0	30,000	Edmed (2), Clarke, Hodgson
19/01	Leicester C	A	0–2	28,000	
02/02	Leeds Utd	A	2–2	10,000	McDougall, Whitehurst
09/02	Everton	H	1–2	55,000	Race
13/02	Manchester Utd	H	2–3	12,000	Hodgson, Done (pen)
23/02	Newcastle Utd	A	2–2	45,000	Edmed, Maitland (o.g.)
09/03	Arsenal	H	2–4	20,000	Hodgson, Edmed
13/03	West Ham Utd	H	2–1	16,000	Lindsay, Davidson
16/03	Birmingham C	A	0–0	20,000	
29/03	Cardiff C	A	2–0	30,000	Hodgson (2)
30/03	Bolton W	A	0–0	25,000	
01/04	Cardiff C	H	2–1	12,000	Race, Done (pen)
06/04	The Wednesday	H	3–2	30,000	Race, Clarke, Hodgson
10/04	Huddersfield T	H	3–1	4,000	Hodgson (2), Wadsworth (o.g.)
13/04	Derby Co	A	5–2	11,516	Race (2), Hodgson, Clarke (2)
17/04	Portsmouth	A	0–0	25,000	
20/04	Sunderland	H	5–2	28,000	Hodgson, Race (3)
27/04	Blackburn R	A	1–2	6,000	Done (pen)
04/05	Manchester C	H	1–1	25,000	Hodgson

Div One Position 5th P42 Pts 46

FA CUP

DATE	OPPOSITION	VENUE	SCORE	ATT.	GOALSCORERS
12/01	Bristol C	A	2–0	28,500	Salisbury, Hodgson
26/01	Bolton W	H	0–0	55,055	
30/01	Bolton W	A	2–5*	41,808	Lindsay, Hodgson (*AET)

1929–30

FOOTBALL LEAGUE DIVISION ONE

DATE	OPPOSITION	VENUE	SCORE	ATT.	GOALSCORERS
31/08	Middlesbrough	A	0–5	28,286	
04/09	Huddersfield T	H	3–0	33,000	Clark, Race, Hodgson
07/09	Everton	A	0–3	45,600	
14/09	West Ham Utd	H	3–1	25,000	Edmed (2), Lindsay
16/09	Huddersfield T	A	0–3	12,000	
21/09	Manchester Utd	A	2–1	22,000	Smith (2)
28/09	Grimsby T	H	2–0	28,000	Hodgson, Race
05/10	Leicester C	A	1–2	20,000	Smith
09/10	Blackburn R	H	1–1	20,000	Race
12/10	Birmingham C	H	1–1	25,000	Smith
19/10	Derby Co	A	2–2	15,840	Smith, Hodgson
26/10	Manchester C	H	1–6	20,000	Smith
02/11	Portsmouth	H	3–3	25,000	Hodgson, Davidson, Smith
09/11	Bolton W	H	3–0	22,000	Race (3)
16/11	Aston Villa	A	3–2	23,000	Murray, Mort (o.g.), Smith
23/11	Leeds Utd	H	1–0	30,000	Smith

30/11	Sheffield Wed	A	1–2	25,000	Hodgson
07/12	Burnley	H	1–3	35,000	Hodgson
14/12	Sunderland	A	3–2	22,000	Smith, Hopkin, Hodgson
21/12	Arsenal	H	1–0	40,000	McPherson
25/12	Sheffield Utd	A	0–4	30,000	
26/12	Sheffield Utd	H	2–0	46,000	Smith, McPherson
28/12	Middlesbrough	H	5–2	23,982	Edmed, Smith (2), Hopkin (2)
04/01	Everton	A	3–3	55,000	Edmed, McPherson, McDougall
18/01	West Ham Utd	A	1–4	25,000	Smith
25/01	Manchester Utd	H	1–0	35,000	Race
01/02	Grimsby T	A	2–3	15,000	Smith (2)
08/02	Leicester C	H	1–1	30,000	Hodgson
15/02	Birmingham C	A	0–1	20,000	
22/02	Derby Co	H	2–2	30,000	Hodgson (2)
01/03	Manchester C	A	3–4	22,000	Smith, McPherson, Hodgson
08/03	Portsmouth	H	2–0	25,000	Hodgson (2)
15/03	Bolton W	A	2–0	20,000	Smith (2)
22/03	Aston Villa	H	2–0	35,000	Gunson, Smith
29/03	Leeds Utd	A	1–1	6,000	Smith
02/04	Arsenal	A	1–0	24.000	McPherson
05/04	Sheffield Wed	H	1–3	30,000	Hodgson
12/04	Burnley	A	1–4	12,000	Smith
18/04	Newcastle Utd	A	1–3	35,000	Smith
19/04	Sunderland	H	0–6	30,000	
21/04	Newcastle Utd	H	0–0	20,000	
03/05	Blackburn R	A	0–1	15,000	

Div One Position 12th   P42 Pts 41

FA CUP

DATE	OPPOSITION	VENUE	SCORE	ATT.	GOALSCORERS
11/01	Cardiff City	H	1–2	50,141	McPherson

1930–31

FOOTBALL LEAGUE DIVISION ONE

DATE	OPPOSITION	VENUE	SCORE	ATT.	GOALSCORERS
30/08	Blackburn R	H	2–1	35,000	Smith (2)
01/09	West Ham Utd	A	0–7	28,000	
06/09	Middlesbrough	A	3–3	16,816	Done (pen), Hodgson, Edmed
10/09	Bolton W	H	7–2	30,000	McPherson (2), Edmed (2) Smith, Hodgson (2)
13/09	Huddersfield T	H	1–4	35,000	Smith
20/09	Aston Villa	A	2–4	34,000	Hodgson (2)
27/09	Chelsea	H	3–1	30,000	Hodgson (3)
04/10	Newcastle Utd	A	4–0	30,000	Smith (2), Hodgson, Edmed
11/10	Sheffield Wed	A	1–2	30,000	Hodgson
18/10	Leeds Utd	H	2–0	30,000	Hodgson (2)
25/10	Blackpool	A	3–1	15,000	Smith (3)
01/11	Manchester C	H	0–2	25,000	
08/11	Derby Co	H	2–2	14,966	Hodgson, McPherson
15/11	Leicester C	H	3–1	20,000	Smith (2), Black (o.g.)
22/11	Portsmouth	A	0–4	18,000	
29/11	Sheffield Utd	H	6–1	25,000	Hodgson (3), McPherson (2), Smith
06/12	Sunderland	A	5–6	22,616	Hopkin, Hodgson, McRorie, Smith (2)
13/12	Arsenal	H	1–1	50,000	Morrison
20/12	Birmingham C	A	0–2	18,000	
25/12	Grimsby T	A	0–0	30,000	
26/12	Grimsby T	H	1–1	30,000	McPherson
27/12	Blackburn R	A	3–3	20,000	Hodgson (2), A.Scott
03/01	Middlesbrough	H	3–1	21,133	Hodgson (2), Done
14/01	Bolton W	A	0–2	9,000	
17/01	Huddersfield T	A	1–2	10,000	McPherson
24/01	Aston Villa	H	1–1	30,000	Hodgson
31/01	Chelsea	A	2–2	40,000	Hodgson, Gunson
07/02	Newcastle Utd	H	4–2	30,000	Wright (3), Barton
14/02	Sheffield Wed	H	5–3	25,000	Wright, Hodgson (4; 1 pen)
21/02	Leeds Utd	A	2–1	15,000	Wright, Hodgson
28/02	Blackpool	H	5–2	15,000	McPherson (2), Hodgson (3; 1 pen)
07/03	Manchester C	A	1–1	18,000	Hodgson
14/03	Derby Co	H	0–0	30,000	
21/03	Leicester C	A	2–3	15,000	Barton (2)
28/03	Portsmouth	H	3–1	20,000	McDougall, Clarke, Wright
03/04	Manchester C	H	1–1	27,000	Hodgson
04/04	Sheffield Utd	A	1–4	12,000	Barton
06/04	Manchester C	A	1–4	8,000	A.Scott
11/04	Sunderland	H	2–4	30,000	McPherson, Hodgson (pen)
15/04	Birmingham C	H	0–0	28,000	
18/04	Arsenal	A	1–3	45,000	Roberts (o.g.) 5
02/05	West Ham Utd	H	2–0	25,000	Hodgson (2)

Div One Position 9th   P42 Pts 42

FA CUP

DATE	OPPOSITION	VENUE	SCORE	ATT.	GOALSCORERS
10/01	Birmingham C	H	0–2	40,500	

LANCASHIRE SENIOR CUP – WINNERS

DATE	OPPOSITION	VENUE	SCORE	ATT.	GOALSCORERS
08/10	Everton	H	5–0		Smith (3), Hodgson, Bradshaw
05/11	Burnley	H	3–1		Barton, McPherson, Morrison
19/11	Preston NE	H	4–2		Smith (2), McPherson, OG
25/04	Manchester U	H	4–0		Wright (2), Hodgson, McPherson

1931–32

FOOTBALL LEAGUE DIVISION ONE 1931–32

DATE	OPPOSITION	VENUE	SCORE	ATT.	GOALSCORERS
29/08	Newcastle Utd	A	1–0	36,000	Hodgson
02/09	Bolton W	H	2–2	30,000	Wright (2)
05/09	Aston Villa	H	2–0	40,000	Wright (2)
09/09	Middlesbrough	A	1–4	20,854	Wright
12/09	Leicester C	A	1–2	15,000	Gunson
16/09	Middlesbrough	H	7–2	20,854	Gunson, Barton (2), Hodgson (2), Smith, Morrison
19/09	Everton	A	1–3	55,000	Wright
26/09	Grimsby T	H	4–0	30,000	Hodgson (2), Savage (2)
03/10	Chelsea	A	0–2	30,000	
10/10	West Ham Utd	H	2–2	25,000	Gunson, Wright

17/10	West Brom A	A	2–1	30,000	Hodgson, Gunson
24/10	Blackpool	H	3–2	25,000	Gunson, Hodgson, Ramsey (o.g.)
31/10	Sheffield Utd	A	0–3	20,000	
07/11	Blackburn R	H	4–2	25,000	Barton (2), Gunson, Hodgson
14/11	Sunderland	A	3–1	17,646	Wright (2), Hodgson
21/11	Manchester C	H	4–3	30,000	McPherson, Hodgson, Done (2; 1 pen)
28/11	Arsenal	A	0–6	35,000	
05/12	Birmingham C	H	4–3	25,000	Hodgson, Wright, Gunson, McRorie
12/12	Portsmouth	A	0–2	16,000	
19/12	Derby Co	H	1–1	25,000	Hodgson
25/12	Sheffield Wed	H	3–1	35,000	Gunson (2), Barton
26/12	Sheffield Wed	A	1–1	35,000	McPherson
02/01	Newcastle Utd	A	4–2	28,000	Barton (2), Gunson, Hodgson
16/01	Aston Villa	A	1–6	25,000	Barton
27/01	Leicester C	H	3–3	30,000	Hodgson, McRorie, Gunson
30/01	Everton	A	1–2	50,000	Wright
06/02	Grimsby T	A	1–5	17,000	Done
20/02	West Ham Utd	A	0–1	18,000	
02/03	West Brom A	H	4–1	23,000	Hodgson (3), Gunson
05/03	Blackpool	A	2–2	15,000	Wright, Hodgson
12/03	Sheffield Utd	H	2–1	30,000	Gunson, Hodgson (pen)
19/03	Blackburn R	A	3–1	10,000	Hodgson, Gunson (2)
26/03	Sunderland	H	1–2	25,000	Hodgson
28/03	Huddersfield T	H	0–3	28,000	
29/03	Huddersfield T	A	3–4	12,000	Hodgson (2), Wright
02/04	Manchester C	A	1–0	20,000	Gunson
06/04	Chelsea	H	2–1	38,000	Hodgson, Hancock
09/04	Arsenal	H	2–1	40,000	Hancock, McRorie
16/04	Birmingham C	A	1–3	10,000	Gunson (pen)
23/04	Portsmouth	H	1–3	20,000	McRorie
30/04	Derby Co	A	2–1	12,000	Hodgson (2)
07/05	Bolton W	A	1–8	8,000	McRorie

Div One Position 10th   P42 Pts 44

FA CUP

DATE	OPPOSITION	VENUE	SCORE	ATT.	GOALSCORERS
09/01	Everton	A	2–1	57,090	Gunson, Hodgson
23/01	Chesterfield	A	4–2	28,393	Barton (4)
13/02	Grimsby T	H	1–0	49,479	Gunson
27/02	Chelsea	H	0–2	57,804	

1932–33

FOOTBALL LEAGUE DIVISION ONE

DATE	OPPOSITION	VENUE	SCORE	ATT.	GOALSCORERS
27/08	Wolves	H	5–1	45,000	Hodgson, Wright, Gunson, Crawford (2)
29/08	Sheffield Utd	A	2–6	25,000	Gunson, Crawford
03/09	Newcastle Utd	A	3–4	26,000	Hodgson (pen), Crawford, Bradshaw
07/09	Sheffield Utd	H	2–2	18,000	Wright (2)
10/09	Aston Villa	H	0–0	40,000	
17/09	Middlesbrough	A	1–0	11,371	Gunson
24/09	Bolton W	H	0–1	30,000	
01/10	Everton	A	1–3	46,000	Gunson
08/10	Leicester C	A	2–1	15,000	Roberts, Hodgson
15/10	Portsmouth	H	4–3	25,000	Wright, Hodgson (3)
22/10	Arsenal	H	2–3	40,000	Wright, Hodgson
29/10	Manchester C	A	1–1	10,000	McPherson
05/11	Leeds Utd	H	0–1	30,000	
12/11	Blackburn R	A	2–2	12,000	Hodgson, Wright
19/11	Derby Co	H	6–1	30,000	Collin (o.g.), Hodgson (3), Wright, Roberts
26/11	Blackpool	H	1–4	12,000	Wright
03/12	Sunderland	H	3–3	20,000	Wright, Barton, Roberts
10/12	Birmingham C	A	0–3	12,000	
17/12	West Brom A	H	2–0	20,000	Hodgson, Barton
24/12	Sheffield Wed	A	0–3	14,000	
26/12	Chelsea	H	3–0	38,000	Bradshaw, Barton, Gunson
27/12	Chelsea	A	2–0	40,000	Bruton, Barton
31/12	Wolves	A	1–3	19,540	Barton
07/01	Newcastle Utd	H	3–0	25,000	Hodgson (pen) (2), Wright
21/01	Aston Villa	A	2–5	25,000	Hodgson, Roberts
01/02	Middlesbrough	H	1–3	9,973	Hanson
04/02	Bolton W	A	3–3	12,000	Taylor, Barton, Done (pen)
11/02	Everton	H	7–4	50,000	Barton (3), Hanson, Morrison, Taylor, Roberts
18/02	Leicester C	H	1–2	15,000	Roberts
25/02	Portsmouth	A	1–2	5,000	Barton
04/03	Arsenal	A	1–0	47,000	Hodgson
11/03	Manchester C	H	1–1	35,000	Hodgson (pen)
18/03	Leeds Utd	A	0–5	10,000	
25/03	Blackburn R	H	2–2	20,000	Hodgson, Barton
01/04	Derby Co	A	1–1	7,200	Barton
08/04	Blackpool	A	4–3	12,000	Hodgson (3), Wright
14/04	Huddersfield T	H	2–2	35,000	Barton, Wright
15/04	Sunderland	A	0–0	8,725	
18/04	Huddersfield T	A	1–3	8,000	Jackson
22/04	Birmingham C	H	1–0	15,000	Hodgson
29/04	West Brom A	H	2–1	12,000	Bradshaw
06/05	Sheffield Wed	H	4–1	15,000	Wright (2), Hodgson (2)

Div One Position 14th   P42 Pts 39

FA CUP

DATE	OPPOSITION	VENUE	SCORE	ATT.	GOALSCORERS
14/01	West Brom A	A	0–2	29,170	

1933–34

FOOTBALL LEAGUE DIVISION ONE

DATE	OPPOSITION	VENUE	SCORE	ATT.	GOALSCORERS
26/08	Wolves	A	2–3	30,000	D.Wright, Hodgson (pen)
30/08	Stoke C	H	1–1	40,000	English
02/09	Sheffield Utd	H	3–2	35,000	English, Hodgson (2)
04/09	Stoke C	A	1–1	28,000	Taylor
09/09	Aston Villa	A	2–4	30,000	Hodgson, English
16/09	Leicester C	H	1–3	25,000	Hanson
23/09	Tottenham H	A	3–0	33,716	English (2), Hanson
30/09	Everton	H	3–2	54,800	Nieuwenhuys, Hanson, English
07/10	Chelsea	H	3–0	35,000	D.Wright, Hodgson, English

DATE	OPPOSITION	VENUE	SCORE	ATT.	
14/10	Sunderland	A	1–4	25,321	English
21/10	Middlesbrough	A	1–4	10,899	English
28/10	Blackburn R	H	4–0	20,000	Hanson, Nieuwenhuys, Hodgson (pen), S.Roberts
04/11	Birmingham C	A	2–1	15,000	English, Hodgson
11/11	Leeds Utd	H	4–3	30,000	Done, English (2), Hanson
18/11	Derby Co	A	1–3	15,733	English
25/11	West Brom A	H	1–1	35,000	English
02/12	Arsenal	A	1–2	38,362	English
09/12	Sheffield Wed	H	1–3	25,000	Hanson
16/12	Manchester C	A	1–2	15,000	Nieuwenhuys
23/12	Newcastle Utd	H	1–2	30,000	Nieuwenhuys
25/12	Portsmouth	H	2–2	30,000	Hanson, English
26/12	Portsmouth	A	0–1	23,000	
30/12	Wolves	H	1–1	30,000	Hanson
01/01	Newcastle Utd	A	2–9	18,000	Taylor, Betton (o.g.)
06/01	Sheffield Utd	A	2–2	12,000	S.Roberts, Hanson
20/01	Aston Villa	H	2–3	40,000	S.Roberts, Done
01/02	Leicester C	A	0–1	15,000	
03/02	Tottenham H	H	3–1	30,000	Hodgson (pen), Nieuwenhuys (2)
10/02	Everton	H	0–0	50,000	
21/02	Chelsea	A	0–2	15,000	
24/02	Sunderland	H	1–1	20,000	Morrison
03/03	Middlesbrough	H	6–2	25,946	Hodgson (3), English (2), Taylor
10/03	Blackburn R	A	1–3	8,000	Hodgson
17/03	Birmingham C	H	4–1	40,000	Hodgson (4)
24/03	Leeds Utd	A	1–5	13,000	Hodgson
30/03	Huddersfield T	H	2–2	35,000	Johnson, Hanson
31/03	Derby Co	H	4–2	35,000	Nieuwenhuys (2), Johnson, Hodgson
03/04	Huddersfield T	A	2–0	26,700	Hodgson, Nieuwenhuys
07/04	West Brom A	A	2–2	16,000	V.Wright, Hodgson
14/04	Arsenal	H	2–3	40,000	V.Wright, Hodgson
21/04	Sheffield Wed	A	1–8	18,000	Hodgson (pen), Hanson
02/05	Manchester C	H	3–2	16,000	Hanson, Hodgson (2)

Div One Position 18th   P42 Pts 38

FA CUP

DATE	OPPOSITION	VENUE	SCORE	ATT.	GOALSCORERS
13/01	Fulham	H	1–1	45,619	Hodgson
17/01	Fulham	A	3–2*	28,319	Hanson, Bradshaw, Roberts
27/01	Tranmere R*	H	3–1	61,036	English (2), Nieuwenhuys
17/02	Bolton W	H	0–3	59,912	

* Tranmere drawn at home but agreed to play at Anfield.

1934–35

FOOTBALL LEAGUE DIVISION ONE

DATE	OPPOSITION	VENUE	SCORE	ATT.	GOAL SCORERS
25/08	Blackburn R	H	2–0	35,000	Wright (2)
29/08	Manchester C	A	1–3	18,000	Hodgson
01/09	Arsenal	A	1–8	57,000	Hanson
05/09	Manchester C	H	2–1	32,000	English, Hodgson
08/09	Portsmouth	H	0–0	30,000	
15/09	Everton	A	0–1	45,000	
22/09	Leeds Utd	A	3–0	10,900	Hodgson, Hanson (2)
29/09	West Brom A	H	3–2	20,000	Hanson, English, Hodgson
06/10	Sheffield Wed	A	1–4	15,000	Hodgson
13/10	Birmingham C	H	5–4	20,000	Wright, McDougall, English, Hodgson (2; 1 pen)
20/10	Grimsby T	H	1–1	35,000	Wright
27/10	Preston NE	A	2–2	15,000	Hodgson, Wright
03/11	Wolves	H	2–0	20,000	Wright, Hodgson
10/11	Huddersfield T	A	0–8	13,000	
17/11	Leicester C	H	5–1	20,000	Hodgson (3), Wright, Taylor
24/11	Derby Co	A	2–1	17,349	Wright (2)
01/12	Aston Villa	H	3–1	20,000	Hodgson (2), Johnson
08/12	Chelsea	A	1–4	30,000	Wright
15/12	Tottenham H	H	4–1	20,000	Hodgson (2), Nieuwenhuys, Wright
22/12	Sunderland	A	3–2	20,000	Wright (2), Hanson
26/12	Middlesbrough	H	2–2	45,936	Nieuwenhuys, Roberts
29/12	Blackburn R	A	2–0	15,000	Nieuwenhuys, English
01/01	Middlesbrough	A	0–2	19,436	
05/01	Arsenal	H	0–2	56,700	
19/01	Portsmouth	A	2–1	15,000	Hodgson, Wright
02/02	Leeds Utd	H	4–2	25,000	Hodgson (3), Hanson
09/02	West Brom A	A	1–1	18,000	Shaw (o.g.)
20/02	Sheffield Wed	H	1–2	16,000	Hanson
23/02	Birmingham C	A	3–1	25,000	English, Hodgson (2)
02/03	Grimsby T	A	2–3	12,000	English, Hodgson
09/03	Preston NE	H	0–0	30,000	
16/03	Wolves	A	3–5	20,000	Hodgson (pen), Hanson, Wright
20/03	Everton	H	2–1	32,000	Hodgson (2,1 pen)
23/03	Huddersfield T	H	3–2	18,000	Johnson (2), Hodgson (pen)
30/03	Leicester C	A	1–3	25,000	Johnson
06/04	Derby Co	H	1–3	20,000	Nieuwenhuys
13/04	Aston Villa	A	2–4	20,000	Howe, Nieuwenhuys
19/04	Stoke C	H	5–0	20,000	Wright (2), Carr, Nieuwenhuys, Howe
20/04	Chelsea	H	6–0	15,000	Wright (2), Nieuwenhuys (2), Howe, Carr
22/04	Stoke C	A	1–1	18,000	Nieuwenhuys
27/04	Tottenham H	A	1–5	16,129	Nieuwenhuys
04/05	Sunderland	H	2–2	20,000	Johnson, Hanson

Div One Position 7th   P42 Pts 45

FA CUP

DATE	OPPOSITION	VENUE	SCORE	ATT.	GOALSCORERS
12/01	Yeovil & Petters	A	6–2	13,000	Nieuwenhuys, Wright, Hodgson (2), Roberts (2)
26/01	Blackburn R	A	0–1	49,546	

1935–36

FOOTBALL LEAGUE DIVISION ONE

DATE	OPPOSITION	VENUE	SCORE	ATT.	GOALSCORERS
31/08	Chelsea	A	2–2	40,000	Nieuwenhuys (2)
04/09	Manchester C	H	0–2	30,000	
07/09	Everton	H	4–0	48,000	Howe (4), Hodgson (2)
11/09	Manchester C	A	0–6	25,000	
14/09	Grimsby T	H	7–2	25,000	Howe (3), Hodgson (2), Carr, Johnson
18/09	Stoke C	H	2–0	23,192	Hodgson (2)
21/09	Leeds Utd	A	0–1	12,000	
28/09	West Brom A	H	5–0	30,000	Nieuwenhuys, Carr (2), Hodgson, Howe
05/10	Sunderland	A	0–2	30,114	
12/10	Birmingham C	H	1–2	30,000	Nieuwenhuys
19/10	Bolton W	H	0–0	15,000	
26/10	Huddersfield T	H	3–0	40,000	Howe (2), Nieuwenhuys
02/11	Middlesbrough	A	2–2	18,104	Carr, Hodgson
09/11	Aston Villa	H	3–2	40,000	Hodgson, Carr (pen), McDougall
16/11	Wolves	A	1–3	20,000	Carr
23/11	Derby Co	H	0–0	30,000	
30/11	Portsmouth	A	1–2	17,000	Howe
07/12	Preston NE	H	2–1	25,000	Glassey, Balmer
14/12	Brentford	A	2–1	20,000	Glassey, Wright
21/12	Sheffield Wed	H	1–0	10,000	Wright
25/12	Arsenal	A	0–1	47,000	
26/12	Arsenal	H	2–1	45,000	Howe (2)
28/12	Chelsea	H	2–3	35,000	Howe, Nieuwenhuys
04/01	Everton	A	0–0	55,000	
18/01	Grimsby T	A	0–0	10,000	
01/02	West Brom A	H	1–6	25,000	Balmer
08/02	Sunderland	H	0–3	35,000	
15/02	Birmingham C	H	0–2	18,000	
22/02	Bolton W	H	1–1	20,000	Balmer
29/02	Aston Villa	A	0–3	12,000	
07/03	Portsmouth	H	2–0	10,000	Wright, Nieuwenhuys
14/03	Huddersfield T	A	0–1	15,000	
18/03	Leeds Utd	H	2–1	20,000	Wright (2)
21/03	Wolves	H	0–2	25,000	
28/03	Derby Co	A	2–2	16,820	Howe, P.Taylor
04/04	Middlesbrough	H	2–2	20,000	Glassey (2)
10/04	Blackburn R	H	2–2	20,000	Busby, Howe
11/04	Preston NE	A	1–3	20,000	Howe
13/04	Blackburn R	A	4–1	30,000	P.Taylor, Nieuwenhuys (2), Wright
18/04	Brentford	H	0–0	30,000	
25/04	Sheffield Wed	A	0–0	10,000	
02/05	Stoke C	A	1–2	14,000	Howe

Div One Position 19th   P42 Pts 38

FA CUP

DATE	OPPOSITION	VENUE	SCORE	ATT.	GOALSCORERS
11/01	Swansea T	H	1–0	33,494	Wright
25/01	Arsenal	H	0–2	53,720	

1936–37

FOOTBALL LEAGUE DIVISION ONE

DATE	OPPOSITION	VENUE	SCORE	ATT.	GOALSCORERS
29/08	Stoke City	H	2–1	30,000	Hanson, Nieuwenhuys
02/09	Portsmouth	A	2–6	18,000	Nieuwenhuys, Hanson
05/09	Charlton A	A	1–1	31,295	Hanson
09/09	Portsmouth	H	0–0	25,000	
12/09	Grimsby T	H	7–1	16,000	Nieuwenhuys, Howe (2), Wright (2), Balmer, Busby
16/09	Chelsea	A	0–2	25,000	
19/09	Everton	A	0–2	57,587	
26/09	Leeds Utd	A	0–2	16,000	
03/10	Birmingham C	H	2–0	25,000	Wright, Taylor
10/10	Middlesbrough	A	3–3	22,858	Howe, Nieuwenhuys, Taylor
17/10	Bolton W	H	0–0	25,000	
24/10	Brentford	A	2–5	30,000	Balmer, Nieuwenhuys
31/10	Arsenal	H	2–1	45,000	Balmer, Howe
07/11	Preston NE	A	1–3	15,000	Nieuwenhuys
14/11	Sheffield Wed	H	2–2	20,000	Howe (2)
21/11	Manchester Utd	A	5–2	25,000	Hanson, Eastham, Howe (3)
28/11	Derby Co	H	3–3	25,000	Barker (o.g.), Nieuwenhuys, Howe
05/12	Wolves	A	0–2	17,000	
12/12	Sunderland	H	4–0	30,000	Hanson (2), Nieuwenhuys, Balmer
19/12	Huddersfield T	A	0–4	14,000	
25/12	West Brom A	H	1–3	30,000	Howe
26/12	Stoke C	A	1–1	16,000	Wright
28/12	West Brom A	H	1–2	35,000	Hanson
02/01	Charlton A	A	1–2	28,000	Howe
09/01	Grimsby T	A	1–2	12,000	Niuewenhuys
23/01	Everton	H	3–2	37,632	Howe, Taylor, Balmer
30/01	Leeds Utd	H	3–0	12,000	Nieuwenhuys (2), Hanson
06/02	Birmingham C	A	0–5	20,000	
13/02	Middlesbrough	H	0–2	22,459	
24/02	Bolton W	A	1–0	18,000	Gosling (o.g.)
27/02	Brentford	H	2–2	18,000	Hanson, Balmer
10/03	Arsenal	A	0–1	21,000	
13/03	Preston NE	H	1–1	10,000	Hanson (pen)
20/03	Sheffield Wed	A	2–1	18,000	Balmer, Hanson
26/03	Manchester C	H	0–5	32,000	
27/03	Manchester Utd	H	2–0	28,000	Hanson, Howe
29/03	Manchester C	A	1–5	25,000	Howe
03/04	Derby Co	A	1–4	13,430	Eastham
10/04	Wolves	H	1–0	30,000	Nieuwenhuys
17/04	Sunderland	A	2–4	14,255	Nieuwenhuys, Hanson
24/04	Huddersfield T	H	1–1	20,000	Howe
01/05	Chelsea	H	1–1	12,000	Balmer

Div One Position 18th   P42 Pts 35

FA CUP

DATE	OPPOSITION	VENUE	SCORE	ATT.	GOALSCORERS
16/01	Norwich C	A	0–3	26,800	

1937–38

FOOTBALL LEAGUE DIVISION ONE

DATE	OPPOSITION	VENUE	SCORE	ATT.	GOAL SCORERS
28/08	Chelsea	A	1–6	42,000	Harston
01/09	Portsmouth	H	3–2	20,000	Harston (2), Nieuwenhuys
04/09	Charlton A	H	1–2	35,000	Balmer
08/09	Portsmouth	A	1–1	17,000	Balmer
11/09	Preston NE	H	1–4	18,000	Nieuwenhuys
15/09	Stoke C	H	3–0	20,000	Niuewenhuys, Hanson (2; 1 pen)
18/09	Grimsby T	H	2–1	30,000	Balmer, Nieuwenhuys

1937–38 (CONTINUED)

25/09	Leeds Utd	A	0–2	18,000	
02/10	Everton	H	1–2	45,000	Nieuwenhuys
09/10	West Brom A	H	0–1	25,000	
16/10	Wolves	A	0–2	28,000	
23/10	Leicester C	H	1–1	20,000	Hanson
30/10	Sunderland	A	3–2	20,000	Fagan, Nieuwenhuys, Hanson
06/11	Brentford	H	3–4	35,000	Hanson, Fagan, Shafto
13/11	Manchester C	A	3–1	25,000	Taylor, Shafto, Fagan
20/11	Huddersfield T	H	0–1	35,000	
27/11	Blackpool	A	1–0	15,000	Hanson
04/12	Derby Co	H	3–4	20,000	Hanson, Nieuwenhuys (2)
11/12	Bolton W	A	0–0	12,000	
18/12	Arsenal	H	2–0	32,000	Shafto, Nieuwenhuys
27/12	Birmingham C	A	2–2	35,000	Taylor, Nieuwenhuys
01/01	Chelsea	H	2–2	40,000	Shafto, Fagan
15/01	Charlton A	A	0–3	23,000	
29/01	Grimsby T	A	0–0	8,000	
02/02	Preston NE	A	2–2	20,000	Balmer, Fagan (pen)
05/02	Leeds Utd	H	1–1	30,000	Nieuwenhuys
16/02	Everton	A	3–1	33,465	Balmer, Shafto (2)
19/02	West Brom A	A	1–5	18,000	Balmer
26/02	Wolves	H	0–1	35,000	
05/03	Leicester C	A	2–2	15,000	Hanson (2)
12/03	Sunderland	H	4–0	30,000	Nieuwenhuys, Balmer (2), Taylor
19/03	Brentford	A	3–1	16,000	Balmer, McInnes, Hanson
26/03	Manchester C	H	2–0	30,000	Balmer, Jones
02/04	Huddersfield T	A	2–1	15,000	Fagan, Balmer
06/04	Birmingham C	H	3–2	15,000	Hanson, Taylor, Fagan
09/04	Blackpool	H	4–2	30,000	Taylor, Hanson, Nieuwenhuys, Fagan (pen)
15/04	Middlesbrough	A	1–1	29,843	Hanson
16/04	Derby Co	A	1–4	16,384	Hanson
18/04	Middlesbrough	H	1–1	32,010	Balmer
23/04	Bolton W	H	2–1	25,000	Balmer, Taylor
30/04	Arsenal	A	0–1	40,000	
07/05	Stoke C	A	0–2	25,000	

Div One Position 11th P42 Pts 41

FA CUP

DATE	OPPOSITION	VENUE	SCORE	ATT	GOALSCORERS
08/01	Crystal P	A	0–0	33,000	
12/01	Crystal P	H	3–1	35,919	Shafto, Collins (o.g.), Fagan (pen)
22/01	Huddersfield Utd	A	1–1	50,264	Hanson
26/01	Sheffield Utd	H	1–0	48,297	Johnson (o.g.)
12/02	Huddersfield T	H	0–1	57,682	

1938–39

FOOTBALL LEAGUE DIVISION ONE

DATE	OPPOSITION	VENUE	SCORE	ATT	GOALSCORERS
27/08	Chelsea	H	2–1	33,933	Taylor (2)
03/09	Preston NE	A	0–1	20,000	
07/09	Manchester Utd	H	1–0	25,070	Nieuwenhuys
10/09	Charlton A	H	1–0	32,701	Busby
14/09	Middlesbrough	H	3–1	25,535	Fagan (2), Nieuwenhuys
17/09	Bolton W	A	1–3	25,000	Taylor
24/09	Leeds Utd	H	3–0	32,197	Fagan, Balmer, Taylor
01/10	Everton	A	1–2	65,076	Fagan (pen)
08/10	Leicester C	A	2–2	12,300	Nieuwenhuys, Van Den Berg
15/10	Aston Villa	H	3–0	41,224	Van Den Berg, Balmer, Fagan
22/10	Wolves	A	2–2	25,000	Taylor, Nieuwenhuys
29/10	Huddersfield T	H	3–3	33,734	Van Den Berg, Fagan (pen), Balmer
05/11	Portsmouth	A	1–1	24,000	Nieuwenhuys
12/11	Arsenal	H	2–2	42,450	Nieuwenhuys (2)
19/11	Brentford	A	1–2	22,000	Nieuwenhuys
26/11	Blackpool	H	1–0	25,000	Kinghorn
03/12	Derby Co	A	2–2	24,753	Taylor, Kinghorn
10/12	Grimsby T	H	2–2	26,500	Nieuwenhuys, Fagan
17/12	Sunderland	A	3–2	15,309	Kinghorn, Bush, Taylor
24/12	Chelsea	A	1–4	7,000	Balmer
26/12	Stoke C	A	1–3	16,000	Fagan
27/12	Stoke C	H	1–0	45,814	Fagan
31/12	Preston NE	H	4–1	40,000	Taylor (2), Fagan (pen), Balmer
02/01	Middlesbrough	A	0–3	25,309	
14/01	Charlton A	A	3–1	24,000	Eastham, Balmer (2)
25/01	Bolton W	H	1–2	18,000	Fagan
28/01	Leeds Utd	A	1–1	13,600	Balmer
04/02	Everton	H	0–3	55,994	
18/02	Aston Villa	A	0–2	40,000	
25/02	Wolves	H	0–2	54,896	
04/03	Leicester C	H	1–1	20,000	Taylor
11/03	Portsmouth	H	4–4	18,000	Fagan, Taylor (2), Nieuwenhuys
15/03	Huddersfield T	H	1–1	7,704	Nieuwenhuys
18/03	Arsenal	A	0–2	35,000	
25/03	Brentford	H	1–0	18,000	Fagan (pen)
01/04	Blackpool	A	1–1	17,000	Fagan
07/04	Birmingham C	H	4–0	30,000	Nieuwenhuys (2), Balmer (2)
08/04	Derby Co	H	2–1	26,209	Taylor (2)
10/04	Birmingham C	A	0–0	20,000	
15/04	Grimsby T	A	1–2	7,000	Nieuwenhuys
22/04	Sunderland	H	1–1	15,000	Kinghorn
06/05	Manchester Utd	A	0–2	14,000	

Div One Position 11th P42 Pts 42

FA CUP

DATE	OPPOSITION	VENUE	SCORE	ATT	GOALSCORERS
07/01	Luton Town	H	3–0	40,431	Balmer (2), Paterson
21/01	Stockport Co	H	5–1	39,407	Nieuwenhuys (2), Eastham, Balmer (2)
11/02	Wolves	A	1–4	61,315	Fagan (pen)

FOOTBALL LEAGUE 1939/40–1945/46

LEAGUE SUSPENDED THREE GAMES INTO 1939–40 SEASON. VARIOUS REGIONAL LEAGUES PLAYED DURING WAR YEARS.

1945–46

FA CUP

DATE	OPPOSITION	VENUE	SCORE	ATT	GOAL SCORERS
05/01	Chester	A	2–0	12,000	Liddell, Fagan
09/01	Chester	H	2–1	11,207	Fagan (2)
26/01	Bolton W	A	0–5	39,692	
30/01	Bolton W	H	2–0	35,247	Balmer, Nieuwenhuys

1946–47

FOOTBALL LEAGUE DIVISION ONE

DATE	OPPOSITION	VENUE	SCORE	ATT	GOAL SCORERS
31/08	Sheffield Utd	A	1–0	30,000	Carney
04/09	Middlesbrough	H	0–1	30,000	
07/09	Chelsea	H	7–4	49,995	Fagan (2), Jones, Liddell (2), Balmer
11/09	Manchester Utd	A	0–5	50,000	
14/09	Bolton W	A	3–1	25,000	Nieuwenhuys, Stubbins, Balmer
21/09	Everton	H	0–0	49,838	
28/09	Leeds Utd	H	2–0	51,042	Balmer, Nieuwenhuys
05/10	Grimsby T	A	6–1	22,000	Stubbins (2), Liddell (2), Balmer, Fagan (pen)
09/10	Middlesbrough	A	2–2	37,382	Liddell (2)
12/10	Charlton A	H	1–1	51,127	Done
19/10	Huddersfield T	H	4–1	17,000	Done (3), Balmer
26/10	Brentford	H	1–0	43,894	Stubbins
02/11	Blackburn R	A	0–0	23,000	
09/11	Portsmouth	H	3–0	50,000	Balmer (3;1 pen)
16/11	Derby Co	A	4–1	28,444	Balmer (4)
23/11	Arsenal	H	4–2	45,000	Balmer (3;1 pen), Stubbins
30/11	Blackpool	A	2–3	23,565	Balmer, Done
07/12	Wolves	H	1–5	52,512	Balmer (pen)
14/12	Sunderland	A	4–1	33,300	Balmer, Liddell, Nieuwenhuys, Stubbins
21/12	Aston Villa	H	4–1	35,650	Balmer (2), Stubbins, Nieuwenhuys
25/12	Stoke C	A	1–2	30,420	Stubbins
26/12	Stoke C	H	2–0	49,494	Nieuwenhuys, Stubbins
28/12	Sheffield Utd	H	1–2	50,961	Stubbins
04/01	Chelsea	A	1–3	58,375	Balmer
18/01	Bolton W	H	0–3	50,000	
29/01	Everton	A	0–1	35,000	
01/02	Leeds Utd	A	2–1	25,000	Stubbins (2)
12/02	Grimsby T	H	5–0	40,000	Done (3), Fagan (2)
22/02	Huddersfield T	H	1–0	35,000	Stubbins
08/03	Blackburn R	H	2–1	49,378	Done, Stubbins
15/03	Portsmouth	A	2–1	30,000	Stubbins (2)
22/03	Derby Co	H	1–1	50,848	Taylor
04/04	Preston NE	A	0–0	30,000	
05/04	Blackpool	H	2–3	47,000	Fagan, Done
07/04	Preston NE	H	3–0	47,000	Stubbins (2), Balmer
19/04	Sunderland	H	1–0	41,589	Stubbins
26/04	Aston Villa	A	2–1	40,000	Watkinson, Fagan
03/05	Manchester Utd	H	1–0	50,000	Stubbins
10/05	Charlton A	A	3–1	35,000	Stubbins (3)
17/05	Brentford	A	1–1	22,000	Priday
24/05	Arsenal	A	2–1	48,000	Balmer, Priday
31/05	Wolves	A	2–1	50,078	Balmer, Stubbins

Div One Position 1st P42 Pts 57

FA CUP

DATE	OPPOSITION	VENUE	SCORE	ATT	GOALSCORERS
11/01	Walsall	A	5–2	18,379	Foulkes (o.g.), Done, Liddell, Balmer (2)
25/01	Grimsby T	H	2–0	42,265	Stubbins, Done
08/02	Derby Co	H	1–0	44,493	Balmer
01/03	Birmingham C	H	4–1	51,911	Stubbins (3), Balmer
29/03	*Burnley	H	0–0	52,570	(a.e.t.) (at Ewood Park)
12/04	**Burnley	H	0–1	72,000	(at Maine Road)

1947–48

FOOTBALL LEAGUE DIVISION ONE

DATE	OPPOSITION	VENUE	SCORE	ATT	GOALSCORERS
23/08	Preston NE	H	3–1	49,353	Liddell, Stubbins (2)
27/08	Manchester Utd	A	0–2	45,000	
30/08	Stoke C	A	2–0	30,000	Liddell (2)
03/09	Manchester Utd	H	2–2	50,000	Stubbins, Balmer (pen)
06/09	Burnley	H	1–1	56,074	Balmer
08/09	Sheffield Utd	A	1–3	40,000	Stubbins
13/09	Portsmouth	A	0–1	32,000	
17/09	Charlton A	A	0–2	40,000	
20/09	Bolton W	H	0–0	43,920	
27/09	Everton	A	3–0	66,576	Balmer, Stubbins, Fagan
04/10	Middlesbrough	H	1–3	41,140	Balmer
11/10	Chelsea	H	3–0	51,449	Priday, Stubbins, Liddell
18/10	Huddersfield T	A	1–1	27,518	Balmer
25/10	Derby Co	H	2–2	49,624	Priday, Balmer
01/11	Blackpool	A	0–2	25,000	
08/11	Grimsby T	H	3–1	36,796	Stubbins, Priday, Baron
15/11	Sunderland	A	1–5	37,258	Liddell
22/11	Blackburn R	A	2–1	35,672	Balmer, Liddell
29/11	Manchester C	A	0–2	37,464	
06/12	Aston Villa	H	3–3	37,732	Spicer, Stubbins, Balmer
13/12	Wolves	A	2–1	32,000	Stubbins, Balmer
20/12	Preston NE	A	3–3	32,000	Jones, Liddell, Stubbins
25/12	Arsenal	H	1–3	50,000	Priday
27/12	Arsenal	A	2–1	59,000	Stubbins, Liddell
01/01	Charlton A	A	2–3	34,533	Stubbins (2)
03/01	Stoke C	H	0–0	48,655	
17/01	Burnley	A	0–3	25,000	
31/01	Portsmouth	H	0–3	23,097	
07/02	Bolton W	A	0–3	20,800	
21/02	Middlesbrough	A	1–0	36,133	
28/02	Chelsea	A	1–3	39,078	Baron
06/03	Huddersfield T	H	4–0	40,000	Stubbins (4)
20/03	Blackpool	H	2–0	48,725	Stubbins (2;1 pen)
26/03	Sheffield Utd	H	4–0	54,797	Fagan (2), Liddell, Stubbins
27/03	Grimsby T	A	2–0	18,000	Balmer, Spicer
31/03	Derby Co	A	4–0	16,277	Stubbins, Balmer (2), Fagan

03/04	Sunderland	H	0–0	49,687	
10/04	Blackburn R	A	2–1	26,000	Stubbins, Balmer
17/04	Manchester C	H	1–1	39,348	Fagan
21/04	Everton	H	4–0	55,035	Stubbins, Liddell, Brierley, Balmer
24/04	Aston Villa	A	1–2	30,000	Stubbins
01/05	Wolves	H	2–1	31,773	Paisley, Balmer

Div One Position 11th   P42 Pts 42

FA CUP

DATE	OPPOSITION	VENUE	SCORE	ATT	GOALSCORERS
10/01	Nottingham F	H	4–1	48,569	Priday, Stubbins (2), Liddell
24/01	Manchester Utd	A	0–3	74,721	(at Goodison Park)

1948–49

FOOTBALL LEAGUE DIVISION ONE

DATE	OPPOSITION	VENUE	SCORE	ATT	GOALSCORERS
21/08	Aston Villa	A	1–2	35,000	Balmer
25/08	Sheffield Utd	H	3–3	37,393	Balmer (2), Liddell
28/08	Sunderland	H	4–0	52,253	Liddell, Fagan, Watkinson, Balmer
30/08	Sheffield Utd	A	2–1	30,000	Shannon, Liddell
04/09	Wolves	A	0–0	40,000	
08/09	Arsenal	A	1–1	46,714	Liddell
11/09	Bolton W	H	0–1	56,561	
15/09	Arsenal	H	0–1	46,714	
18/09	Everton	A	1–1	78,599	Fagan
25/09	Blackpool	A	0–1	30,000	
02/10	Derby Co	H	0–0	53,776	
09/10	Chelsea	H	1–1	42,709	Payne
16/10	Birmingham C	A	0–0	43,000	Done
23/10	Middlesbrough	H	4–0	57,561	Balmer, Stubbins, Liddell (pen), Whitaker (o.g.)
30/10	Newcastle Utd	A	0–1	67,362	
06/11	Portsmouth	H	3–1	43,665	Liddell, Balmer, Done
13/11	Manchester C	A	4–2	21,659	Payne, Done (2), Taylor
20/11	Charlton A	H	1–0	49,377	Done
27/11	Stoke C	A	0–3	35,000	
04/12	Burnley	H	1–1	41,001	Done
11/12	Preston NE	A	2–3	28,000	Done (2)
18/12	Aston Villa	H	1–1	23,866	Done
25/12	Manchester Utd	A	0–0	47,788	
27/12	Manchester Utd	H	0–2	53,273	
01/01	Sunderland	A	2–0	43,109	Hall (o.g.), Liddell (pen)
22/01	Bolton W	A	3–0	30,000	Balmer, Stubbins, Gillies (o.g.)
05/02	Everton	H	0–0	50,132	
19/02	Blackpool	H	1–1	52,294	Balmer
05/03	Chelsea	A	1–2	42,746	Payne
12/03	Birmingham C	H	1–0	43,763	Done
19/03	Charlton A	A	1–2	30,000	Done
26/03	Stoke C	H	4–0	30,791	Stubbins (2), Done, Balmer
02/04	Portsmouth	A	2–3	34,500	Stubbins, Paisley
06/04	Wolves	H	0–0	35,399	
09/04	Manchester C	H	0–1	31,389	
15/04	Huddersfield T	A	1–0	47,319	
16/04	Middlesbrough	A	1–0	32,308	Balmer
18/04	Huddersfield T	H	4–0	22,000	Balmer (2), Baron, Liddell
23/04	Newcastle Utd	H	1–1	43,488	Baron
30/04	Burnley	A	2–0	17,693	Balmer, Stubbins
04/05	Derby Co	A	0–3	22,897	
07/05	Preston NE	H	0–2	31,937	

Div One Position 12th   P42 Pts 40

FA CUP

DATE	OPPOSITION	VENUE	SCORE	ATT	GOALSCORERS
08/01	Nottingham F	A	2–2*	35,000	Fagan, Done
15/01	Nottingham F	H	4–0	52,218	Payne, Balmer (2), Stubbins
29/01	Notts Co	H	1–0	61,003	Liddell
12/02	Wolves	A	1–3	54,983	

1949–50

FOOTBALL LEAGUE DIVISION ONE

DATE	OPPOSITION	VENUE	SCORE	ATT	GOALSCORERS
20/08	Sunderland	H	4–2	49,811	Paisley, Balmer, Baron, Stubbins
22/08	Stoke C	A	0–0	35,000	
27/08	Everton	A	0–0	70,812	
31/08	Stoke C	H	1–1	38,097	Liddell
03/09	Arsenal	A	2–1	56,000	Stubbins (2)
07/09	Manchester Utd	H	1–1	51,857	Stubbins
10/09	Bolton W	A	2–1	44,212	Baron
17/09	Birmingham C	A	3–2	40,000	Done, Liddell (2)
24/09	Derby Co	A	3–1	54,512	Baron, Fagan, Payne
01/12	West Brom A	A	1–0	44,219	Stubbins
08/10	Middlesbrough	H	2–0	49,569	Payne, Lambert (pen)
15/10	Blackpool	A	0–0	32,000	
22/10	Newcastle Utd	H	2–2	48,987	Liddell, Baron
29/10	Fulham	A	1–0	42,000	Liddell
05/11	Manchester C	H	4–0	50,536	Liddell (2; 1 pen), Brierley, Baron
12/11	Charlton A	A	3–1	38,800	Done, Liddell (2; 1 pen)
19/11	Aston Villa	H	2–1	50,293	Liddell, Brierley
26/11	Wolves	A	1–1	55,000	Fagan
03/12	Portsmouth	H	2–2	44,851	Done (2)
10/12	Huddersfield T	A	2–3	25,767	Fagan, Brierley
17/12	Sunderland	A	2–3	46,575	Brierley, Done
24/12	Everton	H	3–1	50,485	Baron (2), Fagan
26/12	Chelsea	A	1–1	55,820	Fagan
27/12	Chelsea	H	2–2	58,757	Fagan
31/12	Arsenal	H	2–0	55,020	Liddell, 1 (o.g.) (name not recorded)
14/01	Bolton W	A	2–3	41,507	Liddell, Fagan
21/01	Birmingham C	H	2–0	37,668	Payne, Stubbins
04/02	Derby Co	A	2–2	36,835	Stubbins, Liddell
18/02	West Brom A	H	2–1	46,634	Stubbins, Brierley
25/02	Middlesbrough	A	1–4	31,804	Stubbins
08/03	Blackpool	H	0–1	33,464	
11/03	Aston Villa	A	0–2	39,035	
15/03	Manchester Utd	A	0–0	30,000	
18/03	Wolves	H	0–2	41,216	

29/03	Manchester C	A	2–1	38,000	Liddell, Payne
01/04	Charlton A	H	1–0	39,721	Liddell (pen)
07/04	Burnley	A	2–0	33,035	Payne, Liddell
08/04	Newcastle Utd	A	1–5	45,000	Fagan
10/04	Burnley	H	0–1	43,716	
15/04	Fulham	H	1–1	36,274	Fagan
22/04	Portsmouth	A	1–2	47,507	Stubbins
03/05	Huddersfield T	H	2–3	35,463	Fagan, Liddell

Div One Position 8th   P42 Pts 48

FA CUP

DATE	OPPOSITION	VENUE	SCORE	ATT	GOALSCORERS
07/01	Blackburn R	A	0–0	52,468	
11/01	Blackburn R	H	2–1	52,221	Payne, Fagan
28/01	Exeter C	H	3–1	45,209	Baron, Fagan, Payne
11/02	Stockport Co	A	2–1	27,833	Fagan, Stubbins
04/03	Blackpool	H	2–1	53,973	Fagan, Liddell
25/03	Everton	N	2–0	72,000	Paisley, Liddell (at Maine Road)
29/04	Arsenal	N	0–2	98,249	(at Wembley)

1950–51

FOOTBALL LEAGUE DIVISION ONE

DATE	OPPOSITION	VENUE	SCORE	ATT	GOALSCORERS
19/08	Wolves	A	0–2	50,622	
23/08	Manchester Utd	H	2–1	30,211	Liddell, Allen (o.g.)
26/08	Sunderland	H	4–0	52,080	Liddell (2), Stubbins (2)
30/08	Manchester Utd	A	0–1	34,835	
02/09	Aston Villa	A	1–1	50,000	Balmer
06/09	Tottenham H	H	2–1	39,015	Balmer, Stubbins
09/09	Derby Co	H	1–0	50,079	Done
16/09	Everton	A	3–1	71,150	Stubbins, Balmer (2)
23/09	Fulham	A	1–2	42,000	Liddell
30/09	Bolton W	H	3–3	44,534	Payne, Balmer (2)
07/10	Stoke C	H	0–0	40,239	
14/10	West Brom A	A	1–1	35,030	Taylor
21/10	Middlesbrough	H	0–0	47,426	
28/10	Sheffield Wed	A	1–1	33,549	Payne
04/11	Newcastle Utd	H	2–4	48,810	Liddell (pen), Payne
11/11	Huddersfield T	A	2–2	25,220	Liddell, Taylor
18/11	Arsenal	H	1–3	44,193	Compton (o.g.)
25/11	Burnley	A	1–1	31,990	Baron
02/12	Chelsea	H	1–0	28,717	Liddell
09/12	Portsmouth	A	3–1	29,470	Payne (2), Balmer
16/12	Wolves	H	1–4	30,959	Liddell (pen)
23/12	Sunderland	A	1–2	30,150	Balmer
25/12	Blackpool	A	0–3	32,000	
26/12	Blackpool	H	1–0	54,121	Balmer
13/01	Derby Co	A	2–1	21,849	Haigh, Liddell
20/01	Everton	H	0–2	48,688	
27/01	Charlton A	A	0–1	25,000	
03/02	Fulham	H	2–0	38,630	Jones, Liddell
10/02	Portsmouth	H	2–1	36,958	Jones, Balmer
17/02	Bolton W	A	1–2	35,824	Liddell
24/02	Stoke C	A	3–2	25,000	Done, Jones, Liddell
03/03	West Brom A	H	1–1	33,654	Paisley
10/03	Middlesbrough	A	1–1	29,247	Liddell
17/03	Sheffield Wed	H	2–1	31,413	Liddell (2; 1 pen)
23/03	Charlton A	H	1–0	31,650	Haigh
24/03	Newcastle Utd	A	1–1	50,000	Done
31/03	Huddersfield T	H	1–4	27,915	Haigh
07/04	Arsenal	A	2–1	42,000	Stubbins, Payne
14/04	Burnley	H	1–0	24,118	Jones
21/04	Chelsea	A	0–1	30,134	
25/04	Aston Villa	H	0–0	23,061	
05/05	Tottenham H	A	1–3	49,072	Stubbins

Div One Position 9th   P42 Pts 43

FA CUP

DATE	OPPOSITION	VENUE	SCORE	ATT	GOALSCORERS
06/01	Norwich C	A	1–3	34,641	Balmer

1951–52

FOOTBALL LEAGUE DIVISION ONE

DATE	OPPOSITION	VENUE	SCORE	ATT	GOALSCORERS
18/08	Portsmouth	H	0–2	42,270	
21/08	Burnley	A	0–0	23,162	
25/08	Chelsea	H	3–1	44,055	Baron, Liddell, Stubbins
29/08	Burnley	H	3–1	32,857	Stubbins, Done, Liddell
01/09	Huddersfield T	H	2–1	39,818	Liddell, Baron
05/09	Arsenal	H	0–0	50,483	
08/09	Wolves	A	1–2	50,000	Brierley
12/09	Arsenal	H	0–0	39,853	
15/09	Sunderland	H	2–2	37,381	Liddell, Baron
22/09	Aston Villa	A	0–2	50,000	
29/09	Derby Co	H	2–0	40,259	Smith, Williams
06/10	Charlton A	A	0–2	33,000	
13/10	Fulham	H	4–0	36,793	Smith, Payne (2), Liddell
20/10	Middlesbrough	H	3–3	26,126	Liddell, Smith, Jones
27/10	West Brom A	A	2–5	34,891	Payne, Liddell (pen)
03/11	Newcastle Utd	A	1–1	50,100	Payne
10/11	Bolton W	H	1–1	49,537	Jackson
17/11	Stoke C	A	2–1	24,000	Baron, Payne
24/11	Manchester Utd	H	0–0	42,378	
01/12	Tottenham H	A	3–2	51,350	Liddell (3,1 pen)
08/12	Preston NE	A	2–2	34,722	Liddell, Hughes
15/12	Portsmouth	A	3–1	29,945	Smith, Liddell (2)
22/12	Chelsea	H	1–1	26,459	Liddell
25/12	Blackpool	H	1–1	41,071	Payne
26/12	Blackpool	A	0–2	27,414	
29/12	Huddersfield T	A	2–1	25,500	Liddell, Payne
05/01	Wolves	H	1–1	44,768	Taylor
19/01	Sunderland	A	0–3	33,549	
26/01	Aston Villa	H	1–2	39,774	Liddell
09/02	Derby Co	A	1–1	22,495	Done

1951–52 (CONTINUED)

DATE	OPPOSITION	VENUE	SCORE	ATT	GOALSCORERS
16/02	Charlton A	H	1–1	33,487	Done
01/03	Fulham	A	1–1	37,000	Payne
08/03	Middlesbrough	H	1–1	41,945	W.H.Jones
15/03	West Brom A	A	3–3	27,133	Liddell, Paisley, Stubbins
22/03	Newcastle Utd	H	3–0	48,966	Smith, Stubbins (2)
29/03	Bolton W	A	1–1	14,571	Liddell
05/04	Stoke City	H	2–1	19,740	Paisley, Baron
11/04	Manchester C	H	2–1	35,305	Baron, Payne
12/04	Manchester Utd	A	0–4	42,970	
14/04	Manchester C	H	1–2	34,404	Smith
19/04	Tottenham H	H	1–1	36,898	Liddell
26/04	Preston NE	A	0–4	32,000	

Div One Position 11th   P42 Pts 43

FA CUP

DATE	OPPOSITION	VENUE	SCORE	ATT	GOALSCORERS
12/01	Workington T	H	1–0	52,581	Payne
02/02	Wolves*	H	2–1	61,905	Paisley, Done
23/02	Burnley	H	0–2	52,070	

* RECORD ATTENDANCE AT ANFIELD.

1952–53

FOOTBALL LEAGUE DIVISION ONE

DATE	OPPOSITION	VENUE	SCORE	ATT	GOALSCORERS
23/08	Preston NE	A	1–0	38,000	Smith
27/08	Sheffield Wed	H	1–0	46,614	Baron
30/08	Stoke C	H	3–2	40,062	Smith, Baron, Liddell
03/09	Sheffield Wed	A	2–0	41,183	Baron, Liddell
06/09	Manchester C	H	2–0	42,965	Baron, Smith
10/09	Tottenham H	H	2–1	49,809	Smith, Liddell (pen)
13/09	Portsmouth	H	1–1	49,771	Williams
15/09	Tottenham H	H	1–3	37,331	Williams
20/09	Middlesbrough	H	4–1	40,750	Payne, Smith, Williams, Baron
27/09	West Brom A	A	0–3	33,774	
04/10	Newcastle Utd	H	5–3	48,002	Liddell, Smith (2), Baron, Paisley
11/10	Bolton W	A	2–2	35,251	Baron, Payne
18/10	Aston Villa	H	0–2	42,573	
25/10	Sunderland	A	1–3	50,555	Liddell
01/11	Wolves	H	2–1	46,487	Payne, Liddell (pen)
08/11	Charlton A	A	2–3	30,000	Williams, Brierley
15/11	Arsenal	H	1–5	45,010	Payne
22/11	Derby Co	A	2–3	20,758	Liddell (pen), Smith
29/11	Blackpool	H	2–2	32,336	Payne (2)
13/12	Manchester Utd	H	1–2	34,450	Liddell
20/12	Preston NE	H	2–2	27,659	Liddell, Baron
25/12	Burnley	A	0–2	35,858	
26/12	Burnley	H	1–1	46,589	Liddell (pen)
03/01	Stoke C	A	1–3	25,000	Baron
17/01	Manchester C	A	0–1	41,191	
24/01	Portsmouth	A	1–3	27,045	Paisley
07/02	Middlesbrough	H	3–2	15,445	Liddell, Smyth, Taylor
14/02	West Brom A	H	3–0	24,980	Liddell, Payne, Smyth
21/02	Newcastle Utd	A	2–1	35,000	Smyth, Taylor
04/03	Bolton W	H	0–0	24,999	
07/03	Aston Villa	A	0–4	30,000	
14/03	Sunderland	H	2–0	40,409	Smyth, A'Court
21/03	Wolves	A	0–3	30,000	
23/03	Chelsea	A	0–3	17,337	
28/03	Charlton A	H	1–2	23,204	Payne
03/04	Cardiff C	H	2–1	52,079	W.Jones, Bimpson
04/04	Arsenal	A	3–5	40,564	Bimpson, A'Court, Liddell
06/04	Cardiff C	A	0–4	20,000	
11/04	Derby Co	H	1–1	34,064	Smyth
18/04	Blackpool	A	1–3	22,073	Smyth
20/04	Manchester Utd	A	1–3	20,869	Smyth
25/04	Chelsea	H	2–0	47,699	W.H.Jones, Bimpson

Div One Position 17th   P42 Pts 36

FA CUP

DATE	OPPOSITION	VENUE	SCORE	ATT	GOALSCORERS
10/01	Gateshead	A	0–1	15,193	

1953–54

FOOTBALL LEAGUE DIVISION ONE

DATE	OPPOSITION	VENUE	SCORE	ATT	GOALSCORERS
19/08	Portsmouth	H	3–1	39,662	W.Jones (2), Liddell
22/08	Manchester Utd	H	4–4	46,725	Bimpson (2), W.Jones, Liddell
26/08	Newcastle Utd	A	2–2	47,263	Baron (2)
29/08	Bolton W	A	0–2	28,277	
02/09	Newcastle Utd	A	0–4	47,000	
05/09	Preston NE	H	1–5	46,928	W.Jones
07/09	Wolves	A	1–2	35,701	Jackson
12/09	Tottenham H	A	1–2	47,535	W.Jones
16/09	Wolves	H	1–1	29,848	W.Jones
19/09	Burnley	H	4–0	36,643	Bimpson (4)
26/09	Charlton A	A	0–6	31,000	
03/10	Sheffield Wed	H	2–2	38,647	Paisley, Bimpson
10/10	Aston Villa	H	6–1	37,759	Liddell, Smyth (2), Paisley, Payne, Blanchflower (o.g.)
17/10	Huddersfield T	A	0–2	30,115	
24/10	Sheffield Utd	H	3–0	37,978	Payne, Smyth (2)
31/10	Chelsea	A	2–5	33,000	Smyth (2)
07/11	Manchester C	H	2–2	30,917	Bimpson, Baron
14/11	Sunderland	A	2–3	36,369	Smyth (2)
21/11	Arsenal	H	1–2	47,814	Bimpson
28/11	Cardiff C	A	1–3	15,000	Bimpson
05/12	Blackpool	H	5–2	47,320	Payne, A'Court (2), Arnell, Smyth
12/12	Portsmouth	A	1–5	23,509	Smyth
19/12	Manchester Utd	A	1–5	26,074	Bimpson
25/12	West Brom A	A	2–5	30,390	A'Court, Lambert (pen)
26/12	West Brom A	H	0–0	51,167	
02/01	Bolton W	H	1–2	44,383	Evans
16/01	Preston NE	H	1–2	27,000	Baron
23/01	Tottenham H	H	2–2	43,592	Liddell, Evans

DATE	OPPOSITION	VENUE	SCORE	ATT	GOALSCORERS
06/02	Burnley	A	1–1	23,000	Anderson
13/02	Sheffield Wed	A	2–3	47,657	Evans, Anderson
24/02	Sheffield A	A	1–1	10,000	Anderson
27/02	Aston Villa	A	1–2	25,000	Bimpson
06/03	Huddersfield T	H	1–3	46,074	Evans
13/03	Sheffield Utd	A	1–3	17,000	Liddell (pen)
20/03	Chelsea	H	2–3	36,292	Anderson
03/04	Sunderland	H	4–3	30,417	Jackson, Evans, Liddell (pen), Anderson
07/04	Manchester C	A	2–0	12,593	Jackson (2)
10/04	Arsenal	A	0–3	33,178	
16/04	Middlesbrough	A	1–0	26,882	Smyth
17/04	Cardiff C	H	0–1	41,340	
19/04	Middlesbrough	H	4–1	22,000	Rowley, Smyth (2), Liddell
24/04	Blackpool	A	0–3	18,651	

Div One Position 22nd   P42 Pts 28

FA CUP

DATE	OPPOSITION	VENUE	SCORE	ATT	GOALSCORERS
09/01	Bolton W	A	0–1	45,341	

1954–55

FOOTBALL LEAGUE DIVISION TWO

DATE	OPPOSITION	VENUE	SCORE	ATT	GOALSCORERS
21/08	Doncaster R	H	3–2	49,741	T.Rowley (3)
23/08	Plymouth A	A	0–1	25,574	
28/08	Derby Co	A	2–3	18,777	Evans, Bimpson
01/09	Plymouth A	H	3–3	32,777	Evans, Arnell (2)
04/09	West Ham Utd	H	1–2	37,593	Payne
06/09	Bristol R	A	0–3	25,574	
11/09	Blackburn R	A	3–4	29,200	Evans (2), Liddell
15/09	Bristol R	H	5–3	31,100	Evans (5)
18/09	Fulham	H	4–1	44,372	Liddell (3;2 pen), Evans
25/09	Swansea T	A	2–3	25,836	Liddell, T.Rowley
02/10	Notts Co	H	3–1	37,639	Anderson (2), Evans
09/10	Rotherham Utd	H	3–1	45,868	A'Court, Liddell, Evans
16/10	Stoke C	A	0–2	23,569	
23/10	Bury	H	1–1	33,310	Anderson
30/10	Lincoln C	A	3–3	13,800	Anderson, Liddell (2)
06/11	Hull C	H	2–1	32,952	Twentyman, Anderson
13/11	Luton T	A	2–3	15,887	Liddell, Evans
20/11	Nottingham F	H	1–0	33,509	Liddell (pen)
27/11	Leeds Utd	A	2–2	12,000	Liddell
04/12	Middlesbrough	H	3–1	26,749	Liddell (2;1 pen), Twentyman
11/12	Birmingham C	A	1–9	17,565	Liddell
18/12	Doncaster R	A	1–4	9,655	Evans
25/12	Ipswich T	H	6–2	24,073	Liddell (4;1 pen), Bimpson, Evans
27/12	Ipswich T	A	2–0	19,481	
01/01	Derby Co	H	2–0	34,327	Jackson, Liddell
22/01	Blackburn R	H	4–1	45,543	Liddell (2;1 pen), Evans (2)
05/02	Fulham	A	2–1	24,000	A.C.Rowley, Evans
12/02	Swansea T	H	1–1	42,249	Twentyman
03/03	Notts Co	A	3–3	11,000	Arnell, A'Court, Rowley
05/03	Stoke C	H	2–4	35,655	Evans (2)
12/03	Bury	A	4–3	16,081	Evans (4)
19/03	Lincoln C	H	2–4	31,805	Liddell (2;1 pen)
26/03	Hull C	A	2–2	6,000	Anderson, Evans
02/04	Luton T	H	4–4	30,710	Evans (2), Anderson, South
08/04	Port Vale	A	3–4	25,000	Anderson, Evans, Liddell
09/04	Nottingham F	A	1–3	15,409	Liddell
11/04	Port Vale	H	1–1	36,285	Jackson
16/04	Leeds Utd	H	2–2	34,950	Payne, A.C.Rowley
23/04	Middlesbrough	A	2–1	11,737	A.C.Rowley, Liddell
26/04	West Ham Utd	A	3–0	9,000	Evans, Anderson (2)
30/04	Birmingham C	H	2–2	38,392	Liddell (2;1 pen)
02/05	Rotherham Utd	H	1–6	17,000	Liddell

Div Two Position 11th   P42 Pts 42

FA CUP

DATE	OPPOSITION	VENUE	SCORE	ATT	GOALSCORERS
08/01	Lincoln C	A	1–1	15,399	Evans
12/01	Lincoln C	H	1–0*	32,179	Evans
29/01	Everton	A	4–0	72,000	Liddell, A'Court, Evans (2)
19/02	Huddersfield T	H	0–2	57,115	

1955–56

FOOTBALL LEAGUE DIVISION TWO

DATE	OPPOSITION	VENUE	SCORE	ATT	GOALSCORERS
20/08	Nottingham F	A	3–1	21,389	A'Court (2), Evans
24/08	Sheffield Wed	H	0–3	41,791	
27/08	Hull City	H	3–0	38,928	Liddell (2), Arnell
31/08	Sheffield Wed	A	1–1	30,853	Liddell
03/09	Blackburn R	A	3–3	30,000	Arnell (2), Liddell
07/09	Bristol R	H	0–2	38,221	
10/09	Lincoln C	A	2–1	39,816	Arnell (2)
17/09	Leicester C	A	1–3	21,356	Liddell
24/09	Middlesbrough	H	1–1	35,312	Liddell
01/10	Plymouth A	H	4–1	34,397	Twentyman (2), A'Court (2)
08/10	Bristol C	H	1–2	25,279	A.C.Rowley
15/10	West Ham Utd	H	3–1	32,187	A'Court, Payne, Liddell
22/10	Bury	A	4–1	12,296	Arnell (2), Liddell (2)
29/10	Rotherham Utd	H	2–0	31,810	Arnell, Liddell
05/11	Swansea T	A	1–2	25,000	Arnell
12/11	Notts Co	H	2–1	32,654	Liddell, Twentyman
19/11	Leeds Utd	A	2–4	22,500	Liddell (pen), Arnell
26/11	Fulham	H	7–0	34,995	Evans, Arnell, Liddell (2), Twentyman, A'Court, Payne
03/12	Port Vale	A	1–1	16,191	Liddell
10/12	Barnsley	H	1–1	26,241	Evans
17/12	Nottingham F	H	5–2	29,248	Evans, Melia, Liddell (3)
24/12	Hull C	A	2–1	19,537	Anderson, Evans
26/12	Stoke C	H	2–2	49,604	Liddell (pen), Evans
27/12	Stoke C	A	2–3	29,133	Twentyman, A.C.Rowley
31/12	Blackburn R	H	1–2	48,071	Anderson
21/01	Leicester C	H	3–1	39,917	Liddell (2;1 pen), Arnell
04/02	Middlesbrough	A	2–1	12,171	Evans, Liddell

11/02	Plymouth A	A	0–4	10,250	
25/02	West Ham Utd	A	0–2	18,800	
29/02	Leeds Utd	H	1–0	21,068	Evans
03/03	Bury	H	4–2	35,535	Evans (2; 1 pen), Liddell, Dickson
10/03	Barnsley	A	5–0	13,678	Anderson (2), Liddell (2), Dickson
17/03	Swansea T	H	4–1	48,217	Liddell, Dickson (2), Anderson
24/03	Notts Co	A	1–0	14,000	Anderson
30/03	Doncaster R	A	0–1	15,000	
31/03	Bristol C	H	2–1	46,713	Arnell, Evans (pen)
02/04	Doncaster R	H	1–2	49,659	Evans
07/04	Fulham	A	1–3	15,750	Liddell
14/04	Port Vale	H	4–1	29,413	A.C.Rowley (3), Twentyman
21/04	Rotherham Utd	A	1–0	9,031	A.C.Rowley
28/04	Bristol R	A	2–1	24,106	Evans, Twentyman
02/05	Lincoln C	H	0–2	11,069	

Div Two Position 3rd   P42 Pts 48

FA CUP

DATE	OPPOSITION	VENUE	SCORE	ATT	GOALSCORERS
07/01	Accrington S*	H	2–0	48,385	Liddell (2)
28/01	Scunthorpe Utd	H	3–3	53,393	Liddell (2), Payne
05/02	Scunthorpe Utd	A	2–1	19,500	Liddell, Arnell (a.e.t.)
18/02	Manchester C	A	0–0	70,640	
22/02	Manchester C	H	1–2	57,528	Arnell

*LIVERPOOL FC WEAR YELLOW SHIRTS, WHITE SHORTS AND RED SOCKS

1956–57

FOOTBALL LEAGUE DIVISION TWO

DATE	OPPOSITION	VENUE	SCORE	ATT	GOAL SCORERS
18/08	Huddersfield T	H	2–3	49,344	Liddell (2; 1 pen)
23/08	Notts Co	A	1–1	14,671	Liddell
25/08	Bury	A	2–0	17,000	Bimpson, Saunders
29/08	Notts Co	H	3–3	41,095	Twentyman (2), Arnell
01/09	Grimsby T	H	3–2	43,222	Bimpson (2), Arnell
03/09	West Ham Utd	A	1–1	25,000	Liddell
08/09	Doncaster R	A	1–1	13,580	Liddell
15/09	Stoke C	H	0–2	47,119	
22/09	Middlesbrough	A	1–1	21,912	Robinson (o.g.)
29/09	Leicester C	H	2–0	41,126	Melia, Liddell
06/10	Blackburn R	H	2–3	41,538	Anderson, Liddell
13/10	Bristol C	A	1–2	26,042	Wheeler
20/10	Fulham	H	4–3	36,735	A'Court, Wheeler, Liddell, Melia
27/10	Barnsley	A	1–4	13,941	Melia
03/11	Port Vale	H	4–1	32,334	Liddell, Wheeler (3)
10/11	Rotherham Utd	A	2–2	11,524	Bimpson, A'Court
17/11	Lincoln C	H	4–0	29,762	Arnell (2), Wheeler (2)
24/11	Swansea T	A	1–1	18,000	Arnell
01/12	Sheffield Utd	H	5–1	34,159	Wheeler, Liddell, Melia, A'Court, Arnell
08/12	Nottingham F	A	0–1	17,624	
15/12	Huddersfield T	H	3–0	11,577	Arnell (3)
22/12	Bury	H	2–0	18,754	Liddell (pen), Melia
25/12	Leyton O	H	1–0	22,001	A'Court
26/12	Leyton O	A	4–0	10,332	A'Court, Arnell, Bimpson, Liddell
29/12	Grimsby T	A	0–0	15,001	
12/01	Doncaster R	H	2–1	35,954	Arnell, Twentyman
19/01	Stoke C	A	0–1	31,144	
02/02	Middlesbrough	H	1–2	38,890	A'Court
09/02	Leicester C	A	2–3	39,622	Liddell, Evans
16/02	Blackburn R	A	2–2	27,100	Wheeler, Liddell
02/03	Fulham	A	2–1	26,500	Evans, Liddell
09/03	Barnsley	H	2–1	30,672	Wheeler, Liddell
16/03	Port Vale	A	2–1	14,241	A.C.Rowley (2)
23/03	Rotherham Utd	H	4–1	33,307	Liddell, Noble (o.g.), A.C.Rowley, A'Court
30/03	Lincoln C	A	3–3	8,449	Jackson (2), A.C.Rowley
06/04	Swansea T	H	2–0	34,773	A'Court (2)
13/04	Sheffield Utd	A	0–3	24,000	
19/04	Bristol R	H	4–1	40,776	Melia, Campbell, Liddell (pen), A.C.Rowley
20/04	Nottingham F	H	3–1	47,621	Liddell, A'Court, A.C.Rowley
22/04	Bristol R	A	0–0	14,794	
27/04	West Ham Utd	H	1–0	36,236	Liddell (pen)
01/05	Bristol C	H	2–1	15,108	A.C.Rowley, Liddell

Div Two Position 3rd   P42 Pts 53

FA CUP

DATE	OPPOSITION	VENUE	SCORE	ATT	GOALSCORERS
05/01	Southend Utd	A	1–2	18,253	Wheeler

1957–58

FOOTBALL LEAGUE DIVISION TWO

DATE	OPPOSITION	VENUE	SCORE	ATT	GOALSCORERS
24/08	Bristol C	A	2–1	28,191	A.C.Rowley (2)
28/08	Huddersfield T	H	1–1	41,447	A'Court
31/08	Cardiff C	H	3–0	45,698	Melia, Liddell, Malloy (o.g.)
04/09	Huddersfield T	A	1–2	16,614	A.C.Rowley
07/09	Fulham	H	2–2	33,000	Liddell, A'Court
14/09	Middlesbrough	A	2–2	33,000	Melia, Rowley
19/09	Rotherham Utd	A	2–2	10,359	Arnell, Melia
21/09	Leyton O	H	3–0	36,077	Wheeler, Rowley, Jackson
23/09	Stoke C	A	2–1	23,231	Bimpson, Rowley
28/09	Charlton A	A	1–5	25,403	Rowley
05/10	Doncaster R	H	5–0	33,701	Rowley (2), Melia (2), Bimpson
12/10	Swansea T	H	4–0	37,204	Rowley (2), Melia, Campbell
19/10	Derby Co	A	1–2	22,631	Rowley
26/10	Bristol R	H	2–0	36,686	Liddell, A'Court
02/11	Lincoln C	A	1–0	9,983	Wheeler
09/11	Notts Co	H	4–0	39,735	Melia, A'Court, Liddell, Rowley
16/11	Ipswich T	A	1–3	20,452	Wheeler
23/11	Blackburn R	H	2–0	55,232	Liddell (2)
27/11	Rotherham Utd	H	2–0	37,518	Wheeler, Liddell
30/11	Sheffield Utd	A	1–1	20,122	Liddell
07/12	West Ham Utd	H	1–1	34,030	Liddell
14/12	Barnsley	A	1–2	15,205	Jackson
21/12	Bristol C	H	4–3	38,051	Rowley (2), McNamara, A'Court
25/12	Grimsby T	A	1–3	17,705	Rowley

26/12	Grimsby T	H	3–2	47,766	Liddell (2, 1 pen), McNamara
28/12	Cardiff C	A	1–6	32,000	Wheeler
11/01	Fulham	H	2–1	51,701	McNamara, Bimpson
18/01	Middlesbrough	H	0–2	39,246	
01/02	Leyton O	A	0–1	18,568	
08/02	Charlton A	H	3–1	38,528	Twentyman, Liddell, Murdoch
19/02	Doncaster R	A	1–1	6,093	Liddell
22/02	Blackburn R	A	3–3	41,700	Liddell (3)
05/03	Derby Co	H	2–0	30,832	Liddell, Murdoch
08/03	Bristol R	A	1–3	19,299	Murdoch
15/03	Lincoln C	H	1–0	31,403	Liddell
22/03	Notts Co	A	2–0	13,040	Melia, Bimpson
29/03	Ipswich T	H	3–1	24,026	Melia, Harrower, A'Court
05/04	Swansea T	A	2–0	13,500	Melia, Murdoch
07/04	Stoke C	H	3–0	39,446	Murdoch, Liddell (2; 1 pen)
12/04	Sheffield Utd	H	1–0	43,222	Liddell
19/04	West Ham Utd	H	1–1	37,750	Liddell
26/04	Barnsley	H	1–1	26,440	Harrower

Div Two Position 4th   P42 Pts 54

FA CUP

DATE	OPPOSITION	VENUE	SCORE	ATT	GOALSCORERS
04/01	Southend Utd	H	1–1	43,454	Smith (o.g.)
08/01	Southend Utd	A	3–2	20,000	Molyneux, White, Rowley
25/01	Northampton T	H	3–1	56,939	Liddell, Collins (o.g.), Bimpson
15/02	Scunthorpe Utd	A	1–0	23,000	Murdoch
01/03	Blackburn R	A	1–2	51,000	Murdoch

1958–59

FOOTBALL LEAGUE DIVISION TWO

DATE	OPPOSITION	VENUE	SCORE	ATT	GOALSCORERS
23/08	Grimsby T	H	3–3	47,502	Melia, Liddell (2;1 pen)
30/08	Sunderland	A	1–2	36,168	Liddell
03/09	Brighton & HA	H	5–0	39,520	Arnell (2), Harrower, Banks, Molyneux
06/09	Middlesbrough	A	1–2	34,714	Harrower
10/09	Sheffield Utd	A	2–1	44,232	Liddell, Twentyman
13/09	Charlton A	H	3–0	43,329	Liddell (2;1 pen), A'Court
15/09	Sheffield Utd	A	0–2	14,727	
20/09	Bristol C	H	3–1	26,896	Liddell (2), Campbell
24/09	Brighton & HA	A	2–2	21,323	Liddell, Morris
27/09	Cardiff C	A	1–2	41,866	Banks
04/10	Huddersfield T	A	0–5	15,934	
11/10	Lincoln C	H	3–2	31,344	Harrower, Morris (2)
18/10	Fulham	H	1–0	32,200	Bimpson
25/10	Sheffield Wed	H	3–2	39,912	Martin (o.g.), Morris (pen), Harrower
01/11	Stoke C	A	2–0	26,919	Bimpson, Melia
08/11	Liverpool	H	3–0	34,920	Twentyman, Bimpson, Melia
15/11	Derby Co	A	2–3	16,907	Mays (o.g.), Bimpson
22/11	Bristol R	H	2–1	39,365	Twentyman, Melia
29/11	Ipswich T	A	0–2	15,637	
06/12	Swansea T	A	4–0	27,561	Bimpson, Morris, Harrower, A'Court
13/12	Scunthorpe Utd	A	2–1	11,194	Melia, A'Court
20/12	Grimsby T	A	3–2	10,004	Morris, Bimpson, A'Court
26/12	Rotherham Utd	A	1–0	12,960	Melia
27/12	Rotherham Utd	H	4–0	44,729	Morris, Bimpson (2), Harrower
03/01	Sunderland	H	3–1	36,953	Wheeler, Bimpson, Morris
31/01	Charlton A	A	1–3	17,566	Twentyman, Morris, Melia
07/02	Bristol C	A	3–2	34,091	Arnell (2), Melia
14/02	Cardiff C	A	0–3	25,000	
21/02	Huddersfield T	H	2–2	28,860	Melia, Morris
28/02	Leyton O	A	3–1	14,064	Melia, Morris, A'Court
07/03	Fulham	H	0–0	43,926	
20/03	Stoke C	H	3–4	35,507	Melia (2), Bimpson
27/03	Barnsley	H	3–2	52,546	Melia, Liddell (2)
28/03	Lincoln C	A	1–2	11,012	Bimpson
30/03	Barnsley	A	2–0	7,517	Melia (2)
04/04	Derby Co	H	3–0	38,879	Liddell, Melia (2)
08/04	Middlesbrough	H	1–2	36,288	Melia
11/04	Bristol R	A	0–3	14,810	
14/04	Sheffield Wed	A	0–1	28,264	
18/04	Ipswich T	H	3–1	16,415	Melia, Liddell, A'Court
22/04	Scunthorpe Utd	H	3–0	11,976	Arnell, Liddell, Morris
25/04	Swansea T	A	3–3	8,000	A'Court, Melia (2)

Div Two Position 4th   P42 Pts 53

FA CUP

DATE	OPPOSITION	VENUE	SCORE	ATT	GOALSCORERS
15/01	Worcester C	A	1–2	15,011	Twentyman (pen)

1959–60

FOOTBALL LEAGUE DIVISION TWO

DATE	OPPOSITION	VENUE	SCORE	ATT	GOALSCORERS
22/08	Cardiff C	A	2–3	34,000	Malloy (2 o.gs.)
26/08	Bristol C	H	4–2	33,071	Liddell (2), Melia (pen), A'Court
29/08	Hull C	H	5–3	35,520	Harrower, Melia, Moran, A'court, Liddell
01/09	Bristol C	A	0–1	22,528	
05/09	Sheffield Utd	A	1–2	25,073	Morrissey
09/09	Scunthorpe Utd	H	2–0	31,713	Melia, Hunt
12/09	Middlesbrough	A	1–2	39,000	Liddell
17/09	Scunthorpe Utd	A	1–1	18,851	Melia
19/09	Derby Co	A	2–1	11,822	A'Court, Hunt
26/09	Plymouth A	H	4–1	29,278	Melia, A'Court, Hunt, Moran
03/10	Swansea T	A	4–5	16,500	Kennedy (o.g.), Melia (pen), Hunt, Moran
10/10	Brighton & HA	H	2–2	30,366	A'Court, Melia
17/10	Stoke C	A	1–1	17,000	Harrower
24/10	Portsmouth	H	1–1	21,075	Moran
31/10	Sunderland	A	1–1	30,208	Hunt
07/11	Aston Villa	H	2–1	49,981	Hickson (2)
14/11	Lincoln City	A	2–4	10,801	Hickson, Hunt
21/11	Leyton O	H	4–3	34,321	Morris (2), Melia, Hickson
28/11	Huddersfield T	A	0–1	16,185	
05/12	Ipswich T	H	3–1	24,843	Hunt (2), Hickson
12/12	Bristol R	A	2–0	15,615	Melia (2)
19/12	Cardiff C	H	0–4	27,291	

1959–60 (CONTINUED)

DATE	OPPOSITION	VENUE	SCORE	ATT	GOALSCORERS
26/12	Charlton A	A	0–3	15,491	
28/12	Charlton A	H	2–0	26,658	A'Court, Hunt
02/01	Hull City	A	1–0	18,681	Melia
16/01	Sheffield Utd	H	3–0	33,297	Melia, Hunt (2)
23/01	Middlesbrough	A	3–3	28,800	Thompson (o.g.), Hickson, Hunt
13/02	Plymouth A	A	1–1	16,996	Hickson
20/02	Swansea Town	H	4–1	31,663	Hickson (2), Hunt (2)
27/02	Brighton & HA	A	2–1	21,118	Hickson (2)
05/03	Stoke C	H	5–1	35,101	Hunt, Harrower (2), Liddell, Hickson
12/03	Portsmouth	A	1–2	14,622	Harrower
19/03	Huddersfield T	H	2–2	30,009	Hickson, Wheeler
30/03	Aston Villa	A	4–4	27,000	Hunt, Hickson (2), Molyneux
02/04	Lincoln C	H	1–3	24,081	Moran (pen)
06/04	Derby Co	A	4–1	19,411	Hunt, A'Court, Wheeler, Hickson
09/04	Leyton O	A	0–2	13,007	
16/04	Bristol R	H	4–0	27,317	Melia, A'Court, Campbell, Hunt
18/04	Rotherham Utd	H	3–0	26,776	Hunt, Hickson
19/04	Rotherham Utd	A	2–2	10,123	Hickson, Hunt
23/04	Ipswich T	A	1–0	12,048	Hickson
30/04	Sunderland	H	3–0	25,916	Hickson, Hunt, Melia

Div Two Position 3rd   P42 Pts 50

FA CUP

DATE	OPPOSITION	VENUE	SCORE	ATT	GOALSCORERS
09/01	Leyton O	H	2–1	40,343	Hunt (2)
30/01	Manchester Utd	H	1–3	56,736	Wheeler

1960–61

FOOTBALL LEAGUE DIVISION TWO

DATE	OPPOSITION	VENUE	SCORE	ATT	GOALSCORERS
20/08	Leeds Utd	H	2–0	43,041	Lewis, Hickson
24/08	Southampton	A	1–4	24,823	Leishman
27/08	Middlesbrough	A	1–1	21,236	Lewis
31/08	Southampton	H	0–1	37,604	
03/09	Brighton & HA	H	2–0	24,390	Harrower (2)
07/09	Luton T	H	2–2	27,339	Hickson, Moran (pen)
10/09	Ipswich T	A	0–1	13,502	
14/09	Luton T	A	1–2	10,055	Moran (pen)
17/09	Scunthorpe Utd	H	3–2	23,797	Harrower, Leishman, Hunt
24/09	Leyton O	A	3–1	10,921	Hickson, A'Court, Morrissey
01/10	Derby Co	H	1–0	24,695	Wheeler
08/10	Lincoln C	A	2–1	6,656	Hunt (2)
15/10	Portsmouth T	H	3–3	26,302	Hickson (2), Hunt
22/10	Huddersfield T	H	4–2	15,719	Lewis, Hunt, A'Court, Hickson
29/10	Sunderland	H	1–1	30,612	Harrower (pen)
05/11	Plymouth A	A	4–0	17,641	A'Court, Hickson, Hunt (2)
12/11	Norwich C	H	2–1	32,473	Hunt, Harrower
19/11	Charlton A	A	3–1	13,439	Lawrie (o.g.), Hunt, Wheeler
26/11	Sheffield Utd	H	4–2	39,999	Harrower (3), Hickson
10/12	Swansea T	H	4–0	25,739	Lewis (2), A'Court, Hickson
17/12	Leeds Utd	A	2–2	11,900	Lewis, Leishman
26/12	Rotherham Utd	H	2–1	39,426	Hunt, Lewis
27/12	Rotherham Utd	A	0–1	17,815	
31/12	Middlesbrough	H	3–4	34,645	A'Court, Lewis (2)
14/01	Brighton & HA	A	1–3	17,495	A'Court
21/01	Ipswich T	H	1–1	23,389	Lewis
04/02	Scunthorpe Utd	A	3–2	7,970	Lewis, Melia, Leishman
11/02	Leyton O	H	5–0	22,131	Hickson (3), Morrissey, Lewis
18/02	Derby Co	A	4–1	16,301	Hickson, Melia (2), Lewis
25/02	Lincoln C	H	2–0	24,759	Morrissey, Lewis
04/03	Portsmouth T	A	2–2	14,301	Banks, Morrissey
11/03	Huddersfield T	H	3–1	29,733	Banks (2), Lewis
18/03	Swansea T	A	0–2	13,181	
24/03	Plymouth A	H	1–1	25,250	Banks
31/03	Bristol R	H	3–0	36,538	Hunt, Wheeler, Hickson
01/04	Sheffield Utd	A	1–1	28,853	Morrissey
04/04	Bristol R	A	3–4	16,522	Lewis (3; 1 pen)
08/04	Charlton A	H	2–1	26,390	Hunt (2)
15/04	Norwich C	A	1–2	21,204	Hickson
22/04	Stoke C	H	3–0	13,389	Hunt, Hickson, Lewis
29/04	Sunderland	A	1–1	30,040	Hunt
03/04	Stoke C	A	1–3	4,463	A'Court

Div Two Position 3rd   P42 Pts 52

FA CUP

DATE	OPPOSITION	VENUE	SCORE	ATT	GOALSCORERS
07/01	Coventry C	H	3–2	50,909	Hunt, Lewis, Harrower
28/01	Sunderland	H	0–2	46,185	

LEAGUE CUP

DATE	OPPOSITION	VENUE	SCORE	ATT	GOALSCORERS
19/10	Luton T	H	1–1	10,503	Leishman
24/10	Luton T	A	5–2	6,125	Lewis (2), Hickson, Hunt (2)
16/11	Southampton	H	1–2	14,036	Hunt

1961–62

FOOTBALL LEAGUE DIVISION TWO

DATE	OPPOSITION	VENUE	SCORE	ATT	GOALSCORERS
19/08	Bristol R	A	2–0	19,438	Lewis, Mills (o.g.)
23/08	Sunderland	H	3–0	48,962	Hunt (2), Lewis
26/08	Leeds Utd	H	5–0	42,950	Hunt (3), Lewis (pen), Melia
30/08	Sunderland	A	4–1	47,261	Hunt (2), St John (2)
02/09	Norwich C	A	2–1	28,049	Hunt (2)
09/09	Scunthorpe Utd	H	2–1	46,837	Hemsted (o.g.), A'Court
16/09	Brighton & HA	A	0–0	18,764	
20/09	Newcastle Utd	H	3–1	38,180	Milne, Heslop (o.g.)
23/09	Bury	H	5–0	46,609	Melia (2), St John, Hunt, Lewis
30/09	Charlton A	A	4–0	14,236	Hunt (2), Lewis, St John
04/10	Newcastle Utd	H	2–0	52,419	Lewis, Hunt
07/10	Middlesbrough	A	0–2	24,123	
14/10	Walsall	H	6–1	42,229	Lewis, Melia, Hunt (3), St John
21/10	Derby Co	A	0–2	27,355	
28/10	Leyton O	H	3–3	36,612	Hunt (2), Leishman

DATE	OPPOSITION	VENUE	SCORE	ATT	GOALSCORERS
04/11	Preston NE	A	3–1	29,243	Milne, Callaghan, St John
11/11	Luton T	H	1–1	34,924	Lewis
18/11	Huddersfield T	A	2–1	23,086	Melia, Hunt
25/11	Swansea T	H	5–0	35,725	Melia (2), Hunt (3)
02/12	Southampton	A	0–2	21,445	
09/12	Plymouth A	H	2–1	32,543	A'Court, St John
16/12	Bristol R	H	2–0	29,957	St John, Hunt
23/12	Leeds Utd	A	0–1	17,214	
26/12	Rotherham Utd	A	0–1	13,577	
13/01	Norwich C	H	5–4	35,576	Melia (2), Hunt (2), A'Court
20/01	Scunthorpe Utd	A	1–1	11,200	St John
03/02	Brighton & HA	H	3–1	36,414	Byrne, Hunt, St John
10/02	Bury	A	3–0	21,872	Hunt (3)
24/02	Middlesbrough	H	5–1	37,629	St John (2), Hunt (3)
03/03	Walsall	A	1–1	13,660	A'Court
10/03	Derby Co	H	4–1	38,152	Hunt (2), Melia (2)
17/03	Leyton O	A	2–2	25,880	A'Court (2)
24/03	Preston NE	H	4–1	39,701	Melia, St John, Hunt (2)
28/03	Rotherham Utd	H	4–1	32,827	Hunt, St John (3)
31/03	Luton T	A	0–1	9,086	
07/04	Huddersfield T	H	1–1	38,022	Hunt
21/04	Southampton	H	2–0	40,410	Lewis (2)
23/04	Stoke C	H	2–1	41,005	Moran (pen), Melia
24/04	Stoke C	A	0–0	15,472	
28/04	Plymouth A	A	3–2	13,427	A'Court, St John, Hunt
30/04	Charlton A	H	2–1	34,327	Hunt, A'Court
04/05	Swansea T	A	2–4	15,000	St John, Hunt

Div Two Position 1st   P42 Pts 62

FA CUP

DATE	OPPOSITION	VENUE	SCORE	ATT	GOALSCORERS
06/01	Chelsea	H	4–3	48,455	St John (2), Hunt, A'Court
27/01	Oldham A	A	2–1	42,000	St John (2)
17/02	Preston NE	H	0–0	54,967	
20/02	Preston NE	A	0–0	37,831	(a.e.t.)
26/02	Preston NE	N	0–1	43,944	(at Old Trafford)

1962–63

FOOTBALL LEAGUE DIVISION ONE

DATE	OPPOSITION	VENUE	SCORE	ATT	GOALSCORERS
18/08	Blackpool	H	1–2	51,207	Lewis
22/08	Manchester C	A	2–2	33,165	Moran (pen), Hunt
26/08	Blackburn R	A	0–1	21,700	
29/08	Manchester C	H	4–1	46,073	St John, Hunt (2), A'Court
01/09	Sheffield Utd	A	2–0	47,742	Callaghan, St John
03/09	West Ham Utd	A	0–1	22,262	
08/09	Nottingham F	A	1–3	24,126	Leishman
12/09	West Ham Utd	H	2–1	39,261	St John (2)
15/09	Ipswich T	H	1–1	40,121	Hunt
22/09	Everton	A	2–2	73,000	Lewis, Hunt
29/09	Wolves	A	2–3	34,368	Melia (2)
06/10	Bolton W	A	1–0	41,155	Hunt
13/10	Leicester C	A	0–3	24,137	
27/10	West Brom A	A	0–1	17,850	
03/11	Burnley	H	1–2	43,870	St John
10/11	Manchester Utd	A	3–3	43,810	St John, Melia, Moran
14/11	Arsenal	H	2–1	38,452	Hunt, Moran (pen)
17/11	Leyton O	H	5–0	30,009	Hunt (3), Stevenson, St John
24/11	Birmingham C	A	2–0	27,050	Hunt (2)
01/12	Fulham	H	2–1	38,267	Hunt, A'Court
08/12	Sheffield Wed	A	2–0	15,939	Lewis, Hunt
15/12	Blackpool	A	2–1	16,271	St John, Hunt
22/12	Blackburn R	H	3–1	35,371	Lewis, St John, Moran
13/02	Aston Villa	H	4–0	46,374	Hunt (2), St John (2)
16/02	Wolves	H	4–1	53,517	Lewis (2), St John (2)
02/03	Leicester C	H	0–2	54,842	
05/03	Ipswich T	A	1–2	14,059	Lewis, St John
09/03	Arsenal	A	2–2	30,496	Lewis, Hunt
20/03	West Brom A	H	2–2	43,977	Hunt, Moran (pen)
23/03	Burnley	A	3–1	28,500	St John, Hunt, Lewis
08/04	Everton	H	0–0	56,060	
12/04	Tottenham H	H	5–2	54,463	Stevenson, Melia (2), St John, Lewis
13/04	Manchester Utd	H	1–0	51,529	St John
15/04	Tottenham H	A	2–7	53,727	Hunt (2)
18/04	Nottingham F	A	0–2	36,599	
20/04	Fulham	A	0–0	18,894	
29/04	Sheffield Wed	H	0–2	29,144	
02/05	Leyton O	A	1–2	8,273	St John
08/05	Birmingham C	H	5–1	23,684	Wallace, St John, Callaghan, Hunt (2)
11/05	Sheffield Utd	H	0–0	18,494	
13/05	Bolton W	A	0–1	15,739	
18/05	Aston Villa	A	0–2	18,000	

Div One Position 8th   P42 Pts 44

FA CUP

DATE	OPPOSITION	VENUE	SCORE	ATT	GOALSCORERS
09/01	Wrexham	A	3–0	29,992	Hunt, Lewis, Melia
26/01	Burnley	A	1–1	49,885	Lewis
21/02	Burnley	H	2–1	57,906	St John, Moran (pen) (a.e.t.)
16/03	Arsenal	A	2–1	55,245	Melia, Moran (pen)
30/03	West Ham Utd	H	1–0	49,036	Hunt
27/04	Leicester C	N	0–1	65,000	(at Hillsborough)

1963–64

FOOTBALL LEAGUE DIVISION ONE

DATE	OPPOSITION	VENUE	SCORE	ATT	GOALSCORERS
24/08	Blackburn R	A	2–1	34,390	Moran (pen), Callaghan
28/08	Nottingham F	H	1–2	49,829	Mackinlay (o.g.)
31/08	Blackpool	A	1–2	42,767	Melia
03/09	Nottingham F	A	0–0	21,788	
07/09	Chelsea	A	3–1	38,202	St John (2), Hunt
09/09	Wolves	A	3–1	25,000	Hunt (2), Melia
14/09	West Ham Utd	H	1–2	45,497	Hunt
16/09	Wolves	H	6–0	44,050	Arrowsmith, Thompson, Callaghan, Hunt (2), Milne

Date	Opposition	Venue	Score	Att	Goalscorers
21/09	Sheffield Utd	A	0–3	24,932	
28/09	Everton	H	2–1	51,973	Callaghan (2)
05/10	Aston Villa	H	5–2	39,106	St John, Callaghan, Thompson, Hunt (2)
09/10	Sheffield Wed	H	3–1	46,107	St John (2), Melia
19/10	West Brom A	H	1–0	43,099	Milne
26/10	Ipswich T	A	2–1	16,356	Melia, Hunt
02/11	Leicester C	H	0–1	47,438	
09/11	Bolton W	A	2–1	23,824	Hunt, Callaghan
16/11	Fulham	H	2–0	38,478	St John, Hunt
23/11	Manchester Utd	A	1–0	54,654	Yeats
30/11	Burnley	H	2–0	42,968	St John, Hunt (pen)
07/12	Arsenal	A	1–1	40,551	Callaghan
14/12	Blackburn R	H	1–2	45,182	Hunt
21/12	Blackpool	A	1–0	13,254	St John
26/12	Stoke C	H	6–1	49,942	St John, Hunt (4), Arrowsmith
11/01	Chelsea	H	2–1	45,848	Hunt, Arrowsmith
18/01	West Ham Utd	A	0–1	25,546	
01/02	Sheffield Utd	H	6–1	43,309	Hunt (2), Thompson, St John (3)
08/02	Everton	A	1–3	66,515	St John
19/02	Aston Villa	A	2–2	13,769	Hunt, Arrowsmith
22/02	Birmingham C	H	2–1	41,823	Moran, St John
04/03	Sheffield Wed	A	2–2	23,703	St John, Stevenson
07/03	Ipswich T	H	6–0	35,575	St John, Hunt (2), Arrowsmith (2), Thompson
14/03	Fulham	A	0–1	14,022	
20/03	Bolton W	H	2–0	38,583	Arrowsmith, St John
27/03	Tottenham H	A	3–1	56,952	Hunt (3)
28/03	Leicester C	A	0–1	31,209	Hunt, Arrowsmith
30/03	Tottenham H	H	3–1	52,904	St John (2), Arrowsmith
04/04	Manchester Utd	H	3–0	52,559	Callaghan, Arrowsmith (2)
14/04	Burnley	A	3–0	34,900	Arrowsmith (2), St John
18/04	Arsenal	H	5–0	48,623	St John, Arrowsmith, Thompson (2), Hunt
22/04	Birmingham C	A	1–3	22,623	Hunt
25/04	West Brom A	A	2–2	19,279	Hunt (2)
29/04	Stoke C	A	1–3	32,149	Arrowsmith

Div One Position 1st   P42 Pts 57

FA CUP

Date	Opposition	Venue	Score	Att	Goalscorers
04/01	Derby Co	H	5–0	46,460	Arrowsmith (4), Hunt
25/01	Port Vale	H	0–0	52,727	
27/01	Port Vale	A	2–1	42,179	Hunt, Thompson (a.e.t.)
15/02	Arsenal	A	1–0	61,295	St John
29/02	Swansea T	H	1–2	52,608	Thompson

1964–65

CHARITY SHIELD

Date	Opposition	Venue	Score	Att	Goal scorers
15/08	West Ham	N	2–2	38,858	Wallace, Byrne (Trophy shared)

FOOTBALL LEAGUE DIVISION ONE

Date	Opposition	Venue	Score	Att	Goal scorers
22/08	Arsenal	H	3–2	47,620	Hunt, Wallace (2)
26/08	Leeds Utd	A	2–4	36,200	Hunt, Milne
29/08	Blackburn R	A	2–3	26,865	Ferns, Smith
02/09	Leeds Utd	H	2–1	52,548	Thompson, Smith
05/09	Blackpool	H	2–2	45,646	Thompson, Hunt
09/09	Leicester C	A	0–2	27,114	
12/09	Sheffield Wed	A	0–1	22,701	
19/09	Everton	H	0–4	52,619	
26/09	Aston Villa	A	5–1	38,940	Graham (3), Callaghan, Hunt
07/10	Sheffield Utd	H	3–1	37,745	Hunt (2), Graham
10/10	Birmingham C	A	0–0	19,850	
13/10	Leicester C	H	0–1	42,558	
17/10	West Ham Utd	H	2–2	36,029	St John, Hunt
24/10	West Brom A	A	0–3	17,500	
31/10	Manchester Utd	H	0–2	52,402	
07/11	Fulham	A	1–1	18,367	Callaghan
14/11	Nottingham F	H	2–0	40,498	Thompson, Hunt
21/11	Stoke C	A	1–1	28,816	Hunt
28/11	Tottenham H	H	1–1	41,198	Hunt
05/12	Burnley	A	5–1	12,490	Hunt (3), Strong, Lawler
12/12	Arsenal	A	0–0	26,171	
19/12	Blackburn R	H	3–2	33,316	Smith, Hunt (2)
26/12	Sunderland	A	3–2	49,902	Milne, Stevenson (2)
28/12	Sunderland	H	0–0	43,528	
02/01	Blackpool	A	3–2	21,863	Hunt (2), St John
16/01	Sheffield Wed	H	4–2	42,422	Hunt (2), Milne, St John
06/02	Aston Villa	H	1–0	24,396	Hunt
13/02	Wolves	H	2–1	40,803	Hunt, Lawler
24/02	Birmingham C	H	4–3	39,253	Callaghan (2), Hunt, Thompson
27/02	West Ham Utd	A	1–2	25,780	Hunt
13/03	Sheffield Utd	A	0–3	19,034	
20/03	Fulham	H	3–2	28,465	Callaghan (2), Milne
01/04	Nottingham F	A	2–2	23,926	Thompson, Hunt
03/04	Stoke C	A	3–2	40,315	Milne, St John, Hunt
06/04	West Brom A	H	0–3	34,152	
09/04	Tottenham H	A	0–3	27,057	
12/04	Everton	A	1–2	62,720	Stevenson (pen)
16/04	Chelsea	A	0–4	62,587	
17/04	Burnley	H	1–1	30,004	Smith
19/04	Chelsea	H	2–0	41,847	Chisnall, Strong
24/04	Manchester Utd	A	0–3	55,772	
26/04	Wolves	A	3–1	13,839	Strong, Sealey, Arrowsmith

Div One Position 7th   P42 Pts 44

FA CUP

Date	Opposition	Venue	Score	Att	Goalscorers
09/01	West Brom A	A	2–1	28,360	Hunt, St John
30/01	Stockport Co	H	1–1	51,587	Milne
03/02	Stockport Co	A	2–0	24,080	Hunt (2)
20/02	Bolton W	A	1–0	52,207	Callaghan
06/03	Leicester C	A	0–0	39,356	
10/03	Leicester C	H	1–0	53,324	Hunt
27/03	Chelsea	N	2–0	67,686	(at Villa Park) Thompson, Stevenson (pen)
01/05	Leeds Utd	N	2–1	100,000	Hunt, St John (a.e.t.) (at Wembley)

EUROPEAN CUP

Date	Opposition	Venue	Score	Att	Goalscorers
17/08	Reykjavik	A	5–0	10,000	Wallace (2), Hunt (2), Chisnall
14/09	Reykjavik	H	6–1	32,597	Byrne, St John (2), Hunt, Graham, Stevenson
25/11	Anderlecht	H	3–0	44,516	St John, Hunt, Yeats
16/12	Anderlecht	A	1–0	60,000	Hunt
10/02	Cologne	A	0–0	40,000	
17/03	Cologne	H	0–0	48,432	
24/03	Cologne	N	2–2	45,000	St John, Hunt (replay at Rotterdam; won on toss of coin)
04/05	Inter Milan (s–f)	H	3–1	54,082	Hunt, Callaghan, St John
12/05	Inter Milan (s–f)	A	0–3	90,000	

1965–66

CHARITY SHIELD

Date	Opposition	Venue	Score	Att	Goal scorers
14/08	Manchester United	N	2–2	48,502	Yeats, Stevenson (Trophy shared, played at Wembley)

FOOTBALL LEAGUE DIVISION ONE 1965–66

Date	Opposition	Venue	Score	Att	Goalscorers
21/08	Leicester C	A	3–1	29,698	Hunt (2), Strong
25/08	Sheffield Utd	H	0–1	47,259	
01/09	Sheffield Utd	A	0–0	20,798	
04/09	Blackpool	A	3–2	25,616	Hunt (2), Callaghan
06/09	West Ham Utd	A	5–1	32,144	Milne, Callaghan, Hunt (3)
11/09	Fulham	H	2–1	46,382	Lawler, Hunt
15/09	West Ham Utd	H	1–1	44,397	Strong
18/09	Tottenham H	A	1–2	46,770	Strong
25/09	Everton	H	5–0	53,557	Smith, Hunt (2), Stevenson, St John
02/10	Aston Villa	A	3–1	43,859	Thompson (2), St John
09/10	Manchester Utd	A	0–2	58,161	
16/10	Newcastle Utd	H	2–0	47,984	Hunt, Callaghan
23/10	West Brom A	A	0–3	30,000	
30/10	Nottingham F	H	4–0	38,420	Stevenson (pen), Hunt (2), St John
06/11	Sheffield Wed	H	2–0	24,456	Hunt, Thompson
13/11	Northampton T	H	5–0	41,904	St John, Stevenson (pen), Hunt, Callaghan, Thompson
17/11	Blackburn R	H	5–2	36,450	Stevenson (pen), St John (2), Hunt, Smith
20/11	Stoke C	A	0–0	28,622	
27/11	Burnley	H	2–1	50,282	Hunt, Milne
04/12	Chelsea	A	1–0	36,839	Hunt
11/12	Arsenal	H	4–2	43,727	Thompson, St John, Strong, Hunt
18/12	Newcastle Utd	A	0–0	42,910	
27/12	Leeds Utd	H	0–1	53,430	
28/12	Leeds Utd	A	1–0	49,192	Milne
01/01	Manchester Utd	H	2–1	53,970	Smith, Milne
08/01	Arsenal	A	1–0	43,917	Yeats
15/01	West Brom A	H	2–2	46,687	Milne, Byrne
29/01	Leicester C	H	1–0	45,409	Lawler
05/02	Blackburn R	A	4–1	30,414	Lawler, Hunt, St John (2)
12/02	Sunderland	H	4–0	43,859	Hunt (3), Yeats
19/02	Blackpool	H	4–1	45,046	Hunt (2), Arrowsmith, Milne
26/02	Fulham	A	0–2	31,626	
12/03	Tottenham H	H	1–0	50,760	Clayton (o.g.)
19/03	Everton	A	0–0	62,537	
26/03	Aston Villa	H	3–0	23,625	Hunt (2), Callaghan
06/04	Sheffield Wed	H	1–0	44,792	Stevenson
09/04	Northampton T	A	0–0	20,029	
11/04	Sunderland	A	2–2	38,355	Lawler (2)
16/04	Stoke C	H	2–0	41,106	Strong, St John
23/04	Burnley	A	0–2	36,741	
30/04	Chelsea	H	2–1	53,754	Hunt (2)
10/05	Nottingham F	A	1–1	22,105	Milne

Div One Position 1st   P42 Pts 61

FA CUP

Date	Opposition	Venue	Score	Att	Goalscorers
22/01	Chelsea	H	1–2	54,097	Hunt

EUROPEAN CUP WINNERS' CUP

Date	Opposition	Venue	Score	Att	Goalscorers
29/09	Juventus	A	0–1	12,000	
13/10	Juventus	H	2–0	51,055	Lawler, Strong
01/12	Standard Liège	H	3–1	46,112	Lawler (2), Thompson
15/12	Standard Liège	A	2–1	35,000	Hunt, St John
01/03	Honved	A	0–0	20,000	
08/03	Honved	H	2–0	54,631	Lawler, St John
14/04	Celtic (s–f)	A	0–1	80,000	
19/04	Celtic (s–f)	H	2–0	54,208	Smith, Strong
05/05	Borussia Dortmund	N	1–2	41,657	Hunt (final played at Hampden Park; a.e.t.)

1966–67

CHARITY SHIELD

Date	Opposition	Venue	Score	Att	Goal scorers
13/08	Everton	A	1–0	63,329	Hunt (Played at Goodison)

FOOTBALL LEAGUE DIVISION ONE

Date	Opposition	Venue	Score	Att	Goalscorers
20/08	Leicester C	H	3–2	49,076	Hunt, Strong, Stevenson (pen)
24/08	Manchester C	A	1–0	50,923	Strong
27/08	Everton	A	1–3	64,318	Smith
30/08	Manchester C	H	3–2	51,645	Hunt (2), Strong
03/09	West Ham Utd	A	1–1	33,000	Strong
05/09	Blackpool	A	2–1	24,375	Hunt, Thompson
10/09	Sheffield Utd	H	1–1	48,717	Strong
17/09	Southampton	A	2–1	28,287	St John, Callaghan
24/09	Sunderland	H	2–2	45,706	Yeats, Hunt
01/10	Aston Villa	A	3–2	24,909	St John, Callaghan, Graham
08/10	Fulham	H	2–2	44,024	Strong, St John
15/10	Nottingham F	H	1–0	32,887	Hunt
29/10	Stoke City	A	0–2	37,933	
05/11	Nottingham F	A	4–0	40,624	Strong, Hunt (2), Thompson
09/11	Burnley	H	2–0	50,124	Lawler, Thompson
12/11	Newcastle Utd	A	2–0	36,910	St John, Hunt≈
19/11	Sheffield Utd	A	5–0	51,014	Lawler, Thompson, Strong (2), St John
26/11	West Brom A	H	1–2	25,900	Strong
03/12	Sheffield Utd	H	1–0	42,762	St John

1966–67 (CONTINUED)

DATE	OPPOSITION	VENUE	SCORE	ATT	GOALSCORERS
10/12	Manchester Utd	A	2–2	62,500	St John (2)
24/12	Chelsea	A	2–1	36,921	Hinton (o.g.), Strong
26/12	Chelsea	H	2–1	51,920	Stevenson, Hunt
31/12	Everton	H	0–0	53,744	
07/01	West Ham Utd	H	2–0	48,518	Thompson (2)
14/01	Sheffield Wed	A	1–0	43,951	Thompson
18/01	Leicester C	A	1–2	32,049	Rodrigues (o.g.)
21/01	Southampton	H	2–1	47,545	Lawler, Arrowsmith
04/02	Sunderland	A	2–2	45,301	Yeats, Thompson
11/02	Aston Villa	H	1–0	45,747	Milne
25/02	Fulham	A	2–2	37,481	St John, Strong
04/03	Stoke City	H	2–1	48,891	Lawler, Hunt
18/03	Burnley	A	0–1	29,388	
25/03	Manchester Utd	H	0–0	53,813	
27/03	Arsenal	H	0–0	46,168	
28/03	Arsenal	A	1–1	35,795	Arrowsmith
01/04	Tottenham H	A	1–2	53,135	Thompson
07/04	Newcastle Utd	H	3–1	44,824	Hunt (2), Callaghan
22/04	West Brom A	H	0–1	39,883	
28/04	Sheffield Utd	A	1–0	19,110	Hunt
03/05	Leeds Utd	A	1–2	36,597	Stevenson (pen)
06/05	Tottenham H	H	0–0	40,845	
13/05	Blackpool	H	1–3	28,773	Thompson

Div One Position 5th **P42 Pts 51**

FA CUP

DATE	OPPOSITION	VENUE	SCORE	ATT	GOALSCORERS
28/01	Watford	A	0–0	33,000	
01/02	Watford	H	3–1	54,451	St John, Hunt, Lawler
18/02	Aston Villa	H	1–0	52,477	St John
11/03	Everton	A	0–1	64,851	(40,149 watched the game live on cctv at Anfield)

EUROPEAN CUP

DATE	OPPOSITION	VENUE	SCORE	ATT	GOALSCORERS
28/09	Petrolul Ploesti	H	2–0	44,463	St John, Callaghan
12/10	Petrolul Ploesti	A	1–3	20,000	Hunt
19/10	Petrolul Ploesti	N	2–0	15,000	St John, Thompson (Played in Brussels)
07/12	Ajax	A	1–5	65,000	Lawler
14/12	Ajax	H	2–2	53,846	Hunt (2)

1967–68

FOOTBALL LEAGUE DIVISION ONE

DATE	OPPOSITION	VENUE	SCORE	ATT	GOALSCORERS
19/08	Manchester C	A	0–0	49,343	
22/08	Arsenal	H	2–0	52,033	Hunt (2)
26/08	Newcastle Utd	H	6–0	51,829	Hateley (3), Hughes, Hunt (2)
28/08	Arsenal	A	0–2	33,420	
02/09	West Brom A	A	2–0	32,737	Hateley, Hunt
05/09	Nottingham F	A	1–0	39,352	Hughes
09/09	Chelsea	H	3–1	53,839	Smith (pen), Hateley (2)
16/09	Southampton	A	0–1	29,512	
23/09	Everton	H	1–0	54,189	Hunt
30/09	Stoke C	H	2–1	50,220	Thompson, Smith (pen)
07/10	Leicester C	A	1–2	25,609	St John
14/10	West Ham Utd	A	3–1	46,951	St John (2), Smith
24/10	Burnley	A	1–1	29,855	Lawler
28/10	Sheffield Wed	H	1–0	50,399	Lawler
04/11	Tottenham H	A	1–1	47,682	Hunt
11/11	Manchester Utd	H	1–2	54,515	Hunt
18/11	Sunderland	A	1–1	29,993	Irwin (o.g.)
25/11	Wolves	H	2–1	43,885	Hateley, Stevenson (pen)
02/12	Fulham	A	1–1	29,330	Hateley
09/12	Leeds Utd	H	2–0	39,676	Hunt, Sprake (o.g.)
16/12	Manchester C	H	1–1	53,268	Hunt
23/12	Newcastle Utd	A	1–1	46,190	St John
26/12	Coventry C	A	1–1	42,209	Hunt
30/12	Coventry C	H	1–0	48,866	Callaghan
06/01	West Brom A	H	4–1	51,092	Strong, Hunt (3)
20/01	Southampton	H	2–0	44,906	Strong, Yeats
03/02	Everton	A	0–1	64,482	
12/02	Chelsea	A	1–3	40,670	Thompson
24/02	Leicester C	H	3–1	41,451	Callaghan, Strong, Hateley
02/03	Wolves	A	1–1	33,207	Hunt
16/03	Burnley	H	3–2	41,114	Hateley (2), Strong
23/03	Sheffield Wed	A	2–1	32,177	Hunt, Arrowsmith
06/04	Manchester Utd	A	2–1	63,050	Yeats, Hunt
12/04	Sheffield Utd	A	1–2	50,422	Hunt
13/04	Sunderland	H	2–1	40,350	Hunt (2)
15/04	Sheffield Utd	H	1–1	22,743	Strong (pen)
20/04	West Ham Utd	A	0–1	33,060	
27/04	Fulham	H	4–1	32,307	Callaghan, Hunt (2), Hateley
29/04	Tottenham H	H	1–1	41,688	Hateley
04/05	Leeds Utd	A	2–1	44,553	Lawler, Graham
11/05	Nottingham F	H	6–1	38,850	Hateley (3), St John, Hunt (2)
15/11	Stoke City	A	1–2	27,693	Hunt

Div One Position 3rd **P42 Pts 55**

FA CUP

DATE	OPPOSITION	VENUE	SCORE	ATT	GOALSCORERS
27/01	Bournemouth	A	0–0	24,388	
30/01	Bournemouth	H	4–1	54,075	Hateley, Thompson, Hunt, Lawler
17/02	Walsall	A	0–0	21,066	
19/02	Walsall	H	5–2	39,113	Hateley (4), Strong
09/03	Tottenham H	A	1–1	54,005	Hateley
12/03	Tottenham H	H	2–1	53,658	Hunt, Smith (pen)
30/03	West Brom A	A	0–0	53,062	
08/04	West Brom A	H	1–1	54,273	Hateley (a.e.t.)
18/04	West Brom A	N	1–2	56,000	Hateley (at Maine Road)

LEAGUE CUP

DATE	OPPOSITION	VENUE	SCORE	ATT	GOALSCORERS
13/09	Bolton W	H	1–1	45,957	Thompson
27/09	Bolton W	A	2–3	31,500	Smith (pen), Callaghan

INTER-CITIES' FAIRS CUP

DATE	OPPOSITION	VENUE	SCORE	ATT	GOALSCORERS
19/09	Malmo	A	2–0	14,314	Hateley (2)
04/10	Malmo	H	2–1	39,795	Yeats, Hunt
07/11	TSV Munchen	H	8–0	44,812	St John, Hateley, Smith (pen), Hunt (2), Thompson, Callaghan (2)
14/11	TSV Munchen	A	1–2	10,000	Callaghan
28/11	Ferencvaros	A	0–1	30,000	
09/01	Ferencvaros	H	0–1	46,892	

1968–69

FOOTBALL LEAGUE DIVISION ONE

DATE	OPPOSITION	VENUE	SCORE	ATT	GOALSCORERS
10/08	Manchester C	H	2–1	51,236	Graham, Thompson
14/08	Southampton	A	0–2	24,453	
17/08	Arsenal	A	1–1	43,535	Hunt
20/08	Stoke C	H	2–1	46,674	Callaghan, Allen (o.g.)
24/08	Sunderland	A	4–1	46,547	Smith, Lawler, Callaghan, Hateley
27/08	Everton	A	0–0	63,898	
31/08	Leeds Utd	A	0–1	38,929	
07/09	Q.P.R.	H	2–0	46,025	Yeats, Graham
14/09	Ipswich T	A	2–0	24,514	Graham, St John
21/09	Leicester C	H	4–0	48,375	Yeats, Smith (pen), Evans, Callaghan
28/09	Wolves	A	6–0	39,310	Hunt (2), Thompson (2), Evans (2)
05/10	Burnley	A	4–0	26,238	Hunt (2), Thompson, Strong
08/10	Everton	H	1–1	54,496	Smith
12/10	Manchester Utd	H	2–0	53,392	St John, Evans
19/10	Tottenham H	A	1–2	44,122	Hunt
26/10	Newcastle Utd	A	2–1	45,223	Evans, Thompson
02/11	West Brom A	A	0–0	34,600	
09/11	Chelsea	H	2–1	47,248	Callaghan, Smith (pen)
16/11	Sheffield Wed	A	2–1	31,245	Lawler, Callaghan
23/11	Coventry C	A	2–0	44,820	Strong, Callaghan
30/11	Nottingham F	H	1–0	25,175	Hunt (equals Gordon Hodgson's lge goal record (233))
03/12	Southampton	H	1–0	40,527	Callaghan
07/12	West Ham Utd	H	2–0	48,632	Hughes, Thompson
14/12	Manchester Utd	A	0–1	59,000	
21/12	Tottenham H	H	1–0	43,843	Hughes
26/12	Burnley	H	1–1	52,515	Lawler
11/01	West Brom A	H	1–0	47,587	Thompson
18/01	Chelsea	A	2–1	51,872	Hunt, Evans (Hunt breaks lge scoring record)
01/02	Sheffield Wed	H	1–0	45,406	Hunt
15/02	Nottingham F	H	0–2	42,359	
22/02	West Ham Utd	A	1–1	36,498	Hunt
15/03	Sunderland	H	2–0	17,855	St John, Evans
29/03	Q.P.R.	A	2–1	16,792	Smith (pen), Hunt
31/03	Arsenal	H	1–1	44,843	Smith (pen)
05/04	Wolves	H	1–0	45,399	Hunt (Hunt's 300th club goal)
07/04	Stoke C	A	0–0	27,389	
12/04	Leicester C	H	2–1	28,671	Hughes, Callaghan
19/04	Ipswich T	H	4–0	40,449	Thompson, Graham (2), St John
22/04	Coventry C	A	0–0	35,106	
28/04	Leeds Utd	H	0–0	53,750	
12/05	Manchester C	A	0–1	28,309	
17/05	Newcastle Utd	A	1–1	34,910	Hunt

Div One Position 2nd **P42 Pts 61**

FA CUP

DATE	OPPOSITION	VENUE	SCORE	ATT	GOALSCORERS
04/01	Doncaster R	H	2–0	48,330	Hunt, Callaghan
25/01	Burnley	H	2–1	53,667	Smith (pen), Hughes
01/03	Leicester C	A	0–0	42,002	
03/03	Leicester C	H	0–1	54,666	

LEAGUE CUP

DATE	OPPOSITION	VENUE	SCORE	ATT	GOALSCORERS
04/09	Sheffield Utd	H	4–0	32,358	Hunt, Lawler, Callaghan, Thompson
25/09	Swansea T	H	2–0	31,051	Lawler, Hunt
15/10	Arsenal	A	1–2	39,299	Lawler

INTER-CITIES' FAIRS CUP

DATE	OPPOSITION	VENUE	SCORE	ATT	GOALSCORERS
18/09	Athletico Bilbao	A	1–2	35,000	Hunt
02/10	Athletico Bilbao	H	2–1	49,567	Lawler, Hughes (Liverpool FC lose on toss of coin)

1969–70

FOOTBALL LEAGUE DIVISION ONE

DATE	OPPOSITION	VENUE	SCORE	ATT	GOALSCORERS
09/08	Chelsea	H	4–1	48,383	Lawler, St John (2), Strong
12/08	Manchester C	H	3–2	51,959	St John (2), Hunt
16/08	Tottenham H	A	2–0	50,474	Hughes, Lawler
20/08	Manchester C	A	2–0	47,888	Graham (2)
23/08	Burnley	H	3–3	51,113	Smith (2;1 pen), Graham
27/08	Crystal P	A	3–1	36,369	Hughes, Hunt, Thompson
30/08	Sheffield Wed	A	1–1	33,600	Lawler
06/09	Coventry C	H	2–1	48,337	St John, Strong
09/09	Sunderland	H	2–0	46,370	Strong, Smith
13/09	Manchester Utd	A	0–1	59,387	
20/09	Stoke C	H	3–1	45,745	Hunt, Hughes, Callaghan
27/09	West Brom A	A	2–2	34,343	Graham, Hunt
04/10	Nottingham F	H	1–1	44,859	Chapman (o.g.)
07/10	Tottenham H	H	0–0	46,518	
11/10	Newcastle Utd	A	0–1	43,830	
18/10	Ipswich T	A	2–2	23,263	Graham, Lindsay
25/10	Southampton	A	4–1	41,611	Hughes, Hunt (2), Byrne (o.g.)
01/11	Derby Co	A	0–4	40,993	
08/11	Wolves	H	0–0	39,114	
15/11	West Ham Utd	A	2–0	39,668	Lawler, Graham
22/11	Leeds Utd	A	1–1	43,293	Yeats
29/11	Arsenal	A	0–1	40,295	
06/12	Everton	A	3–0	57,026	Hughes, Brown (o.g.), Graham
13/12	Manchester Utd	H	1–4	47,682	Hughes
26/12	Burnley	A	5–1	22,944	Ross, Graham, Lawler, Thompson, Callaghan
10/01	Stoke C	A	2–0	30,038	Graham, Thompson
17/01	West Brom A	H	1–1	43,526	Lawler

DATE	OPPOSITION	VENUE	SCORE	ATT	GOALSCORERS
31/01	Nottingham F	A	0–1	30,838	
16/02	Newcastle Utd	H	0–0	38,218	
28/02	Derby Co	H	0–2	43,594	
03/03	Coventry C	A	3–2	29,497	Hughes, Evans (2)
07/03	Leeds Utd	H	0–0	51,435	
11/03	Southampton	A	1–0	23,239	Evans
14/03	Arsenal	A	1–2	32,333	Yeats
16/03	Sheffield Wed	H	3–0	31,931	Lawler, Yeats, Graham
21/03	Everton	H	0–2	54,496	
24/03	Ipswich T	H	2–0	29,548	Callaghan, Smith (pen)
28/03	West Ham Utd	A	0–1	38,239	
30/03	Wolves	A	1–0	32,754	Lawler
03/04	Crystal P	H	3–0	30,999	Graham (2), Lawler
15/04	Sunderland	A	1–0	33,007	Lawler
18/04	Chelsea	A	1–2	36,521	Graham

Div One Position 5th   P42 Pts 51

FA CUP

DATE	OPPOSITION	VENUE	SCORE	ATT	GOALSCORERS
07/01	Coventry C	A	1–1	33,688	Graham
12/01	Coventry C	H	3–0	51,261	Ross, Thompson, Graham
24/01	Wrexham	H	3–1	54,096	Graham (2), St John
07/02	Leicester C	H	0–0	53,785	
11/02	Leicester C	A	2–0	42,100	Evans (2)
21/02	Watford	A	0–1	34,047	

LEAGUE CUP

DATE	OPPOSITION	VENUE	SCORE	ATT	GOALSCORERS
03/09	Watford	A	2–1	21,149	Slater (o.g.), St John
24/09	Manchester Utd	H	2–3	28,019	Evans, Graham

INTER-CITIES' FAIRS CUP

DATE	OPPOSITION	VENUE	SCORE	ATT	GOALSCORERS
16/09	Dundalk	H	10–0	32,562	Evans (2), Lawler, Smith (2), Graham (2), Lindsay, Thompson, Callaghan
30/09	Dundalk	A	4–0	6,000	Thompson (2), Graham, Callaghan
12/11	Vitoria Setubal	A	0–1	16,000	
26/11	Vitoria Setubal	H	3–2	41,633	Smith (pen), Evans, Hunt (LFC lose on away goals

1970–71

FOOTBALL LEAGUE DIVISION ONE

DATE	OPPOSITION	VENUE	SCORE	ATT	GOALSCORERS
15/08	Burnley	A	2–1	26,702	A.Evans, Hughes
17/08	Blackpool	A	0–0	28,818	
22/08	Huddersfield T	H	4–0	52,628	McLaughlin (2), A.Evans (2)
25/08	Crystal P	H	1–1	47,612	Graham
29/08	West Brom A	A	1–1	31,624	A.Evans
05/09	Manchester Utd	H	1–1	52,541	A.Evans
12/09	Newcastle Utd	A	0–0	35,501	
19/09	Nottingham F	H	3–0	42,676	Graham, Thompson, A.Evans
26/09	Southampton	A	0–1	26,155	
03/10	Chelsea	H	1–0	46,196	A.Evans
10/10	Tottenham H	A	0–1	44,457	
17/10	Burnley	H	2–0	40,804	Yeats, Heighway
24/10	Ipswich T	A	1–0	22,577	
31/10	Wolves	H	2–0	43,391	Smith (pen), A.Evans
07/11	Derby Co	A	0–0	33,004	
14/11	Coventry C	H	0–0	40,303	
21/11	Everton	H	3–2	53,777	Heighway, Toshack, Lawler
28/11	Arsenal	A	0–2	45,097	
05/12	Leeds Utd	H	1–1	51,357	Toshack
12/12	West Ham Utd	A	2–1	27,459	Whitham, Boersma
19/12	Huddersfield T	H	0–0	25,033	
26/12	Stoke C	H	0–0	47,103	
09/01	Blackpool	H	2–2	42,939	Heighway, Craven (o.g.)
12/01	Manchester C	H	0–0	45,985	
16/01	Crystal P	A	0–1	28,253	
30/01	Arsenal	H	2–0	43,847	Toshack, Smith
06/02	Leeds Utd	A	1–0	48,425	Toshack
16/02	West Ham Utd	H	1–0	38,032	Toshack
20/02	Everton	A	0–0	56,846	
27/02	Wolves	A	0–1	32,290	
13/03	Coventry C	A	0–1	27,687	
20/03	Derby Co	H	2–0	40,990	Mackay (o.g.), Lawler
29/03	Ipswich T	A	2–0	42,017	A.Evans, Graham
02/04	West Brom A	H	1–1	43,580	A.Evans
06/04	Newcastle Utd	H	1–1	44,289	Lawler
10/04	Stoke C	A	0–1	28,810	Thompson
12/04	Chelsea	A	0–1	38,705	
17/04	Tottenham H	H	0–0	49,363	
19/04	Manchester Utd	A	2–0	44,004	Heighway, Edwards (o.g.)
24/04	Nottingham F	A	1–0	20,678	Hall
26/04	Manchester C	A	2–2	17,975	Graham (2)
01/05	Southampton	H	1–0	38,427	Hughes

Div One Position 5th   P42 Pts 51

FA CUP

DATE	OPPOSITION	VENUE	SCORE	ATT	GOALSCORERS
02/01	Aldershot	A	1–0	45,500	McLaughlin
23/01	Swansea C	H	3–0	47,229	Toshack, St John, Lawler
13/02	Southampton	H	1–0	50,226	Lawler
06/03	Tottenham H	H	0–0	54,731	
16/03	Tottenham H	A	1–0	56,283	Heighway
27/03	Everton	N	2–1	62,144	A.Evans, Hall (at Old Trafford)
08/03	Arsenal	N	1–2	100,000	Heighway (a.e.t.) (at Wembley)

LEAGUE CUP

DATE	OPPOSITION	VENUE	SCORE	ATT	GOALSCORERS
08/09	Mansfield T	A	0–0	12,532	
22/09	Mansfield T	H	3–2	31,087	Hughes, Smith (pen), A.Evans (a.e.t.)
06/1	Swindon T	A	0–2	23,992	

INTER-CITIES' FAIRS CUP

DATE	OPPOSITION	VENUE	SCORE	ATT	GOALSCORERS
15/09	Ferencvaros	H	1–0	37,531	Graham
29/09	Ferencvaros	A	1–1	25,000	Hughes

21/10	Dinamo Bucharest	H	3–0	36,525	Lindsay, Lawler, Hughes
04/11	Dinamo Bucharest	A	1–1	45,000	Boersma
09/12	Hibernian	A	1–0	30,296	Toshack
22/12	Hibernian	H	2–0	37,815	Heighway, Boersma
10/03	Bayern Munich	H	3–0	45,616	A.Evans (3)
24/03	Bayern Munich	A	1–1	23,000	Ross
14/04	Leeds Utd (s–f)	H	0–1	52,577	
28/04	Leeds Utd (s–f)	A	0–0	40,462	

1971–72

CHARITY SHIELD

DATE	OPPOSITION	VENUE	SCORE	ATT	GOALSCORERS
07/08	Leicester City	A	0–1	25, 014	(Played at Filbert Street)

FOOTBALL LEAGUE DIVISION ONE

DATE	OPPOSITION	VENUE	SCORE	ATT	GOALSCORERS
14/08	Nottingham F	H	3–1	51,427	Keegan, Smith (pen), Hughes
17/08	Wolves	H	3–2	51,869	Toshack, Heighway, Smith (pen)
21/08	Newcastle Utd	A	2–3	39,720	Hughes, Keegan
24/08	Crystal P	A	1–0	29,489	Toshack
28/08	Leicester C	H	3–2	50,970	Heighway, Keegan, Toshack
01/09	Manchester C	A	0–1	45,144	
04/09	Tottenham H	A	0–2	50,124	
11/09	Southampton	H	1–0	45,878	Toshack
18/09	Leeds Utd	A	0–1	41,381	
25/09	Manchester Utd	H	2–2	55,634	Graham, Hall
02/10	Stoke City	A	0–0	28,698	
09/10	Chelsea	H	0–0	48,464	
16/10	Nottingham F	A	3–2	20,945	Hughes, Heighway, Smith (pen)
23/10	Huddersfield T	H	2–0	41,627	Smith (pen), Evans
30/10	Sheffield Utd	A	1–1	39,023	Keegan
06/11	Arsenal	H	3–2	46,929	Hughes, Callaghan, Ross
13/11	Everton	A	0–1	56,563	
20/11	Coventry C	A	2–0	25,325	Whitham (2)
27/11	West Ham Utd	H	1–0	43,399	Hughes
04/12	Ipswich T	A	0–0	21,359	
11/12	Derby Co	H	3–2	44,601	Whitham (3)
18/12	Tottenham H	H	0–0	43,409	
27/12	West Brom A	A	0–1	43,804	
01/01	Leeds Utd	A	0–2	53,847	
08/01	Leicester C	A	0–0	26,421	
22/01	Wolves	A	0–0	33,692	
29/01	Crystal P	H	4–1	39,538	Lawler (2), Callaghan, Keegan
12/02	Huddersfield T	A	1–0	18,702	Whitham
19/02	Sheffield Utd	H	2–0	42,005	Toshack (2)
26/02	Manchester C	H	3–0	50,074	Lloyd, Keegan, Graham
04/03	Everton	H	4–0	53,922	Wright (o.g.), McLaughlin (o.g.), Lawler, Hughes
11/03	Chelsea	A	0–0	38,691	
18/03	Newcastle Utd	H	5–0	43,899	Lawler, Keegan, Toshack, Hughes, Heighway
25/03	Southampton	A	1–0	21,680	Toshack
28/03	Stoke C	A	2–1	42,489	Burrows (o.g.), Keegan
01/04	West Brom A	H	2–0	46,564	Smith (pen), Lawler
03/04	Manchester Utd	A	3–0	54,000	Lawler, Toshack, Hughes
08/04	Coventry C	H	3–1	50,628	Keegan, Smith (pen), Toshack
15/04	West Ham Utd	A	2–0	32,660	Toshack, Heighway
22/04	Ipswich T	H	2–0	54,316	Toshack (2)
01/05	Derby Co	A	0–1	39,420	
08/05	Arsenal	A	0–0	39,285	

Div One Position 3rd   P42 Pts 57

FA CUP

DATE	OPPOSITION	VENUE	SCORE	ATT	GOALSCORERS
15/01	Oxford Utd	A	3–0	18,000	Keegan (2), Lindsay
05/02	Leeds Utd	H	0–0	56,300	
09/02	Leeds Utd	A	0–2	45,821	

LEAGUE CUP

DATE	OPPOSITION	VENUE	SCORE	ATT	GOALSCORERS
07/09	Hull C	H	3–0	31,612	Lawler, Heighway, Hall (pen)
05/10	Southampton	H	1–0	28,964	Heighway
27/10	West Ham Utd	A	1–2	40,898	Graham

EUROPEAN CUP WINNERS' CUP

DATE	OPPOSITION	VENUE	SCORE	ATT	GOALSCORERS
15/09	Servette Geneva	A	1–2	16,000	Lawler
29/09	Servette Geneva	H	2–0	38,591	Hughes, Heighway
20/10	Bayern Munich	H	0–0	42,949	
03/11	Bayern Munich	A	1–3	40,000	Evans

1972–73

FOOTBALL LEAGUE DIVISION ONE

DATE	OPPOSITION	VENUE	SCORE	ATT	GOALSCORERS
12/08	Manchester C	H	2–0	55,383	Hall, Callaghan
15/08	Manchester Utd	H	2–0	54,779	Toshack, Heighway
19/08	Crystal P	A	1–1	30,054	Hughes
23/08	Chelsea	A	2–1	35,375	Toshack, Callaghan
26/08	West Ham Utd	H	3–2	50,491	Toshack, Ferguson (o.g.), Hughes
30/08	Leicester C	A	2–3	28,694	Toshack (2)
02/09	Derby Co	A	1–2	32,524	Toshack
09/09	Wolves	H	4–2	43,386	Hughes, Cormack, Smith (pen), Keegan
16/09	Arsenal	A	0–0	47,597	
23/09	Sheffield Utd	H	5–0	42,940	Boersma, Lindsay, Heighway, Cormack, Keegan (pen)
30/09	Leeds Utd	A	2–1	46,468	Lloyd, Boersma
07/10	Everton	H	1–0	55,975	Cormack
14/10	Southampton	A	1–1	24,110	Lawler
21/10	Stoke C	H	2–1	45,604	Hughes, Callaghan
28/10	Norwich C	A	1–1	36,625	Cormack
04/11	Chelsea	H	3–1	48,932	Toshack (2), Keegan
11/11	Manchester Utd	A	0–2	53,944	
18/11	Newcastle Utd	A	3–2	46,153	Cormack, Lindsay, Toshack
25/11	Tottenham H	A	2–1	45,399	Heighway, Keegan
02/12	Birmingham C	H	4–3	45,407	Lindsay (2), Cormack, Toshack
09/12	West Brom A	H	1–1	27,213	Boersma
16/12	Ipswich T	A	1–1	25,693	Heighway
23/12	Coventry C	H	2–0	41,550	Toshack (2)

1972–73 (CONTINUED)

DATE	OPPOSITION	VENUE	SCORE	ATT	GOALSCORERS
26/12	Sheffield Utd	A	3–0	34,040	Boersma, Lawler, Heighway
30/12	Crystal P	H	1–0	50,862	Cormack
06/01	West Ham Utd	A	1–0	34,480	Keegan
20/01	Derby Co	H	1–1	45,996	Toshack
27/01	Wolves	A	1–2	32,957	Keegan
10/02	Arsenal	H	0–2	49,896	
17/02	Manchester C	A	1–1	40,528	Boersma
24/02	Ipswich T	H	2–1	43,875	Heighway, Keegan
03/03	Everton	A	2–0	54,269	Hughes (2)
10/03	Southampton	H	3–2	41,674	Lloyd, Keegan (2)
17/03	Stoke C	A	1–0	33,540	Mahoney (o.g.)
24/03	Norwich C	H	3–1	42,995	Lawler, Hughes, Hall
31/03	Tottenham H	H	1–1	48,477	Keegan
07/04	Birmingham C	A	1–2	48,114	Smith
14/04	West Brom A	H	1–0	43,853	Keegan (pen)
17/04	Coventry C	A	2–1	27,280	Boersma (2)
21/04	Newcastle Utd	A	1–2	37,240	Keegan
23/04	Leeds Utd	H	2–0	55,738	Cormack, Keegan
28/04	Leicester C	H	0–0	56,202	

Div One Position 1st   P42 Pts 60

FA CUP

DATE	OPPOSITION	VENUE	SCORE	ATT	GOALSCORERS
13/01	Burnley	A	0–0	35,730	
16/01	Burnley	H	3–0	56,124	Toshack (2), Cormack
03/02	Manchester C	H	0–0	56,296	
07/02	Manchester C	A	0–2	49,572	

LEAGUE CUP

DATE	OPPOSITION	VENUE	SCORE	ATT	GOALSCORERS
05/09	Carlisle Utd	A	1–1	16,257	Keegan
19/09	Carlisle Utd	H	5–1	22,128	Keegan, Boersma (2), Lawler, Heighway
03/10	West Brom A	A	1–1	17,756	Heighway
10/10	West Brom A	H	2–1	26,461	Hughes, Keegan (a.e.t.)
31/10	Leeds Utd	H	2–2	44,609	Keegan, Toshack
22/11	Leeds Utd	A	1–0	34,856	Keegan
04/12	Tottenham H	H	1–1	48,677	Hughes
06/12	Tottenham H	A	1–3	34,565	

UEFA CUP

DATE	OPPOSITION	VENUE	SCORE	ATT	GOALSCORERS
12/09	Eintracht Frankfurt	H	2–0	33,380	Keegan, Hughes
26/09	Eintracht Frankfurt	A	0–0	20000	
24/10	AEK Athens	H	3–0	31,906	Boersma, Cormack, Smith (pen)
07/11	AEK Athens	A	3–1	25,000	Hughes (2), Boersma
29/11	Dynamo Berlin	A	0–0	19,000	
13/12	Dynamo Berlin	H	3–1	34,140	Boersma, Heighway, Toshack
07/03	Dynamo Dresden	H	2–0	33,270	Hall, Boersma
21/03	Dynamo Dresden	A	1–0	35,000	Keegan
10/04	Tottenham H (s–f)	H	1–0	42,174	Lindsay
25/04	Tottenham H (s–f)	A	1–2	46,919	Heighway (LFC win on away goals)
10/05	Borussia M'g'bach	H	3–0	41,169	Keegan (2), Lloyd
23/05	Borussia M'g'bach	A	0–2	35,000	(agg win)

1973–74

FOOTBALL LEAGUE DIVISION ONE

DATE	OPPOSITION	VENUE	SCORE	ATT	GOALSCORERS
25/08	Stoke C	H	1–0	52,935	Heighway
28/08	Coventry C	A	0–1	29,305	
01/09	Leicester C	A	1–1	29,347	Toshack
04/09	Derby Co	H	2–0	45,237	Thompson, Keegan (pen)
08/09	Chelsea	H	1–0	47,016	Keegan
12/09	Derby Co	A	1–3	32,867	Boersma
15/09	Birmingham C	A	1–1	35,719	Hall
22/09	Tottenham H	H	3–2	42,901	Lawler (2), Lindsay (pen)
29/09	Manchester Utd	A	0–0	53,882	
06/10	Newcastle Utd	H	2–1	45,612	Cormack, Lindsay (pen)
13/10	Southampton	A	0–1	22,018	
20/10	Leeds Utd	A	0–1	44,811	
27/10	Sheffield Utd	H	1–0	40,641	Keegan
03/11	Arsenal	A	2–0	39,827	Hughes, Toshack
10/11	Wolves	H	1–0	38,088	Heighway
17/11	Ipswich T	H	4–2	37,420	Keegan (3; 1 pen), Cormack
24/11	Q.P.R.	A	2–2	26,254	Lloyd, Toshack
01/12	West Ham Utd	H	1–0	34,857	Cormack
08/12	Everton	A	1–0	56,098	Waddle
15/12	Norwich C	H	1–1	20,628	Cormack
22/12	Manchester Utd	H	2–0	40,420	Keegan (pen), Heighway
26/12	Burnley	A	1–2	24,404	Cormack
29/12	Chelsea	A	1–0	32,901	Cormack
01/01	Leicester C	H	1–1	39,110	Cormack
12/01	Birmingham C	H	3–2	39,094	Keegan (2), Thompson
19/01	Stoke C	A	1–1	32,789	Smith
02/02	Norwich C	H	1–0	31,742	Cormack
05/02	Coventry C	H	2–1	21,656	Lindsay (pen), Keegan
23/02	Newcastle Utd	A	0–0	41,727	
26/02	Southampton	H	1–0	27,015	Boersma
02/03	Burnley	H	1–0	42,562	Toshack
16/03	Leeds Utd	H	1–0	56,003	Heighway
23/03	Wolves	A	1–0	35,867	Hall
06/04	Q.P.R.	H	2–1	54,027	Lindsay (pen), Mancini (o.g.)
08/04	Sheffield Utd	A	0–1	31,809	
12/04	Manchester C	H	1–1	43,284	Cormack
13/04	Ipswich T	A	1–1	33,285	Hughes
16/04	Manchester C	A	4–0	50,781	Hall (2), Boersma, Keegan
20/04	Everton	H	0–0	55,858	
24/04	Arsenal	H	0–1	47,997	
27/04	West Ham Utd	A	2–2	36,160	Toshack, Keegan
08/05	Tottenham H	A	1–1	24,178	Heighway

Div One Position 2nd   P42 Pts 57

FA CUP

DATE	OPPOSITION	VENUE	SCORE	ATT	GOALSCORERS
05/01	Doncaster R	H	2–2	31,483	Keegan (2)
08/01	Doncaster R	A	2–0	22,499	Heighway, Cormack

DATE	OPPOSITION	VENUE	SCORE	ATT	GOALSCORERS
26/01	Carlisle Utd	H	0–0	47,211	
29/01	Carlisle Utd	A	2–0	21,262	Boersma, Toshack
16/02	Ipswich T	A	2–0	45,340	Hall, Keegan
09/03	Bristol C	A	1–0	37,671	Toshack
30/03	Leicester C	N	0–0	60,000	(at Old Trafford)
03/04	Leicester C	N	3–1	55,619	Hall, Keegan, Toshack (at Villa Park)
04/05	Newcastle Utd	N	3–0	100,000	Keegan (2), Heighwat (at Wembley)

LEAGUE CUP

DATE	OPPOSITION	VENUE	SCORE	ATT	GOALSCORERS
08/10	West Ham Utd	A	2–2	25,823	Cormack, Heighway
29/10	West Ham Utd	H	1–0	26,002	Toshack
21/11	Sunderland	A	2–0	36,208	Keegan, Toshack
27/11	Hull C	A	0–0	19,748	
04/12	Hull C	H	3–1	17,120	Callaghan (3)
19/12	Wolves	A	0–1	15,242	

EUROPEAN CUP

DATE	OPPOSITION	VENUE	SCORE	ATT	GOALSCORERS
19/09	Jeunesse D'Esch	A	1–1	5,000	Hall
03/10	Jeunesse D'Esch	H	2–0	28,714	Mond (o.g.), Toshack
24/10	Red Star Belgrade	A	1–2	40,000	Lawler
06/11	Red Star Belgrade	A	1–2	41,744	Lawler

1974–75

CHARITY SHIELD

DATE	OPPOSITION	VENUE	SCORE	ATT	GOALSCORERS
10/08	Leeds United	N	1–1	67,000	Boersma (Played at Wembley; LFC won 6–5 on pens scorers: Lindsay, Hughes, Hall, Smith, Cormack, Callaghan)

FOOTBALL LEAGUE DIVISION ONE

DATE	OPPOSITION	VENUE	SCORE	ATT	GOALSCORERS
17/08	Luton T	A	2–1	21,062	Smith, Heighway
20/08	Wolves	A	0–0	33,499	
24/08	Leicester C	H	2–1	49,398	Lindsay (2 pens)
27/08	Wolves	H	2–0	42,449	Heighway, Toshack
31/08	Chelsea	A	3–0	39,461	Kennedy, Boersma (2)
07/09	Tottenham H	H	5–2	47,538	Boersma (3), Hughes, Kennedy
14/09	Manchester C	A	45,194		
21/09	Stoke C	H	3–0	51,423	Ritchie (o.g.), Boersma, Heighway
24/09	Burnley	A	0–1	44,639	
28/09	Sheffield Utd	A	0–1	29,443	
05/10	Carlisle Utd	A	1–0	20,844	Kennedy
12/10	Middlesbrough	H	2–0	52,590	Callaghan, Keegan (pen)
19/10	Q.P.R.	A	1–0	27,392	Hall
26/10	Leeds Utd	H	1–0	54,996	Heighway
02/11	Ipswich T	A	0–1	30,564	
09/11	Arsenal	H	1–3	43,850	Kennedy
16/11	Everton	A	0–0	56,797	
23/11	West Ham Utd	H	1–1	46,348	Smith
30/11	Coventry C	A	1–1	23,089	Kennedy
07/12	Derby Co	H	2–2	41,058	Kennedy, Heighway
14/12	Luton T	H	2–0	35,151	Toshack, Heighway
21/12	Birmingham C	A	1–3	23,608	Toshack
26/12	Manchester C	H	4–1	46,062	Hall (2), Toshack, Heighway
11/01	Derby Co	A	0–0	33,463	
18/01	Coventry C	H	2–1	43,668	Heighway, Keegan
01/02	Arsenal	A	0–2	43,028	
08/02	Ipswich T	H	5–2	47,421	Hall, Toshack (2), Lindsay, Cormack
12/02	Newcastle Utd	A	1–4	38,115	Hall
19/02	West Ham Utd	A	0–0	40,256	
22/02	Everton	H	0–0	55,853	
01/03	Chelsea	H	2–2	42,762	Heighway, Cormack
08/03	Burnley	A	1–1	31,812	McDermott
15/03	Sheffield Utd	H	0–0	40,862	
19/03	Leicester C	A	1–1	28,012	Toshack
22/03	Tottenham H	A	2–0	34,331	Keegan, Cormack
25/03	Newcastle Utd	H	4–0	41,147	Keegan, Toshack (2), McDermott
29/03	Birmingham C	H	1–0	49,454	Keegan (pen)
31/03	Stoke C	A	0–2	45,954	
05/04	Carlisle Utd	H	2–0	34,971	Keegan (2)
12/04	Carlisle Utd	H	2–0	46,073	Toshack, Keegan
19/04	Middlesbrough	A	0–1	34,027	
26/04	Q.P.R.	H	3–1	42,546	Toshack (2), Keegan (pen)

Div One Position 2nd   P42 Pts 51

FA CUP

DATE	OPPOSITION	VENUE	SCORE	ATT	GOALSCORERS
04/01	Stoke C	H	2–0	48,723	Heighway, Keegan
25/01	Ipswich T	A	0–1	34,708	

LEAGUE CUP

DATE	OPPOSITION	VENUE	SCORE	ATT	GOALSCORERS
10/09	Brentford	H	2–1	21,413	Kennedy, Boersma
08/10	Bristol C	A	0–0	25,573	
16/10	Bristol C	H	4–0	23,694	Heighway (2), Kennedy (2)
12/11	Middlesbrough	H	0–1	24,906	

EUROPEAN CUP–WINNERS' CUP

DATE	OPPOSITION	VENUE	SCORE	ATT	GOALSCORERS
17/09	Stromsgodset Dr	H	11–0	24,743	Lindsay (pen), Boersma (2), Thompson (2), Heighway, Cormack, Hughes, Smith, Callaghan, Kennedy
01/10	Stromsgodset Dr	A	1–0	17,000	Kennedy
23/10	Ferencvaros	H	1–1	35,027	Keegan
05/11	Ferencvaros	A	0–0	30,000	

1975–76

FOOTBALL LEAGUE DIVISION ONE

DATE	OPPOSITION	VENUE	SCORE	ATT	GOAL SCORERS
16/08	Q.P.R.	A	0–2	27,113	
19/08	West Ham Utd	H	2–2	40,564	Callaghan, Toshack
23/08	Tottenham H	H	3–2	42,729	Keegan (pen), Case, Heighway
26/08	Leeds Utd	H	3–0	36,186	Kennedy, Callaghan (2)
30/08	Leicester C	A	1–1	25,008	Keegan
06/09	Sheffield Utd	H	1–0	37,340	Kennedy

DATE	OPPOSITION	VENUE	SCORE	ATT	GOALSCORERS
13/09	Ipswich T	A	0–2	28,132	
30/09	Aston Villa	H	3–0	42,779	Toshack, Keegan, Case
27/09	Everton	A	0–0	55,570	
04/10	Wolves	H	2–0	36,391	Hall, Case
11/10	Birmingham C	H	3–1	36,532	Toshack (3)
18/10	Coventry C	A	0–0	20,695	
25/10	Derby Co	H	1–1	46,324	Toshack
01/11	Middlesbrough	A	1–0	30,952	McDermott
08/11	Manchester Utd	H	3–1	49,136	Heighway, Toshack, Keegan
15/11	Newcastle Utd	A	2–1	39,686	Hall, Kennedy
22/11	Coventry C	H	1–1	36,929	Toshack
29/11	Norwich C	H	1–3	34,780	Hughes
02/12	Arsenal	H	2–2	27,447	Neal (2 pens)
06/12	Burnley	A	0–0	18,426	
13/12	Tottenham H	A	4–0	29,891	Keegan, Case, Neal, Heighway
20/12	Q.P.R.	H	2–0	39,182	Toshack, Neal (pen)
26/12	Stoke C	A	1–1	32,092	Toshack
27/12	Manchester C	H	1–0	53,386	Cormack
10/01	Ipswich T	H	3–3	40,547	Keegan (2), Case
17/01	Sheffield Utd	A	0–0	31,255	
31/01	West Ham Utd	H	4–0	26,741	Toshack (3), Keegan
07/02	Leeds Utd	H	2–0	54,525	Keegan, Toshack
18/02	Manchester Utd	A	0–0	59,709	
21/02	Newcastle Utd	H	2–0	43,404	Keegan, Case
24/02	Arsenal	A	0–1	36,127	
28/02	Derby Co	A	1–1	32,800	Kennedy
06/03	Middlesbrough	H	0–2	41,391	
13/03	Birmingham C	A	1–0	31,797	Neal (pen)
20/03	Norwich C	A	1–1	29,038	Fairclough
27/03	Burnley	H	2–0	36,708	Fairclough (2)
03/04	Everton	A	1–0	54,632	Fairclough
06/04	Leicester C	H	1–0	35,290	Keegan
10/04	Aston Villa	A	0–0	44,250	
17/04	Stoke City	H	5–3	44,069	Neal (pen), Toshack, Kennedy, Hughes, Fairclough
19/04	Manchester C	A	3–0	50,439	Heighway, Fairclough (2)
04/05	Wolves	A	3–1	48,900	Keegan, Toshack, Kennedy

1st Div Position 1st   P42   Pts 60

FA CUP
DATE	OPPOSITION	VENUE	SCORE	ATT	GOALSCORERS
03/01	West Ham Utd	A	2–0	32,363	Keegan, Toshack
24/01	Derby Co	A	0–1	38,200	

LEAGUE CUP
DATE	OPPOSITION	VENUE	SCORE	ATT	GOALSCORERS
10/09	York C	A	1–0	9,421	Lindsay (pen)
07/10	Burnley	H	1–1	24,607	Case
14/10	Burnley	A	0–1	20,022	

UEFA CUP
DATE	OPPOSITION	VENUE	SCORE	ATT	GOALSCORERS
17/09	Hibernian	A	0–1	19,219	
30/09	Hibernian	H	3–1	29,963	Toshack (3)
22/10	Real Sociedad	A	3–1	20,000	Heighway, Callaghan, Thompson
04/11	Real Sociedad	H	6–0	23,796	Toshack, Kennedy (2), Fairclough, Heighway, Neal
26/11	Slask Wroclaw	A	2–1	46,000	Kennedy, Toshack
10/11	Slask Wroclaw	H	3–0	17,886	Case (3)
03/03	Dynamo Dresden	A	0–0	33,000	
17/03	Dynamo Dresden	H	2–1	39,300	Case, Keegan
30/03	Barcelona (s–f)	A	1–0	70,000	Toshack
14/04	Barcelona (s–f)	H	1–1	55,104	Thompson
28/04	Bruges (final)	H	3–2	49,981	Kennedy, Case, Keegan (pen)
19/05	Bruges (final)	A	1–1	33,000	Keegan

1976–77

CHARITY SHIELD
DATE	OPPOSITION	VENUE	SCORE	ATT	GOALSCORERS
14/08	Southampton	N	1–0	76,500	Toshack (Played at Wembley)

FOOTBALL LEAGUE DIVISION ONE
DATE	OPPOSITION	VENUE	SCORE	ATT	GOALSCORERS
21/08	Norwich C	H	1–0	49,753	Heighway
25/08	West Brom A	A	1–0	30,334	Toshack
28/08	Birmingham C	A	1–2	33,228	Johnson
04/09	Coventry C	H	3–1	40,371	Keegan, Johnson, Toshack
11/09	Derby Co	A	3–2	26,833	Kennedy, Toshack, Keegan
18/09	Tottenham H	H	2–0	47,421	Johnson, Heighway
25/09	Newcastle Utd	A	0–1	33,204	
02/10	Middlesbrough	H	0–0	45,107	
16/10	Everton	H	3–1	55,141	Heighway, Neal (pen), Toshack
23/10	Leeds Utd	H	1–1	44,696	Kennedy
27/10	Leicester C	A	1–0	29,384	Toshack
30/10	Aston Villa	H	3–0	51,751	Callaghan, McDermott, Keegan
06/11	Sunderland	A	1–0	39,956	Fairclough
09/11	Leicester C	H	5–1	39,581	Heighway, Toshack, Neal (pen), Jones, Keegan (pen)
20/11	Arsenal	A	1–1	45,016	Kennedy
27/11	Bristol C	H	2–1	44,323	Keegan, Jones
04/12	Ipswich T	A	0–1	35,082	
11/12	Q.P.R.	H	3–1	37,154	Toshack, Keegan, Kennedy
15/12	Aston Villa	A	1–5	42,851	Kennedy
18/12	West Ham Utd	A	0–2	24,175	
27/12	Stoke C	H	4–0	50,371	Thompson, Neal (pen), Keegan, Johnson
29/12	Manchester C	A	1–1	50,020	Watson (o.g.)
01/01	Sunderland	H	2–0	44,687	Kennedy, Thompson
15/01	West Brom A	H	1–1	39,195	Fairclough
22/01	Norwich C	A	1–2	25,913	Neal (pen)
05/02	Birmingham C	H	4–1	41,072	Neal (pen), Toshack (2), Heighway
16/02	Manchester Utd	A	0–0	57,487	
19/02	Derby Co	H	3–1	44,202	Toshack, Jones, Keegan
05/03	Newcastle Utd	H	1–0	45,553	Heighway
09/03	Tottenham H	A	0–1	32,098	
12/03	Middlesbrough	A	1–0	29,166	Hughes
22/03	Everton	A	0–0	56,562	
02/04	Leeds Utd	H	3–1	48,791	Neal (pen), Fairclough, Heighway
09/04	Manchester C	H	2–1	55,283	Keegan, Heighway
11/04	Stoke C	A	0–0	29,905	
16/04	Arsenal	H	2–0	48,174	Neal, Keegan
30/04	Ipswich T	H	2–1	56,044	Kennedy, Keegan
03/05	Manchester Utd	H	1–0	53,046	Keegan
07/05	Q.P.R.	A	1–1	29,382	Case
10/05	Coventry C	A	0–0	38,032	
14/05	West Ham Utd	H	0–0	55,675	
16/05	Bristol C	A	1–2	38,688	Johnson

1st Div Position 1st   P42   Pts 57

FA CUP
DATE	OPPOSITION	VENUE	SCORE	ATT	GOALSCORERS
08/01	Crystal P	H	0–0	44,730	
11/01	Crystal P	A	3–2	27,664	Keegan, Heighway (2)
29/01	Carlisle Utd	H	3–0	45,358	Keegan, Toshack, Heighway
26/02	Oldham A	A	3–1	52,455	Keegan, Case, Neal (pen)
19/03	Middlesbrough	H	2–0	55,881	Fairclough, Keegan
23/04	Everton	N	2–2	52,637	McDermott, Case (at Maine Road)
27/04	Everton	N	3–0	52,579	(at Maine Road) Neal (pen), Case, Kennedy
21/05	Manchester Utd	N	1–2	100,000	(at Wembley) Case

LEAGUE CUP
DATE	OPPOSITION	VENUE	SCORE	ATT	GOALSCORERS
31/08	West Brom A	H	1–1	23,378	Callaghan
06/09	West Brom A	A	0–1	22,662	

EUROPEAN CUP
DATE	OPPOSITION	VENUE	SCORE	ATT	GOALSCORERS
14/09	Crusaders	H	2–0	22,442	Neal (pen), Toshack
28/09	Crusaders	A	5–0	10,500	Keegan, Johnson (2), McDermott, Heighway
20/10	Trabzonspor	A	0–1	25,000	
03/11	Trabzonspor	H	3–0	42,275	Heighway, Johnson, Keegan
02/03	St Etienne	A	0–1	38,000	
16/03	St Etienne	H	3–1	55,043	Keegan, Kennedy, Fairclough
06/04	FC Zurich (s–f)	A	3–1	30,500	Neal (2,1pen), Heighway
20/04	FC Zurich (s–f)	H	3–0	50,611	Case (2), Keegan
25/05	Borussia M'g'bach	N	3–1	57,000	McDermott, Smith, Neal (pen) (Played in Rome)

1977–78

FOOTBALL LEAGUE DIVISION ONE
DATE	OPPOSITION	VENUE	SCORE	ATT	GOALSCORERS
20/08	Middlesbrough	A	1–1	30,805	Dalglish
23/08	Newcastle Utd	H	2–0	48,267	Dalglish, McDermott
27/08	West Brom A	H	3–0	48,525	Dalglish, Heighway, Case
03/09	Birmingham C	H	1–0	28,239	R.Kennedy
10/09	Coventry C	H	2–0	45,574	Fairclough, Dalglish
17/09	Ipswich T	A	1–1	29,658	Dalglish
24/09	Derby Co	H	1–0	48,359	McDermott
01/10	Manchester Utd	A	0–2	55,109	
04/10	Arsenal	A	0–0	47,110	
08/10	Chelsea	H	2–0	40,499	Dalglish, Fairclough
15/10	Leeds Utd	A	2–1	45,500	Case (2)
22/10	Everton	H	0–0	51,668	
29/10	Manchester C	A	1–3	49,207	Fairclough
05/11	Aston Villa	H	1–2	50,436	Carrodus (o.g.)
12/11	Q.P.R.	A	0–2	25,625	
19/11	Bristol C	A	1–1	41,053	Dalglish
26/11	Leicester C	H	4–0	26,051	Fairclough, Heighway, Dalglish, McDermott
03/12	West Ham Utd	A	2–0	39,659	Dalglish, Fairclough
10/12	Norwich C	A	1–2	24,983	Thompson
17/12	Q.P.R.	H	1–0	38,249	Neal (pen)
26/12	Nottingham F	H	1–1	47,218	Heighway
27/12	Wolves	A	1–0	50,294	Neal (pen)
31/12	Newcastle Utd	A	2–0	36,456	Thompson, Dalglish
02/01	Middlesbrough	H	2–0	49,305	Johnson, Heighway
14/01	West Brom A	H	1–0	35,809	Johnson
21/01	Birmingham C	H	2–3	48,401	Thompson, R.Kennedy
04/02	Coventry C	A	0–1	28,965	
25/02	Manchester Utd	H	3–1	49,590	Souness, R.Kennedy, Case
04/03	Chelsea	A	1–3	35,550	Neal (pen)
08/03	Derby Co	H	2–4	23,413	Fairclough, Dalglish
11/03	Leeds Utd	H	1–0	48,233	Dalglish
25/03	Wolves	A	3–1	27,531	Case, Dalglish (2)
01/04	Aston Villa	H	3–0	40,190	Dalglish (2), Kennedy
05/04	Everton	A	1–0	52,759	Johnson
08/04	Leicester C	H	3–2	42,979	Smith (2), Lee
15/04	Bristol C	A	1–1	31,471	Heighway
18/04	Ipswich T	H	2–2	40,044	Dalglish, Souness
22/04	Norwich C	H	3–0	44,857	Ryan (o.g.), Fairclough (2)
24/04	Arsenal	A	1–0	38,318	Fairclough
29/04	West Ham Utd	H	2–0	37,448	McDermott, Fairclough
01/05	Manchester C	H	4–0	44,528	Dalglish (3), Neal (pen)
04/05	Nottingham F	H	0–0	50,021	

Div One Position 2nd   P42   Pts 57

FA CUP
DATE	OPPOSITION	VENUE	SCORE	ATT	GOALSCORERS
07/01	Chelsea	A	2–4	45,449	Johnson, Dalglish

LEAGUE CUP
DATE	OPPOSITION	VENUE	SCORE	ATT	GOALSCORERS
30/08	Chelsea	H	2–0	33,170	Dalglish, Case
26/10	Derby Co	H	2–0	30,400	Fairclough (2)
29/11	Coventry C	H	2–2	33,817	Fairclough, Neal (pen)
20/12	Coventry C	A	2–0	36,105	Case, Dalglish
17/01	Wrexham	A	3–1	25,641	Dalglish (3)
07/02	Arsenal	H	2–1	44,764	Dalglish, Kennedy
14/02	Arsenal	A	0–0	49,561	
18/03	Nottingham F	N	0–0	100,000	(a.e.t.) (at Wembley)
22/03	Nottingham F	N	0–1	54,375	(at Old Trafford)

EUROPEAN CUP
DATE	OPPOSITION	VENUE	SCORE	ATT	GOALSCORERS
19/10	Dynamo Dresden	H	5–1	39,835	Hansen, Case (2), Neal (pen), Kennedy
02/11	Dynamo Dresden	A	1–2	33,000	Heighway
01/03	Benfica	A	2–1	70,000	Case, Hughes
15/03	Benfica	H	4–1	48,364	Callaghan, Dalglish, McDermott, Neal
29/03	Borussia M'g'bach	A	1–2	66,000	Johnson

1977–78 (CONTINUED)

DATE	OPPOSITION	VENUE	SCORE	ATT	GOALSCORERS
12/04	Borussia M'g'bach	H	3–0	51,500	Kennedy, Dalglish, Case
10/05	FC Bruges	N	1–0	92,000	(at Wembley) Dalglish

EUROPEAN SUPER CUP

DATE	OPPOSITION	VENUE	SCORE	ATT	GOALSCORERS
22/11	SV Hamburg	A	1–1	16,000	Fairclough
06/12	SV Hamburg	H	6–0	34,931	Thompson, McDermott (3), Fairclough, Dalglish. (Won 7-1 on agg)

1978–79

FOOTBALL LEAGUE DIVISION ONE

DATE	OPPOSITION	VENUE	SCORE	ATT	GOALSCORERS
19/08	Q.P.R.	H	2–1	50,793	Dalglish, Heighway
22/09	Ipswich T	A	3–0	28,114	Souness, Dalglish (2)
26/09	Manchester C	A	4–1	46,710	Souness (2), Heighway, Dalglish
02/09	Tottenham H	H	7–0	50,705	Dalglish (2), R.Kennedy, Johnson (2), Neal (pen), McDermott
09/09	Birmingham C	A	3–0	31,740	Souness (2), A.Kennedy
16/09	Coventry C	H	1–0	51,130	Souness
23/09	West Brom A	H	1–1	33,834	Dalglish
30/09	Bolton W	H	3–0	47,099	Case (3)
07/10	Norwich C	A	4–1	25,632	Heighway (2), Johnson, Case
14/10	Derby Co	H	5–0	47,475	Johnson, R.Kennedy (2), Dalglish (2)
21/10	Chelsea	H	2–0	45,775	Johnson, Dalglish
28/10	Everton	A	0–1	53,131	
04/11	Leeds Utd	H	1–1	51,657	McDermott (pen)
11/11	Q.P.R.	A	3–1	26,626	Heighway, R.Kennedy, Johnson
18/11	Manchester C	H	1–0	47,765	Neal (pen)
22/11	Tottenham H	A	0–0	50,393	
25/11	Middlesbrough	H	2–0	39,812	McDermott, Souness
02/12	Arsenal	A	0–1	51,902	
09/12	Nottingham F	H	2–0	51,469	McDermott (2; 1 pen)
16/12	Bristol City	A	0–1	28,722	
26/12	Manchester Utd	A	3–0	54,940	R.Kennedy, Case, Fairclough
03/02	West Brom A	H	2–1	52,211	Dalglish, Fairclough
13/02	Birmingham C	H	1–0	35,207	Souness
21/02	Norwich C	H	6–0	35,754	Dalglish (2), Johnson (2), A.Kennedy, R.Kennedy
24/02	Derby Co	A	2–0	27,859	Dalglish, R.Kennedy
03/03	Chelsea	A	0–0	40,594	
06/03	Coventry C	A	0–0	26,629	
13/03	Everton	H	1–1	52,352	Dalglish
20/03	Wolves	H	2–0	39,695	McDermott, Johnson
24/03	Ipswich T	H	2–0	43,343	Dalglish, Johnson
07/04	Arsenal	H	3–0	47,297	Case, Dalglish, McDermott
10/04	Wolves	A	1–0	30,857	Hansen
14/04	Manchester Utd	H	2–0	46,608	Dalglish, Neal
16/04	Aston Villa	A	1–3	44,029	Johnson
21/04	Bristol City	H	1–0	43,191	Dalglish
24/04	Southampton	A	1–1	23,181	Johnson
28/04	Nottingham F	A	0–0	41,598	
01/05	Bolton W	A	4–1	35,200	Johnson, R.Kennedy (2), Dalglish
05/05	Southampton	H	2–0	46,687	Neal (2)
08/05	Aston Villa	H	3–0	50,576	A.Kennedy, Dalglish, McDermott
11/05	Middlesbrough	A	1–0	32,244	Johnson
17/05	Leeds Utd	A	3–0	41,324	Johnson (2), Case

Div One Position 1st   P42 Pts 68 (conceded 16, scored 85 – still a League record)

FA CUP

DATE	OPPOSITION	VENUE	SCORE	ATT	GOALSCORERS
10/01	Southend Utd	A	0–0	31,033	
17/01	Southend Utd	H	3–0	37,797	Case, Dalglish, R.Kennedy
30/01	Blackburn R	A	1–0	43,432	Dalglish
28/02	Burnley	H	3–0	47,161	Johnson (2), Souness
10/03	Ipswich T	A	1–0	31,322	Dalglish
31/03	Manchester Utd	N	2–2	52,584	Dalglish, Hansen (at Maine Road)
04/04	Manchester Utd	N	0–1	53,069	(at Goodison Park)

LEAGUE CUP

DATE	OPPOSITION	VENUE	SCORE	ATT	GOALSCORERS
28/08	Sheffield Utd	A	0–1	35,753	

EUROPEAN CUP

DATE	OPPOSITION	VENUE	SCORE	ATT	GOALSCORERS
13/09	Nottingham F	A	0–2	38,316	
27/09	Nottingham F	H	0–0	51,679	

EUROPEAN SUPER CUP

DATE	OPPOSITION	VENUE	SCORE	ATT	GOALSCORERS
04/12	Anderlecht	A	1–3	35,000	Case
19/12	Anderlecht	H	2–1	23,598	Hughes, Fairclough. (LFC lost 3–4 on aggregate)

1979–80

CHARITY SHIELD

DATE	OPPOSITION	VENUE	SCORE	ATT	GOALSCORERS
11/08	Arsenal	N	3–1	92,000	McDermott (2), Dalglish (Played at Wembley)

FOOTBALL LEAGUE DIVISION ONE

DATE	OPPOSITION	VENUE	SCORE	ATT	GOALSCORERS
21/08	Bolton W	H	0–0	45,960	
25/08	West Brom A	H	3–1	48,021	Johnson (2), McDermott
01/09	Southampton	A	2–3	21,402	Johnson, Irwin
08/09	Coventry C	H	4–0	39,926	Johnson (2), Case, Dalglish
15/09	Leeds Utd	A	1–1	39,779	McDermott
22/09	Norwich City	H	0–0	44,120	
29/09	Nottingham F	A	0–1	28,262	
06/10	Bristol C	H	4–0	38,213	Johnson, Dalglish, R.Kennedy, McDermott
09/10	Bolton W	A	1–1	25,571	Dalglish
13/10	Ipswich T	A	2–1	25,310	Hunter (o.g.), Johnson
20/10	Everton	H	2–2	52,201	Lyons (o.g.), R.Kennedy
27/10	Manchester C	H	4–0	48,128	Johnson, Dalglish (2), R.Kennedy
03/11	Wolves	H	3–0	49,541	Dalglish (2), R.Kennedy
10/11	Brighton & HA	A	4–1	29,682	R.Kennedy, Dalglish, Johnson
17/11	Tottenham H	H	2–1	51,092	McDermott (2)
24/11	Arsenal	A	0–0	55,561	
01/12	Middlesbrough	H	4–0	39,885	McDermott, Hansen, Johnson, R.Kennedy
08/12	Aston Villa	A	3–1	41,160	R.Kennedy, Hansen, McDermott

DATE	OPPOSITION	VENUE	SCORE	ATT	GOALSCORERS
15/12	Crystal P	H	3–0	42,898	Case, Dalglish, McDermott
22/12	Derby Co	A	3–1	24,945	Davies (o.g.), McDermott (pen), Johnson
26/12	Manchester Utd	H	2–0	51,073	Hansen, Johnson
29/12	West Brom A	A	2–0	34,915	Johnson (2)
12/01	Southampton	H	1–1	44,655	McDermott (pen)
19/01	Coventry C	A	0–1	31,578	
09/02	Norwich C	A	5–3	25,624	Fairclough (3), Dalglish, Case
19/02	Nottingham F	H	2–0	45,093	McDermott, R.Kennedy
23/02	Ipswich T	H	1–1	47,566	Fairclough
26/02	Wolves	A	0–1	36,693	
01/03	Everton	A	2–1	53,013	Johnson, Neal (pen)
11/03	Manchester C	H	2–0	40,443	Caton (o.g.), Souness
15/03	Bristol C	A	3–1	27,187	R.Kennedy, Dalglish (2)
19/03	Leeds Utd	H	3–0	37,008	Johnson (2), A.Kennedy
22/03	Brighton & HA	H	1–0	42,747	Hansen
29/03	Tottenham H	A	0–2	34,115	
01/04	Stoke C	H	1–0	36,415	Dalglish
05/04	Manchester Utd	A	1–2	57,342	Dalglish
08/04	Derby Co	H	3–0	40,932	Irwin, Johnson, Osgood (o.g.)
19/04	Arsenal	H	1–1	46,878	Dalglish
23/04	Stoke C	A	2–0	32,000	Johnson, Fairclough
26/04	Crystal P	A	0–0	45,583	
03/05	Aston Villa	H	4–1	51,541	Johnson (2), Cohen, Blake (o.g.)
06/05	Middlesbrough	A	0–1	24,458	

Div One Position 1st   P42 Pts 60

FA CUP

DATE	OPPOSITION	VENUE	SCORE	ATT	GOALSCORERS
05/01	Grimsby T	H	5–0	49,706	Souness, Johnson (3), Case
26/01	Nottingham F	A	2–0	33,277	Dalglish, McDermott (pen)
16/02	Bury	H	2–0	43,769	Fairclough (2)
08/03	Tottenham H	A	1–0	48,033	McDermott
12/04	Arsenal	N	0–0	50,174	(at Hillsborough)
16/04	Arsenal	N	1–1	40,769	Fairclough (a.e.t.) (at Villa Park)
28/04	Arsenal	N	1–1	42,975	Dalglish (a.e.t.) (at Villa Park)
01/05	Arsenal	N	0–1	35,335	(at Coventry)

LEAGUE CUP

DATE	OPPOSITION	VENUE	SCORE	ATT	GOALSCORERS
29/08	Tranmere R	A	0–0	16,759	
04/09	Tranmere R	H	4–0	24,785	Thompson, Dalglish (2), Fairclough
25/09	Chesterfield	H	3–1	20,960	Fairclough, Dalglish, McDermott
30/10	Exeter C	H	2–0	21,019	Fairclough (2)
05/12	Norwich C	A	3–1	23,000	Johnson (2), Dalglish
22/01	Nottingham F	A	0–1	32,234	
12/02	Nottingham F	H	1–1	50,880	Fairclough

EUROPEAN CUP

DATE	OPPOSITION	VENUE	SCORE	ATT	GOALSCORERS
19/09	Dynamo Tbilisi	H	2–1	35,270	Johnson, Case
03/10	Dynamo Tbilisi	A	0–3	80,000	

1980–81

CHARITY SHIELD

DATE	OPPOSITION	VENUE	SCORE	ATT	GOALSCORERS
09/08	West Ham	N	1–0	90,000	McDermott (Played at Wembley)

FOOTBALL LEAGUE DIVISION ONE

DATE	OPPOSITION	VENUE	SCORE	ATT	GOALSCORERS
16/08	Crystal P	H	3–0	42,777	Dalglish, R.Kennedy, A.Kennedy
19/08	Coventry C	A	0–0	22,807	
23/08	Leicester C	A	0–2	28,455	
30/08	Norwich C	H	4–1	35,315	Hansen, McDermott, A.Kennedy, Johnson
06/09	Birmingham C	A	1–1	27,042	Dalglish
13/09	West Brom A	H	4–0	36,792	McDermott (pen), Souness, Fairclough (2)
20/09	Southampton	A	2–2	24,085	Souness, Fairclough
27/09	Brighton & HA	H	4–1	35,836	Souness (2), McDermott (pen), Fairclough
04/10	Manchester C	A	3–0	41,022	Dalglish, Souness, Lee
07/10	Middlesbrough	H	4–2	28,204	McDermott (2; 1 pen), R.Kennedy, Dalglish
11/10	Ipswich T	H	1–1	48,084	McDermott (pen)
18/10	Everton	A	2–2	52,565	Lee, Dalglish
25/10	Arsenal	H	1–1	40,310	Souness
01/11	Stoke City	A	2–2	22,864	Johnson, Dalglish
08/11	Nottingham F	H	0–0	43,143	
11/11	Coventry C	H	2–1	26,744	Johnson (2)
15/11	Crystal P	A	2–2	31,154	R.Kennedy, McDermott
22/11	Aston Villa	H	2–1	48,114	Dalglish (2)
25/11	Wolves	A	1–4	25,497	Neal
29/11	Sunderland	A	4–2	32,340	Johnson, McDermott, Lee (2)
06/12	Tottenham H	H	2–1	39,545	Johnson, R.Kennedy
13/12	Ipswich T	A	1–1	32,274	Case
20/12	Wolves	H	1–0	33,563	R.Kennedy
26/12	Manchester Utd	A	0–0	57,073	
27/12	Leeds Utd	H	0–0	44,086	
10/01	Aston Villa	A	0–2	47,960	
17/01	Norwich C	H	1–0	23,829	McDermott
31/01	Leicester C	H	1–2	35,154	Young (o.g.)
07/02	West Brom A	A	0–2	27,905	
14/02	Birmingham C	H	2–2	32,199	Johnson, Neal
21/02	Brighton & HA	A	2–2	23,275	Johnson, McDermott
28/02	Southampton	H	2–0	41,575	R.Kennedy, McDermott
21/03	Everton	H	1–0	49,743	Bailey (o.g.)
28/03	Arsenal	A	0–1	47,058	
03/04	Stoke City	H	3–0	33,308	Whelan, McDermott (2)
11/04	Nottingham F	A	0–0	27,363	
14/04	Manchester Utd	H	0–1	31,276	
18/04	Leeds Utd	A	0–0	39,206	
25/04	Tottenham H	A	1–1	35,334	Gayle
02/05	Sunderland	H	0–1	40,337	
05/05	Middlesbrough	A	2–1	19,102	R.Kennedy, Irwin
19/05	Manchester C	H	1–0	24,462	R.Kennedy

Div One Position 5th   P42 Pts 51

FA CUP

DATE	OPPOSITION	VENUE	SCORE	ATT	GOALSCORERS
03/01	Altrincham	H	4–1	37,170	McDermott, Dalglish (2), R.Kennedy
24/01	Everton	A	1–2	53,804	Case

LEAGUE CUP

DATE	OPPOSITION	VENUE	SCORE	ATT	GOALSCORERS
27/08	Bradford C	A	0–1	16,232	
02/09	Bradford C	H	4–0	21,017	Dalglish (2), R.Kennedy, Johnson
23/09	Swindon T	H	5–0	16,566	Lee (2), Dalglish, Cockerill (o.g.), Fairclough
28/10	Portsmouth	H	4–1	32,021	Dalglish, Johnson (2), Souness
05/12	Birmingham C	H	3–1	30,236	Dalglish, McDermott, Johnson
14/01	Manchester C	A	1–0	48,045	R.Kennedy
10/02	Manchester C	H	1–1	46,711	Dalglish
14/03	West Ham Utd	N	1–1	100,000	A.Kennedy (a.e.t.) (at Wembley)
01/04	West Ham Utd	N	2–1	36,693	Dalglish, Hansen (at Villa Park)

EUROPEAN CUP

DATE	OPPOSITION	VENUE	SCORE	ATT	GOALSCORERS
17/09	Oulu Palloseura	A	1–1	14,000	McDermott
01/10	Oulu Palloseura	H	10–1	21,013	Souness (3,1 pen), Lee, McDermott (3), R.Kennedy, Fairclough
22/10	Aberdeen	A	1–0	24,000	McDermott
05/11	Aberdeen	H	4–0	36,182	Miller (o.g.), Neal, Dalglish, Hansen
04/03	CSKA Sofia	H	5–1	37,255	Souness (3), Lee, McDermott
18/03	CSKA Sofia	A	1–0	65,000	Johnson
08/04	Bayern Munich (s-f)	A	0–0	44,543	
22/04	Bayern Munich (s-f)	A	1–1	77,600	R.Kennedy (LFC win on away goals)
27/05	Real Madrid	N	1–0	48,360	A.Kennedy (Played in Paris)

1981–82

FOOTBALL LEAGUE DIVISION ONE

DATE	OPPOSITION	VENUE	SCORE	ATT	GOAL SCORERS
29/08	Wolves	A	0–1	28,001	
01/09	Middlesbrough	H	1–1	31,963	Neal (pen)
05/09	Arsenal	H	2–0	35,269	McDermott, Johnson
12/09	Ipswich T	A	0–2	26,703	
19/09	Aston Villa	H	0–0	37,474	
22/09	Coventry C	A	2–1	16,731	A.Kennedy, McDermott (pen)
26/09	West Ham Utd	A	1–1	30,802	Johnson
03/10	Swansea C	H	2–2	48,645	McDermott (2; 1 pen)
10/10	Leeds Utd	H	3–0	35,840	Rush (2), Cherry (o.g.)
17/10	Brighton & HA	A	3–3	26,321	Dalglish, R.Kennedy, McDermott
24/10	Manchester Utd	H	1–2	41,438	McDermott (pen)
31/10	Sunderland	A	2–0	27,854	Souness, McDermott
07/11	Everton	H	3–1	48,861	Dalglish (2), Rush
21/11	West Brom A	A	1–1	20,871	Dalglish
28/11	Southampton	H	0–1	37,189	
05/12	Nottingham F	A	2–3	24,521	Lawrenson, R.Kennedy
26/12	Manchester C	H	1–3	37,929	Whelan
05/01	West Ham Utd	H	3–0	28,427	McDermott, Whelan, Dalglish
15/01	Wolves	H	2–1	26,438	Whelan, Dalglish
26/01	Notts Co	A	4–0	14,407	Whelan, Rush (3)
30/01	Aston Villa	A	3–0	35,947	Rush, McDermott (2)
06/02	Ipswich T	H	4–0	41,316	McDermott, Rush, Dalglish, Whelan
16/02	Swansea C	A	0–2	22,604	
20/02	Coventry C	H	4–0	28,286	Souness, Lee, Rush, McDermott (pen)
27/02	Leeds Utd	A	2–0	33,689	Souness, Rush
06/03	Brighton	H	0–1	28,574	
09/03	Stoke C	A	5–1	16,758	McDermott, Dalglish, Souness, Lee, Whelan
20/03	Sunderland	H	1–0	30,344	Rush
27/03	Everton	A	3–1	51,847	Whelan, Souness, Johnston
30/03	Birmingham C	H	3–1	24,224	Rush (2), McDermott
02/04	Notts Co	H	1–0	30,126	Dalglish
07/04	Manchester Utd	A	1–0	50,969	Johnston
10/04	Manchester C	A	5–0	40,112	Lee, Neal (pen), Johnston, A.Kennedy, Rush
13/04	Stoke C	H	2–0	30,419	A.Kennedy, Johnston
17/04	West Brom A	H	1–0	34,286	Dalglish
24/04	Southampton	A	3–2	24,704	Rush, Whelan (2)
01/05	Nottingham F	H	2–0	34,321	Johnston (2)
03/05	Tottenham H	A	2–2	38,091	Dalglish (2)
08/05	Birmingham C	H	1–0	26,381	Rush
11/05	Arsenal	A	1–1	30,932	Rush
15/05	Tottenham H	H	3–1	48,122	Lawrenson, Dalglish, Whelan
18/05	Middlesbrough	A	0–0	17,431	

Div One Position 1st   P42 Pts 87

FA CUP

DATE	OPPOSITION	VENUE	SCORE	ATT	GOALSCORERS
02/01	Swansea C	A	4–0	24,179	Hansen, Rush (2), Lawrenson
23/01	Sunderland	H	3–0	28,582	Dalglish (2), Rush
13/02	Chelsea	A	0–2	41,422	

LEAGUE CUP (MILK CUP)

DATE	OPPOSITION	VENUE	SCORE	ATT	GOALSCORERS
07/10	Exeter C	H	5–0	11,478	Rush (2), McDermott, Dalglish, Whelan
28/10	Exeter C	A	6–0	11,740	Rush (2), Dalglish, Neal, Sheedy, Marker (o.g.)
10/11	Middlesbrough	A	4–1	16,145	Sheedy, Rush, Johnston (2)
01/12	Arsenal	A	0–0	37,917	
08/12	Arsenal	H	3–0	21,375	Johnson, McDermott (pen), Dalglish (a.e.t.)
12/01	Barnsley	H	0–0	33,707	
19/01	Barnsley	A	3–1	29,639	Souness, Johnson, Dalglish
02/02	Ipswich T	A	2–0	26,690	McDermott, Rush
09/02	Ipswich T	H	2–2	34,933	Rush, Dalglish
13/03	Tottenham H	N	3–1	100,000	Whelan (2), Rush (a.e.t.) (at Wembley)

EUROPEAN CUP

DATE	OPPOSITION	VENUE	SCORE	ATT	GOALSCORERS
16/09	Oulu Palloseura	A	1–0	8,400	Dalglish
30/09	Oulu Palloseura	H	7–0	20,789	Dalglish, Rush, McDermott (2), R.Kennedy, Johnson, Lawrenson
21/10	AZ67 Alkmaar	A	2–2	15,000	Johnson, Lee
04/11	AZ67 Alkmaar	H	3–2	29,703	McDermott (pen), Rush, Hansen
03/03	CSKA Sofia	H	1–0	27,388	Whelan
17/03	CSKA Sofia	A	0–2	60,000	

WORLD CLUB CHAMPIONSHIP

DATE	OPPOSITION	VENUE	SCORE	ATT	GOALSCORERS
13/12	Flamengo	N	0–3	62,000	(Played in Tokyo)

1982–83

CHARITY SHIELD

DATE	OPPOSITION	VENUE	SCORE	ATT	GOALSCORERS
21/08	Tottenham H	N	1–0	82,500	Rush (Played at Wembley)

FOOTBALL LEAGUE DIVISION ONE 1982–83

DATE	OPPOSITION	VENUE	SCORE	ATT	GOALSCORERS
28/08	West Brom A	H	2–0	35,652	Lee, Neal (pen)
31/08	Birmingham C	A	0–0	20,176	
04/09	Arsenal	A	2–0	36,429	Hodgson, Neal
07/09	Nottingham F	H	4–3	27,145	Hodgson (2), Souness, Rush
11/09	Luton T	H	3–3	33,694	Souness, Rush, Johnston
18/09	Swansea T	A	3–0	20,322	Rush (2), Johnston
25/09	Southampton	H	5–0	32,996	Whelan (2), Souness, Lawrenson (2)
02/10	Ipswich T	A	0–1	24,342	
09/10	West Ham Utd	H	1–3	32,500	Souness
16/10	Manchester Utd	H	0–0	40,853	
23/10	Stoke C	A	1–1	29,411	Lawrenson
30/10	Brighton & HA	H	3–1	27,929	Lawrenson, Dalglish (2)
06/11	Everton	A	5–0	52,741	Rush (4), Lawrenson
13/11	Coventry C	H	4–0	27,870	Dalglish, Rush (3)
20/11	Notts Co	A	2–1	16,914	Johnston, Dalglish
27/11	Tottenham H	H	3–0	40,691	Neal (pen), Dalglish (2)
04/12	Norwich C	A	0–1	22,909	
11/12	Watford	H	3–1	36,690	Rush, Neal (2 pens)
18/12	Aston Villa	H	4–2	34,568	Hodgson, Dalglish, Kennedy, Rush
27/12	Manchester C	H	5–2	44,664	Dalglish (3), Neal, Rush
28/12	Sunderland	A	0–0	35,041	
01/01	Notts Co	H	5–1	33,643	Rush (3), Dalglish (2)
03/01	Arsenal	H	3–1	37,713	Rush, Souness, Dalglish
15/01	West Brom A	A	1–0	24,560	Rush
22/01	Birmingham C	H	1–1	30,986	Neal
05/02	Luton T	A	3–1	18,434	Rush, Kennedy, Souness
12/02	Ipswich T	H	1–0	34,976	Dalglish
26/02	Manchester Utd	H	1–1	57,397	Dalglish
05/03	Stoke C	H	5–1	30,020	Dalglish (2), Neal, Johnston, Souness
12/03	West Ham Utd	H	3–0	28,511	Pike (o.g.), Lee, Rush
19/03	Everton	H	0–0	44,737	
22/03	Brighton & HA	A	2–2	25,030	Rush (2)
02/04	Sunderland	H	1–0	35,821	Souness
04/04	Manchester C	A	4–0	35,647	Souness, Fairclough (2), Kennedy
09/04	Swansea T	H	3–0	30,010	Rush, Lee, Fairclough
12/04	Coventry C	A	0–0	14,821	
16/04	Southampton	A	3–2	25,578	Dalglish, Johnston
23/04	Norwich C	H	0–2	37,022	
30/04	Tottenham H	A	0–2	44,907	
02/05	Nottingham F	A	0–1	25,107	
07/05	Aston Villa	H	1–1	39,939	Johnston
14/05	Watford	A	1–2	27,173	Johnston

Div One Position 1st   P42 Pts 82

FA CUP

DATE	OPPOSITION	VENUE	SCORE	ATT	GOALSCORERS
08/01	Blackburn R	A	2–1	21,967	Hodgson, Rush
29/01	Stoke C	H	2–0	36,666	Dalglish, Rush
20/02	Brighton & HA	H	1–2	44,868	Johnston

LEAGUE CUP (MILK CUP)

DATE	OPPOSITION	VENUE	SCORE	ATT	GOALSCORERS
05/10	Ipswich T	A	2–1	19,328	Rush (2)
26/10	Ipswich T	H	2–0	17,698	Whelan, Lawrenson
11/11	Rotherham Utd	H	1–0	20,412	Johnston
30/11	Norwich C	A	2–0	13,235	Lawrenson, Fairclough
18/01	West Ham Utd	H	2–1	23,935	Hodgson, Souness
08/02	Burnley	H	3–0	33,520	Souness, Neal (pen), Hodgson
15/02	Burnley	A	0–1	20,000	
26/03	Manchester Utd	N	2–1	100,000	Kennedy, Whelan (a.e.t.) (at Wembley)

EUROPEAN CUP

DATE	OPPOSITION	VENUE	SCORE	ATT	GOALSCORERS
14/09	Dundalk	A	4–1	16,500	Whelan (2), Rush, Hodgson
28/09	Dundalk	H	1–0	12,021	Whelan
19/10	JK Helsinki	A	0–1	5,722	
02/11	JK Helsinki	H	5–0	16,434	Dalglish, Johnston, Neal, Kennedy (2)
02/03	Widzew Lodz	A	0–2	45,531	
16/03	Widzew Lodz	H	3–2	44,494	Neal (pen), Rush, Hodgson

1983–84

CHARITY SHIELD

DATE	OPPOSITION	VENUE	SCORE	ATT	GOALSCORERS
20/08	Manchester United	N	0–2	92,000	(Played at Wembley)

FOOTBALL LEAGUE DIVISION ONE

DATE	OPPOSITION	VENUE	SCORE	ATT	GOALSCORERS
27/08	Wolves	A	1–1	26,249	Rush
31/08	Norwich C	A	1–0	23,859	Souness
03/09	Nottingham F	H	1–0	31,376	Rush
06/09	Southampton	H	1–1	26,331	Rush
10/09	Arsenal	A	2–0	47,896	Johnston, Dalglish
17/09	Aston Villa	H	2–1	34,246	Dalglish, Rush
24/09	Manchester Utd	A	0–1	56,121	
01/10	Sunderland	H	0–1	29,534	
15/10	West Ham Utd	A	3–1	32,555	Robinson (3)
22/10	Q.P.R.	A	1–0	27,140	Nicol
29/10	Luton T	H	6–0	31,940	Rush (5), Dalglish
06/11	Everton	H	3–0	40,875	Rush, Robinson, Nicol
12/11	Tottenham H	A	2–2	45,032	Robinson, Rush
19/11	Stoke C	H	1–0	26,529	Rush
26/11	Ipswich T	A	1–1	23,826	Dalglish
03/12	Birmingham C	H	1–0	24,791	Rush
10/12	Coventry C	A	0–4	20,586	
17/12	Notts Co	H	5–0	22,436	Nicol, Souness (2; 1 pen), Hunt (o.g.), Rush
26/12	West Brom A	A	2–1	25,139	Nicol, Souness
27/12	Leicester C	A	2–2	33,664	Lee, Rush
31/12	Nottingham F	A	1–0	29,692	Rush

1983–84 (CONTINUED)

DATE	OPPOSITION	VENUE	SCORE	ATT	GOALSCORERS
02/01	Manchester Utd	H	1–1	45,122	Johnston
14/01	Wolves	H	0–1	23,325	
20/01	Aston Villa	A	3–1	19,566	Rush (3)
01/02	Watford	H	3–0	20,746	Rush, Nicol, Whelan
04/02	Sunderland	A	0–0	25,646	
11/02	Arsenal	H	2–1	34,642	Kennedy, Neal
18/02	Luton T	A	0–0	14,877	
25/02	Q.P.R.	H	2–0	32,206	Rush, Robinson
03/03	Everton	A	1–1	51,245	Rush
10/03	Tottenham H	A	3–1	36,718	Dalglish, Whelan, Lee
16/03	Southampton	A	0–2	19,698	
31/03	Watford	A	2–0	21,293	Wark, Rush
07/04	West Ham Utd	H	6–0	38,359	Rush (2), Dalglish, Whelan, Souness (2)
14/04	Stoke C	A	0–2	24,372	
18/04	Leicester C	A	3–3	26,553	Whelan, Rush, Wark
21/04	West Brom A	H	3–0	35,320	McNaught (o.g.), Souness, Dalglish
28/04	Ipswich T	H	2–2	32,069	Kennedy, Rush
05/05	Birmingham C	A	0–0	18,809	
07/05	Coventry C	H	5–0	33,393	Rush (4; 1 pen), Hansen
12/05	Notts Co	A	0–0	18,745	
15/05	Norwich C	H	1–1	38,837	Rush

Div One Position 1st   P42   Pts 80

FA CUP

DATE	OPPOSITION	VENUE	SCORE	ATT	GOALSCORERS
06/01	Newcastle Utd	H	4–0	33,566	Robinson, Rush (2), Johnston
29/01	Brighton & HA	A	0–2	19,057	

LEAGUE CUP (MILK CUP)

DATE	OPPOSITION	VENUE	SCORE	ATT	GOALSCORERS
05/10	Brentford	A	4–1	17,859	Rush (2), Robinson, Souness
25/10	Brentford	H	4–0	9,902	Souness (pen), Hodgson, Dalglish, Robinson
08/11	Fulham	A	1–1	20,142	Rush
22/11	Fulham	H	1–1	15,783	Dalglish
29/11	Fulham	A	1–0	20,905	Souness (a.e.t.)
20/12	Birmingham C	A	1–1	17,405	Souness
22/12	Birmingham C	H	3–0	11,638	Nicol, Rush (2,1 pen)
17/01	Sheffield Wed	A	2–2	49,357	Nicol, Neal (pen)
25/01	Sheffield Wed	H	3–0	40,485	Rush (2), Robinson
07/02	Walsall	H	2–2	31,073	Whelan (2)
14/02	Walsall	A	2–0	18,591	Rush, Whelan
25/03	Everton	N	0–0	100,000	(a.e.t.) (at Wembley)
28/03	Everton	N	1–0	52,089	Souness (at Maine Road)

EUROPEAN CUP

DATE	OPPOSITION	VENUE	SCORE	ATT	GOALSCORERS
14/09	BK Odense	A	1–0	30,000	Dalglish
28/09	BK Odense	H	5–0	14,985	Robinson (2), Dalglish (2), Clausen (o.g.)
19/10	Atletico Bilbao	H	0–0	33,063	
02/11	Atletico Bilbao	A	1–0	47,500	Rush
07/03	Benfica	H	1–0	39,096	Rush
21/03	Benfica	A	4–1	70,000	Whelan (2), Johnston, Rush
11/04	Dinamo Bucharest	H	1–0	36,941	Lee
25/04	Dinamo Bucharest	A	2–1	60,000	Rush (2)
30/05	AS Roma	N	1–1	69,693	Neal (a.e.t) (Liverpool won 4–2 on penalties) (in Rome)

1984–85

CHARITY SHIELD

DATE	OPPOSITION	VENUE	SCORE	ATT	GOALSCORERS
18/08	Everton	N	0–1	100,000	(Played at Wembley)

FOOTBALL LEAGUE DIVISION ONE

DATE	OPPOSITION	VENUE	SCORE	ATT	GOALSCORERS
25/08	Norwich C	A	3–3	22,005	Bruce (o.g.), Dalglish, Neal (pen)
27/08	West Ham Utd	H	3–0	32,633	Walsh, Wark (2)
01/09	Q.P.R.	H	1–1	33,982	Whelan
04/09	Luton T	A	2–1	14,127	Neal (pen), Dalglish
08/09	Arsenal	A	1–3	50,006	Kennedy
15/09	Sunderland	A	1–1	34,044	Walsh
22/09	Manchester Utd	A	1–1	56,638	Walsh
29/09	Sheffield Wed	H	0–2	40,196	
06/10	West Brom A	H	0–0	29,346	
12/10	Tottenham A	A	0–1	28,599	
20/10	Everton	H	0–1	45,545	
28/10	Nottingham F	A	2–0	19,838	Whelan, Rush
03/11	Stoke C	A	1–0	20,611	Whelan
10/11	Southampton	H	1–1	36,382	Rush
18/11	Newcastle Utd	A	2–0	28,003	Nicol, Wark
24/11	Ipswich T	H	2–0	34,918	Wark (2)
01/12	Chelsea	A	1–3	40,972	Molby
04/12	Coventry C	H	3–1	27,237	Wark (2), Rush (pen)
15/12	Aston Villa	A	0–0	24,007	
21/12	Q.P.R.	A	2–0	11,007	Wark, Rush
26/12	Leicester C	H	1–2	38,419	Neal (pen)
29/12	Luton T	H	1–0	35,403	Wark
01/01	Watford	A	1–1	27,073	Rush
19/01	Norwich C	H	4–0	30,627	Wark, Rush (2), Dalglish
02/02	Sheffield Wed	A	1–1	48,246	Lawrenson
12/02	Arsenal	H	3–0	28,645	Rush, Neal, Whelan
23/02	Stoke C	H	2–0	31,368	Nicol, Dalglish
02/03	Nottingham F	H	1–0	35,696	Wark (pen)
16/03	Tottenham H	A	0–1	43,852	
23/03	West Brom A	A	5–0	20,500	Nicol, Dalglish, Wark (3)
31/03	Manchester Utd	H	0–1	34,886	
03/04	Sunderland	A	3–0	24,096	Rush (2), Wark
06/04	Leicester C	A	1–0	22,942	Whelan
20/04	Newcastle Utd	H	3–1	34,733	Wark, Gillespie, Walsh
27/04	Ipswich T	A	0–0	24,484	
04/05	Chelsea	H	4–3	33,733	Whelan, Nicol (2), Rush
06/05	Coventry C	A	2–0	18,951	Walsh (2)
11/05	Aston Villa	H	2–1	33,001	Whelan, Rush
14/05	Southampton	A	1–0	23,001	Wark
17/05	Watford	H	4–3	29,130	Rush (2), Dalglish, Wark (pen)
20/05	West Ham Utd	A	3–0	22,408	Walsh (2), Beglin
23/05	Everton	A	0–1	51,045	

Div One Position 2nd   P42   Pts 77

FA CUP

DATE	OPPOSITION	VENUE	SCORE	ATT	GOALSCORERS
05/01	Aston Villa	H	3–0	36,877	Rush (2), Wark
27/01	Tottenham H	H	1–0	27,905	Rush
16/02	York C	A	1–1	13,485	Rush
20/02	York C	H	7–0	43,010	Whelan (2), Wark (3), Neal, Walsh
10/03	Barnsley	A	4–0	19,838	Rush (3), Whelan
13/04	Manchester Utd	N	2–2	51,690	Whelan, Walsh (a.e.t.) (at Goodison Park)
17/04	Manchester Utd	N	1–2	45,775	McGrath (o.g.) (at Maine Road)

LEAGUE CUP (MILK CUP)

DATE	OPPOSITION	VENUE	SCORE	ATT	GOALSCORERS
24/09	Stockport Co	A	0–0	11,169	
09/10	Stockport Co	N	2–0	13,422	Robinson, Whelan (a.e.t.)
31/10	Tottenham H	A	0–1	38,690	

EUROPEAN CUP

DATE	OPPOSITION	VENUE	SCORE	ATT	GOALSCORERS
19/09	Lech Poznan	A	1–0	35,000	Wark
03/10	Lech Poznan	H	4–0	22,143	Wark (3), Walsh
24/10	Benfica	H	3–1	27,733	Rush (3)
07/11	Benfica	A	0–1	50,000	
06/03	Austria Vienna	A	1–1	21,000	Nicol
20/03	Austria Vienna	H	4–1	32,761	Walsh (2), Nicol, Obermayer (o.g.)
10/04	Panathinaikos (s–f)	H	4–0	39,488	Wark, Rush (2), Beglin
24/04	Panathinaikos (s–f)	A	1–0	60,000	Lawrenson
29/05	Juventus	N	0–1	—	(Played in Brussels)

WORLD CLUB CHAMPIONSHIP

DATE	OPPOSITION	VENUE	SCORE	ATT	GOALSCORERS
09/12	Independiente	N	0–1	62,000	(Played in Tokyo)

EUROPEAN SUPER CUP

DATE	OPPOSITION	VENUE	SCORE	ATT	GOALSCORERS
16/01	Juventus	A	0–2	60,000	(Played in Turin)

1985–86

FOOTBALL LEAGUE DIVISION ONE

DATE	OPPOSITION	VENUE	SCORE	ATT	GOAL SCORERS
17/08	Arsenal	H	2–0	38,261	Whelan, Nicol
21/08	Aston Villa	A	2–2	20,197	Rush, Molby
24/08	Newcastle Utd	A	0–1	29,670	
26/08	Ipswich T	H	5–0	29,383	Nicol, Rush (2), Molby, Johnston
31/08	West Ham Utd	A	2–2	19,762	Johnston, Whelan
03/09	Nottingham F	H	2–0	27,135	Whelan (2)
07/09	Watford	H	3–1	31,395	Neal (pen), Johnston, Rush
14/09	Oxford Utd	A	2–2	11,474	Rush, Johnston
21/09	Everton	A	3–2	51,509	Dalglish, Rush, McMahon
28/09	Tottenham H	H	4–1	41,521	Lawrenson, Rush, Molby (2 pens)
05/10	Q.P.R.	A	1–2	24,621	Walsh
12/10	Southampton	H	1–0	31,070	McMahon
19/10	Manchester Utd	A	1–1	54,492	Johnston
26/10	Luton T	H	3–2	31,488	Walsh (2), Molby
02/11	Leicester C	H	1–0	31,718	Rush
09/11	Coventry C	A	3–0	16,947	Beglin, Walsh, Rush
16/11	West Brom A	H	4–1	28,407	Nicol, Molby, Lawrenson, Walsh
23/11	Birmingham C	A	2–0	15,062	Rush, Walsh
30/11	Chelsea	H	1–1	38,482	Molby (pen)
07/12	Aston Villa	H	3–0	29,418	Molby, Walsh, Johnston
14/12	Arsenal	A	0–2	35,048	
21/12	Newcastle Utd	H	1–1	30,746	Nicol
26/12	Manchester C	A	0–1	35,584	
28/12	Nottingham F	A	1–1	27,141	MacDonald
01/01	Sheffield Wed	H	2–2	38,964	Rush, Walsh
12/01	Watford	A	3–2	16,967	Walsh (2), Rush
18/01	West Ham Utd	H	3–1	41,056	Molby (pen), Rush, Walsh
01/02	Ipswich T	A	1–2	20,551	Whelan
09/02	Manchester Utd	H	1–1	35,064	Wark
22/02	Everton	H	0–2	45,445	
02/03	Tottenham H	A	2–1	16,436	Molby, Rush
08/03	Q.P.R.	H	4–1	26,219	McMahon (2), Rush (Rush's 100th Lge goal), Wark
15/03	Southampton	A	2–1	19,784	Wark, Rush
22/03	Oxford Utd	H	6–0	37,861	Rush (2), Lawrenson, Whelan, Molby (2; 1 pen)
29/03	Sheffield Wed	A	0–0	37,946	
31/03	Manchester C	H	2–0	43,316	McMahon (2)
12/04	Coventry C	H	5–0	42,729	Whelan (3), Molby, Rush
16/04	Luton T	A	1–0	15,390	Johnston
19/04	West Brom A	A	2–1	22,010	Dalglish, Rush
26/04	Birmingham C	A	5–0	42,021	Rush, Gillespie (3; 1 pen), Molby (pen)
30/04	Leicester C	A	2–0	25,799	Rush, Whelan
03/05	Chelsea	A	1–0	43,900	Dalglish

Div One Position 1st   P42   Pts 88

FA CUP

DATE	OPPOSITION	VENUE	SCORE	ATT	GOAL SCORERS
04/01	Norwich C	H	5–0	29,082	MacDonald, Walsh, McMahon, Whelan, Wark
26/01	Chelsea	A	2–1	33,625	Rush, Lawrenson
15/02	York C	A	1–1	12,443	Molby (pen)
18/02	York C	H	3–1	29,362	Wark, Molby (pen), Dalglish (a.e.t.)
11/03	Watford	H	0–0	36,775	
17/03	Watford	A	2–1	28,097	Molby (pen), Rush (a.e.t.)
05/04	Southampton	N	2–0	44,605	Rush (2) (a.e.t.) (at White Hart Lane)
10/05	Everton	N	3–1	98,000	Rush (2), Johnston (at Wembley)

LEAGUE CUP (MILK CUP)

DATE	OPPOSITION	VENUE	SCORE	ATT	GOALSCORERS
24/09	Oldham A	H	3–0	16,150	McMahon (2), Rush
09/10	Oldham A	A	5–2	7,719	Whelan (2), Wark, Rush, MacDonald (agg 8–2)
29/10	Brighton & H A	H	4–0	15,291	Walsh (3), Dalglish
26/11	Manchester Utd	H	2–1	41,291	Molby (2,1 pen)
21/01	Ipswich Town	H	3–0	19,762	Walsh, Whelan, Rush
12/02	Q.P.R.	A	0–1	15,051	
05/03	Q.P.R.	H	2–2	23,863	MacMahon, Johnston (agg 2–3)

SCREEN SPORT SUPER CUP

DATE	OPPOSITION	VENUE	SCORE	ATT	GOALSCORERS
17/09	Southampton	H	2–1	16,189	Molby, Dalglish
22/10	Southampton	A	1–1	10,503	Walsh
03/12	Tottenham H	H	2–0	14,855	MacDonald, Walsh
14/01	Tottenham H	A	3–0	10,078	Rush (2), Lawrenson
05/02	Norwich C	A	1–1	15,330	Dalglish
06/05	Norwich C	H	3–1	26,696	MacDonald, Molby (pen), Johnston

1986–87

CHARITY SHIELD

DATE	OPPOSITION	VENUE	SCORE	ATT	GOALSCORERS
16/08	Everton	N	1–1	88,231	Rush (Trophy shared, played at Wembley)

SCREEN SPORT SUPER CUP FINAL

DATE	OPPOSITION	VENUE	SCORE	ATT	GOALSCORERS
16/09	Everton	H	3–1	20,660	Rush (2), McMahon
30/09	Everton	A	4–1	26,068	Rush (3), Nicol

FOOTBALL LEAGUE DIVISION ONE

DATE	OPPOSITION	VENUE	SCORE	ATT	GOALSCORERS
23/08	Newcastle Utd	A	2–0	33,306	Rush (2)
25/08	Manchester C	H	0–0	39,989	
30/08	Arsenal	H	2–1	38,637	Molby (pen), Rush
03/09	Leicester C	A	1–2	16,344	Dalglish
06/09	West Ham Utd	A	5–2	29,807	Whelan, Johnston, Dalglish (2), Rush
13/09	Charlton A	H	2–0	37,413	Molby (pen), Rush
20/09	Southampton	A	1–2	20,452	McMahon
27/09	Aston Villa	H	3–3	38,298	Wark (2; 1 pen), McMahon
04/10	Wimbledon	A	3–1	15,978	Molby, Rush (2)
11/10	Tottenham H	H	0–1	43,139	
18/10	Oxford Utd	H	4–0	34,512	Rush (2), Dalglish, Molby (pen)
25/10	Luton T	A	1–4	13,140	Molby (pen)
01/11	Norwich C	H	6–2	36,915	Nicol, Walsh (3), Rush (2)
08/11	Q.P.R.	A	3–1	24,045	Rush, Nicol, Johnston
16/11	Sheffield Wed	H	1–1	28,020	Rush
23/11	Everton	A	0–0	48,247	
29/11	Coventry C	H	2–0	31,614	Molby (pen), Wark
06/12	Watford	A	0–2	23,954	
14/12	Chelsea	H	3–0	25,856	Whelan, Rush, Nicol
20/12	Charlton A	A	0–0	16,564	
26/12	Manchester Utd	H	0–1	40,663	
27/12	Sheffield Wed	A	1–0	40,959	Rush
01/01	Nottingham F	A	1–1	32,854	Rush
03/01	West Ham Utd	H	1–0	41,286	McMahon
17/01	Manchester C	A	1–0	35,336	Rush
24/01	Newcastle Utd	H	2–0	38,054	Walsh, Rush
14/02	Leicester C	H	4–3	34,259	Walsh, Rush (3)
21/02	Aston Villa	A	2–2	32,093	Johnston, Walsh
28/02	Southampton	H	1–0	33,133	Aldridge
07/03	Luton T	H	2–0	32,433	Molby (pen), Donaghy (o.g.)
10/03	Arsenal	A	1–0	47,777	Rush
14/03	Oxford Utd	A	3–1	14,211	Wark (2), Rush
18/03	Q.P.R.	H	2–1	28,988	Rush (2)
22/03	Tottenham H	A	0–1	32,763	
28/03	Wimbledon	H	1–2	36,409	Dalglish
11/03	Norwich C	A	1–2	22,879	Rush
18/03	Nottingham F	H	3–0	37,359	Dalglish, Whelan, Ablett
20/04	Manchester Utd	A	0–1	54,103	
25/04	Everton	H	3–1	44,827	McMahon, Rush (2)
02/05	Coventry C	A	0–1	26,209	
04/05	Watford	H	1–0	40,150	Rush
09/05	Chelsea	A	3–3	29,245	Rush, McMahon, Aldridge

Div One Position 2nd   P42 Pts 77

FA CUP

DATE	OPPOSITION	VENUE	SCORE	ATT	GOALSCORERS
11/01	Luton T	A	0–0	11,085	
26/01	Luton T	H	0–0	34,822	
28/01	Luton T	A	0–3	14,687	

LEAGUE CUP (LITTLEWOODS CUP)

DATE	OPPOSITION	VENUE	SCORE	ATT	GOALSCORERS
23/09	Fulham	H	10–0	13,498	Rush (2), Wark (2), Whelan, McMahon (4), Nicol
07/10	Fulham	A	3–2	7,864	McMahon, Parker (o.g.), Molby (pen)
29/10	Leicester C	A	4–1	20,248	McMahon (3), Dalglish
19/11	Coventry C	A	0–0	26,385	
26/11	Coventry C	H	3–1	19,179	Molby (3 pens)
21/01	Everton	H	1–0	53,325	Rush
11/02	Southampton (s–f)	A	0–0	22,818	
25/02	Southampton (s–f)	H	3–0	38,481	Whelan, Dalglish, Molby
05/04	Arsenal	N	1–2	96,000	Rush (at Wembley)

1987–88

FOOTBALL LEAGUE DIVISION ONE

DATE	OPPOSITION	VENUE	SCORE	ATT	GOALSCORERS
15/08	Arsenal	A	2–1	54,703	Aldridge, Nicol
29/08	Coventry C	A	4–1	27,637	Nicol (2), Aldridge (pen), Beardsley
05/09	West Ham Utd	A	1–1	29,865	Aldridge (pen)
12/09	Oxford Utd	H	2–0	42,266	Aldrige, Barnes
15/09	Charlton A	H	3–2	36,637	Aldridge (pen), Hansen, McMahon
20/09	Newcastle Utd	A	4–1	24,141	Nicol (3), Aldridge
29/09	Derby Co	H	4–0	43,405	Beardsley, Aldridge (3; 2 pens)
03/10	Portsmouth	H	4–0	44,366	Beardsley, McMahon, Aldridge (pen), Whelan
17/10	Q.P.R.	H	4–0	43,735	Johnston, Aldridge (pen), Barnes (2)
24/10	Luton T	A	1–0	12,452	Gillespie
01/11	Everton	H	2–0	44,260	McMahon, Bearsley
04/11	Wimbledon	A	1–1	13,544	Houghton
15/11	Manchester Utd	A	1–1	47,106	Aldridge
21/11	Norwich C	H	0–0	37,446	
24/11	Watford	H	4–0	32,396	McMahon, Houghton, Aldridge, Barnes
28/11	Tottenham H	A	2–0	47,362	McMahon, Johnston
06/12	Chelsea	H	2–1	31,211	Aldridge (pen), McMahon
12/12	Southampton	A	2–2	19,507	Barnes (2)
19/12	Sheffield Wed	H	1–0	35,383	Gillespie

DATE	OPPOSITION	VENUE	SCORE	ATT	GOALSCORERS
26/12	Oxford Utd	A	3–0	13,680	Aldridge, Barnes, McMahon
28/12	Newcastle Utd	H	4–0	44,637	McMahon, Aldridge (2; 1 pen), Houghton
01/01	Coventry C	A	4–0	38,790	Beardsley (2), Aldridge, Houghton
16/01	Arsenal	H	2–0	44,294	Aldridge, Beardsley
23/01	Charlton A	A	2–0	28,095	Beardsley, Barnes
06/02	West Ham Utd	H	0–0	42,049	
13/02	Watford	A	4–1	23,838	Beardsley (2), Aldridge, Barnes
27/02	Portsmouth	H	2–0	28,117	Barnes
05/03	Q.P.R.	A	1–0	23,171	Barnes
16/03	Derby Co	A	1–1	26,356	Johnston
20/03	Everton	A	0–1	44,162	
26/03	Wimbledon	H	2–1	36,464	Aldridge, Barnes
02/04	Nottingham F	A	1–2	29,188	Aldridge (pen)
04/04	Manchester Utd	H	3–3	43,497	Beardsley, Gillespie, McMahon
13/04	Nottingham F	H	5–0	39,535	Houghton, Aldridge (2), Gillespie, Beardsley
20/04	Norwich C	A	0–0	22,509	
23/04	Tottenham H	H	1–0	44,798	Beardsley
30/04	Chelsea	H	1–1	35,625	Barnes
02/05	Southampton	H	1–1	37,610	Aldridge
07/05	Sheffield Wed	A	5–1	35,893	Johnston (2), Barnes, Beardsley (2)
09/05	Luton T	H	1–1	30,736	Aldridge

Div One Position 1st   P40 Pts 90

FA CUP

DATE	OPPOSITION	VENUE	SCORE	ATT	GOALSCORERS
09/01	Stoke C	A	0–0	31,979	
12/01	Stoke C	H	1–0	39,147	Beardsley
31/01	Aston Villa	A	2–0	46,324	Barnes, Beardsley
21/02	Everton	A	1–0	48,270	Houghton
13/03	Manchester C	A	4–0	44,047	Houghton, Beardsley (pen), Johnston, Barnes
09/04	Nottingham F (s–f)	N	2–0	51,627	Aldridge (2,1 pen) (at Hillsborough)
14/05	Wimbledon	N	0–1	98,203	(at Wembley)

LEAGUE CUP (LITTLEWOODS CUP)

DATE	OPPOSITION	VENUE	SCORE	ATT	GOALSCORERS
23/09	Blackburn R	A	1–1	13,924	Nicol
06/10	Blackburn R	H	1–0	28,994	Aldridge
28/10	Everton	H	0–1	44,071	

1988–89

CHARITY SHIELD

DATE	OPPOSITION	VENUE	SCORE	ATT	GOALSCORERS
20/08	Wimbledon	N	2–1	54,887	Aldridge (2) (Played at Wembley)

MERCANTILE CREDIT TROPHY (FOOTBALL LEAGUE CENTENARY)

DATE	OPPOSITION	VENUE	SCORE	ATT	GOALSCORERS
29/08	Nottingham F	H	4–1	20,141	Venison, Molby (pen), Houghton, Barnes
20/09	Arsenal	A	1–2	29,135	Staunton

FOOTBALL LEAGUE DIVISION ONE

DATE	OPPOSITION	VENUE	SCORE	ATT	GOALSCORERS
27/08	Charlton A	A	3–0	21,389	Aldridge (3)
03/09	Manchester Utd	H	1–0	42,026	Molby (pen)
10/09	Aston Villa	A	1–1	41,409	Houghton
17/09	Tottenham H	H	1–1	40,929	Beardsley
24/09	Southampton	A	3–1	21,046	Aldridge, Beardsley, Molby (pen)
01/10	Newcastle Utd	H	1–2	39,139	Gillespie
08/10	Luton T	A	0–1	12,117	
22/10	Coventry C	H	0–0	38,742	
26/10	Nottingham F	A	1–2	29,755	Rush
29/10	West Ham Utd	A	2–0	30,198	Rush, Beardsley
05/11	Middlesbrough	H	3–0	39,489	Rush, Aldridge, Beardsley
12/11	Millwall	H	1–1	41,966	Nicol
19/11	Q.P.R.	A	1–0	20,063	Aldridge
26/11	Wimbledon	H	1–1	36,188	Houghton
04/12	Arsenal	A	1–1	31,863	Barnes
11/12	Everton	H	1–1	42,372	Houghton
17/12	Norwich C	H	1–0	34,325	
26/12	Derby Co	A	1–0	25,213	Rush
01/01	Manchester Utd	A	1–3	44,745	Barnes
03/01	Aston Villa	H	1–0	39,014	Whelan
14/01	Sheffield Wed	A	2–2	31,524	Nicol, Aldridge
21/01	Southampton	H	2–2	35,565	Aldridge, Rush
04/02	Newcastle Utd	A	2–2	30,966	Rush, Aldridge
01/03	Charlton A	A	2–0	30,283	Bearsdley, Aldridge (pen)
11/03	Middlesbrough	A	4–0	25,197	Beardsley, Houghton, Aldridge, McMahon
14/03	Luton T	H	5–0	31,447	Aldridge (3; 1 pen), Beardsley, McMahon
22/03	Coventry C	A	2–1	23,807	Barnes, Aldridge, Whelan
26/03	Tottenham H	A	2–1	30,012	Aldridge (pen), Beardsley
29/03	Derby Co	H	1–0	42,518	Barnes
01/04	Norwich C	A	1–0	26,338	Whelan
08/04	Sheffield Wed	H	5–1	39,672	McMahon, Beardsley (2), Houghton, Barnes
11/04	Millwall	A	2–1	22,130	Barnes, Aldridge
03/05	Everton	A	0–0	45,994	
10/05	Nottingham F	H	1–0	39,793	Aldridge (pen)
13/05	Wimbledon	A	2–1	14,730	Aldridge, Barnes
16/05	Q.P.R.	H	2–0	38,368	Aldridge, Whelan
23/05	West Ham Utd	A	5–1	41,855	Aldridge, Houghton (2), Rush, Barnes
26/05	Arsenal	H	0–2	41,718	

1st Div Position 2   P38 Pts 76

FA CUP

DATE	OPPOSITION	VENUE	SCORE	ATT	GOALSCORERS
07/01	Carlisle Utd	A	3–0	18,556	Barnes, McMahon (2)
29/01	Millwall	A	2–0	23,615	Aldridge, Rush
18/02	Hull C	A	3–2	20,058	Barnes, Aldridge (2)
18/03	Brentford	H	4–0	42,376	McMahon, Barnes, Beardsley (2)
15/04	Nottingham F (s–f)	N		53,000	(abandoned after 6 mins, at Hillsborough)
07/05	Nottingham F (s–f)	N	3–1	38,000	Aldridge (2), Laws (o.g.) (at Old Trafford)
20/05	Everton	N	3–2	82,800	Aldridge, Rush (2) (at Wembley)

LEAGUE CUP (LITTLEWOODS CUP)

DATE	OPPOSITION	VENUE	SCORE	ATT	GOALSCORERS
28/09	Walsall	H	1–0	18,084	Gillespie
12/10	Walsall	A	3–1	12,015	Barnes, Rush, Molby (pen)
02/11	Arsenal	H	1–1	31,951	Barnes

1988–89 (CONTINUED)

DATE	OPPOSITION	VENUE	SCORE	ATT	GOALSCORERS
09/11	Arsenal	A	0–0	54,029	
23/11	Arsenal	N	2–1	21,708	McMahon, Aldridge
30/11	West Ham Utd	A	1–4	26,971	Aldrdige (pen)

1989–90

CHARITY SHIELD

DATE	OPPOSITION	VENUE	SCORE	ATT	GOALSCORERS
12/08	Arsenal	N	1–0	63,149	Beardsley (Played at Wembley)

FOOTBALL LEAGUE DIVISION ONE

DATE	OPPOSITION	VENUE	SCORE	ATT	GOALSCORERS
19/08	Manchester C	H	3–1	37,628	Barnes (pen), Beardsley, Nicol
23/08	Aston Villa	A	1–1	35,796	Barnes
26/08	Luton T	A	0–0	11,124	
09/09	Derby Co	A	3–0	20,034	Rush, Barnes (pen), Beardsley
12/09	Crystal P	H	9–0	35,779	Nicol (2), McMahon, Rush, Gillespie, Beardsley, Aldridge (pen), Barnes, Hysen
16/09	Norwich C	H	0–0	36,885	
23/09	Everton	A	3–1	42,453	Barnes, Rush (2)
14/10	Wimbledon	A	2–1	13,510	Beardsley, Whelan
21/10	Southampton	A	1–4	20,501	Beardsley (pen)
29/10	Tottenham H	H	1–0	36,550	Barnes
04/11	Coventry C	A	0–1	36,433	
11/11	Q.P.R.	A	2–3	18,304	Barnes (2;1 pen)
19/11	Millwall	A	2–1	13,547	Barnes, Rush
26/11	Arsenal	H	2–1	36,983	McMahon, Barnes
29/11	Sheffield Wed	A	0–2	32,732	
02/12	Manchester C	A	4–1	31,641	Rush (2), Beardsley, McMahon
09/12	Aston Villa	H	1–1	37,435	Beardsley
16/12	Chelsea	H	5–2	31,005	Beardsley, Rush (2), Houghton, McMahon
23/12	Manchester Utd	H	0–0	37,426	
26/12	Sheffield Wed	H	2–1	37,488	Molby, Rush
30/12	Charlton A	H	1–0	36,678	Barnes
01/01	Nottingham F	A	2–2	24,518	Rush (2)
13/01	Luton T	H	2–2	35,312	Barnes, Nicol
20/01	Crystal P	A	2–0	29,807	Rush, Beardsley
03/02	Everton	H	2–1	38,730	Barnes, Beardsley (pen)
10/02	Norwich C	A	0–0	20,210	
03/03	Millwall	H	1–0	36,427	Gillespie
18/03	Manchester Utd	A	2–1	46,629	Barnes (2; 1 pen)
21/03	Tottenham H	A	0–1	25,656	
31/03	Southampton	H	3–2	37,027	Barnes, Osman (o.g.), Rush
03/04	Wimbledon	H	2–1	33,319	Rush, Gillespie
11/04	Charlton A	A	4–0	13,982	Rosenthal (3), Barnes
14/04	Nottingham F	H	2–2	37,265	Rosenthal, McMahon
18/04	Arsenal	A	1–1	33,395	Barnes
21/04	Chelsea	H	4–1	38,481	Rosenthal, Nicol (2), Rush
28/04	Q.P.R.	H	2–1	37,758	Rush, Barnes (pen)
01/05	Derby Co	H	1–0	38,038	Gillespie
05/05	Coventry City	A	6–1	23,204	Rush, Barnes (3), Rosenthal (2)

1st Div Position 1st   P38 Pts 79

FA CUP

DATE	OPPOSITION	VENUE	SCORE	ATT	GOALSCORERS
06/01	Swansea C	A	0–0	16,098	
09/01	Swansea C	H	8–0	29,194	Barnes (2), Whelan, Rush (3), Beardsley, Nicol
28/01	Norwich C	A	0–0	23,152	
31/01	Norwich C	H	3–1	29,339	Nicol, Barnes, Beardsley (pen)
17/02	Southampton	H	3–0	35,961	Rush, Beardsley, Nicol
11/03	QPR	A	2–2	21,057	Barnes, Rush
14/03	QPR	H	1–0	38,090	Beardsley
08/04	Crystal Palace	N	3–4	38,389	Rush, McMahon, Barnes (pen)

LEAGUE CUP (LITTLEWOODS CUP)

DATE	OPPOSITION	VENUE	SCORE	ATT	GOALSCORERS
19/09	Wigan Athletic	H	5–2	19,231	Hysen, Rush (2), Beardsley, Barnes
04/10	Wigan Athletic	N	3–0	17,954	Staunton (3) (Wigan chose to play at Anfield)
25/10	Arsenal	A	0–1	40.814	

1990–91

CHARITY SHIELD

DATE	OPPOSITION	VENUE	SCORE	ATT	GOALSCORERS
18/08	Manchester Utd	N	1–1	66,558	Barnes (Played at Wembley)

FOOTBALL LEAGUE DIVISION ONE

DATE	OPPOSITION	VENUE	SCORE	ATT	GOALSCORERS
25/08	Sheffield Utd	A	3–1	27,009	Barnes, Houghton, Rush
28/08	Nottingham F	A	2–0	33,663	Rush, Beardsley
01/09	Aston Villa	H	2–1	38,061	Beardsley, Barnes
08/09	Wimbledon	A	2–1	12,364	Barnes, Whelan
16/09	Manchester Utd	H	4–0	35,726	Beardsley (3), Barnes
22/09	Everton	A	3–2	39,847	Beardsley (2), Barnes (pen)
29/09	Sunderland	A	1–0	31,107	Houghton
06/10	Derby Co	H	2–0	37,036	Houghton, Beardsley
20/10	Norwich C	A	1–1	21,275	Gillespie
27/10	Chelsea	H	2–0	38,463	Rush, Nicol
04/11	Tottenham H	A	3–1	35,003	Rush (2), Beardsley
10/11	Luton T	H	4–0	35,207	Rush (2), Molby (pen), Beardsley
17/11	Coventry C	A	1–0	22,571	Beardsley
24/11	Manchester C	H	2–2	37,849	Rush, Rosenthal
02/12	Arsenal	A	0–3	40,419	
15/12	Sheffield Utd	H	2–0	33,516	Barnes, Rush
22/12	Southampton	A	3–2	31,894	Rosenthal (2), Houghton
26/12	Q.P.R.	A	1–1	17,848	Barnes
30/12	Crystal P	A	0–1	26,280	
01/01	Leeds Utd	H	3–0	36,975	Barnes, Rosenthal, Rush
12/01	Aston Villa	A	0–0	40,026	
19/01	Wimbledon	H	1–1	35,030	Barnes
03/02	Manchester Utd	A	1–1	43,690	Speedie
09/02	Everton	H	3–1	38,129	Molby, Speedie (2)
23/02	Luton T	A	1–3	12,032	Molby (pen)
03/03	Arsenal	H	0–1	37,221	
09/03	Manchester C	A	3–0	35,150	Molby (2 pens), Barnes
16/03	Sunderland	H	2–1	37,582	Rush, Owers (o.g.)
23/03	Derby Co	A	7–1	20,531	Molby (pen), Barnes (2), Rush, Nicol (2), Houghton
30/03	Q.P.R.	H	1–3	37,251	Molby (pen)
01/04	Southampton	A	0–1	20,255	
09/04	Coventry C	H	1–1	31,063	Rush
13/04	Leeds Utd	A	5–4	31,460	Houghton, Molby (pen), Speedie, Barnes (2)
20/04	Norwich C	H	3–0	37,065	Barnes, Houghton, Rush
23/04	Crystal P	H	3–0	36,767	Rush, Barnes, McGoldrick (o.g.)
04/05	Chelsea	A	2–4	32,266	Speedie, Rosenthal
06/05	Nottingham F	A	1–2	26,151	Molby (pen)
11/05	Tottenham H	H	2–0	36,192	Rush, Speedie

Div One Position 2nd   P38 Pts 76

FA CUP

DATE	OPPOSITION	VENUE	SCORE	ATT	GOALSCORERS
05/01	Blackburn R	A	1–1	18,524	Atkins (o.g.)
08/01	Blackburn R	H	3–0	34,175	Houghton, Rush, Staunton
26/01	Brighton HA	A	2–2	32,670	Rush (2)
30/01	Brighton HA	A	3–0	14,392	McMahon (2), Rush
17/02	Everton	H	0–0	38,323	
20/02	Everton	A	4–4	37,766	Beardsley (2), Rush, Barnes
27/02	Everton	A	0–1	40,201	

LEAGUE CUP (RUMBELOWS CUP)

DATE	OPPOSITION	VENUE	SCORE	ATT	GOALSCORERS
25/09	Crewe Alexandra	H	5–1	17,228	McMahon, Gillespie, Houghton, Rush (2)
09/10	Crewe Alexandra	A	4–1	7,200	Rush (3), Staunton
31/10	Manchester United	A	1–3	42,033	Houghton

1991–92

FOOTBALL LEAGUE DIVISION ONE

DATE	OPPOSITION	VENUE	SCORE	ATT	GOAL SCORERS
17/08	Oldham A	H	2–1	38,841	Houghton, Barnes
21/08	Manchester C	A	1–2	37,322	McManaman
24/08	Luton T	A	0–0	11,132	
27/08	Q.P.R.	H	1–0	32,700	Saunders
31/08	Everton	H	3–1	39,072	Burrows, Saunders, Houghton
07/09	Notts Co	A	2–1	16,051	Rosenthal, Walters (pen)
14/09	Aston Villa	H	1–1	38,400	Walters (pen)
21/09	Leeds Utd	A	0–1	32,917	
28/09	Sheffield Wed	H	1–1	37,071	Houghton
06/10	Manchester Utd	A	0–0	44,997	
19/10	Chelsea	A	2–2	30,230	McManaman, Rush
26/10	Coventry C	H	1–0	33,339	Houghton
02/11	Crystal P	H	1–2	34,231	Hysen
17/11	West Ham Utd	A	0–0	23,569	
23/11	Wimbledon	H	0–0	13,373	
30/11	Norwich C	H	2–1	34,881	Molby, Houghton
07/12	Southampton	A	1–1	19,503	Redknapp
14/12	Nottingham F	H	2–0	35,285	McMahon, Molby
18/12	Tottenham H	A	2–1	27,434	Saunders, Houghton
21/12	Manchester C	H	2–2	36,743	Saunders, Nicol
26/12	Q.P.R.	A	0–0	21,693	
28/12	Everton	A	1–1	37,681	Tanner
01/01	Sheffield Utd	H	2–1	35,993	Houghton, Saunders
11/01	Luton T	H	2–1	35,095	McManaman, Saunders
18/01	Oldham A	A	3–2	18,952	McManaman, Saunders, Thomas
29/01	Arsenal	H	2–0	33,753	Molby (pen), Houghton
01/02	Chelsea	H	1–2	38,681	Rosenthal
08/02	Coventry C	A	0–0	21,540	
22/02	Norwich C	A	0–3	20,411	
29/02	Southampton	H	0–0	34,449	
11/03	West Ham Utd	H	1–0	30,821	Saunders
14/03	Crystal P	A	0–1	23,680	
21/03	Tottenham H	H	2–1	36,968	Saunders (2)
28/03	Sheffield Utd	A	0–2	26,943	
31/03	Notts Co	H	4–0	25,457	Thomas, McManaman, Rush, Venison
08/04	Wimbledon	A	2–3	26,134	Thomas, Rosenthal
11/04	Aston Villa	A	0–1	35,755	
18/04	Leeds Utd	H	0–0	37,186	
20/04	Arsenal	A	0–4	38,517	
22/04	Nottingham F	A	1–1	23,787	Rush
26/04	Manchester Utd	H	2–0	38,669	Rush, Walters
02/05	Sheffield Wed	A	0–0	34,861	

Div One Position 6th   P42 Pts 64

FA CUP

DATE	OPPOSITION	VENUE	SCORE	ATT	GOALSCORERS
06/01	Crewe A	A	4–0	7,400	McMahon, Barnes (3,1 pen)
05/02	Bristol R	A	1–1	9,464	Saunders
11/02	Bristol R	H	2–1	30,142	McMahon, Saunders
16/02	Ipswich T	A	0–0	26,140	
26/02	Ipswich T	H	3–2	27,335	Houghton, Molby, McManaman
08/03	Aston Villa	H	1–0	29,109	Thomas
05/04	Portsmouth (s–f)	N	1–1	41,869	Whelan (at Highbury)
13/04	Portsmouth (s–f)	N	0–0	40,077	(a.e.t.) (Liverpool win on penalties)
09/05	Sunderland	N	2–0	79,544	Thomas, Rush (at Wembley)

LEAGUE CUP (RUMBELOWS CUP)

DATE	OPPOSITION	VENUE	SCORE	ATT	GOALSCORERS
25/09	Stoke City	H	2–2	18,389	Rush (2)
09/10	Stoke City	A	3–2	22,335	McManaman, Saunders, Walters
29/10	Port Vale	H	2–2	21,533	McManaman, Rush
20/11	Port Vale (replay)	A	4–1	18,725	McManaman, Walters, Houghton, Saunders
03/12	Peterborough Utd	A	0–1	14,114	

UEFA CUP

DATE	OPPOSITION	VENUE	SCORE	ATT	GOALSCORERS
18/09	Kuusysi Lahti	H	6–1	17,131	Saunders (4), Houghton (2)
02/10	Kuusysi Lahti	A	0–1	8,435	
23/10	Auxerre	A	0–2	16,500	
06/11	Auxerre	H	3–0	23,094	Molby (pen), Marsh, Walters
27/11	Swarovski Tirol	A	2–0	12,500	Saunders (2)
11/12	Swarovski Tirol	H	4–0	16,007	Saunders (3), Venison
04/03	Genoa (q–f)	A	0–2	40,000	
18/03	Genoa (q–f)	H	1–2	38,840	Rush

1992–93

CHARITY SHIELD

DATE	OPPOSITION	VENUE	SCORE	ATT	GOALSCORERS
08/08	Leeds U	N	3–4	61,201	Rush (2), Saunders (o.g.) (Played at Wembley)

PREMIER LEAGUE

DATE	OPPOSITION	VENUE	SCORE	ATT	GOALSCORERS
16/08	Nottingham F	A	0–1	20,038	
19/08	Sheffield Utd	H	2–1	33,107	Walters, Stewart
23/08	Arsenal	H	0–2	34,961	
25/08	Ipswich T	A	2–2	20,109	Walters, Molby (pen)
29/08	Leeds Utd	A	2–2	29,597	Whelan, Molby (pen)
01/09	Southampton	H	1–1	30,024	Wright
05/09	Chelsea	A	2–1	34,199	Saunders, Redknapp
12/09	Sheffield Utd	A	0–1	20,632	
19/09	Aston Villa	H	2–4	37,863	Walters, Rosenthal
26/09	Wimbledon	H	2–3	29,574	Molby (pen), McManaman
03/10	Sheffield Wed	H	1–0	35,785	Hutchison
18/10	Manchester Utd	A	2–2	33,243	Hutchison, Rush
25/10	Norwich C	H	4–1	36,318	Thomas, Hutchison, Burrows, Walters (pen)
31/10	Tottenham H	A	0–2	32,917	
07/11	Middlesbrough	H	4–1	34,974	Rosenthal (2), McManaman, Rush
23/11	Q.P.R.	A	1–0	21,056	Rosenthal
28/11	Crystal P	H	5–0	36,380	McManaman (2), Marsh, Rosenthal, Hutchison
07/12	Everton	A	1–2	35,826	Wright
13/12	Blackburn R	H	2–1	43,668	Walters
19/12	Coventry C	A	1–5	19,779	Redknapp
28/12	Manchester C	H	1–1	43,037	Rush
09/01	Aston Villa	A	1–2	40,826	Barnes
16/01	Wimbledon	A	0–2	11,294	
31/01	Arsenal	H	1–0	27,580	Barnes (pen)
06/02	Nottingham F	H	0–0	40,463	
10/02	Chelsea	A	0–0	20,981	
13/02	Southampton	A	1–2	17,216	Hutchison
20/02	Ipswich T	H	0–0	36,680	
27/02	Sheffield Wed	A	1–1	33,964	Hutchison
06/03	Manchester Utd	H	1–2	44,374	Rush
10/03	Q.P.R.	H	1–0	30,370	Rush
13/03	Middlesbrough	A	2–1	22,463	Hutchison, Rush
20/03	Everton	H	1–0	44,619	Rosenthal
23/03	Crystal P	A	1–1	18,688	Rush
03/04	Blackburn R	A	1–4	15,032	Rush
10/04	Oldham A	H	1–0	36,129	Rush
12/04	Manchester C	A	1–1	28,098	Rush
17/04	Coventry C	H	4–0	33,328	Walters (3; 1 pen), Burrows
21/04	Leeds Utd	H	2–0	34,992	Barnes, Walters (pen)
01/05	Norwich C	A	0–1	20,610	
05/05	Oldham A	A	2–3	15,381	Rush (2)
08/05	Tottenham H	H	6–2	43,385	Rush (2), Barnes (2), Harkness, Walters (pen)

Premier League Position 6th P42 Pts 59

FA CUP

DATE	OPPOSITION	VENUE	SCORE	ATT	GOALSCORERS
03/01	Bolton W	A	2–2	21,502	Winstanley (o.g.), Rush
13/01	Bolton W	H	0–2	34,790	

LEAGUE CUP (COCA-COLA CUP)

DATE	OPPOSITION	VENUE	SCORE	ATT	GOALSCORERS
22/09	Chesterfield	H	4–4	12,533	Rosenthal, Hutchinson, Walters, Wright
06/10	Chesterfield	A	4–1	10,632	Hutchinson, Redknapp, Walters, Rush
28/10	Sheffield Utd	A	0–0	17,856	
11/11	Sheffield Utd	H	3–0	17,654	McManaman (2), Marsh (pen)
01/12	Crystal P	H	1–1	18,525	Marsh (pen)
16/12	Crystal P	A	1–2	19,622	Marsh (pen)

EUROPEAN CUP WINNERS' CUP

DATE	OPPOSITION	VENUE	SCORE	ATT	GOALSCORERS
16/09	Apollon Limassol	H	6–1	12,769	Stewart (2), Rush (4)
29/09	Apollon Limassol	A	2–1	8,000	Rush, Hutchison
22/10	Spartak Moscow	A	2–4	60,000	Wright, McManaman
04/11	Spartak Moscow	H	0–2	37,993	

1993–94

PREMIER LEAGUE

DATE	OPPOSITION	VENUE	SCORE	ATT	GOAL SCORERS
14/08	Sheffield Wed	H	2–0	44,004	Clough (2)
18/08	Q.P.R.	A	3–1	19,635	Nicol, Clough, Rush
22/08	Swindon T	A	5–0	17,017	Ruddock, Whelan, McManaman (2), Marsh
25/08	Tottenham H	H	1–2	42,456	Clough
28/08	Leeds Utd	H	2–0	44,068	Molby (pen), Rush
01/09	Coventry C	A	0–1	16,740	
12/09	Blackburn R	H	0–1	37,355	
18/09	Everton	A	0–2	38,157	
25/09	Chelsea	A	0–1	31,271	
02/10	Arsenal	H	0–0	42,750	
16/10	Oldham Ath	H	2–1	32,661	Fowler, Barlow (o.g.)
23/10	Manchester C	A	1–1	30,403	Rush
30/10	Southampton	H	4–2	32,818	Rush, Fowler (3)
06/11	West Ham Utd	A	2–0	42,254	Clough, Martin (o.g.)
21/11	Newcastle Utd	A	0–3	36,374	
28/11	Aston Villa	H	2–1	38,484	Redknapp, Fowler
04/12	Sheffield Wed	A	1–3	32,177	Fowler
08/12	Q.P.R.	H	3–2	24,561	Molby (pen), Barnes, Rush
11/12	Swindon T	H	2–2	32,739	Wright, Barnes
18/12	Tottenham H	A	3–3	31,394	Redknapp, Fowler (2,1 pen)
26/12	Sheffield Utd	A	0–0	22,932	
28/12	Wimbledon	H	1–1	32,232	Scales (o.g.)
01/01	Ipswich T	H	2–1	22,355	Ruddock, Rush
04/01	Manchester Utd	H	3–3	42,795	Ruddock, Clough (2)
15/01	Oldham A	H	3–0	14,573	Dicks, Redknapp, Fowler
22/01	Manchester C	H	2–1	41,872	Rush (2)
05/02	Norwich C	H	2–2	19,746	Barnes, Culverhouse (o.g.)
14/02	Southampton	A	2–4	18,306	Dicks (pen), Rush
19/02	Leeds Utd	A	0–2	40,053	
26/02	Coventry C	H	1–0	38,547	Rush
05/03	Blackburn R	A	0–2	20,831	
13/03	Everton	H	2–1	44,281	Rush, Fowler
19/03	Chelsea	H	2–1	38,629	Rush, Burley (o.g.)
26/03	Arsenal	A	0–1	35,556	
30/03	Manchester Utd	A	0–1	44,751	
02/04	Sheffield Utd	H	1–2	36,642	Rush
04/04	Wimbledon	A	1–1	13,819	Redknapp
09/04	Ipswich T	H	1–0	30,485	Dicks (pen)
16/04	Newcastle Utd	H	0–2	44,601	
23/04	West Ham Utd	A	2–1	26,096	Rush, Fowler
30/04	Norwich C	H	0–1	44,339	
07/05	Aston Villa	A	1–2	45,347	Fowler

Premier League Position 8th P42 Pts 60

FA CUP

DATE	OPPOSITION	VENUE	SCORE	ATT	GOALSCORERS
19/01	Bristol C	A	1–1	21,718	Rush
25/01	Bristol C	H	0–1	36,720	

LEAGUE CUP (COCA-COLA CUP)

DATE	OPPOSITION	VENUE	SCORE	ATT	GOALSCORERS
22/09	Fulham	A	3–1	13,599	Clough, Rush, Fowler
05/10	Fulham	H	5–0	12,541	Fowler (5)
27/10	Ipswich T	H	3–2	19,058	Rush (3)
01/12	Wimbledon	H	1–1	19,290	Molby (pen)
14/12	Wimbledon	A	2–2	11,343	Ruddock, Segers (o.g.) (a.e.t.)
					(Wimbledon won 4–3 on penalties)

1994–95

PREMIER LEAGUE

DATE	OPPOSITION	VENUE	SCORE	ATT	GOALSCORERS
20/08	Crystal P	A	6–1	18,084	Molby (pen), McManaman (2), Fowler, Rush (2)
28/08	Arsenal	H	3–0	30,017	Fowler (3)
31/08	Southampton	A	2–0	15,190	Fowler, Barnes
10/09	West Ham Utd	H	0–0	30,907	
17/09	Manchester Ud	A	0–2	43,740	
24/09	Newcastle Utd	A	1–1	34,435	Rush
01/10	Sheffield Wed	H	4–1	31,493	McManaman (2), Walker (o.g.), Rush
08/10	Aston Villa	H	3–2	32,158	Ruddock, Fowler (2)
15/10	Blackburn R	A	2–3	30,263	Fowler, Barnes
22/10	Wimbledon	H	3–0	31,139	McManaman, Fowler, Barnes
29/10	Ipswich T	A	3–1	22,513	Barnes, Fowler (2)
31/10	Q.P.R.	A	1–2	18,295	Barnes
05/11	Nottingham F	H	1–0	33,329	Fowler
09/11	Chelsea	H	3–1	32,855	Fowler (2), Ruddock
21/11	Everton	A	0–2	39,866	
26/11	Tottenham H	H	1–1	35,007	Fowler (pen)
03/12	Coventry C	A	1–1	21,029	Rush
11/12	Crystal P	H	0–0	30,972	
18/12	Chelsea	A	0–0	27,050	
26/12	Leicester C	A	2–1	21,393	Fowler (pen), Rush
28/12	Manchester C	H	2–0	38,122	Fowler, Phelan (o.g.)
31/12	Leeds Utd	A	2–0	38,563	Redknapp, Fowler
02/01	Norwich C	H	4–0	34,709	Scales, Fowler (2), Rush
14/01	Ipswich T	H	0–1	32,733	
24/01	Everton	H	0–0	39,505	
04/02	Nottingham F	A	1–1	25,418	Fowler
11/02	Q.P.R.	H	1–1	35,996	Scales
25/02	Sheffield Wed	A	2–1	31,964	Barnes, McManaman
04/03	Newcastle Utd	H	2–0	39,300	Fowler, Rush
14/03	Coventry C	H	2–3	27,183	Molby (pen), D.Burrows (o.g.)
19/03	Manchester Utd	A	2–0	38,906	Bruce (o.g.), Redknapp
22/03	Tottenham H	A	0–0	31,988	
05/04	Southampton	H	3–1	29,881	Rush (2), Fowler (pen)
09/04	Leeds Utd	H	0–1	37,454	
12/04	Arsenal	A	1–0	38,036	Fowler
14/04	Manchester C	A	1–2	27,055	McManaman
17/04	Leicester C	H	2–0	36,012	Fowler, Rush
29/04	Norwich C	A	2–1	21,843	Harkness, Rush
02/05	Wimbledon	A	0–0	12,041	
06/05	Aston Villa	A	0–2	40,154	
10/05	West Ham Utd	A	0–3	22,446	
14/05	Blackburn R	H	2–1	40,014	Barnes, Redknapp

Premier League Position 4th P42 Pts 74

FA CUP

DATE	OPPOSITION	VENUE	SCORE	ATT	GOALSCORERS
07/01	Birmingham C	A	0–0	25,326	
18/01	Birmingham C	H	1–1	36,275	Redknapp (a.e.t.) (Liverpool won 2–0 on penalties)
28/01	Burnley	A	0–0	20,511	
07/02	Burnley	H	1–0	32,109	Barnes
19/02	Wimbledon	H	1–1	25,124	Fowler
28/02	Wimbledon	A	2–0	12,553	Barnes, Rush
11/03	Tottenham H	H	1–2	39,592	Fowler

LEAGUE CUP (COCA-COLA CUP)

DATE	OPPOSITION	VENUE	SCORE	ATT	GOALSCORERS
21/09	Burnley	H	2–0	23,359	Sclaes, Fowler
05/10	Burney	A	4–1	19,032	Redknapp (2), Fowler, Clough
25/10	Stoke C	H	2–1	32,060	Rush (2)
30/11	Blackburn R	A	3–1	30,115	Rush (3)
11/01	Arsenal	H	1–0	36,004	Rush
15/01	Crystal P (s–f)	H	1–0	25,480	Fowler
08/03	Crystal P (s–f)	H	1–0	18,224	Fowler
02/04	Bolton W	N	2–1	75,595	McManaman (2) (at Wembley)

1995–96

PREMIER LEAGUE

DATE	OPPOSITION	VENUE	SCORE	ATT	GOAL SCORERS
19/08	Sheffield Wed	H	1–0	40,535	Collymore
21/08	Leeds Utd	A	0–1	35,852	
26/08	Tottenham H	A	3–1	31,254	Barnes (2), Fowler
30/08	Q.P.R.	H	1–0	37,548	Ruddock
09/09	Wimbledon	A	0–1	19,530	

1995–96 (CONTINUED)

DATE	OPPOSITION	VENUE	SCORE	ATT	GOALSCORERS
16/09	Blackburn R	H	3–0	39,502	Redknapp, Fowler, Collymore
23/09	Bolton W	H	5–2	40,104	Fowler (4), Harkness
01/10	Manchester Utd	A	2–2	34,934	Fowler (2)
14/10	Coventry C	H	0–0	39,079	
22/10	Southampton	A	3–1	15,245	McManaman (2), Redknapp
28/10	Manchester C	H	6–0	39,267	Rush (2), Redknapp, Fowler (2), Ruddock
04/11	Newcastle Utd	A	1–2	36,547	Rush
18/11	Everton	H	1–2	40,818	Fowler
22/11	West Ham Utd	A	0–0	24,324	
25/11	Middlesbrough	A	1–2	29,390	Ruddock
02/12	Southampton	H	1–1	38,007	Collymore
09/12	Bolton W	A	1–0	21,042	Collymore
17/12	Manchester Utd	H	2–0	40,546	Fowler (2)
23/12	Arsenal	H	3–1	39,806	Fowler (3)
30/12	Chelsea	A	2–2	31,137	McManaman (2)
01/01	Nottingham F	H	4–2	39,206	Fowler (2), Collymore, Cooper (o.g.)
13/01	Sheffield Wed	A	1–1	32,747	Rush
20/01	Leeds Utd	H	5–0	40,254	Ruddock (2), Fowler (2, 1 pen), Collymore
31/01	Aston Villa	A	2–0	39,332	Collymore, Fowler
03/02	Tottenham H	H	0–0	40,628	
11/02	Q.P.R.	A	2–1	18,405	Wright, Fowler
24/02	Blackburn R	A	3–2	33,168	Collymore (2), Thomas
03/03	Aston Villa	H	3–0	39,568	McManaman, Fowler (2)
13/03	Wimbledon	H	2–2	34,063	Collymore, McManaman
16/03	Chelsea	H	2–0	40,820	Wright, Fowler
20/03	Leeds Utd	A	0–1	30,812	McManaman, Fowler
23/03	Nottingham F	A	0–1	29,058	
03/04	Newcastle Utd	H	4–3	40,702	Fowler (2), Collymore (2)
06/04	Coventry C	A	0–1	23,137	
08/04	West Ham Utd	H	2–0	40,326	Collymore, Barnes
16/04	Everton	A	1–1	39,022	Fowler
27/04	Middlesbrough	H	1–0	40,782	Collymore
01/05	Arsenal	A	0–0	38,323	
05/05	Manchester C	A	2–2	31,436	Lomas (o.g.), Barnes

Premier League Position 3rd P42 Pts 71

FA CUP

DATE	OPPOSITION	VENUE	SCORE	ATT	GOALSCORERS
06/01	Rochdale	H	7–0	28,126	McAteer, Collymore (3), Rush, Fowler, Valentine (o.g.)
18/02	Shrewsbury	A	4–0	7,752	McAteer, Collymore, Fowler, Walton (o.g.)
28/02	Charlton	A	2–1	36,818	Fowler, Collymore
10/03	Leeds Utd	A	0–0	34,632	
20/03	Leeds Utd	H	3–0	30,812	McManaman (2), Fowler
31/03	Aston Villa (s–f)	N	3–0	39,072	Fowler (2), McAteer
17/05	Manchester Utd	N	0–1	79,007	(at Wembley)

LEAGUE CUP (COCA-COLA CUP)

DATE	OPPOSITION	VENUE	SCORE	ATT	GOALSCORERS
20/09	Sunderland	H	2–0	25,579	McManaman, Thomas
04/10	Sunderland	A	1–0	20,560	Fowler
25/10	Manchester C	H	4–0	29,394	Scales, Fowler, Rush, Harkness
29/11	Newcastle Utd	H	0–1	40,077	

UEFA CUP

DATE	OPPOSITION	VENUE	SCORE	ATT	GOALSCORERS
12/09	Spartak Vladikavkaz	A	2–1	43,000	McManaman, Redknapp
26/09	Spartak Vladikavkaz	H	0–0	35,042	
17/10	Brondby	A	0–0	37,648	
31/10	Brondby	H	0–1	35,878	

1996–97

PREMIER LEAGUE

DATE	OPPOSITION	VENUE	SCORE	ATT	GOALSCORERS
17/08	Middlesbrough	A	3–3	30,039	Bjornebye, Barnes, Fowler
19/08	Arsenal	H	2–0	38,103	McManaman (2)
24/08	Sunderland	H	0–0	40,508	
04/09	Coventry C	A	1–0	23,021	Babb
07/09	Southampton	H	2–1	39,189	Collymore, McManaman
15/09	Leicester C	A	3–0	20,987	Berger (2), Thomas
21/09	Chelsea	H	5–1	40,739	Fowler, Barnes, Berger (2), Myers (o.g.)
29/09	West Ham Utd	A	2–1	25,064	Collymore, Thomas
12/10	Manchester Utd	A	0–1	55,128	
27/10	Derby Co	H	2–1	39,515	Fowler (2)
03/11	Blackburn R	A	0–3	29,598	
16/11	Leeds Utd	A	2–0	39,981	Ruddock, McManaman
20/11	Everton	H	1–1	40,751	Fowler
23/11	Wimbledon	H	1–1	39,027	Collymore
02/12	Tottenham H	A	2–0	32,899	Thomas, McManaman
07/12	Sheffield Wed	H	0–1	39,507	
14/12	Middlesbrough	H	5–1	39,491	Fowler (4), Bjornebye
17/12	Nottingham F	H	4–2	36,126	Collymore (2), Fowler, Lyttle (o.g.)
23/12	Newcastle Utd	A	1–1	36,570	Fowler
26/12	Leicester C	H	1–1	40,786	Collymore
29/12	Southampton	A	1–0	15,222	Barnes
01/01	Chelsea	A	0–1	38,329	
11/01	West Ham Utd	H	0–0	40,102	
18/01	Aston Villa	H	3–0	40,489	Carragher, Collymore, Fowler
01/02	Derby Co	A	1–0	18,102	Collymore
19/02	Leeds Utd	H	4–0	38,957	Fowler, Collymore (2), Redknapp
22/02	Blackburn R	H	0–0	40,747	
02/03	Aston Villa	A	0–1	39,839	
10/03	Newcastle Utd	H	4–3	40,751	McManaman, Berger, Fowler (2)
15/03	Nottingham F	A	1–1	29,181	Fowler
24/03	Arsenal	A	2–1	36,068	Collymore, McAteer
06/04	Coventry C	H	1–2	40,079	Fowler
03/04	Sunderland	A	2–1	22,938	Fowler, McManaman
16/04	Everton	A	1–1	40,177	Thomsen (o.g.)
19/04	Manchester Utd	H	1–3	40,892	Barnes
03/05	Tottenham H	H	2–1	40,003	Collymore, Berger
06/05	Wimbledon	A	1–2	20,016	Owen
11/05	Sheffield Wed	A	1–1	38,943	Redknapp

Premier League Position 4th P38 Pts 68

FA CUP

DATE	OPPOSITION	VENUE	SCORE	ATT	GOALSCORERS
04/01	Burnley	H	1–0	33,252	Collymore
26/01	Chelsea	A	2–4	27,950	Fowler, Collymore

LEAGUE CUP (COCA-COLA CUP)

DATE	OPPOSITION	VENUE	SCORE	ATT	GOALSCORERS
23/10	Charlton	H	1–1	15,000	Fowler
13/11	Charlton	A	4–1	20,714	Wright, Redknapp, Fowler (2)
27/11	Arsenal	H	4–2	32,814	McManaman, Fowler (2; 1pen), Berger
08/01	Middlesbrough	A	1–2	28,670	McManaman

EUROPEAN CUP WINNERS' CUP

DATE	OPPOSITION	VENUE	SCORE	ATT	GOALSCORERS
12/09	MyPa	A	1–0	5,500	Bjornebye
26/09	MyPa	H	3–1	39,013	Berger, Collymore, Barnes
17/10	FC Sion	A	2–1	16,500	Fowler, Barnes
31/10	FC Sion	H	6–3	38,514	McManaman, Bjornebye, Barnes, Fowler (2), Berger
06/03	Brann Bergen	A	1–1	12,700	Fowler
20/03	Brann Bergen	H	3–0	40,326	Fowler (2, 1 pen), Collymore
10/04	Paris St Germain	A	0–3	35,142	
24/04	Paris St Germain	H	2–0	38,954	Fowler, Wright

1997–98

PREMIER LEAGUE

DATE	OPPOSITION	VENUE	SCORE	ATT	GOALSCORERS
09/08	Wimbledon	A	1–1	26,106	Owen (pen)
13/08	Leicester C	H	1–2	35,007	Ince
23/08	Blackburn R	A	1–1	30,187	Owen
26/08	Leeds Utd	A	2–0	39,775	McManaman, Riedle
13/09	Sheffield Wed	A	2–1	34,705	Ince, Thomas
20/09	Southampton	A	1–1	15,252	Riedle
22/09	Aston Villa	H	3–0	34,843	Fowler (pen), McManaman, Riedle
27/09	West Ham Utd	A	1–2	25,908	Fowler
05/10	Chelsea	H	4–2	36,647	Berger, Fowler (3)
18/10	Everton	A	0–2	40,112	
25/10	Derby Co	H	4–0	38,017	Fowler (2), Leonhardsen, McManaman
01/11	Bolton W	A	1–1	25,000	Fowler
08/11	Tottenham H	A	4–0	38,006	McManaman, Leonhardsen, Redknapp, Owen
22/11	Barnsley	H	0–1	41,011	
30/11	Arsenal	A	1–0	38,094	McManaman
06/12	Manchester Utd	H	1–3	41,027	Fowler (pen)
13/12	Crystal P	A	3–0	25,790	McManaman, Owen, Leonhardsen
20/12	Coventry C	H	1–0	39,707	Owen
26/12	Leeds Utd	H	3–1	43,854	Owen, Fowler (2)
28/12	Newcastle Utd	A	2–1	36,702	McManaman (2)
10/01	Wimbledon	H	2–0	38,011	Redknapp (2)
17/01	Leicester C	A	0–0	21,633	
20/01	Newcastle Utd	H	2–1	42,791	Owen
31/01	Blackburn R	H	0–0	43,980	
07/02	Southampton	A	2–3	43,550	Owen (2)
14/02	Sheffield Wed	A	3–3	34,405	Owen (3)
23/02	Everton	H	1–1	44,501	Ince
28/02	Aston Villa	A	1–2	39,372	Owen (pen)
07/03	Bolton W	H	2–1	44,532	Ince, Owen
14/03	Tottenham H	H	3–3	30,245	McManaman (2), Ince
28/03	Barnsley	A	3–2	18,648	Riedle (2), McManaman
10/04	Manchester Utd	A	1–1	55,171	Owen
13/04	Crystal P	H	2–1	43,007	Leonhardsen, Thompson
19/04	Coventry C	A	1–1	22,721	Owen
25/04	Chelsea	A	1–4	34,639	Riedle
02/05	West Ham Utd	H	5–0	44,414	Owen, McAteer (2), Leonhardsen, Ince
06/05	Arsenal	H	4–0	44,417	Ince (2), Owen, Leonhardsen
10/05	Derby Co	A	0–1	30,492	

Premier League Position 3rd P38 Pts 65

FA CUP

DATE	OPPOSITION	VENUE	SCORE	ATT	GOALSCORERS
03/01	Coventry City	H	1–3	33,888	Redknapp

LEAGUE CUP (COCA-COLA CUP)

DATE	OPPOSITION	VENUE	SCORE	ATT	GOALSCORERS
15/10	West Brom	A	2–0	21,986	Berger, Fowler
18/11	Grimsby T	H	3–0	28,515	Owen (3; 1 pen)
07/01	Newcastle Utd	A	2–0	33,207	Owen, Fowler
27/01	Middlesbrough	H	2–1	33,438	Redknapp, Fowler
18/01	Middlesbrough	A	0–2	29,828	

UEFA CUP

DATE	OPPOSITION	VENUE	SCORE	ATT	GOALSCORERS
16/09	Celtic	A	2–2	48,526	Owen, McManaman
30/09	Celtic	H	0–0	38,205	(won on away goals rule)
21/10	Strasbourg	A	0–3	18,813	
04/11	Strasbourg	H	2–0	32,426	Fowler (pen), Riedle

1998–99

PREMIER LEAGUE

DATE	OPPOSITION	VENUE	SCORE	ATT	GOALSCORERS
16/08	Southampton	A	2–1	15,202	Riedle, Owen
22/08	Arsenal	H	0–0	44,429	
30/08	Newcastle Utd	A	4–1	36,740	Owen (3), Berger
09/09	Coventry C	H	2–0	41,771	Berger, Redknapp
12/09	West Ham Utd	A	1–2	26,029	Riedle
19/09	Charlton A	H	3–3	44,526	Fowler (2), Berger
24/09	Manchester Utd	A	0–2	55,181	
04/10	Chelsea	H	1–1	44,404	Redknapp
17/10	Everton	A	0–0	40,185	
24/10	Nottingham F	H	5–1	44,595	Owen (4), McManaman
31/10	Leicester C	A	0–1	21,837	
07/11	Derby Co	H	1–2	44,020	Redknapp
14/11	Leeds Utd	A	1–3	44,305	Fowler
20/11	Aston Villa	H	4–2	39,241	Ince, Fowler (3)
29/11	Blackburn R	A	2–0	41,753	Ince, Owen
05/12	Tottenham H	A	1–2	36,521	Berger
13/12	Wimbledon	A	0–1	26,080	

DATE	OPPOSITION	VENUE	SCORE	ATT	GOALSCORERS
19/12	Sheffield Wed	H	2–0	40,003	Berger, Owen
26/12	Middlesbrough	A	3–1	34,626	Owen, Redknapp, Heggem
28/12	Newcastle Utd	A	4–2	44,605	Owen (2), Riedle (2)
09/01	Arsenal	A	0–0	38,107	
16/01	Southampton	H	7–1	44,011	Fowler (3), Matteo, Carragher, Owen, Thompson
30/01	Coventry C	A	1–2	23,056	McManaman
06/02	Middlesbrough	H	3–1	44,384	Owen, Heggem, Ince
13/02	Charlton A	A	0–1	20,043	
20/02	West Ham Utd	H	2–2	44,511	Fowler, Owen
27/02	Chelsea	A	1–2	34,822	Owen
13/03	Derby Co	A	2–3	32,913	Fowler (2; 1 pen)
03/04	Everton	H	3–2	44,852	Fowler (2; 1 pen), Berger
05/04	Nottingham F	A	2–2	28,374	Redknapp, Owen
12/04	Leeds Utd	A	0–0	39,451	
17/04	Aston Villa	H	0–1	44,306	
21/04	Leicester C	A	0–1	36,019	
24/04	Blackburn R	A	3–1	29,944	McManaman, Redknapp, Leonhardsen
01/05	Tottenham H	H	3–2	44,007	Redknapp, Ince, McManaman
05/05	Manchester Utd	H	2–2	44,702	Redknapp (pen), Ince
08/05	Sheffield Wed	A	0–1	27,383	
16/05	Wimbledon	H	3–0	44,000	Riedle, Berger, Ince

Premier League Position 7th P38 Pts 54

FA CUP

DATE	OPPOSITION	VENUE	SCORE	ATT	GOALSCORERS
03/01	Port Vale	A	3–0	16,557	Fowler, Owen, Ince
24/01	Manchester Utd	A	1–2	54,591	Owen

LEAGUE CUP (WORTHINGTON CUP)

DATE	OPPOSITION	VENUE	SCORE	ATT	GOALSCORERS
27/10	Fulham	H	3–1	22,296	Morgan (o.g.), Fowler (pen), Ince
10/11	Tottenham H	H	1–3	20,772	Owen

UEFA CUP

DATE	OPPOSITION	VENUE	SCORE	ATT	GOALSCORERS
15/09	Kosice	A	3–0	4,500	Berger, Riedle, Owen
29/09	Kosice	H	5–0	23,792	Redknapp (2), Ince, Fowler (2)
20/10	Valencia	H	0–0	26,004	
03/11	Valencia	A	2–2	53,000	McManaman, Berger (Liverpool win on away goals)
24/11	Celta Vigo	A	1–3	24,600	Owen
08/12	Celta Vigo	H	0–1	30,289	

1999–00

PREMIER LEAGUE

DATE	OPPOSITION	VENUE	SCORE	ATT	GOALSCORERS
07/08	Sheffield Wed	A	2–1	34,853	Fowler, Camara
14/08	Watford	H	0–1	44,174	
21/08	Middlesbrough	A	0–1	34,783	
23/08	Leeds Utd	A	2–1	39,703	Camara, Radebe (o.g.)
28/08	Arsenal	H	2–0	44,886	Fowler, Berger
11/09	Manchester Utd	H	2–3	44,929	Hyypia, Berger
18/09	Leicester C	A	2–2	21,623	Owen (2;1 pen)
27/09	Everton	H	0–1	44,802	
02/10	Aston Villa	A	0–0	39,127	
15/10	Chelsea	H	1–0	44,826	Thompson
23/10	Southampton	A	1–1	15,241	Camara
27/10	West Ham Utd	H	1–0	44,012	Camara
01/11	Bradford C	A	3–1	40,483	Camara, Redknapp (pen), Heggem
06/11	Derby Co	H	2–0	44,467	Murphy, Redknapp
20/11	Sunderland	A	2–0	42,015	Owen, Berger
27/11	West Ham Utd	A	0–1	26,043	
05/12	Sheffield Wed	H	4–1	42,517	Hyypia, Murphy, Gerrard, Thompson
18/12	Coventry C	H	2–0	44,024	Owen, Camara
26/12	Newcastle Utd	A	2–2	36,445	Owen (2)
28/12	Wimbledon	H	3–1	44,107	Owen, Berger, Fowler
03/01	Tottenham H	A	0–1	36,044	
15/01	Watford	A	3–2	21,367	Berger, Thompson, Smicer
22/01	Middlesbrough	H	0–0	44,324	
05/02	Leeds Utd	H	3–1	44,793	Hamann, Berger, Murphy
13/02	Arsenal	A	1–0	38,098	Camara
04/03	Manchester Utd	A	1–1	61,592	Berger
11/03	Sunderland	H	1–1	44,693	Berger (pen)
15/03	Aston Villa	H	0–0	43,615	
18/03	Derby Co	A	2–0	33,378	Owen, Camara
25/03	Newcastle Utd	H	2–1	44,743	Camara, Redknapp
01/04	Coventry C	A	3–0	23,098	Owen (2), Heskey
09/04	Tottenham H	H	2–0	44,536	Berger, Owen
16/04	Wimbledon	A	2–1	26,102	Heskey (2)
21/04	Everton	A	0–0	40,052	
29/04	Chelsea	A	0–2	34,957	
03/05	Leicester C	H	0–2	43,536	
07/05	Southampton	H	0–0	43,456	
14/05	Bradford C	A	0–1	18,276	

Premier League Position 4th P38 Pts 67

FA CUP

DATE	OPPOSITION	VENUE	SCORE	ATT	GOALSCORERS
12/12	Huddersfield T	A	2–0	23,678	Camara, Matteo
10/01	Blackburn R	H	0–1	32,839	

WORTHINGTON CUP

DATE	OPPOSITION	VENUE	SCORE	ATT	GOALSCORERS
14/09	Hull C	A	5–1	10,034	Murphy (2), Meijer (2), Staunton
21/09	Hull C	H	4–2	24,318	Murphy, Maxwell, Riedle (2)
13/10	Southampton	A	1–2	13,822	Owen

2000–01

PREMIER LEAGUE

DATE	OPPOSITION	VENUE	SCORE	ATT	GOALSCORERS
19/08	Bradford C	H	1–0	44,183	Heskey
21/08	Arsenal	A	0–2	38,014	
26/08	Southampton	A	3–3	15,202	Owen (2), Hyypia
06/09	Aston Villa	H	3–1	43,360	Owen (3)
09/09	Manchester C	H	3–2	44,692	Owen, Hamann (2)

DATE	OPPOSITION	VENUE	SCORE	ATT	GOALSCORERS
17/09	West Ham Utd	A	1–1	25,998	Gerrard
23/09	Sunderland	H	1–1	44,713	Owen
01/10	Chelsea	A	0–3	34,966	
15/10	Derby Co	A	4–0	30,532	Heskey (3), Berger
21/10	Leicester C	H	1–0	44,395	Heskey
29/10	Everton	H	3–1	44,718	Barmby, Heskey, Berger (pen)
04/11	Leeds Utd	A	3–4	40,055	Hyypia, Ziege, Smicer
12/11	Coventry C	H	4–1	43,701	McAllister, Gerrard, Heskey (2)
19/11	Tottenham H	H	1–2	36,036	Fowler
26/11	Newcastle Utd	A	1–2	51,949	Heskey
02/12	Charlton A	H	3–0	43,515	Fish (o.g.), Heskey, Babbel
10/12	Ipswich T	H	0–1		
17/12	Manchester Utd	A	1–0	67,533	Murphy
23/12	Arsenal	H	4–0	44,144	Gerrard, Owen, Berger, Fowler
26/12	Middlesbrough	A	0–1	34,696	
01/01	Southampton	H	2–1	38,474	Gerrard, Babbel
13/01	Aston Villa	A	3–0	41,336	Murphy (2), Gerrard
20/01	Middlesbrough	H	0–0	43,042	
31/01	Manchester C	A	1–1	34,629	Heskey
03/02	West Ham Utd	H	3–0	44,045	Smicer, Fowler (2)
10/02	Sunderland	A	1–1	47,533	Litmanen (pen)
03/03	Leicester C	A	0–2	21,924	
18/03	Derby Co	H	1–1	43,362	Owen
31/03	Manchester Utd	H	2–0	44,806	Gerrard, Fowler
10/04	Ipswich T	A	1–1	23,504	Heskey
13/04	Leeds Utd	H	1–2	44,115	Gerrard
16/04	Everton	A	3–2	40,260	Heskey, Babbel, McAllister
22/04	Tottenham H	H	3–1	43,547	Heskey, McAllister (pen), Fowler
28/04	Coventry C	A	2–0	23,063	Hyypia, McAllister
01/05	Bradford C	A	2–0	22,057	Owen, McAllister
05/05	Newcastle Utd	H	3–0	44,363	Owen (3)
08/05	Chelsea	H	2–2	43,588	Owen (2)
19/05	Charlton A	A	4–0	20,043	Fowler (2), Murphy, Owen

Premier League Position 3rd P38 Pts 69

FA CUP

DATE	OPPOSITION	VENUE	SCORE	ATT	GOALSCORERS
06/01	Rotherham Utd	H	3–0	30,689	Heskey (2), Hamann
27/01	Leeds Utd	A	2–0	37,108	Barmby, Heskey
18/02	Manchester C	H	4–2	36,231	Litmanen (pen), Heskey, Smicer (pen), Babbel
11/03	Tranmere R	A	4–2	16,334	Murphy, Owen, Gerrard, Fowler (pen)
08/04	Wycombe W (s–f)	N	2–1	40,037	Heskey, Fowler (at Villa Park)
12/05	Arsenal	N	2–1	74,200	Owen (2) (final played at Millennium Stadium, Cardiff)

WORTHINGTON CUP

DATE	OPPOSITION	VENUE	SCORE	ATT	GOALSCORERS
01/11	Chelsea	H	2–1	29,370	Murphy, Fowler
29/11	Stoke C	A	8–0	27,109	Ziege, Smicer, Babbel, Fowler (3;1 pen), Hyypia, Murphy
13/12	Fulham	H	3–0	20,144	Owen, Smicer, Barmby
10/01	Crystal P (s–f)	A	1–2	25,933	Smicer
24/01	Crystal P (s–f)	H	5–0	41,854	Smicer, Murphy (2), Biscan, Fowler
25/02	Birmingham C	N	1–1	73,500	Fowler (a.e.t.) (Liverpool won 5–4 on penalties) (Played at Millennium Stadium, Cardiff)

UEFA CUP

DATE	OPPOSITION	VENUE	SCORE	ATT	GOALSCORERS
14/09	Rapid Bucharest	A	1–0	12,000	Barmby
28/09	Rapid Bucharest	H	0–0	37,954	
26/10	Slovan Liberec	H	1–0	29,662	Heskey
09/11	Slovan Liberec	A	3–2	6,808	Barmby, Heskey, Owen
23/11	Olympiakos	A	2–2	43,855	Barmby, Gerrard
07/12	Olympiakos	H	2–0	35,484	Heskey, Barmby
15/02	Roma	A	2–0	59,718	Owen (2)
22/02	Roma	H	0–1	43,688	
08/03	Porto	A	0–0	21,150	
15/03	Porto	H	2–0	40,502	Murphy, Owen
05/03	Barcelona (s–f)	A	0–0	90,000	
19/04	Barcelona (s–f)	H	1–0	44,203	McAllister (pen)
16/05	Alaves	N	5–4	65,000	Babbel, Gerrard, McAllister (pen), Fowler, Geli (o.g.)

2001–02

FA CHARITY SHIELD

DATE	OPPOSITION	VENUE	SCORE	ATT	GOALSCORERS
12/08	Manchester Utd	N	2–1	70,227	Owen, McAllister (Played at Millennium Stadium, Cardiff)

EUROPEAN SUPER CUP

DATE	OPPOSITION	VENUE	SCORE	ATT	GOALSCORERS
24/08	Bayern Munich	N	3–2	15,000	Heskey, Owen, Riise (Played in Monaco)

PREMIER LEAGUE

DATE	OPPOSITION	VENUE	SCORE	ATT	GOALSCORERS
17/08	West Ham Utd	H	2–1	43,935	Owen (2)
27/08	Bolton W	A	1–2	27,205	Heskey
08/09	Aston Villa	H	1–3	44,102	Gerrard
15/09	Everton	A	3–1	39,554	Gerrard, Owen (pen), Riise
22/09	Tottenham H	H	1–0	44,116	Litmanen
30/09	Newcastle Utd	A	2–0	52,095	Riise, Murphy
13/10	Leeds Utd	A	1–1	44,352	Murphy
20/10	Leicester C	A	4–1	21,886	Fowler (3), Hyypia
27/10	Charlton A	A	2–0	22,887	Redknapp, Owen
04/11	Manchester Utd	H	3–1	44,361	Owen (2), Riise
17/11	Blackburn R	A	1–1	28,859	Owen
25/11	Sunderland	H	1–0	43,437	Heskey
01/12	Derby Co	A	1–0	33,289	Owen
08/12	Middlesbrough	A	2–0	43,674	Owen, Berger
12/12	Fulham	H	0–0	37,153	
16/12	Chelsea	A	0–4	41,174	
23/12	Arsenal	H	1–2	44,297	Litmanen
26/12	Aston Villa	A	2–1	42,602	Litmanen, Smicer
29/12	West Ham Utd	A	1–1	35,103	Owen
01/01	Bolton W	H	1–1	43,710	Gerrard
09/01	Southampton	A	0–2	31,527	
13/01	Arsenal	A	1–1	38,132	Riise
19/01	Southampton	H	1–1	43,710	Owen
22/01	Manchester Utd	A	1–0	67,599	Murphy
30/01	Leicester C	H	1–0	42,305	Heskey
03/02	Leeds Utd	A	4–0	40,216	Ferdinand (o.g.), Heskey (2), Owen

2001–02 (CONTINUED)

Date	Opposition	Venue	Score	Att	Goalscorers
09/02	Ipswich T	A	6–0	25,608	Xavier, Heskey (2), Hyypia, Owen (2)
23/02	Everton	H	1–1	44,371	Anelka
02/03	Fulham	A	2–0	21,103	Anelka, Litmanen
06/03	Newcastle Utd	H	3–0	44,204	Murphy (2), Hamann
16/03	Middlesbrough	A	2–1	31,253	Heskey, Riise
24/03	Chelsea	H	1–0	44,203	Smicer
30/03	Charlton A	A	2–0	44,094	Smicer, Owen
13/04	Sunderland	A	1–0	48,335	Owen
20/04	Derby Co	H	2–0	43,510	Owen (2)
27/04	Tottenham H	A	0–1	36,017	
08/05	Blackburn R	H	4–3	40,663	Murphy, Anelka, Hyypia, Heskey
11/05	Ipswich T	H	5–0	44,088	Riise (2), Owen, Smicer, Anelka

Premier League Position 2nd P38 Pts 80

FA CUP

DATE	OPPOSITION	VENUE	SCORE	ATT	GOALSCORERS
05/01	Birmingham C	H	3–0	40,875	Anelka, Owen (2)
27/01	Arsenal	A	0–1	38,092	

LEAGUE CUP (WORTHINGTON CUP)

DATE	OPPOSITION	VENUE	SCORE	ATT	GOALSCORERS
09/10	Grimsby T	H	1–2*	32,672	McAllister (pen)

CHAMPIONS LEAGUE

DATE	OPPOSITION	VENUE	SCORE	ATT	GOALSCORERS
08/08	FC Haka	A	5–0	44,940	Heskey, Owen (3), Hyypia
21/08	FC Haka	H	4–1	31,602	Fowler, Redknapp, Heskey, Wilson (o.g.)
11/09	Boavista	H	1–1	30,015	Owen
19/08	Borussia Dortmund	A	0–0	50,000	
26/09	Dynamo Kiev	H	1–0	33,513	Litmanen
16/10	Dynamo Kiev	A	2–1	55,000	Murphy, Gerrard
24/10	Boavista	A	1–1	6,000	Murphy
30/10	Borussia Dortmund	H	2–0	41,507	Smicer, Wright
20/11	Barcelona	A	1–3	41,521	Owen
05/12	Roma	A	0–0	57,819	
20/02	Galatasaray	A	0–0	41,605	
26/02	Galatasaray	A	1–1	22,105	Heskey
13/03	Barcelona	H	0–0	75,362	
19/03	Roma	H	2–0	41,794	Litmanen (pen), Heskey
03/04	Bayer L'kusen (q–f)	H	1–0	42,454	Hyypia
09/04	Bayer L'kusen (q–f)	A	2–4	22,500	Xavier, Litmanen (Liverpool lose 3–4 on aggregate)

2002–03

COMMUNITY SHIELD

11/08	Arsenal	N	0–1	67,337	(Played at Millennium Stadium, Cardiff)

PREMIER LEAGUE

18/08	Aston Villa	A	1–0	41,183	Riise
24/08	Southampton	H	3–0	43,058	Diouf (2), Murphy
28/08	Blackburn Rovers	A	2–2	29,207	Murphy, Riise
02/09	Newcastle U	H	2–2	43,241	Owen, Hamann
11/09	Birmingham C	H	2–2	43,113	Murphy, Gerrard
14/09	Bolton Wanderers	A	3–2	27,328	Baros (2), Heskey
21/09	WBA	H	2–0	43,830	Baros, Riise
28/09	Manchester C	A	3–0	35,131	Owen (3)
06/10	Chelsea	H	1–0	43,856	Owen
19/10	Leeds U	H	1–0	40,178	Diao
26/10	Tottenham H	H	2–1	44,084	Owen, Murphy
02/11	West Ham u	H	2–0	44,048	Owen (2)
09/11	Middlesbrough	A	0–1	34,747	
17/11	Sunderland	H	0–0	43,074	
23/11	Fulham	A	2–3	18,144	Baros, Hamann
01/12	Manchester U	H	1–2	44,250	Hyypia
07/12	Charlton Athletic	A	0–2	26,694	
15/12	Sunderland	A	1–2	37,118	Baros
22/12	Everton	H	0–0	44,025	
26/12	Blackburn Rovers	H	1–1	43,075	Riise
29/12	Arsenal	A	1–1	38,074	Murphy
01/01	Newcastle U	A	·0–1	52,147	
11/01	Aston Villa	H	1–1	43,210	Owen
18/01	Southampton	A	1–0	32,104	Heskey
28/01	Arsenal	H	2–2	42,668	Heskey, Riise
02/02	West Ham U	A	3–0	35,033	Baros, Heskey, Gerrard
08/02	Middlesbrough	H	1–1	42,247	Riise
23/02	Birmingham City	A	1–2	29,449	Owen
08/03	Bolton Wanderers	H	2–0	41,462	Owen, Diouf
16/03	Tottenham H	A	3–2	36,077	Owen, Heskey, Gerrard
23/03	Leeds Utd	H	3–1	43,021	Owen, Murphy, Gerrard
05/04	Manchester Utd	A	0–4	67,639	
12/04	Fulham	H	2–0	42,120	Heskey, Owen
19/04	Everton	A	2–1	40,169	Owen, Murphy
21/04	Charlton Athletic	H	2–1	42,010	Hyypia, Gerrard
26/04	West Brom A	A	6–0	27,128	Owen (4),Baros (2)
03/05	Manchester C	H	1–2	44,220	Baros
11/05	Chelsea	H	1–2	41,911	Hyypia

Premier League   Position 5th P38 pts 64

FA CUP

05/01	Manchester C	A	1–0	28,586	Murphy
26/01	Crystal Palace	A	0–0	26,054	
05/02	Crystal Palace	H	0–2	35,109	

LEAGUE CUP (WORTHINGTON CUP)

06/11	Southampton	H	3–1	35,870	Baros, Diouf, Berger
04/12	Ipswich Town	H	1–1	26,305	Diouf (aet, Liverpool won 5–4 on penalties. Scorers Baros, Carragher, Diouf, Gerrard, Riise)
18/12	Aston Villa	A	4–3	38,530	Baros, Murphy (2), Gerrard
08/01	Sheffield Utd	A	1–2	30,095	Mellor
21/01	Sheffield utd	H	2–0	43,837	Diouf, Owen (aet)
02/03	Manchester Utd	N	2–0	74,500	Gerrard, Owen (At Millennium Stadium, Cardiff)

EUROPEAN CHAMPIONS LEAGUE

17/09	Valencia	A	0–2	43,000	
25/09	FC Basel	H	1–1	37,634	Baros
02/10	Spartak Moscow	H	5–0	40,812	Hyyia, Heskey (2), Diao, Cheyrou
22/10	Spartak Moscow	A	3–1	15,000	Owen (3)
30/10	Valencia	H	0–1	41,831	
12/11	FC Basel	A	3–3	35,000	Smicer, Owen, Murphy

UEFA CUP

28/11	Vitesse Arnhem	A	1–0	28,000	Owen
12/12	Vitesse Arnhem	H	1–0	23,576	Owen
20/02	Auxerre	A	1–0	20,452	Hyypia
27/02	Auxerre	H	2–0	34,252	Owen, Murphy
13/03	Celtic	A	1–1	59,759	Heskey
20/03	Celtic	H	0–2	44,238	

2003–04

BARCLAYCARD PREMIERSHIP

17/08	Chelsea	H	1–2	44,082	Owen
24/08	Aston Villa	A	0–0	42,573	
27/08	Tottenham H	H	0–0	43,778	
30/08	Everton	A	3–0	40,200	Kewell, Owen (2)
13/09	Blackburn R	A	3–1	30,074	Kewell, Owen (2)
20/09	Leicester C	H	2–1	44,094	Heskey, Owen
28/09	Charlton Athletic	A	2–2	26,508	Smicer, Owen (pen)
04/10	Arsenal	H	1–2	44,374	Kewell
18/10	Portsmouth	A	0–1	20,123	
25/10	Leeds U	H	3–1	43,599	Owen, Murphy, Sinana–Pongolle
02/11	Fulham	A	2–1	17,682	Heskey, Murphy
09/11	Manchester U	H	1–2	44,159	Kewell
22/11	Middlesbrough	A	0–0	34,268	
30/11	Birmingham C	H	3–1	42,683	Gerrard, Kewell, Heskey
06/12	Newcastle Utd	A	1–1	52,151	Murphy
13/12	Southampton	H	1–2	41,762	Heskey
26/12	Bolton Wanderers	H	3–1	42,987	Hyypia, Sinama–Pongolle, Smicer
28/12	Manchester C	H	2–2	47,201	Smicer, Hamann
07/01	Chelsea	A	1–0	41,420	Cheyrou
10/01	Aston Villa	H	1–0	43,771	Delaney o.g
17/01	Tottenham H	A	1–2	36,104	Kewell
21/01	Wolves	A	1–1	29,380	Cheyrou
31/01	Everton	H	0–0	44,056	
07/02	Bolton W	A	2–2	27,552	Hyypia, Gerrard
11/02	Man City	A	2–1	43,257	Owen, Gerrard
29/02	Leeds Utd	A	2–2	39,932	Kewell, Baros
14/03	Southampton	A	0–2	32,056	
17/03	Portsmouth	H	3–0	34,663	Hamann, Owen (2)
20/03	Wolves	H	1–0	43,795	Hyypia
27/03	Leicester	A	0–0	32,013	
04/04	Blackburn R	H	4–0	41,559	Owen (2),Todd o.g, Heskey
10/04	Arsenal	A	2–4	38,119	Hyypia, Owen
12/04	Charlton A	H	0–1	40,003	
17/04	Fulham	H	0–0	42,042	
24/04	Man Utd	A	1–0	67,647	Murphy (pen)
01/05	Middlesbrough	H	2–0	42,031	Murphy (pen), Heskey
08/05	Birmingham C	A	3–0	29,533	Owen, Heskey, Gerrard
15/05	Newcastle United	H	1–1	44,172	Hyypia

Premiership   Position 4th P38 pts 60

FA CUP

04/01	Yeovil	A	2–0	9,348	Heskey, Murphy
24/01	Newcastle United	H	2–1	41,365	Cheyrou (2)
15/02	Portsmouth	H	1–1	34,669	Owen
22/02	Portsmouth (R)	A	0–1	19,529	

LEAGUE CUP (CARLING CUP)

29/10	Blackburn Rovers	A	4–3	16,918	Murphy (pen), Heskey (2), Kewell
03/12	Bolton Wanderers	H	2–3	33,185	Murphy, Smicer

UEFA CUP

24/09	Olimpija Ljubljana	A	1–1	10,000	Owen
15/10	Olimpija Ljubljana	H	3–0	42,880	Le Tallec, Heskey, Kewell
06/11	Steaua Bucuresti	A	1–1	25,000	Traore
27/11	Steaua Bucuresti	H	1–0	42,837	Kewell
25/02	Levski Sofia	H	2–0	39,149	Gerrard, Kewell
03/03	Levski Sofia	A	4–2	40,281	Gerrard, Owen, Hamann, Hyypia
11/03	Marseille	H	1–1	41,270	Baros
25/03	Marseille	A	1–2	50,000	Heskey (LFC lose 2–3 on aggregate)

Football League Champions – *18*

1900–01, 1905–06, 1921–22, 1922–23, 1946–47, 1963–64, 1965–66, 1972–73, 1975–76,
1976–77, 1978–79, 1979–80, 1981–82, 1982–83, 1983–84, 1985–86, 1987–88, 1989–90

Division Two Winners – *4*

1893–94, 1895–96, 1904–05, 1961–62

Lancashire League Winners – *1*

1892–93

Football Association Challenge Cup Winners – *6*

1964–65, 1973–74, 1985–86, 1988–89, 1991–92, 2000–2001

League Cup Winners – *7*

1980–81, 1981–82, 1982–83, 1983–84, 1994–95, 2000–01, 2002–03

Football Association Charity Shield/Community Shield Winners – *15*

1906, 1964*, 1965*, 1966, 1974, 1976, 1977*, 1979, 1980, 1982, 1986*, 1988, 1989, 1990*, 2001

European Cup Winners – *4*

1976–77, 1977–78, 1980–81, 1983–84

UEFA Cup Winners – *3*

1972–73, 1975–76, 2000–01

European Super Cup Winners – *2*

1977–78, 2001–02

Dubai Super Cup Winners – *1*

1985–86

Carlsberg Trophy – *3*

1997–98, 1998–99, 1999–2000

Reserves Division One Winners – *16*

1956–57, 1968–69, 1969–70, 1970–71, 1972–73, 1973–74, 1974–75, 1975–76,
1976–77, 1978–79, 1980–81, 1981–82, 1983–84, 1984–85, 1989–90, 1999–2000

FA Youth Cup Winners – *1*

1995–96

(*denotes shared trophy)

RECORDS

Appearances

Most first team appearances **Ian Callaghan (857)**
Most League appearances **Ian Callaghan (640)**
Most FA Cup appearances **Ian Callaghan (79)**
Most League Cup appearances **Ian Rush (78)**
Most European appearances **Ian Callaghan (89)**
Oldest player **JE "Ted" Doig, 41 yrs & 165 days v Newcastle United (a) 11 April 1908**
Youngest player **Max Thompson, 17 yrs & 129 days v Tottenham Hotspur (a) 8 May 1974**
Most seasons as an ever-present **Phil Neal (9)**
Most consecutive appearances **Phil Neal (417) 23 October 1976 to 24 September 1983**
Longest-serving player **Elisha Scott – 21 yrs & 52 days: 1913 to 1934**
Oldest debutant **JE "Ted" Doig, 37 yrs & 307 days v Burton United (h) 1 September 1904**

Goals

Most first team goals **Ian Rush (346)**
Most League goals **Roger Hunt (245)**
Most FA Cup goals **Ian Rush (39)**
Most League Cup goals **Ian Rush (48)**
Most European goals **Michael Owen (22)**
Highest-scoring substitute **David Fairclough (18)**
Most hat-tricks **Gordon Hodgson (17)**
Most hat-tricks in a season **Roger Hunt (5 in 1961-62)**
Most penalties scored **Jan Molby (42)**
Most games without scoring **Ephraim Longworth (372)**
Youngest goalscorer **Michael Owen, 17 yrs & 144 days v Wimbledon (a) 6 May 1997**
Oldest goalscorer **Billy Liddell, 38 yrs & 55 days v Stoke City (h) 5 March 1960**

Internationals

Most-capped player **Emlyn Hughes (59) England**
Most international goals **Ian Rush (26) Wales**

Honours

Most medals **Phil Neal (20)**

Matches

Record League Win **10-1 v Rotherham Town (h), Division Two, 18 February 1896**
Record FA Cup Win **8-0 v Swansea City (h), 3rd Round replay, 9 January 1990**
Record League Cup Win **10-0 v Fulham (h), 2nd Round 1st Leg, 23 September 1986**
Record European Win **11-0 v Stromgodset (h), Cup Winners' Cup 1st Round 1st Leg, 17 September 1974**
Record League Defeat **1-9 v Birmingham City (a), Division Two, 11 December 1954**
Record FA Cup Defeat **1-5 v Derby County (h), 3rd Round replay, 2 March 1898**
Record League Cup Defeat **1-4 v West Ham United (a), 4th Round, 30 November 1988**
Record European Defeat **1-5 v Ajax (a), European Cup 1st Round 1st Leg, 7 December 1966**

Attendances

Highest League attendance **58,757 v Chelsea, Division One, 27 December 1949**
Highest FA Cup attendance **61,905 v Wolves, 5th Round, 2 February 1952**
Highest League Cup attendance **50,880 v Nottingham Forest, Semi-final 2nd leg, 12 February 1980**
Highest European attendance **55,104 v Barcelona, UEFA Cup Semi-final 2nd leg, 14 April 1976**
Lowest League attendance **1,000 v Loughborough Town, Division Two, 7 December 1895**
Lowest League attendance (post-war) **11,976 v Scunthorpe United, Division Two, 22 April 1959**
Lowest FA Cup attendance **4,000 v Newtown, 2nd Qualifying Round, 29 October 1892**
Lowest FA Cup attendance (post-war) **25,124 v Wimbledon, 5th Round, 19 February 1995**
Lowest League Cup attendance **9,902 v Brentford, 2nd Round 2nd leg, 25 October 1983**
Lowest European attendance **12,021 v Dundalk, European Cup 1st Round 1st leg, 28 September 1982**

CLUB TELEPHONE NUMBERS

Main Switchboard **0151 263 2361**

Ticket Office General **0870 220 2345**
Credit Card Booking Line **0870 220 2151**
UEFA Champions League Bookings **0870 220 0034**
FA Cup/League Cup Booking Line **0870 220 0056**
Priority Booking Line (Priority Ticket Scheme – members only) **0870 220 0408**
24 hour information line **0870 444 4949**

Mail Order Hotline (UK) **0870 6000532**
International Mail Order **00 44 1386 852035**

Conference and Banqueting (for your events at Anfield) **0151 263 7744**
Corporate Sales **0151 263 9199**
Public Relations **0151 260 1433**
Development Association **0151 263 6391**
Caring in the Community **0151 260 1433**
Museum & Tour Centre **0151 260 6677**
Membership Department **0151 261 1444**
Club Store (Anfield) **0151 263 1760**
Club Store (City Centre) **0151 330 3077**
Liverpool Football Club Credit Card
(available to over-18s) **0800 028 2440**

BECOME A MEMBER OF LIVERPOOL FC
& JOIN THE OFFICIAL LIVERPOOL SUPPORTERS CLUB
To join, please call: **08707 02 02 07**
International: **+44 151 261 1444**

SUBSCRIBE TO THE OFFICIAL LFC PROGRAMME AND WEEKLY MAGAZINE
To take out a subscription please call: **0845 1430001**

LFC TEXT MESSAGE SERVICE
Sign up for the official LFC Text Message Service including, Match 2 U, LFC News and LFC 4U services, allowing you to keep in touch when you're on the move.
To sign up go to **www.liverpoolfc.tv/mobilezone**

E SEASON TICKET
Sign up for an e Season Ticket to see Premier League goals & highlights, TV channels and follow the team live through Turnstile.
To sign up go to **www.liverpoolfc.tv**

LFC SAVE & SUPPORT ACCOUNT WITH BRITANNIA
For more information visit **www.britannia.co.uk/lfc** call **0800 915 0503** or visit any Britannia branch.

ASSOCIATION OF INTERNATIONAL BRANCHES:

AUSTRALIA
John O'Connell
257 Crimea Street
Noranda
Perth
6062 WA

Paul Holton
PO Box 194
Annerley
Queensland 4103

BELGIUM
Mikael Roufosse
Rue Colonel
Piron 159
4624 Rousse

BULGARIA
Aleksandar Darakchiev
Velingrad
5 Mayakovsky Str
Pazardjik District
4600

CANADA
Dara Mottahead
1874 Hennessy Crescent
Orleans (Ottawa)
Ontario KA4 3XB

Andrew Cashin
39 Beaumaris Crescent
Brooklin
Ontario
L1M 2H3

CHINA
Gu Jian 289 Guangzhaouda
Dao Zhong
Guangzhao

Bruce Xue
No3/807 791
Nong Lingling Road
Shanghai

CYPRUS
Simos Sakka
Tritonos 2
Larnaca 6047

DENMARK
Per Knudsen
Blegkilde Alle 26 1.TV
9000 Aalborg

Carsten Lymann
Grofthojparken 152 St2
Viby DK-8260

FAROE ISLANDS
Roi Joensen
Bringsnagota
5MH
FO 100
Torshavn

FRANCE
George Quintard
59 Rue de Marsinval
78540 Vernouillet

Dennis Gosioso
3 Rue Feuderic Sauvage
Ecopolis Sud BP 39
Martigues Cedex 13691

GERMANY
David Coultous
Westend Strasse 51
Kempten
D-87439

Ray Latham
Farnweg 6
Wegberg
D-41844

GHANA
Aristo Dotse
PO Box NT 267
Accra New Town
Accra 00233

GIBRALTAR
Julian Sene
32 Durban Road
Harbour Views
Gibraltar

GREECE
John Skotidas
PO Box 16767
Athens
11502

Nassos Siotropos
LFC – OSC Hellenic Branch
PO Box 34 111
10029
Athens

Panagioties Damianidis
Kalavriton 11
GR-564 30
Thessaloniki

HOLLAND
Mick Kennedy
Dudokkwartier 6
Bilthoven
3723 AV

Herman Post
Postbus 407
Dordrecht
3300 AK

HONG KONG
Philip Chu
Shop 2013
2/F United Centre
Admiralty

Douglas Leung
PO Box 24605
Aberdeen Post Office

Chris Davies
18A Glamour Court
Discovery Bay
Lantau Island

ICELAND
Kristmann Palmasson
PO Box 8220
128 Reykjavik

ITALY
Filippo Rossi
CP 107
50018 Scandicci

JAPAN
Katsumi Kashimura
1351-8
Inada
Hitachinaka
Ibaraki
312-0061

LUXEMBOURG
Mark Clintworth
Black Stuff
Val Du Hamm
L-2950

MALAYSIA
John Chew
21C Jalan
Tengku
Ampuan
Zabedah
F9/F Shah Alam
Selangor 40100

MALTA
Matthew Pace
The Kop
Valletta Road
Mosta

MAURTITIUS
Jean Carl Palmyre
Morrison Street
Pamplemousses

NEW ZEALAND
John Corson
62 Nelson Street
Forbury
Dunedin
9001

NORWAY
Tore Hansen
Scandinavian Branch
PO Box 2142
Molde
N-6402

SINGAPORE
James Lim
30 Maxwell Road
#01-100 Singapore 069114

SOUTH AFRICA
Lester Smith
103 Tallent Street
Parow West
Cape Town
7500

Dick Hearns
PO Box 890783
Lyndhurst
2106

SPAIN
Chris Medway
Edifico Indason III
2 C/Cictat de reus 6-1
43840 Salou
Tarragona

SWEDEN
Rolf Rundstrom
Laxgatan 11
Skelleftea
S-931 64

SWITZERLAND
Florian Thurler
PO Box 945
Biel Bienne
CH-2501

George Rossier
PO Box 919
Delemont
CH-2800

THAILAND
Buke Bhornlerts
79-16 Sukhumit 15
Sukhumit Road
Klongtoey 1011
Bangkok

USA
Bernie Grimes
135 Eight Lots Road
Sutton
MA 01590

Daragh Kennedy
PO Box 7071 FDR Station
New York
NY 10150

Adi Anand
5800 Airport Blvrd
Austin
TX 78752

Roy Yates
4024 East Eastridge Drive
Pompano Beach
33064 Florida

ZAMBIA
Karl O'Donohoe
17119 Katima Mulilo Rd
Olympia Park
Lusaka

For details of branches in Republic of Ireland and the UK please visit **www.liverpoolfc.tv**

ACKNOWLEDGEMENTS

The publishers would like to thank the following sources for their kind permission to reproduce the pictures in this book:

Action Images 135b, 145tr, 149bc, 151tr, 151bl, 152, 153bc, 153tr, 169bl /Mirror Syndication 87tl, 112, 121bc,

Adrian Killen 75 (3 colour pics), 78, 93bc

Allsport UKLtd 85, 88, 97, 101tl, 113tr, 113bc, 127br, 129mr, 129tl, 130tl, 134, 136, 137tr, 138, 139tr, 139br, 140bc, 141tc, 141bc, 142tr, 143tc, 144tc, 144bc, 146tc, 146bc, 147tc, 147bc, 147,148, 149tc, 154, 155t, 158, 163, 165tc, 167tr, 169tc, 171tl, 173tl, 178bc/ Shaun Botterill 161tl, 161tr, 162tl, 175b, 193bl, Clive Brunskill 6, 156, 157tr, 157b, 160bc, 164br, 164mr, 164tr, 165bc, 167br, 169br, 170br, 172, 173mr, 173tr, 175tr, 176, 179bc, 187bc , 188tc, 191tl, 191tr, 191br, Graham Chadwick 162bc, 170bl, 171bc, Phil Cole 180tr, 180br, 192bc, Mike Cooper 159bl, 170tc, Stu Forster 179tc, Mike Hewitt 188bc, Ross Kinnaird 173br, 177tc, 177bc, 178tc, 184tr, 190tr, Alex Livesey 181tr, Gary M Prior 186tr,186br, 190tl, 192tl, 193tc, Ben Radford 168tl, 168tr, 174,184br, 185, 187tc, Michael Steele 181bc, 182, 183, 189tc, 189bc, Mark Thompson 160tc

Colorsport 23tr, 29, 32bl, 34, 35tr, 37, 38, 45, 47tr, 51tl, 56tr, 58, 62tr, 62tl, 65l, 66, 67t, 69tr, 70, 71t, 78bl, 79tr, 81, 82tr, 83tr,91tr, 96, 100bm, 102bl, 103, 106bc, 107, 108tr, 110, 111br, 115t, 116, 125bl, 133br, 155bc

Corbis 28

Empics Ltd 5, 19, 24, 86, 90tl/ Alpha 84, 117b, 143bc, Barratts

60b, 65tr, 68, 73t, 84t, Bild Byran 142bc, Mike Egerton 195, 196, 200, Magi Haroun, 132tl, Paul Marriott 115b, Tony Marshall 111tr, Peter Robinson 5tr, 13b, 17, 91b, 95bc, 101mb, 104, 105tl, 108tl, 108bl, 109tr, 109tl, 118tr, 118bc, 122tc, 123tr, 123b, 124tc, 124bc, 126, 127tr, 127mr, 128, 129tr, 130bc, 131, 132br, 133tr,135tr, 139mr, 139bmr, 140tc, 145bc, S&G 33br, 79b, 92, 98t, Neal Simpson 194, 197, 201

Hulton Archive 23, 32br, 40t, 56bl, 60tl, 60tr, 63, 84bl, 84ml, 86bm, 98bl, 114, 121tl

Illustrated London News Picture Library 32tr, 33tl, 33tr

LFC 198, 199, 202-203

Liverpool Central Library 11tc

From the Collection of Liverpool Football Club Museum 4, 11br, 14, 15, 16, 20, 21, 22, 26, 27tr, 30, 35, 39, 40bl, 41, 42, 44, 45, 46, 47b, 48, 49, 50, 52, 53, 54, 55, 56, 57, 59, 64, 67b,71b, 72br, 72tl, 73br, 74, 76, 77, 80, 82, 83b 86m, 87br, 93t, 94, 95, 99tr, 100tl, 102tl, 105tr, 106t, 117t, 118tl, 119, 142br, 161bc, 166, 168bc /Ben Dabbs Collection 43, 61

Ordinance Survey 9tr

Keith Osborne 10

Popperfoto 4, 12, 18tr, 18tl, 25, 69, 89b

John K. Rowlands 8, 9b

Every effort has been made to acknowledge correctly and contact the source and/or copyright holder of each picture, and Carlton Books Limited apologises for any unintentional errors or omissions

which will be corrected in future editions of this book.
The Publishers wish to express their sincere gratitude to Stephen Done and everybody associated with Liverpool Football Club Museum who has contributed to this project.

ACKNOWLEDGEMENTS

Although a great many people have assisted with the preparation of this book, special thanks must go to Rogan Taylor, of Liverpool University, and John Williams, of the University of Leicester, for allowing access to their extensive bank of taped interviews with former players and fans. The interviews, conducted for their book Three Sides Of The Mersey, provide a rare and entertaining insight into life at Anfield in the years before, and immediately after, World War Two. Thanks are also due to John K. Rowlands who conducted detailed research into the life of LFC founder John Houlding, and whose book Everton FC, 1880–1945 gives a comprehensive account of the split that led to Liverpool's formation. The author would also like to express his appreciation to Don Jones and Tim Hill at Granada TV Sport for allowing access to various Liverpool FC-related programmes and interviews, including the 1998 series Reds In Europe. Stephen Done would like to thank Eric Doig for his considerable effort in researching and checking the stats of LFC, and whose grandfather kept goal so well for the Reds! Thanks also to Brian Barwick and Paul Tyrrell at ITV, Gordon Lock (Everton FC) Gordon Lawton (Oldham Athletic FC), plus Terry Anderson, John Gill, Adrian Killen, Rob Lewis, Michelle Round and George Sephton. Finally, a big thanks to Mary, Rory, Ciaran, Rosie and Mairead Anderson for their patience and understanding.

CLUB TELEPHONE NUMBERS

Main Switchboard
0151 263 2361
Ticket Office
0870 220 2345
24-hour Match Ticket Information Line
0151 260 9999
Credit Card Hotline
0870 220 2151
Mail Order Hotline
0870 60000532
International Mail Order Hotline
00 44 1386 852035
Conference and Banqueting
0151 263 7744
Corporate Sales
0151 263 9199
Public Relations
0151 260 1433
Development Association
0151 263 6391
Caring in the Community
0151 260 1433
Museum & Tour Centre
0151 260 6677
Membership Department
0151 261 1444
Club Store (Anfield)
0151 263 1760
Club Store (City Centre)
0151 330 3077
Liverpool Football Club Credit Card
0800 028 2440
Official Website
www.liverpoolfc.tv